Augusto Wiegand Cruz

Human Dignity in the General Theory of Fundamental Rights

Nomos

Online Version
Nomos eLibrary

The Deutsche Nationalbibliothek lists this publication in the Deutsche Nationalbibliografie; detailed bibliographic data are available on the Internet at http://dnb.d-nb.de

a.t.: Regensburg, Univ., Diss., 2024

Original title:
Human Dignity in the General Theory of Fundamental Rights. A Proposal for the Chilean Constitutional Order Considering the German Experience

ISBN 978-3-7560-2324-0 (Print)
978-3-7489-4973-2 (ePDF)

1st Edition 2025

To my wife Alejandra

Preface

This book is the result of many wonderful years as a doctoral researcher at the University of Regensburg and is based on my dissertation, which was accepted in the summer semester of 2024 by the university's Faculty of Law. It is often claimed that doctoral research is an individual and even solitary enterprise. However, at least in my case, this statement is only true to a limited extent; the present work, insofar as it may contribute to scholarship, was only possible thanks to the support of many others whose contributions I am pleased to be able to acknowledge here.

To begin with, it is difficult to convey in a few lines my gratitude to Prof. Dr. Alexander Graser, who – as anyone who has worked under his supervision would testify – embodies the German concept of *Doktorvater.* On the one hand, his supervision included constant guidance, meticulous revisions and corrections, wise advice and multiple conversations about German constitutional law and comparative law practice – conversations that were always encouraging, enlightening, and inexhaustible sources of learning. On the other hand, he bestowed the freedom to pursue my academic goals and trusted in my ability to achieve them. But that was not all: his concern always went beyond the purely academic.

Moreover, at Prof. Dr. Graser's *Lehrstuhl* – a unique space of hard work and commitment surrounded by an atmosphere of friendliness and warmth – I had the privilege of meeting many brilliant colleagues, whose support and advice were indispensable. I am deeply indebted to Elke Stadler, who from the outset kindly accompanied me on this journey and selflessly guided me through a multitude of tasks. My deepest thanks also go to Prof. Dr. Thorsten Kingreen for agreeing to be the second examiner of my dissertation and for his generous and enlightening *Gutachten.*

I would also like to acknowledge the contribution of my sponsors, the German Academic Exchange Service (*Deutscher Akademischer Austauschdienst* – DAAD) and the Chilean National Research and Development Agency (*Agencia Nacional de Investigación y Desarrollo* – ANID), whose generous scholarship made my doctoral research in Germany possible. I am, in addition, deeply grateful to the Alumni Association of the Law Faculty of the University of Regensburg for awarding me the Juratisbona Prize for my doctoral thesis, which was a great honour. Lastly, I wish to thank the Directors of the Max Planck Institute for Comparative Public Law and International Law, Prof. Dr. Dr. h. c. Anne Peters and Prof. Dr. Dr. h. c. mult. Armin von Bogdandy, for including this work in the institute's publication series.

Finally, I would like to thank my parents, Augusto and María del Pilar, for their unconditional support. They have been and will continue to be a central pillar in my life. I would also like to thank my children, Elena and Augusto for their patience in enduring many long working days, including weekends. My final word goes to the person to whom this book is dedicated. It is impossible to describe the magnitude of the courage and generosity of my wife, Alejandra, and the depth of my gratitude and admiration for her. I owe her a debt that I will never be able to repay.

Regensburg, October 2024 Augusto Wiegand Cruz

Table of Contents

Abbreviations

BGB	German Civil Code
BGH	German Federal Supreme Court of Justice
BVerfG	German Federal Constitutional Court
BVerfGE	German Federal Constitutional Court Decision
BVerwG	German Federal Administrative Court
BVerwGE	German Federal Administrative Court Decision
CCT	Chilean Constitutional Tribunal
CSNC	Commission of Studies of the New Constitution
CPR	Constitution of Chile
GG	German Basic Law
GRoP	General right of personality
iVm	In conjunction with
MSI	Right to a minimum subsistence income in accordance with human dignity.
UN	United Nations
UDHR	Universal Declaration of Human Rights
WRV	Imperial Constitution of Weimar

I
Introduction and Antecedents

§ 1 Introduction

Following World War Two, and particularly through the influence of German constitutional case law, doctrine, and jurisprudence, the legal notion of human dignity was incorporated into multiple international instruments and domestic legal systems, achieving a widespread impact. The Chilean constitutional order was no exception.

This research examines the legal doctrine and jurisprudence of human dignity in the general theory of fundamental rights in the Chilean constitutional order. The study thereby contributes both to the legal doctrine of basic rights and the jurisprudence of dignity in the Chilean scholarship and literature. Although the latter has unanimously considered dignity the supreme value or principle of the constitution, its treatment has developed in a somewhat precarious manner. Accordingly, the present study takes a comparative perspective to examine how the constitutional concept of human dignity has been treated in Germany, where the doctrinal work has led to unparalleled development in this area of law.

Against this background, the knowledgeable reader might well question what a new work could contribute to this subject. Existing research on human dignity is plentiful, especially in Germany, where many prominent scholars have dealt with the topic. However, this potential objection can be countered in two ways. First, while there exists an ocean of literature on dignity in the field of comparative law, relatively little research focuses on the Chilean context, as indicated above. Providing a parallel view of the development of this concept in German law enables the Chilean case to be brought into sharper focus.

Moreover, while there exists a copious amount of research into human dignity, the topic is far from exhausted, as the plethora of recent publications attests. Indeed, the existence of the concept of human dignity in law is novel, and this novelty in part explains the controversies that surround it, pointing to the need for further investigation. Hence, it is reasonable to believe that a focus on the particular Chilean situation may furnish new insights that enrich the global debate. Accordingly, the current study contributes to this ongoing discussion from the perspective of the Chilean case.

Importantly, the comparative methodology deployed in this study is not strictly symmetrical, with the German context used to illuminate the investigation of its Chilean counterpart. Given the knowledgeability of human dignity in the latter jurisdiction, it is unnecessary to provide an exhaustive account of the former. Yet the present study's overall aim of investigating key debates on the legal doctrine [*Rechtsdogmatik*] of fundamental rights and their connection to human dignity enables its second potential contribution: that of indicating how German juridical science might influence Chilean approaches to the topic while simultaneously contributing to internal German debates through an external doctrinal lens.

The book presents a fourfold division. Part IV expounds an original interpretation of the human dignity clause of the Chilean constitution and the role it should play in three elements of the general theory of fundamental rights [*Allgemeine Lehre*]. Although human dignity is highly relevant to other elements of the theory of fundamental rights, the most compelling questions on the treatment of the concept of dignity in the Chilean constitutional order concern the foundation, ownership and restrictions of basic rights. To arrive at the aforementioned original interpretation, part IV builds on the previous sections of the book.

Part II presents the results of exhaustive research on how dignity has been treated in Chilean constitutional scholarship and case law and its role in the foundation, ownership and restrictions of basic rights. Each chapter (§) of this part ends by critiquing the treatment of dignity during the period and defines the crucial points to be tackled later, in the fourth part of the book.

Part III does the same for the German jurisdiction while only presenting the central discussion on each topic. This selective focus arises, on the one hand, due to the impossibility of encompassing the vast German literature and case law on dignity in the current work and, on the other hand, that this is not even necessary, considering the goals of this research.

In this sense, the first chapter of the aforementioned Part IV (§ 11) summarizes the principal findings of parts I, II, and III of this book, describing their main conclusions and open questions as well as presenting a comparative analysis of the treatment of the human dignity clause in Germany and Chile.

Finally, Part I consist of this introduction and the subsequent chapter (§ 2), which provides an overview of the legal, academic, and historical context in which the concept has operated since the study of the concept of human dignity in the Chilean constitutional order requires some preliminary considerations.

§ 2 Antecedents

1. *Historical context*

Chile is a former colony of the once-extensive Spanish empire,[1] becoming an independent republic in 1818.[2] Since then, it has enjoyed a period of relative institutional stability, as evidenced by its constitutional history. After a short period of anarchy marked by the failure of various constitutional ventures,[3] the so-called Constitution of 1833 established how the country would be ruled for almost a century,[4] until 1925, when a new constitution came into force.[5] This legal instrument endured until 1973, when a military coup ejected the democratically elected government.[6] The constitutional order was suspended, and the junta started to rule the country via a series of proclamations and decrees.[7]

In 1974, shortly after the coup, the junta tasked a group of jurists loyal to the new military regime with drafting the new constitution.[8] The "Com-

1 See Simon Collier and William F. Sater, *A History of Chile, 1808–2002* (2004) 1–31.
2 ibid 32–51.
3 ibid 46–51.
4 For the origins of the Constitution of 1833 and its main institutional characteristics, see ibid 54 ff.
5 ibid 209 ff.
6 ibid 352 ff.
7 ibid 352–359.
8 This group was originally formed by Sergio Diez Urzúa, Jaime Guzmán Errazuriz, Enrique Ortúzar Escobar, Jorge Ovalle Quiroz, Enrique Evans de la Cuadra, Gustavo Lorca Rojas and Alejandro Silva Bascuñan. See Comisión de Estudios de la Nueva Constitución, *Actas Oficiales de la Comisión Constituyente. Tomo I.*, p. 2, 1st session, 24 September 1973. In December of 1973, a female member, Alicia Romo Román was incorporated, see Eduardo Aldunate Lizana, *Derechos Fundamentales* (2008) 301, fn 559. However, in 1977, on account of severe political differences respecting the ruling form of the junta, the commissioners Alejandro Silva Bascuñan, Comisión de Estudios de la Nueva Constitución, *Actas Oficiales de Comisión Constituyente. Tomo VIII*, p. 855 ff, 278th session, 22 March 1977; Enrique Evans de la Cuadra, ibid 834 ff, 277th session, 17 March 1977; and Jorge Ovalle Quiroz, Comisión de Estudios de la Nueva Constitución, *Actas Oficiales de la Comisión Constituyente. Tomo IX.*, p. 319 ff, 294th session, 24 May 1977, resigned from the CSNC. They were replaced by Luz Bulnes Aldunate, Raul Bertesen Reppeto y Juan de Dios Carmona Peralta, see ibid 330 ff, 296th session, 9 June 1977.

mission of Studies of the New Constitution"[9] [*Comisión de Estudios de la Nueva Constitución*] delivered its proposal in 1978.[10] This was reviewed between 1978 and 1980 by a second committee, the "Council of State" [*Consejo de Estado*], which redrafted some clauses[11] before the very military junta made further modifications to the text.[12] Finally, in 1981, after a referendum (1980) conducted without democratic guarantees, the constitution of the military regime entered into force.[13]

However, the work of the CSNC as a constituent power severely lacked legitimacy.[14] Because its members were not democratically elected but chosen directly by the junta, it represented a highly restricted set of ideologies, political traditions, and beliefs. Naturally, this configuration produced a constitutional text whose contents merely reflected the views and interests of the small group that participated in its creation, not Chilean society as a whole.

Since then, the democratic forces of the country have struggled to make the constitutional order more democratic. Consequently, the Constitution of 1980 has been substantially reformed.[15] The two most important groups of reforms occurred in 1989 and 2005.[16] Nevertheless, both due to its origins and some remaining contents, it is still severely criticized by significant

9 Hereafter also referred to as "CSNC." The CSNC is also colloquially known as the "Ortuzar Commission" [*Comisión Ortuzar*], in reference to its president Enrique Ortúzar Escobar.

10 See Comisión de Estudios de la Nueva Constitución, *Actas Oficiales de la Comisión Constituyente. Tomo XI*, p. 1233 ff., 417th session, 5 October 1978.

11 Firstly, at Consejo de Estado, 'Actas del Consejo de Estado, 54th Session, 14 November 1978'; finally, at Consejo de Estado, 'Actas del Consejo de Estado. 111th Session, 22 July 1980'.

12 There are no proceedings on the changes incorporated by the military junta, see Aldunate Lizana, *Derechos Fundamentales* (n 8) 301.

13 A description in German of this process is in Augusto Wiegand Cruz, 'Die aktuelle Prozess des Verfassungswandels in Chile' (*JuWissBlog*, 2010) 3. Available at <http://juwiss.de/117-2020/> accessed 8 August 2022.

14 Moreover, the CSNC can be considered simply as an assistant council. The constituent power was indeed the junta, as also recognized by the Chilean Constitutional Tribunal in the case Rol 3729–2017, par. 30. In this sense, see also Aldunate Lizana, *Derechos Fundamentales* (n 8) 301–302.

15 Hereafter also referred to as "CPR".

16 For a description of the reforms to the CPR, including those carried out in 1989 and 2005, see José Luis Cea Egaña, *Derecho Constitucional Chileno Tomo I* (2017) 133–152.

social, political, and academic quarters.[17] In this context, two democratic deficits are noteworthy. On the one hand, until very recently, the CPR provided that legislation on several matters may only be adopted by a qualified parliamentary majority, ranging from an absolute majority to three-fifths of the members in office of both chambers (House of Representatives and Senate) that form the Chilean legislative branch.[18] Of particular importance here were the so-called Constitutional Organic Laws, which demanded for their enaction, modification, or abolition a majority of four-sevenths of the legislature, because these laws regulate matters such as public administration (Art. 38, par. 1 CPR), the electoral system (Art. 18, par. 1 CPR) and the education system (Art. 19, no. 11, par. 5 CPR).[19] The junta wished to regulate all these legislative matters before relinquishing power, which allowed proposed reforms to be blocked by a minority. On the other hand, the Chilean Constitutional Tribunal – as detailed in the following subsection – may review some bills prior to their enactment as part of the legislative process.

In this context, the prospect of replacing the CPR entirely gained force over time. During the last government of Michelle Bachelet (2014–2018), a process was initiated to enact a new constitution.[20] However, the process remained incomplete, with the proposed constitution lying dormant in the Chilean parliament.[21] But in November 2019, during the second pres-

17 For strong criticism of the CPR in this sense, see e.g., Jaime Bassa Mercado, Juan Carlos Ferrada Borquéz and Christián Viera Álvarez (eds), *La Constitución Chilena* (2015).

18 These requirements were watered down only a few years ago. Thanks to two constitutional reforms from 2022 and 2023, the qualified parliamentary majority required to approve this legislation now ranges from an absolute majority to four-sevenths of the members in office of both chambers. See Act 21.481 of 23 August 2022 <https://www.bcn.cl/leychile/navegar?idNorma=242302> and Act 21.535 of 27 January 2023, <https://www.bcn.cl/leychile/navegar?idNorma=1188344&idParte=10402301&idVersion=2023-01-27> accessed 08 October 2024.

19 See the previous Art. 66 CPR. Thanks to the constitutional reform of 2023 mentioned in the previous footnote, the "Constitutional Organics Laws" only require an absolute majority of the serving members of both chambers in order to pass. See the current Art. 66 CPR.

20 For a general overview of this process and for different perspectives, see Rodrigo Araya (ed), *Doscientas mil voces: Ecos y Aprendizajes del proceso constituyente de Michelle Bachelet* (2020).

21 See "Boletín N°11.617 – 07. Proyecto de reforma constitucional, iniciado en mensaje de S.E la Presidenta de la República, para modificar la Constitución Política de la República." <https://www.plataformaconstitucionalcep.cl/propuestas-de-contenidos-para-la-nueva-constitucion/proceso-constituyente-michelle-bachelet-2014-2018/antecedentes-proceso-constituyente-2014-2018> accessed 8 August 2022.

idential term of Sebastian Piñera (2018–2022), weeks of demonstrations and protests on the streets prompted parliament to begin the process of potentially enacting a new constitution.[22] The process was regulated by a reform to the CPR and consisted of three main steps.[23] First, a referendum was held that required citizens to decide whether they wanted a new constitution, and if so, whether this should be drafted by (1) a constitutional convention consisting of members of parliament and persons elected for this purpose, or (2) a constitutional assembly elected solely for the same purpose.[24] The referendum took place in October 2020 and resulted in an overwhelming victory for the second alternative.[25] Accordingly, the second step in the process occurred in May 2021, when elections for the constitutional assembly were held.[26] The constitutional assembly worked for one year and presented its draft constitution in July 2022.[27] The third step was a referendum on the draft constitution. Complying with Art. 142 CPR a referendum date of September 4, 2022 was set by presidential decree (Supreme Decree No 2.078, July 4, 2022). However, the proposed constitution was rejected by more than 60% of voters.[28]

22 See Wiegand Cruz (n 13).

23 See Arts. 130 – 142 CPR.

24 Art. 130, pars. 1 – 3 CPR.

25 The option to draft a new constitution secured 78.27 % of available votes, with 78.99 % of votes in favour of electing an assembly to draft the new constitution. See the official results on the webpage of the Chilean Electoral Office [Servicio Nacional Electoral] <https://www.servel.cl/resultados-provisorios-plebiscito-nacional-2020/> accessed 8 August 2022.

26 Art. 130, last par. CPR.

27 Art. 137 CPR. The proposal of the new constitution is available on the official webpage of the constituent assembly. See <https://www.chileconvencion.cl/> accessed 8 August 2022.

28 See the official results on the webpage of the Chilean electoral office [Servicio Nacional Electoral] <https://www.servel.cl/resultados-definitivos-plebiscito-constitucional-2022/> accessed 10 December 2022. After the rejection of this proposal in December 2022, the Chilean parliament agreed to start a new three-stage process to replace the constitution ("Agreement for Chile"). First, a commission of experts ("the Expert Commission") was appointed by parliament to draft the new constitution (March–June 2023). Then, a 50-member elected assembly ("the Constitutional Council") worked on the basis of the draft prepared by the Commission of Experts on a new draft constitution (June–November 2023). A vote on whether to adopt this draft constitution was held on 17 December 2023. However, like the previous proposal, the new draft constitution was rejected, with 55.76% of votes against it. For a detailed breakdown of the official results, see the Chilean electoral office [Servicio Nacional Electoral] website <https://www.servel.cl/resultado-plebiscito-constitucional-2023/> accessed 10 October 2024. A detailed explanation and all official documents recording

Despite its negative peculiarities, and particularly during the first 25 years of the current constitution, the CSNC's proceedings have been widely utilized by scholarship and case law as the determinant canon to interpret constitutional dispositions.[29] However, over the previous three lustrums, this practice has been increasingly challenged, labeled as a technique to legitimate, reproduce, and preserve the institutional legacy of the dictatorship,[30] or to halt meaningful discussions on constitutional interpretation without further deliberation.[31] Hence, it has even been affirmed that an impartial reading of the constitution should avoid referring to the constitutional proceedings altogether.[32]

Against this background, *Ruiz-Tagle* suggests that the fundamental constitutional rights, along with those enshrined in ratified international human rights treaties, form a constitutional block or subsystem of fundamental rights,[33] the understanding of which requires neither the opinion of the CSNC's members nor the case law of any court during the dictatorship.[34] In that sense, even some supporters of the CPR have come to accept that the CSNC proceedings should be viewed as just another hermeneutic resource.[35] Though somewhat late, a few relatively recent judgments of the Chilean Constitutional Tribunal[36] have favorably reacted to these critics as well.[37]

---

this second constitutional process can be found on its official webpage: <https://www.procesoconstitucional.cl/> (Spanish).

29 Aldunate Lizana, *Derechos Fundamentales* (n 8) 301–302, provides some convincing reasons behind this practice.

30 Pablo Contreras Vásquez and Constanza Salgado Muñoz, 'Introducción' in Pablo Contreras Vásquez and Constanza Salgado Muñoz (eds), *Manual sobre Derechos Fundamentales* (2017) 9.

31 Jaime Bassa Mercado, 'La Pretension de Objetividad en la Interpretación Constitucional' in Jaime Bassa Mercado, Juan Carlos Ferrada Bórquez and Christian Viera Álvarez (eds), *La Constitución Chilena* (2015) 14.

32 Jaime Bassa Mercado, *El Estado Constitucional de Derecho: Efectos sobre la Constitución Vigente y Derechos Sociales* (2008) 109 ff.

33 Pablo Ruiz-Tagle Vial, 'Una Visión Democrática y Liberal de los Derechos Fundamentales para la Constitución Constitución Chilena del Bicentenario' in Andrés Bordalí Salamanca (ed), *Justicia Constitucional y Derechos Fundamentales* (2006) 110.

34 ibid 70–71.

35 Angela Vivanco Martínez, *Disposición sobre la Vida Humana y Principios Constitucionales* (2014) 224.

36 Hereafter also referred to as "CCT."

37 CCT Rol 3729–2017, par 30: "(...) Thereby, the use of this type of interpretative criteria [the constitutional proceedings] should not be central nor decisive, but only auxiliary. Also, it should only be used in highly justified cases and never to rigidize

2. The general theory of fundamental rights in Chile

In Chile, the general theory of fundamental rights remains underdeveloped, as many scholars have long claimed.[38] As long ago as 2006, *Aldunate* claimed that "the treatment of fundamental rights lacks a developed methodology",[39] while *Acattino* remarked that this shortcoming had played a substantial role in nurturing a Chilean constitutional practice that produces the highest possible level of legal uncertainty.[40] Such views are widely corroborated by other scholars.[41] On this account, *Ruiz-Tagle* may not have been exaggerating when he proposed, also in 2006, to "introduce" the doctrinal category of fundamental rights into Chilean legal doctrine.[42]

Indeed, it is unusual for any Chilean handbook or treatise of constitutional law to include a separate section on the elements of the theory of fundamental rights; even when such a section exists, it is invariably incomplete.[43] Most of the meagre output on this subject is found in journal articles that deal with a solitary aspect of fundamental rights, or chapter books in which each author does the same. The richest contribution, both for its systematicity and quality, is *Aldunate's* "Fundamental Rights"

the meaning of the text." [Por lo mismo, el uso de este tipo de criterios interpretativos debiera ser auxiliar, no central ni decisivo. También, en casos muy justificados y no para rigidizar el sentido del texto.] (Surprisingly, the CCT proceeds next to materialize a meticulous revision of the relevant proceedings). Ten years prior, a dissident opinion had for the first time argued along these lines. See CCT Rol 740–2007, dissenting opinion of Justice Hernán Vodanovic Schnake, point B. All translations contained in this work, except when a different source is indicated, were carried out by the author.

38 For a review of one of the first publications highlighting this situation, see, e.g., Fernando Atria Lemaitre, *Los Peligros de la Constitución ["The Dangers of the Constitución"]* (1st edn, Universidad Diego Portales 1997) 17.

39 Eduardo Aldunate Lizana, 'Tutela Jurisdiccional y Configuración Constitucional del Derecho de Propiedad' in Andrés Bordalí Salamanca (ed), *Justicia Constitucional y Derechos Fundamentales* (2006) 179 [Por otro lado, el tratamiento de los derechos constitucionales en Chile carece de una metodología desarrollada (...).]

40 Daniela Accatino Scagliotti, 'La Interpretación de los Derechos Fundamentales y la Seguridad Jurídica. Una Mirada a la Practica Constitucional Chilena' in Andrés Bordalí Salamanca (ed), *Justicia Constitucional y Derechos Fundamentales* (2006) 18–19.

41 See Felipe Paredes Paredes, *La Garantía Jurisdiccional de los Derechos Fundamentales* (2014) 56.

42 Ruiz-Tagle Vial (n 33) 104.

43 One of the first attemps to produce a significant work in the field of the dogmatics of fundamental rights is Humberto Nogueira Alcalá's *Dogmática Constitucional* (1997).

(2008),[44] a book-length work in which the author himself remarks on the situation described.[45] Fifteen years later, the situation he describes has not substantially changed. In fact, the editors of one significant recent work on the topic urge scholars working on the Chilean context to prioritize the construction of a more sophisticated doctrine of fundamental rights.[46] On the other hand, as discussed below, the institutional architecture of constitutional remedies can be viewed as a determining factor in the current state of affairs.

3. The Chilean system of constitutional justice

The Chilean system of constitutional jurisdiction is bicephalous. The CCT heads the constitutional review of laws and statutes, in a general sense.[47] Reviews can be *a priori*, whereby the CCT scrutinizes the constitutionality of a bill before its promulgation, in a way similar to the French *Conseil Constitutionnel*.[48] Some laws defined by the CPR always undergo this test,[49] while the remainder do so only when requested by one of the chambers that form the parliament, a parliamentary group, or the president of the republic.[50] The CCT can also review a particular law already in force, in a similar way to the US Supreme Court.[51] The CCT only proceeds with this *a posteriori* review in the context of a controversy brought before ordinary jurisdiction, by request either of the judge or one of the parties involved in the trial who challenges the constitutionality of one or more infra-constitutional statutes.[52] Here, the CCT can rule that the practical application of a valid norm produces unconstitutional effects in the relevant case and may declare its "inapplicability". In addition, the CCT, independently or upon request, may review the constitutionality of a norm in the abstract that had previously been declared inapplicable to one or more concrete cases.[53] If

44 For a general overview, see Aldunate Lizana, *Derechos Fundamentales* (n 8).
45 ibid 105–108.
46 Contreras Vazquez and Salgado Munoz (n 30) 9.
47 The powers of the CCT are enshrined in Art. 93 CPR.
48 Gastón Gómez Bernales, *Las Sentencias del Tribunal Constitucional y sus Efectos sobre la Jurisdicción Común* (2013) 17.
49 Art. 93, no. 1 CPR.
50 Art. 93, no. 3 CPR.
51 Gómez Bernales (n 48) 17.
52 Art. 93, no. 6 CPR.
53 Art. 93, no. 7 CPR.

the CCT determines that no constitutional interpretation of that norm is possible, it proceeds to declare its unconstitutionality, but now *erga omnes.* Consequently, the given statute loses its validity and is deleted from the legal system.[54]

3.1. The "remedy of protection"

3.1.1. Description

Alongside the work of the CCT, the concrete protection of fundamental rights depends on the ordinary courts. The remedy of protection [*recurso de protección*] is the most common mechanism by which fundamental rights are protected,[55] since it has been designated by the CPR to safeguard the majority of such rights.[56] Art 20 CPR states that any person suffering "privation, disturbance or threat" in the "legitimate exercise" of the rights there mentioned, due to "arbitrary or illegal actions or omissions", may resort to the relevant court of appeals.[57] As prescribed by this norm, the court of appeals with jurisdiction shall immediately take the necessary measures to re-establish the rule of law and protect the affected person. If necessary, an appeal before the Supreme Court is permissible.

This remedy has some peculiar characteristics worth mentioning.[58] Firstly, it is highly summary in character. Moreover, it works without prejudice to any other rights that could be claimed before the lower courts through

54 Gómez Bernales (n 48) 19 describes the consequences of this declaration thus.

55 Paredes Paredes (n 41) 117.

56 On the one hand, some constitutional rights are protected by other remedies, as in the case of *Habeas Corpus* (Art. 21 CPR) – it is important to remark that all such cases are brought before ordinary courts. On the other hand, some rights from the Bill of Rights of the CPR are not covered by concrete means of protection through remedies, e.g., Art. 19, no. 10, par. 1 CPR [right to education].

57 [El que por causa de *actos u omisiones arbitrarios o ilegales sufra privación, perturbación o amenaza* en el *legítimo ejercicio de los derechos y garantías* establecidos en el artículo 19, números 1°, 2°, 3° inciso quinto, 4°, 5°, 6°, 9° inciso final, 11°,12°, 13°, 15°, 16° en lo relativo a la libertad de trabajo y al derecho a su libre elección y libre contratación, y a lo establecido en el inciso cuarto, 19°, 21°, 22°, 23°, 24°, y 25° podrá ocurrir por sí o por cualquiera a su nombre, a la Corte de Apelaciones respectiva, la que adoptará de inmediato las providencias que juzgue necesarias para restablecer el imperio del derecho y asegurar la debida protección del afectado, *sin perjuicio de los demás derechos* que pueda hacer valer ante la autoridad o los tribunales correspondientes.] (emphasis added)

58 This paragraph mostly follows Paredes Paredes (n 41) 123 and ff.

ordinary legal actions. Accordingly, the given ruling merely produces the effect of formal *res judicata*. Besides, its procedure is neither described by the constitution nor by the law, but only by rules created by the Supreme Court itself. Finally, its legal nature is not clear. For some scholars, this remedy is solely an injunctive action, incapable of deciding on the merits or substance of the issue, while others, conversely, believe that the rulings on these remedies in practice determine the existence of rights.

A remedy of protection can be brought before the courts not only against acts of the public power but also against private individuals. Accordingly, this remedy, at least in practice, implies an acceptance that basic rights have direct effects on third parties [*unmittelbare Drittwirkung*] in the Chilean jurisdiction.[59]

3.1.2. Analysis

Evaluations of the remedy of protection have varied considerably. While some scholarship has characterized it as the most effective means to protect fundamental rights, especially praising its speed of response,[60] it has also been subject to sound criticism. *Paredes*, for one, considers that rulings on the remedy of protection fail to state reasons in most cases.[61] *Paredes* also contends that the uncertain legal status of the remedy of protection means that the courts do not always review the merits of a particular case, severely harming the potential judicial protection of fundamental rights it affords.[62]

Additionally, the remedy harms the possibility of advancing a robust theory of fundamental rights for the Chilean constitutional order. In particular, *Paredes* highlights two adverse effects: the meagre production of doctrines on fundamental rights and the low constitutional density of judgments on the remedy of protection.[63] Concerning the former, he concludes

---

59 On the origins of the effects on third parties of basic rights in Chile, see Aldunate Lizana, *Derechos Fundamentales* (n 8) 211–224; Andrés Jana Linetzki, 'La Eficacia Horizontal de los Derechos Fundamentales' in Departamento de Derecho Privado de la Facultad de Derecho de la Universidad de Chile (ed), *Derecho Civil y Constitución* (2021); in the German jurisdiction, see § 7, subsection 1.3.

60 Emilio Pfeffer Urquiaga, 'El Recurso de Protección y su Eficacia en la Tutela de los Derechos Constitucionales en Chile' (2006) 4 Estudios Constitucionales 87, 87.

61 Paredes Paredes (n 41) 131.

62 ibid 136.

63 ibid 150.

that, given its characteristics, it is hard to expect this remedy would have a different outcome.[64] On the latter, he remarks that such judgments are typically not grounded in the legal doctrine of basic rights but in legal arguments.[65]

By the same token, *Bordalí* has claimed that the remedy of protection provokes a "triple dysfunctionality" in the Chilean system of constitutional justice.[66] First, decisions on these remedies create "a secondary rule of constitutional law" [*regla secundaria de derecho constitucional*], similar to the decisions of the CCT, thereby preventing unified constitutional interpretations. Also, considering its extremely summary nature, the decisions taken lack all the guarantees of the due process of law. Third, similar cases are resolved in different ways, as the Supreme Court decides on them not in plenary but in separate chambers. Consequently, *Bordalí* concludes, as does *Paredes*, that the rulings on this action do not allow coherent legal doctrines of fundamental rights to be assembled,[67] a view supported by other scholars.[68]

4. The positive text on human dignity in the CPR

4.1. The constitutional chapter on "Institutional Foundations"

As mentioned above, the CPR has been modified in numerous ways since its promulgation. However, few alterations have been made to the constitutional chapter that introduced the conceptof human dignity. The current first section of Art. 1 par. 1 CPR is almost identical to the original:

Persons are born free and equal in dignity and rights.[69]

This norm belongs to the first chapter of the constitution ("Institutional Foundations"). The chapter contains nine articles, each stipulating one or

64 ibid 159.

65 ibid 160.

66 Andrés Bordalí Salamanca, 'La Tutela de los Derechos Fundamentales bajo un Sistema Dual de Justicia Constitucional' in Andrés Bordalí Salamanca (ed), *Justicia Constitucional y Derechos Fundamentales* (2006) 52–53.

67 ibid 53.

68 See, e.g., Gastón Gómez Bernales, *Derechos Fundamentales y Recurso de Protección* (2005) 43.

69 [Las personas nacen libres e iguales en dignidad y derechos]. In the original version, the constitution used the term "men" [los hombres] instead of "persons". See *infra* subsection 4.2.2.

more constitutional principles, values, or duties. Following the norm on dignity, the constitution declares that the family is the core of society (Art. 1, par. 2). The following two paragraphs enshrine the so-called principle of subsidiarity; then, in par. 5, some general duties of the state. Art. 2 defines the national emblems, while the next two articles state that the Chilean State is unitary (Art. 3) and a democratic republic (Art. 4). Art. 5 establishes that sovereignty lies with the nation and proclaims the limits of this sovereignty. The next three articles respectively prescribe the principles of constitutional supremacy, legality, and integrity in the exercise of public office. Finally, the ninth and last article of the chapter sets out a cluster of norms on terrorism.

The Institutional Foundations chapter – in conjunction with Chapter III of the CPR on Constitutional Rights and Duties[70]– forms the doctrinal part of the constitutional text.[71] In this context, Chapter I of the CPR constitutes the "cluster of political and juridical institutions,"[72] or the "juridical philosophy"[73] that shape the Constitution. In other words, the chapter contains the "fundamental decisions" of the constituent.[74] Accordingly, this group of norms has an outstanding hermeneutical function since its contents influence the understanding of the entire constitutional text, acting "as a parameter to the constitutional judge"[75] and functioning as a milestone that "orient(s) the process of creation and transformation of constitutional law,"[76] thereby setting up its most basic interpretative pattern.[77] As such, these articles constitute directly enforceable law.[78]

---

70 Cea Egaña, *Derecho Constitucional Chileno Tomo I.* (n 16) 104–119.

71 Emilio Pfeffer Urquiaga, Luz Bulnes Aldunate and Mario Verdugo Marinkovic, *Manual de Derecho Constitucional. Tomo I.* (1985) 201.

72 Hernan Molina Guaita, *Derecho Constitucional* (2006) 58 [conjunto de instituciones políticas y jurídicas].

73 Alejandro Silva Bascuñan, *Tratado de Derecho Constitucional. Tomo IV.* (1997) 17 [filosofía jurídica].

74 José Manuel Díaz de Valdés Juliá, 'Bases de la Institucionalidad: una Revisión Propositiva' in José Francisco García García (ed), *Nueva Constitución o Reforma* (2014) 95 [decisiones fundamentales].

75 Vivanco Martínez, *Disposición Sobre la Vida Humana y Principios Constitucionales* (n 35) 240 [guía o parámetro para el juez constitucional].

76 Pfeffer Urquiaga, Bulnes Aldunate and Verdugo Marinkovic (n 71) 201 [orientan el proceso de creación y transformación del derecho constitucional].

77 Thus, e.g., Angela Vivanco Martínez, 'La Importancia del Concepto Constitucional de Persona y la Protección de la Vida en la Carta Fundamental de 1980' in José Francisco García García (ed), *Nueva Constitución o Reforma* (2014) 130.

78 Díaz de Valdés Juliá (n 74) 95, providing several examples in fn 11.

The latter views have been supported by settled constitutional case law.[79] Furthermore, the CCT also commented that the norms of the Institutional Foundations chapter, as well as those of the Bill of Rights of the CPR, are:

> (...) inspired by a humanistic thought. This understanding manifests itself, on the one hand, in the primacy that its dispositions [those of the first chapter] concede to the human person, his dignity and natural freedom and, on the other hand, as they prescribe an obligation of respect, promotion and protection of the essential rights that emanate from the human nature. This obligation constitutes an unconditional duty to all state bodies.[80]

Against this background, two facts have somehow militated against separate and distinctive reflection on the normative consequences of the concept of dignity in the doctrine of fundamental rights. First, as mentioned above,[81] most Chilean handbooks and treatises of constitutional law fail to adequately address a general theory of fundamental rights. Second, these works focus on the meaning and legal function of dignity when commenting on the Institutional Foundations chapter,[82] in other words, they do not dedicate a particular section to dealing with this topic.

79 See, e.g., CCT Rol 19–1983, par. 9; CCT Rol 46–1987, pars. 19–21; CCT Rol 591–2006, par. 3; CCT Rol 740–2007, par. 20.

80 CCT Rol 2410–2013, par. 11. [Que el contenido del artículo 19 de la Carta Fundamental, conjuntamente con sus artículos 1º, 4º y 5º, inciso segundo, configuran principios y valores básicos de fuerza obligatoria que impregnan toda la Constitución de una finalidad humanista que se irradia en la primacía que asignan sus disposiciones a la persona humana, a su dignidad y libertad natural, así como en el respeto, promoción y protección a los derechos esenciales que emanan de la naturaleza humana, que se imponen como limitación del ejercicio de la soberanía y como deber de los órganos del Estado.] Note about grammatical gender and translations: in this work, words that are neutral nouns in English such as "person," "human being," "individual," or similar are repeatedly used. German and Spanish class these words as either masculine, feminine or neutral with all translations in this text using the former for the sake of simplicity and fidelity to the source whereas the author's own text uses both male and female pronoun forms to maximize inclusivity.

81 See *supra* subsection 2.

82 See § 3, subsection 1.1.

4.2. Antecedents of the dignity clause of the CPR

4.2.1. Previous constitutional texts

In its modern sense, the concept of human dignity entered into the Chilean constitutional order with Act 17.398 of 9 January 1971, which reformed the Constitution of 1925. However, these reforms were curtailed by the 1973 coup.

This Act introduced a new version of Art. 10, no. 14 of the 1925 constitution. In its first paragraph, the new provision stated that:

> Every person shall have the right to labor, to freely choose the latter, and to a proper remuneration, which shall guarantee the person's and his family's well-being according to human dignity (...).[83]

The Act also incorporated a no. 16 to the same which stated that:

> The state shall adopt all the measures required to satisfy all the social, economic and cultural rights that are necessary for the development of human personality and dignity (...).[84]

Before this reform, other constitutional texts had used the word "dignity," but either in the sense of "rank in a hierarchy" or "merit." In its latter sense, the word was employed in the second paragraph of the Preamble of the Constitutional Regulations [*Reglamento Constitucional*] of 1812, and Art. 260 of the Constitution of 1823; in its former sense, it was implemented in Arts. 4 and 9 of the Provisory Regulation of Government [*Reglamento para el Gobierno Provisorio*] of 1814; Arts. 18, no. 3 and 97 of the Constitution of 1822; Arts. 28 and 145, no. 4 of the Constitution of 1823; and the Constitution of 1833, in its articles 82, no. 8, 102, and 104, no. 3. The CPR also uses the word "dignity" in this meaning in Art. 30, par. 2 when referring to the "official dignity of former President of the Republic."[85]

---

83 [Toda persona tiene derecho al trabajo, a la libre elección de éste, a una remuneración suficiente que asegure a ella y su familia un bienestar acorde con la dignidad humana y a una justa participación en los beneficios que de su actividad provengan.]

84 [El Estado adoptará todas las medidas que tiendan a la satisfacción de los derechos sociales, económicos y culturales necesarios para el libre desenvolvimiento de la personalidad y de la dignidad humanas, para la protección integral de la colectividad y para propender a una equitativa redistribución de la renta nacional.]

85 [El que haya desempeñado este cargo por el período completo, asumirá, inmediatamente y de pleno derecho, la dignidad oficial de Ex Presidente de la República.]

4.2.2. Materials of the CPR

4.2.2.1. The proceedings of the CSNC

The proceedings of the CSNC demonstrate how it progressed through a series of changes to eventually reach a definitive proposal of a norm on human dignity that would become Art. 1 par. 1 of the CPR. They also indicate the CSNC's operational context and how it understood its task as a fight, grounded in traditional Christian values, against Marxist thought. Already in its second session, just a few weeks after the coup, the CSNC proposed a draft decree for consideration by the junta that aimed to prohibit Marxist political parties and associations. The first paragraph of its proposal reads:

> Whereas Marxist doctrine embodies a concept of man and society that is offensive to the spiritual dignity of the human being and harms the libertarian and Christian values that are part of national tradition.[86]

The statements of several members of the CSNC reaffirmed this attitude in the early phase of its work. Thus, *Evans* presented a document in which he affirmed that one goal of the CPR was to organize a state under the rule of law that could protect the rights and dignity of persons.[87] Similarly, *Ortuzar* mentioned human dignity as a principle belonging to the Christian view of the human being that the CPR had to support.[88] An orienting document for the CSNC, prepared by *Ortuzar*, *Diez*, *Evans*, and *Ovalle*, thus crystallized an approach in which human dignity, freedom, and basic rights preceded the state;[89] the Bill of Rights of the CPR had to receive its understanding of law and human dignity from the Hispanic past;[90] and duties supported the "dignity of freedoms."[91]

---

86 Comisión de Estudios de la Nueva Constitución, *Actas Oficiales de La Comisión Constituyente. Tomo I* (n 8) 13, 2nd session, 25 September 1973. [Que la doctrina marxista encierra un concepto del hombre y de la sociedad que lesiona la dignidad espiritual del ser humano y atenta en contra de los valores libertarios y cristianos que son parte de la tradición nacional.] The junta accepted the proposal almost verbatim in Law Decree 77, 13 October 1973, see ibid 19.

87 Comisión de Estudios de la Nueva Constitución, *Actas Oficiales de La Comisión Constituyente. Tomo I* (n 8) 64, 9th session, 23 October 1973.

88 ibid 77, 10th session, 25 October 1973.

89 ibid 191, 18th session, 22 November 1973.

90 ibid 193, 18th session, 22 November 1973.

91 ibid, 18th session, 22 November 1973.

However, the first concrete proposals for a norm on dignity only appeared in session 38, when members were discussing the first chapter of the CPR. *Silva*, for one, suggested incorporating into that chapter, as Art 8, a norm identical to the one introduced into the Constitution of 1925 under Art. 10, no. 16 as part of the 1971 reforms.[92] *Evans,* in turn, suggested a clause (Art. 4) declaring the State's obligation to protect [*amparar*] the dignity of human beings and their inalienable rights.[93] In session 40, *Diez* suggested recognizing dignity in par. 2 of Art. 1 CPR, by which State action had to be directed at "promoting the complete development of the human personality and guarantee guaranteeing human freedom and the respect of the dignity of the human personality."[94] These proposals were mostly largely discussed by the CSNC,[95] and were ultimately reformulated as follows by *Guzman*:

> The action of the State shall promote the common good or the ensemble of social conditions that allow each and every member of the national community to achieve his highest possible personal fulfillment, both spiritual and material, assuring freedom and respecting the dignity of the human being.[96]

This wording was strongly criticized by other members of the committee – not with reference to dignity but to the other concepts invoked by the phrase.[97] However, as *Diez* remarked, the differences lay not in their grounding but rather in how to better express those concepts, with the CPR subsequently required to demonstrate how dignity would be respected in

---

92 ibid 812, 38th session, 7 May 1974. See *supra* subsection 4.2.1.

93 ibid 810, 38th session, 7 May 1974. [El Estado de Chile sirve a todos los seres humanos que forman la comunidad nacional y ampara su dignidad y sus derechos inalienables. En consecuencia, la acción del Estado procura el pleno desarrollo de la persona humana y su participación activa en la vida cívica, social, económica y cultural, debiendo remover los obstáculos que limiten, en el hecho, la libertad y la igualdad de las personas y de los grupos intermedios lícitos en que aquellas se integren.]

94 ibid 871, 40th session, 14 May 1974. [Su acción [del Estado] está encaminada al bien común, a procurar un desarrollo pleno de la personalidad humana y a asegurar su libertad y el respeto a su dignidad.]

95 ibid 954, 957, 960, 963, 965.

96 ibid 974, 46th session, 18 June 1974. [La acción del Estado se encamina a promover el bien común o conjunto de condiciones sociales que permitan a todos y a cada uno de los integrantes de la comunidad nacional, alcanzar su más plena realización personal posible, tanto espiritual como material, asegurando la libertad y respetando la dignidad del ser humano]

97 ibid 974 ff, 46th session, 18 June 1974.

its specific dispositions.[98] Indeed, the members agreed that the concepts under discussion were relevant to the Christian understanding of the human being, with the main points of difference being how and to what extent these concepts should be described by the constitution.[99] Specifically, the discussion concerned whether the CPR needed to define the concept of "common good" and whether human dignity and freedom should be incorporated into this definition.[100] By this token, *Ortuzar* proposed the following wording for Art. 1, par. 2 of the CPR, which was approved despite the dissenting votes of *Evans* and *Ovalle*:

> The action of the State shall promote the common good by creating the social conditions that allow each and every member of the national community to reach the highest possible personal fulfillment, both spiritual and material, and thus ensure the freedom and dignity of the human being.[101]

In the next session, *Ortuzar* suggested deleting the word "thus" [*así*] from the approved norm, since retaining it could signify agreement with the Marxism doctrine that those in poverty did not have freedom or dignity. The proposal was subsequently approved by the other members. The last part of the article thus read: "(...) spiritual and material, with full respect to the freedom and dignity of the human being."[102] Further discussions among the CSNC resulted in a few additional modifications[103] until the norm was

98 ibid 977, 46th session, 18 June 1974.
99 ibid 977 ff, 46th session, 18 June 1974.
100 ibid 986 ff, 46th session, 18 June 1974.
101 ibid 986–987 ff, 46th session, 18 June 1974. [La acción del Estado debe promover el bien común creando las condiciones sociales que permitan a todos y a cada uno de los integrantes de la comunidad nacional alcanzar su más plena realización personal posible, tanto espiritual como material, y asegurar así la libertad y dignidad del ser humano.]
102 ibid 989, 47th session, 20 June 1974. [La acción del Estado debe promover el bien común, creando las condiciones sociales que permitan a todos y a cada uno de los integrantes de la comunidad nacional alcanzar su mayor realización personal posible, espiritual y material, con pleno respeto a la libertad y dignidad del ser humano.]
103 ibid 998, 47th session, 20 June 1974. [La acción del Estado debe promover el bien común, creando las condiciones sociales que permitan a todos y cada uno de los integrantes de la comunidad nacional, alcanzar su mayor realización personal posible, espiritual y material, con pleno respeto a la libertad y dignidad del ser humano y a su derecho a participar en la vida nacional]; ibid 1020–1021, 48th session, 25 June 1974 [(...) alcanzar su mayor realización espiritual y material posible, con pleno

sent to the State Council as par. 4 of Art. 1 of the committee's draft CPR proposal:

> The State shall contribute to create the social conditions that allow each and every member of the national community to reach the highest possible spiritual and material fulfillment, with full respect for the security, freedom, and dignity of the human being and his right to participate with equal opportunities in the national life.[104]

Several months later, as it began drafting Chapter III of the CPR on basic rights, the CSNC discussed an additional norm on dignity. This would ultimately become the CPR's unique clause on human dignity. From the outset, *Ortuzar* recalled how the dignity clause of the German Basic Law connected human dignity with basic rights.[105] The concept of human dignity was evoked by *Evans* in the same manner – the constitution had to recognize everyone's right to dignity in conjunction with the right to life and personality.[106] Similarly, *Silva* suggested that basic rights were grounded in dignity and equality.[107]

The discussion went further, encompassing other doctrinal nuances. *Ortuzar* asserted that the CPR had to consider rights unprescribed by the Constitution of 1925, such as the right to life and free development, and that the dignity of a human being should also be mentioned.[108] Next, in the context of discussing the right to life and the death penalty, the CNSC examined the first three articles of the UN's[109] Universal Declaration of Hu-

---

respeto a la libertad y dignidad del ser humano y a su derecho a participar en la vida nacional]; Comisión de Estudios de la Nueva Constitución, *Actas Oficiales de La Comisión Constituyente. Tomo XI* (n 10) 35, 373rd session, 23 May 1978; ibid 708, 402nd session, 14 July 1978.

104 Comisión de Estudios de la Nueva Constitución, *Actas Oficiales de La Comisión Constituyente. Tomo XI* (n 10) p. 1020, 411st session, 30 August 1978. [El Estado debe contribuir a crear las condiciones sociales que permitan a todos y a cada uno de los integrantes de la comunidad nacional, alcanzar su mayor realización espiritual y material posible, con pleno respeto a la seguridad, libertad y dignidad del ser humano y a su derecho a participar con igualdad de oportunidades en la vida nacional.]

105 Comisión de Estudios de la Nueva Constitución, *Actas Oficiales de la Comisión Constituyente. Tomo III* 16, 83th session, 31 October 1974.

106 ibid 18–19 84th session, 4 November 1973.

107 ibid 21, 84th session, 4 November 1974.

108 ibid 22–28, 84th session, 4 November 1974.

109 Hereafter also referred to as "UN."

man Rights.[110] As a result, *Ortuzar* suggested that adopting the terminology of Art. 1 of the UDHR for the CPR might protect any rights that were not explicitly prescribed in the CPR.

The members then debated whether to recognize a right to dignity as such.[111] *Ovalle* recommended incorporating dignity along with freedom and equality since all other guarantees of the CPR would emanate from these principles.[112] However, *Evans* considered that these concepts did not represent constitutional guarantees or institutions, but would comprise a crucial declaration of principles. *Ovalle* and *Silva* agreed with *Evans* and proposed drafting the opening clause of the chapter on basic rights as follows – next should be listed the Bill of Rights:

> Men are born free and equal in dignity and rights and, therefore, the constitution guarantees to every inhabitant of the Republic (...).[113]
> [1.The right to life (...)
> 2.(...)
> (...).]

Guzman then reopened the discussion by suggesting that the opening norm should instead state that men were "essentially equal" because not all would enjoy the same rights that had to be listed in the Bill of Rights.[114] *Silva* added that referring to "equality of rights" in this opening clause could be repetitive because the CPR also had to enumerate equality before the law in the concrete Bill of Rights.[115] *Evans* recalled that, generally speaking, the concept of dignity was crucial.[116] Consequently, *Guzman* proposed rephrasing the opening norm as "men are born free and equal in their dignity, and therefore, the constitution (...)," a formulation that clarified how the rights, freedoms and equalities listed originated in dignity.[117] The proposal

110 Hereafter also referred to as "UDHR." See Comisión de Estudios de la Nueva Constitución, *Actas Oficiales de La Comisión Constituyente. Tomo III* (n 105) p. 36, 84th session, 4 November 1974.

111 ibid 109, 87th session, 14 November 1974.

112 ibid 214, 90th session, 25 November 1974.

113 ibid 218, 90th session, 25 November 1974.

114 ibid 218 ff, 90th session, 25 November 1974.

115 ibid 220, 90th session, 25 November 1974.

116 ibid 221, 90th session, 25 November 1974.

117 ibid 270, 92nd session, 2 December 1974. Next *Evans* ibid 271, 92nd session, 2 December 1974, stated that it should be a matter of record that the statement *Men are born equal in rights* had been eliminated "(...) because it was considered an unnecessary repetition, since what the Constitution will guarantee next is precisely

was discussed,[118] and after some additional minor alterations,[119] appeared in the following form:

> Men are born free and equal in dignity and, therefore, the constitution guarantees to all persons:
> 1.- The right to life (...).[120]

Several years later (in 1978), the CSNC returned once again to Chapter I for its final revision. At this point, the CNSC opted to include the first section of the aforementioned rule as the first norm of the constitution. Thus, while the Bill of Rights had to start with the simple phrase that the "[C]onstitution guarantees to all persons: 1.- (...),"[121] Art. 1, par. 1 of the CPR was left as "Men are born equal in dignity"[122] and was sent to the State Council in that form.[123]

---

the recognition of those rights. With this clarification on record, Mr. Guzmán's suggestion is declared to be accepted because he is concerned that whoever reads the text approved by this Commission would undoubtedly conclude that it had been taken – as it indeed is – from Art. 1 of the Universal Declaration of Human Rights. This is perhaps the best-known expression of said declaration and, consequently, it is striking that the expression 'Men are born equal in rights' has been deleted." [Después, podría dejarse expresa constancia en el acta de que se eliminó la igualdad de derechos que se había propuesto, no en razón de estimarse que la disposición no procedía sino porque se consideró una repetición innecesaria, por cuanto lo que la Constitución garantizará a continuación es, precisamente, el reconocimiento de aquellos derechos ya enunciados en el encabezamiento. Con esa aclaración en el acta, declara aceptar la sugerencia del señor Guzmán, porque le preocupa el hecho de que quien lea el texto que esta Comisión apruebe, concluirá, sin duda, de que éste fue tomado —y así es— del artículo 1° de la Declaración Universal de los Derechos Humanos. Es tal vez la expresión más conocida de dicha Declaración y, en consecuencia, llamará la atención que se haya eliminado la expresión "los hombres nacen iguales en derechos."]

118 Comisión de Estudios de la Nueva Constitución, *Actas Oficiales de la Comisión Constituyente. Tomo III* (n 105) pp. 270–278, 92nd session, 2 December 1974.

119 ibid 279, 92nd session, 2 December 1974.

120 Comisión de Estudios de la Nueva Constitución, *Actas Oficiales de la Comisión Constituyente. Tomo V*, p. 863, 178, 156th session, 7 October 1975. [Los hombres nacen libres e iguales en dignidad y, en consecuencia, la Constitución asegura a todas las personas: 1. – El derecho a la vida (...).]

121 Comisión de Estudios de la Nueva Constitución, *Actas Oficiales de la Comisión Constituyente. Tomo XI* (n 10) p. 1025, 411th session, 6 September 1978.

122 ibid 724, 402nd session, 14 July 1978.

123 ibid 1020, 411th session, 6 September 1978.

The commission also proposed a preamble, which in its third paragraph stated that:

> [the Chilean nation] proclaims that the human being has natural rights, prior and superior to the State, and that his creative initiative, an expression of his dignity and freedom, constitute an essential element for the integral development of his personality and the spiritual and material progress of the Nation.[124]

The CSNC reconsidered the modern sense of the term "dignity" in further norms of its draft proposal, but these were not adopted in later revisions.[125]

4.2.2.2. The proceedings of the State Council

In one of the first sessions for reviewing the CSNC's draft proposal, the State Council discussed Art. 1, par. 1 of the CPR. The official record only describes this process; at the behest of one member, the word "rights" was restored to the end of the first sentence, and the norm of the CPR was reinstated using the first sentence of Art. 1 UDHR: "Men are born free and equal in dignity and rights."[126] The junta maintained this modification by the State Council.[127] Additionally, the State Council deleted both the pream-

124 ibid 1019, 411th session, 6 September 1978. [[la nación chilena] Proclama que el ser humano tiene derechos naturales, anteriores y superiores al Estado, y que su iniciativa creadora, expresión de su dignidad y libertad, constituye un elemento esencial para el desarrollo integral de su personalidad y el progreso espiritual y material de la Nación].

125 In Art. 8, par. 1 CPR, regarding the illegality of doctrines against human dignity, see ibid 1021, 411th session, 6 September 1978. The reference to dignity in this article was, however, omitted by the State Council, see Consejo de Estado, 'Actas del Consejo de Estado, 56th session, 28 November 1978', p. 8; in Art. 19, no. 15 CPR, on the right to free labor, considering that the human being had a right to a salary that may allow him and his family to live in conditions according to human dignity, see Comisión de Estudios de la Nueva Constitución, *Actas Oficiales de la Comisión Constituyente. Tomo XI* (n 10), p. 1045, 412th session, 7 September 1978. The State Council maintained this wording, but the military junta rephrased the article without any reference to human dignity.

126 Consejo de Estado, 'Actas Del Consejo de Estado, 56th Session, 28 November 1978' (n 125) 9.

127 Aldunate Lizana, *Derechos Fundamentales* (n 8) 421.

ble,[128] and par. 4 of Art. 1[129] of the CSNC's draft proposal. This was later reinserted by the military junta, but was rephrased to elide the reference to human dignity:[130] this version remains in the Chilean constitution today.[131]

5. Some introductory remarks on dignity and Art 5, par. 2 of the CPR

Art. 5, par. 2 of the CPR declares:

> The exercise of sovereignty recognizes as a limitation the respect for the essential rights which emanate from human nature. It is the duty of the organs of the State to respect and promote those rights, guaranteed by this Constitution, as well as by the international treaties ratified by Chile and which are in force.

The paragraph enshrines a complex norm. Accordingly, it is not surprising that it has attracted considerable discussion.

5.1. Status of international treaties on human rights

Firstly, there is absolutely no consensus on the legal status which the CPR confers on the ratified international human rights instruments. This is only natural - the CPR does not contain any norm defining the hierarchy of international treaties, therefore leaving the resolution of this problem *de facto* open to interpretation.[132] Accordingly, scholarly interpretations of such treaties vary, ranking them as either supra-constitutional, constitutional, above ordinary law but below the constitution, or as legal statutes. [133] In several decisions, the CCT seems to have disregarded the two highest options without defining precisely which of the other two is appropriate.[134]

---

128 ibid.

129 Consejo de Estado, 'Actas Del Consejo de Estado, 56th Session, 28 November 1978' (n 125) 7.

130 Aldunate Lizana, *Derechos Fundamentales* (n 8) 422.

131 For a doctrinal analysis of this clause in conjunction with Art. 1, par. 1 CPR, see § 13, subsection 1.4.2.1.3.

132 Miriam Lorena Henríquez Viñas, 'Jerarquía de los tratados de derechos humanos: análisis jurisprudencial desde el método de casos' (2008) 6 Estudios Constitucionales 73, 113.

133 Díaz de Valdés Juliá (n 74) 108.

134 ibid, referring, in fn 42, to the relevant case law of the CCT.

Yet this discussion extends well beyond the theoretical, as the following paragraphs show.

5.2. "Essential rights which emanate from human nature:" analysis

In interpreting the norm quoted above, most scholars concur that the CPR is informed by the classical tradition of human rights and its acknowledgement that the law does not create rights but only recognizes them.[135] Hence, the constitutional catalog of rights should not be considered exhaustive. The clearest summary of this position is provided by *Evans*, who writes that:

> (...) all the fundamental rights of men, be they or be they not in the constitutional text, are protected by the latter, as can be deduced from the nature of these rights and the second paragraph of Art 5 of the Constitution.[136]

This interpretation was echoed by the CCT, which, interpreting the first phrase of Art 5, par. 2 of the CPR, concluded:

> (...) it means that men hold rights as such, [therefore] their constitutional assurance [positive enshrinement] is not necessary for them [those rights] to enjoy constitutional protection (...).[137]

135 Thus, e.g., Cea Egaña, *Derecho Constitucional Chileno Tomo I* (n 16) 264–265; Silva Bascuñan (n 73) 106–109; Emilio Pfeffer Urquiaga, 'Breves Reflexiones y Algunas Propuestas en Torno a los Derechos, Garantías y Deberes Constitucionales' in José Francisco García García (ed), *Nueva Constitución o Reforma* (1st edn, Thomson Reuters 2014) 171; Cristóbal Orrego Sanchéz, 'Vigencia de los Derechos Esenciales que Emanan de la Naturaleza Humana y su Reconocimiento en el Ordenamiento Jurídico Chileno' 20 Revista Chilena de Derecho (Pontificia Universidad Católica de Chile) 59, 65, in fn 21; Vivanco Martínez, *Disposición Sobre La Vida Humana y Principios Constitucionales* (n 35) 328; Molina Guaita (n 72) 60–61.

136 Enrique Evans de la Cuadra, *Los Derechos Constitucionales. Tomo I.* (1999) 23–24. [La enunciación del artículo 19° no es taxativa. Todos los derechos del hombre, estén o no en el texto constitucional, están cautelados por él. Así se desprende de la naturaleza de estos derechos, anteriores al Estado, y del inciso segundo del artículo 5° de la Constitución.]

137 CCT Rol 226–1995, par. 25. [(...) los hombres son titulares de derechos por ser tales, sin que sea menester que se aseguren constitucionalmente para que gocen de protección constitucional.]

Silva soon noted that the main issue would now be to define what is understood by "essential rights" that "emanate from human nature."[138] However, neither the aforementioned scholars, nor others of a similar view,[139] nor the CCT have provided clear hermeneutic criteria to approach that key task, besides some broad references to human dignity.[140] *Nogueira,* while agreeing with the premises of the position noted above, has drafted a concrete proposal of hermeneutical rationalization. After acknowledging the link between the question of which rights are inherent to the human person and the philosophical foundation of human rights, he proposes considering such rights as those recognized by international law in a broad sense.

Finally, some other scholars maintain that Art 5, par. 2 CPR should be understood rather narrowly. As a result, the definition of essential rights is shaped by the following sentence of the norm: "rights that emanate from human nature" are those "guaranteed" by the CPR and "international treaties", in the sense of those expressly enshrined in both sources of law.[141] While these discussions are ongoing, meaningful, and sound, they have rarely considered how a robust conceptualization of dignity could provide coherent doctrinal definitions of the meaning of essential rights in the Chilean context.

6. *Final considerations*

From the reviewed antecedents, several important implications arise for the development of the upcoming sections of this book. First, the institution-

138 Silva Bascuñan (n 73) 107.

139 See, e.g., Cecilia Rosales Rigol, 'Algunas Reflexiones en Torno a la Dignidad y a la Vida Humana a Propósito de una Posible Reforma Constitucional' (2007) 69 Revista de Derecho Público 118, 126, where she suggests that the content of nature in this context means "the reality of the being that nature allows us to discover, which is usually one and common to the individual reason, notwithstanding the will of transient majorities." [El contenido de lo natural (...), es decir la realidad del ser que se nos ofrece la naturaleza para ser descubierta, suele ser una misma y común a la razón individual, a pesar dela voluntad transitoria de una mayoría.] This kind of definition does not provide the interpreter with many hermeneutic criteria.

140 The resort to dignity may be a valid criterion to recognize implicit constitutional rights but this would first require a strong conceptualization of the notion. To explore this doctrinal task is one of the objectives of this work.

141 Pablo Contreras Vásquez, '¿Derechos implícitos? Notas sobre la identificación de normas de derecho fundamental' in José Ignacio Núñez Leiva (ed), *Nuevas perspectivas en derecho público* (2011) 176–177.

al character and design of the remedy of protection and the compelling scholarly critique of its performance indicate that the present work should exclude analysis of the judgments on this remedy, even though several such judgments have dealt with the constitution's norm on dignity. Moreover, the Chilean Supreme Court has resorted to dignity to justify its rulings in cases that do not involve the remedy of protection, as in several judgments on cases about human rights violations.[142] However, these rulings share the lack of doctrinal development of the concept of human dignity with those rulings on the remedy of protection.[143] Accordingly, only the relevant case law of the CCT will be examined. Secondly, the genealogy of the CPR is indeed problematic. Democracy demands a constitutional interpretation, free from authoritarian voices. Hence, the present study combines a hermeneutical approach to the CPR with substantive reservations regarding the proceedings of the CNSC and the Council of State. In addition, the recourse of these sources has been so fully explored that they would scarcely constitute a new contribution to the scholarship.

However, this does not mean that the genealogy of the legal concepts of the CPR lacks importance. On the contrary, it plays a significant role in disciplining judicial discretion – a point particularly relevant when interpreting open-ended legal clauses like human dignity. One challenge of this research will be to explore this genealogy by broader means than referring to the CNCS proceedings alone. Indeed, while the current investigation deals primarily with the Chilean constitutional text in its current form, it aims to avoid the obsolescence that might arise from further changes to the CPR, since its ultimate goal is to contribute to the theory of fundamental rights and the role of dignity.

142 For an overview of Supreme Court decisions on various cases linked to dignity, see Miguel Ángel Fernández González, 'La Dignidad Humana ante la Jurisprudencia de la Corte Suprema' in Arturo Fernandois Vohringer (ed), *Principios, Valores e Instituciones* (2016) 31–36.

143 Criticism in this sense in ibid 36, and Amaya Álvez Marín, 'Norma y Tipicidad iusfundamental' in Pablo Contreras Vazquez and Constanza Salgado Munoz (eds), *Manual sobre Derechos Fundamentales* (2017) 65.

II
Human Dignity in Chile

§ 3 Content of human dignity

1. Scholarship

1.1. Description of sources

Chilean constitutional scholarship has taken a range of approaches to the concept of human dignity, and three broad sets of sources inform the current discussion. Firstly, while most handbooks and general treatises on the CPR review the concept, their treatment varies markedly in its extent, depth, and quality. This treatment ranges from a few lines to complete chapters, and from virtual repetitions of comparative law to thought of great substance and originality.[144]

The second set of sources consists of journal articles and book chapters dealing with dignity as a primary topic – a goal pursued by relatively few authors.[145] Moreover, some of these works either take a general comparative

144 Cf. Aldunate Lizana, *Derechos Fundamentales* (n 8) 96–100; 348–352; Evans de la Cuadra (n 136) 24 ff; Jorge Mario Quinzio Figuereido, *Tratado de Derecho Constitucional* (2006) 1; Molina Guaita (n 72) 57–61; Silva Bascuñan (n 73) 21–33; Mario Verdugo Marinkovic, Emilio Pfeffer Urquiaga and Humberto Nogueira Alcalá, *Derecho Constitucional. Volume I* (2002) 109–111; José Luis Cea Egaña, *Derecho Constitucional Chileno Tomo II. Derechos, deberes y garantías* (2019) 44–50; Cea Egaña, *Derecho Constitucional Chileno Tomo I.* (n 16) 105; 204–208; Nogueira Alcalá, *Dogmática Constitucional* (n 43) 107–152.

145 Luz Bulnes Aldunate, 'Principios y Valores Constitucionales. La Dignidad de la Persona frente a la Jurisprudencia' (2004) 10 Actualidad Jurídica. La Revista de Derecho de la Universidad del Desarrollo; José Luis Cea Egaña, 'Un caso real de Violación de la Dignidad Humana', *XXV Jornadas de Derecho Público. Tomo II.* (1995); José Luis Cea Egaña, 'Dignidad de la Persona y Discrecionalidad Estatal' (2001) 4 Ius Publicum 201; Fernández González (n 142); Humberto Nogueira Alcalá, 'Dignidad de la Persona y Bloque Constitucional de Derechos' (2006) 13 Revista de Derecho (Universidad Católica del Norte) 67; Rosales Rigol (n 139);

perspective,[146] or contribute more fully to the fields of ethics, philosophy, or jurisprudence.[147] And among those examining the concept from the standpoint of constitutional law, some scholars accentuate the role of dignity as the foundation of fundamental rights,[148] or only treat human dignity in a somewhat rhetorical manner even when their work might lie within the field of public law.[149] The final group is comprised of journal articles, book chapters, and monographs that, despite focusing on other topics or themes, encompass the concept of dignity in some way or another.[150]

1.2. Dignity as a value or principle

Broadly speaking, dignity has not been viewed as a right by scholars of Chilean law. As will be seen, there are good reasons to think that when

---

Mauricio Tapia Rodríguez, 'Dignidad humana en el Derecho Civil' in Departamento de Derecho Privado Facultad de Derecho Universidad de Chile (ed), *Derecho Civil y Constitución* (2021); Gino Viale Costa, 'Derecho Penal del Enemigo y Dignidad Humana ¿es Posible Conciliar ambos Institutos' (2012) 25 Revista de Derecho (Universidad Católica de la Santísima Concepción) 71.

146 Cf., with a critical account of the performance of this concept in constitutional law, José Ignacio Martinez Estay, 'Valor de la Incorporación de Conceptos Meta-jurídicos al Lenguaje del Derecho Constitucional. El Caso de la Dignidad Humana' (2001) XXII Revista de Derecho de la Universidad Católica de Valparaíso 115, 115–121; Ignacio Covarrubias Cuevas, '¿Puede la Dignidad Humana Ser un Principio Comúnmente Compartido en Materia de Adjudicación Constitucional?' (2014) 29 Actualidad Jurídica 147, 147–166.

147 Thus, e.g., Carlos Dorn Garrido, 'La Dignidad de la Persona: Límite a la Autonomía Individual' (2011) 26 Revista de Derecho 71.

148 Eduardo Soto Kloss, 'La Dignidad de la Persona. Fundamento de los Derechos Humanos. Antecedentes Veterotestamentarios' [1987] Revista de Derecho Público 49; Jaime Williams Benavente, 'La Dignidad de la Persona Humana en la Constitución de 1980' (2001) 2 Actualidad Jurídica. La Revista de Derecho de la Universidad del Desarrollo 31.

149 Hernan Molina Guaita, 'La Dignidad del Hombre es Sagrada' (1994) LXII Revista de Derecho (Universidad de Concepción) 93; Enrique Navarro Beltrán, 'El Divorcio y la Dignidad de la Persona a la luz de la Constitución de 1980', *XXV Jornadas de Derecho Público. Tomo II.* (1995) 173–174.

150 Humberto Nogueira Alcalá, *Derechos Fundamentales y Garantías Constitucionales. Tomo I* (2018); Humberto Nogueira Alcalá, *Lineamientos de Interpretación Constitucional y del Bloque Constitucional de Derechos* (2006); Álvez Marín (n 143); Marisol Peña Torres, 'La Jurisprudencia de Valores del Tribunal Constitucional' in Arturo Fernandois Vohringer (ed), *Principios, Valores e Instituciones.* (2016); Viviana Ponce de León Solís, 'El Nudge, su Aplicación en el Derecho Chileno y sus Potenciales Problemas de Constitucionalidad' (2019) 46 Revista Chilena de Derecho 345.

a "right to dignity" is mentioned (a rare occurrence), this is without any obvious intention of affirming a doctrinal proposition. In this sense, without exception, Chilean scholarship has assumed that human dignity is a constitutional "value" or "principle." However, the differences between the meanings of these words are rarely explored, with scholars tending to use them rather indistinctly. Besides, the characterization of dignity in the literature quite frequently overlaps with other values.[151] In this vein, there is almost complete agreement that human dignity should be considered one of the most fundamental constitutional values, along with freedom and equality. Nevertheless, for some scholars, these values share the same legal status, while others rank dignity more highly.

The first of these two groups includes the position of *Ruiz-Tagle*, who maintains that fundamental rights serve as an "effective guarantee and direct enforcement" of the values of freedom, democracy, equality, and dignity.[152] He highlights a robust bond between dignity and equality, which produces three egalitarian consequences. First off, "dignity is a way to specify equality between individuals of the human race." Hence, each human being has the same right to pursue his or her life's project. Next, dignity implies the equal recognition "of nationals and foreigners, between all individuals of the human race, whether or not they belong to our same political community." Finally, dignity has a republican and democratic nature: it rejects tiers and hierarchies. In this respect, dignity relates to citizenship, "whose foundation is the equality of merits [between individuals] produced by the only fact of birth."[153] Without the same conceptual clarity, *Evans* seems to agree that dignity, equality, and freedom share the same status, although he defines them as precepts. This triad should be understood as guiding the CPR, and should take precedence in the event of any conflict with other constitutional rules.[154]

On the opposite side of the spectrum, *Nogueira* affirms the constitutional precedence of dignity, since it represents "the backbone of the whole constitutional order and is the source of all fundamental rights."[155] Along the same lines, *Cea* claims the superiority of dignity as an "absolute, intangible,

151 See, e.g., Verdugo Marinkovic, Pfeffer Urquiaga and Nogueira Alcalá (n 144) 107 ff; similarly, Ponce de León Solís (n 150) 354 ff.

152 Ruiz-Tagle Vial (n 33) 95.

153 ibid 103.

154 Evans de la Cuadra (n 136) 24

155 Nogueira Alcalá, 'Dignidad de La Persona y Bloque Constitucional de Derechos' (n 145) 69. [La dignidad de la persona se constituye en el valor supremo, columna ver-

inviolable, irreducible, illimitable and universal value and, for the same reason, a principle of equality and freedom of the human being since his conception."[156] This primacy also places it above fundamental rights, adds *Ivaceta.*[157] Human rights are legal and moral principles aim to preserve human dignity.[158] Numerous other scholars share similar viewpoints, thereby comprising most of the scholarship on this matter.[159] As will be shown, the CCT has considered dignity a value, too.

1.3. Conceptualizations of dignity

1.3.1. The concept of human dignity in the work of Humberto Nogueira

As the Chilean scholar who has explored human dignity in the greatest depth, *Nogueira* warrants a separate section.[160] His work foregrounds the crucial role played by the concept in constitutional and international law since World War Two. He has also frequently underlined the leading position that dignity should occupy in the Chilean constitutional order. His line of argument is presented below.

In one of his first lengthy treatises, *Nogueira* presented a negative approach to dignity that denies the possibility of reaching a precise conceptu-

---

tebral básica de todo el ordenamiento constitucional y fuente de todos los derechos fundamentales.]

156 Cea Egaña, *Derecho Constitucional Chileno Tomo II. Derechos, Deberes y Garantías* (n 144) 50. [(...) absoluto, intangible, inviolable, irreductible e ilimitable, universal y, por idéntica razón, principio de la igualdad y libertad del ser humano desde su concepción.]

157 David Ibaceta Medina, 'Protección de la Dignidad de las Personas Privadas de Libertad en el Bloque de Constitucionalidad' (2008) 70 Revista de Derecho Público 149, 150.

158 Quinzio Figuereido (n 144) 8.

159 See Fernández González (n 142) 30; Pfeffer Urquiaga, 'Breves Reflexiones y Algunas Propuestas en Torno a los Derechos, Garantías y Deberes Constitucionales' (n 135) 227; Rosales Rigol (n 139) 119; Viale Costa (n 145) 114.

160 See, among others, Humberto Nogueira Alcalá, 'Dignidad de la Persona, Derechos Fundamentales y Bloque Constitucional de Derechos: una Aproximación desde Chile y América Latina' (2010) 5 Revista de Derecho (Universidad Católica de Uruguay) 79; Nogueira Alcalá, *Dogmática Constitucional* (n 43) 107–151; Nogueira Alcalá, 'Dignidad de La Persona y Bloque Constitucional de Derechos' (n 145); Nogueira Alcalá, *Derechos Fundamentales y Garantías Constitucionales. Tomo I* (n 150) 11–87; Humberto Nogueira Alcalá, *Derechos Fundamentales y Garantías Constitucionales. Tomo III* (2019) 353–356.

alization while admitting only that dignity can be recognized in concrete cases of its violation. As examples of the latter, he advances any "perturbation or thread or disposal of the essential rights of the person," when "the person is humiliated, discriminated," "obstacles are set out to prevent [the person's] full deployment" or "the person is transformed into a mere object, or he is constituted as a simple means for reaching other ends."[161] Roughly a decade later, however, Nogueira came to provide a positive concept of dignity as the:

> [D]istinctive feature of the human being when compared with the remainder of living beings. This feature constitutes the person as an end-in-itself preventing him from being considered as an instrument or a means to achieve other goals. Dignity also bestows the capacity of self-determination and the free development of his personality.[162]

These two points are characterized by *Nogueira* as the areas of human dignity that should be applied directly from Art. 1, par. 1 CPR; namely, its "deontological" and "ontological" dimensions.[163] Notwithstanding this ambitious definition, *Nogueira* considers human dignity a vague and polysemous term engaged in an ongoing process of development, concretion, and delimitation.[164]

Be that as it may, *Nogueira* emphasizes two aspects of the content protected by dignity. On the one hand, dignity implies respecting the autonomy of the person; on the other, the protection of his or her dignity. This second realm is accomplished by the state through concrete acts, such as welfare measures. Also, *Nogueira* believes that only human beings – and therefore not moral or juridical persons – possess dignity, from conception until death.[165] This entitlement is independent of their "age, intellectual capacity or state of conscience."[166]

---

161 Nogueira Alcalá, *Dogmática Constitucional* (n 43) 108.

162 Nogueira Alcalá, 'Dignidad de la Persona y Bloque Constitucional de Derechos' (n 145) 68. [(…) rasgo distintivo del ser humano respecto de los demás seres vivos, la que constituye a la persona como un fin en sí mismo, impidiendo que sea considerada un instrumento o un medio para otro fin, además de dotarle de capacidad de autodeterminación y de realización libre de la personalidad.]

163 Nogueira Alcalá, 'Dignidad de la Persona, Derechos Fundamentales y Bloque Constitucional de Derechos: Una Aproximación Desde Chile y América Latina' (n 160) 86.

164 ibid 88.

165 Nogueira Alcalá, *Dogmática Constitucional* (n 43) 107.

166 ibid 108.

Nogueira generously sketches out the versatility of dignity, which represents a constitutional "material order of values."[167] On that account, it forms a limit that protects everyone against the abusive exercise of rights by third parties,[168] as well as helping to determine the essential content of each basic right.[169] The constitution's norm on dignity is directly applicable, immediately annulling any rule that ignores or contradicts it.[170] It is also a crucial aspect of constitutional interpretation and guarantees the protection of basic rights,[171] acting as the very foundation of democracy.[172] Finally, *Nogueira* believes that "the dignity of the person calls for the recognition of one's legal personality and of all that the person needs to live according to human dignity."[173]

Quoting *Maihofer*, Nogueira once implied that dignity may be considered a subjective right.[174] Exploring this idea further, he stated that "(...) [there] exists a right to dignity, which operates even when the other rights of the constitution have expired."[175] However, he neither explained what

167 Nogueira Alcalá, 'Dignidad de La Persona y Bloque Constitucional de Derechos' (n 145) 70.

168 Nogueira Alcalá, 'Dignidad de La Persona, Derechos Fundamentales y Bloque Constitucional de Derechos: Una Aproximación Desde Chile y América Latina' (n 160) 84.

169 Nogueira Alcalá, *Lineamientos de Interpretación Constitucional y Del Bloque Constitucional de Derechos* (n 150) 352.

170 Nogueira Alcalá, 'Dignidad de La Persona y Bloque Constitucional de Derechos' (n 145) 69.

171 Nogueira Alcalá, 'Dignidad de La Persona, Derechos Fundamentales y Bloque Constitucional de Derechos: Una Aproximación Desde Chile y América Latina (n 160) 84.

172 ibid 87.

173 Nogueira Alcalá, *Dogmática Constitucional* (n 43) 108.

174 ibid 114. Here *Nogueira*, following Maihofer's ideas, suggests that the human dignity clause has a triple legal meaning for the Chilean constitutional order: "Firstly, it constitutes itself an essential right, from which the other elements of the system of human or essential rights can be deduced; secondly, it constitutes a fundamental norm of the Constitution, in relation to which the other norms that compose the latter must be evaluated; thirdly, it constitutes the material basis on which the organizational structure of the state is constructed." [En primer lugar, se constituye en derecho esencial, a partir del cual se pueden deducir todos los demás components del sistema de derechos esenciales o derechos humanos; en segundo lugar, constituye una norma fundamental de la Carta Fundamental, por relación a la cual cabe dirimir la validez de otras normas que la componen; en tercer lugar, constituye la base material sobre la cual se construye la estructura organizativa del Estado.]

175 ibid. [Existe así un derecho a la dignidad, el cual opera aun cuando caduquen todos los demás derechos asegurados en la Carta Fundamental.]

the content of this right would be, nor its normative or procedural consequences. Since he does not consider dignity as an individual right in any of his later works, he may have subsequently abandoned this view.

1.3.2. José Luis Cea's approach to dignity

José Luis Cea, former Chief Justice of the CCT, is the second Chilean scholar to deal extensively with dignity.[176] During his tenure as a constitutional judge, the CCT orientated most closely to his conceptualization of dignity.[177] As seen before, *Cea* believes that dignity is the first and most important value of the CPR,[178] describing it as "the feature of the human being, which can be predicated only and exclusively as one's attribute (...)."[179] Every human being has dignity, no matter what one's condition, from conception onwards, since it is an "egalitarian feature" of each person.[180] Besides affirming the source of the concept in the theory of natural law, *Cea* expands on the matter, claiming that dignity means that every human person as such:

> (...) is born and has to co-exist with the feature of dignity, namely, as a being that is transcendent in history, as a free subject and an equal to his neighbor. The destiny of the human being is to develop a personal plan for his life.[181]

176 José Luis Cea Egaña, 'Dignidad, Derechos y Garantías en el Régimen Constitucional Chileno', *Práctica Constitucional y Derechos Fundamentales ["Constitutional Practice and Fundamental Rights"]* (1996); Cea Egaña, 'Un Caso Real de Violación de La Dignidad Humana' (n 145); Cea Egaña, 'Dignidad de La Persona y Discrecionalidad Estatal' (n 145); Cea Egaña, *Derecho Constitucional Chileno Tomo II. Derechos, Deberes y Garantías* (n 144) 44–50; Cea Egaña, *Derecho Constitucional Chileno Tomo I* (n 16) 105; 204–8.

177 As will be seen, traces of *Cea's* approach to human dignity are visible in several of the CCT's decisions. Accordingly, Fernández González (n 142) 29, in fn 26, suggests that this conception was followed by the court in decisions such as CCT Rol 389-2003, par. 17 and CCT Rol 433-2005, par. 24.

178 See *supra* subsection 1.3.

179 Cea Egaña, *Derecho Constitucional Chileno Tomo II. Derechos, Deberes y Garantías* (n 144) 44.

180 Cea Egaña (n 176) 21.

181 Cea Egaña, *Derecho Constitucional Chileno Tomo I* (n 16) 207.

Despite these expositions, and similar to *Nogueira*, *Cea* believes that in legal practice, dignity is a concept that is hard to grasp.[182] *Cea* has suggested that dignity is both a value and a subjective right. After describing some situations that constitute an encroachment on dignity, he concludes that any person has the right to respect for his or her dignity.[183] Yet, once again, this position is neither further developed nor explained.

1.3.3. Other understandings of human dignity

1.3.3.1. Summary of other understandings

Alongside the explanations provided above are several other conceptualizations of dignity deployed by other scholars including *Luis Rodríguez*, *Sergio Diez*, *David Ibaceta*, *Angela Vivanco*, *Viviana Ponce de León*, *Miguel Angel Fernández*, and *Pablo Contreras*.

Rodríguez is one of the few scholars to deduce some normative consequences from the norm on dignity linked to another constitutional rule of the constitution.[184] He suggests that the meaning of dignity derives from viewing the human individual as a subject and an autonomous and superior being. The latter facts carry three legal implications. The first feature (subjectivity) prevents the law from considering a human being as an object. The second (autonomy), grounds his or her right to self-determination, as recognized in Art. 1, par. 4 CPR.[185] Last, the superiority of the human being entails his or her precedence over the state and because superiority is predicated equally on each individual, the law cannot consider one individual or a group as superior to another.

---

182 Cea Egaña (n 176) 22.

183 ibid 21

184 Luis Rodríguez Collao, 'Honor y Dignidad de la Persona' (1999) 20 Revista de Derecho de la Pontificia Universidad Católica de Valparaíso 9, 12.

185 Art. 1, par. 4 CPR declares that "[t]he State is at the service of the human person and its end is to promote the common good, for which it must help to create the social conditions which may allow each and every one of the members of the national community his greatest possible spiritual and material [self-]realization possible, with total respect for the rights and guarantees that this Constitution establishes." [El Estado está al servicio de la persona humana y su finalidad es promover el bien común, para lo cual debe contribuir a crear las condiciones sociales que permitan a todos y a cada uno de los integrantes de la comunidad nacional su mayor realización espiritual y material posible, con pleno respeto a los derechos y garantías que esta Constitución establece.]

Diez, a former member of the CSNC, believes that dignity is the respect due to each person as such;[186] it is the treatment that persons deserve "according to his nature."[187] On the other hand, dignity is an inherent attribute of each human being. Thereby, human life and human dignity are inseparable, irrespective of the individual's age, intellectual capacities, or state of conscience. Human beings cannot lose dignity, claims *Diez*, since it is an attribute independent of personal behaviors.[188] Finally, he claims that dignity implies the state will guarantee certain aspects of welfare provision, and that the state must provide the conditions required for a person to freely develop his or her personality.[189]

Akin to this, *Ibaceta* describes dignity as:

> [T]he quality or essential condition of each person, notwithstanding his moral degree of development. Thus, a person deserves favorable treatment without distinctions or arbitrary discriminations, be the latter an act of the state or its organs, or of any person, regarding his development or his capacities. All the above are in harmony with respect for his fundamental rights (...).[190]

Ibaceta claims that all human beings possess dignity as inherent to their nature. Moreover, dignity is a permanent and unwaivable condition of the individual, from conception until death,[191] although the author also states that dignity, as the "most basic value that characterizes the human species" can be destroyed by certain acts.[192] Similarly, *Fernández* views dignity as a value that the CPR has highlighted as a distinctive characteristic of human beings from conception onward, which gives rise to inalienable human rights.[193]

Vivanco accords dignity a central role, since "every human person has dignity as such." She therefore maintains that a person must not "be treated

186 Sergio Diez Urzúa, *Personas y Valores. Su Protección Constitucional* (1999) 45.
187 ibid 47.
188 ibid.
189 ibid.
190 Ibaceta Medina (n 157) 152. [(...) la calidad o condición esencial de toda persona, al margen de su grado moral de desarrollo, que lo hace merecedor de un tratamiento favorable, sin distinciones ni discriminaciones arbitrarias, sea por el Estado, sus organismos e incluso, por toda persona, en el desarrollo de sus propias capacidades y en armonía con el respeto por sus derechos fundamentales (...).]
191 ibid.
192 ibid 155–156.
193 Fernández González (n 142) 30.

in an undignified way" and expresses this duty through the language of rights. Each human being thus has the right to be treated with dignity throughout his or her life, which includes "dying with dignity."[194] For *Vivanco*, dignity covers the freedoms of conscience, opinion, and moral autonomy, as these create the status of equality of freedom between human beings, which forms the central element of what it means to be treated with dignity.[195]

Contreras critiques some of these approaches, using *Cea's* viewpoint as a paradigmatic example of a position based on natural law, and specifically in Catholic teachings on dignity. Beginning with the CCT's definition of dignity,[196] *Contreras* deduces two aspects of dignity: dignity as autonomy, understood as respect for the free moral agency of subjects; and dignity as equality; namely, equal statuses between legal subjects of the political community.[197] Similar to *Contreras*, *Ponce de León* remarks that one of the main features of dignity is that it covers the person's ability to define his or her own aims, as well as the proper means to achieve them.[198] By the same token, *Tapia* suggests that dignity in the CPR is a legal translation of Kant's commandment that prohibits the instrumentalization of self and others.[199]

Finally, though other approaches to the term are available, these are either too briefly formulated (e.g., dignity as the nobility of the person,[200] or the inwardness that allows man to be an end-in-himself)[201] or lack some elemental features that would constitute a full conceptualization of the term.[202]

---

194 Angela Vivanco Martínez, 'El Derecho a la Vida y a la Integridad Física y Psíquica en la Carta Fundamental de 1980' in Enrique Navarro Beltrán (ed), *20 Años de la Constitución Chilena: 1981–2001* (2001) 149.

195 Angela Vivanco Martínez, *Curso de Derecho Constitucional. Vol.II* (2006) 44.

196 Pablo Contreras Vásquez, 'Titularidad de los Derechos Fundamentales', in Pablo Contreras Vásquez and Constanza Salgado Muñoz (eds), *Manual sobre Derechos Fundamentales* (2017) 122. Contreras values the CCT's conceptualization of human dignity, which he believes is conducive to doctrinal development.

197 Contreras Vásquez, 'Titularidad de Derechos Fundamentales' (n 196) 122.

198 Ponce de León Solís (n 150) 355.

199 Tapia Rodríguez (n 145) 40.

200 Julio Alvear Téllez, 'La Persona en la Constitución de 1980: Fundamentos de los Derechos y Garantías Constitucionales' in Enrique Navarro Beltran (ed), *20 Años de la Constitución Chilena: 1981–2001* (2001) 62.

201 Hernán Corral Talciani, 'El Respeto y Protección de la Vida Privada en la Constitución de 1980' in Enrique Navarro Beltrán (ed), *20 Años de la Constitución Chilena: 1981–2001* (2001) 199.

202 Silva Bascuñan (n 73) 31; Molina Guaita (n 72) 92.

1.3.3.2. The remarks of Eduardo Aldunate

Aldunate's primary concern is to identify the theoretical grounds as well as the challenges around the legal doctrine on human dignity that should be avoided by Chilean scholarship and case law.[203] He argues that, because the semantic indeterminacy of constitutional dignity allows several different attributions of meaning, it is necessary to agree on the minimum content required of any conceptualization of dignity.[204] Accordingly, dignity may be defined as an individual attribution inherent in certain features of a human being, such as his or her freedom and rationality, which in turn entitles all persons to claim respect from the community. Human dignity is consequently:

> [T]he value of the potential of individual human development towards the realization of the free rational self-determination of every person, a value that is present in human relationships.[205]

The legal implications are, at minimum, that every human being must be recognized as a legal person and holder of rights – a rather late development in human rights history, remarks *Aldunate.*[206]

1.4. Foundation of human dignity

1.4.1. Ruling opinion

Chilean constitutional scholarship has not focused on this topic, with the core of the ruling opinion reducible to two basic points. First, dignity is held to derive from some inherent human features. For instance, a well-known handbook maintains that "(...) dignity is the product of [a human's] character as a conscious, rational, perfectible (...) and affective being."[207] *Silva,* similarly, states that the "essential characteristic of man, which separates him from the rest of the creatures, consists in the fact

203 Aldunate Lizana, *Derechos Fundamentales ["Fundamental Rights"]* (n 8) 96–98; 100.
204 ibid 99.
205 ibid. [Se llega así a formular una idea de dignidad como el valor de la potencia de desarrollo humano individual hacia la realización de la autodeterminación racional y libre de cada persona, presente en las relaciones humanas.]
206 ibid. On this development, see § 12.
207 Verdugo Marinkovic, Pfeffer Urquiaga and Nogueira Alcalá (n 144) 110.

that he is gifted with intelligence (...) and free will."[208] This moral, free, and rational nature, *Nogueira* asserts, makes the human superior to other created beings.[209] Therefore, continues *Fernández*, dignity is an inherent attribute of human beings, and does not depend on any state, societal, or constitutional recognition.[210] In other words, dignity is grounded in the fact that each human being is his or her "own master."[211]

Second, the inherent features of human beings that ground dignity are conceived of as *transcendental gifts*, particularly in the sense of traditional Catholic teachings on the matter. The ultimate justification for dignity then rests on the belief that humans were created in God's image.[212] *Diez* suggests that this grounding is acknowledged by the CPR when it specifies that one goal of the state is to achieve the maximal spiritual and material development of each member of the national community.[213] Consequently, this divine foundation, alongside inherent human characteristics, constitutes the "dual root of the dignity of man."[214] Thus, constitutional dignity must be considered "spiritual".[215] On this account, *Nogueira* claims that dignity constitutes "an ontological and supra-constitutional reality"; one that the "state only recognises and guarantees, but does not create."[216] Other authors follow a similar line of reasoning.[217]

---

208 Silva Bascuñan (n 73) 30. [(...) la característica esencial del hombre, que lo separa de las demás creaturas, consiste en estar dotado de *inteligencia* (...) y de *libre albedrio.*]

209 Nogueira Alcalá, *Dogmática Constitucional* (n 43) 108.

210 Fernández González (n 142) 29.

211 Alvear Téllez (n 200) 62.

212 Cea Egaña, *Derecho Constitucional Chileno Tomo II. Derechos, Deberes y Garantías* (n 144) 45; Diez Urzúa (n 186) 175; Nogueira Alcalá, *Dogmática Constitucional* (n 43) 107–108; Silva Bascuñan (n 73) 31; Soto Kloss (n 148) 52.

213 Diez Urzúa (n 186) 45.

214 Silva Bascuñan (n 73) 31.

215 Quinzio Figuereido (n 144) 1.

216 Nogueira Alcalá, *Dogmática Constitucional* (n 43) 108. Also, Nogueira Alcalá, 'Dignidad de La Persona y Bloque Constitucional de Derechos' (n 145) 70, which states that human dignity is a concept shared by Christian and secular humanism, from liberalism to democratic socialism.

217 See Evans de la Cuadra (n 136) 24, where the author, commenting on Art. 1, par. 1 CPR, recalls that the ideas behind dignity come from Christian doctrine on man and society. In a similar sense, see also Williams Benavente (n 148) 55; Bulnes Aldunate (n 145) 121. The ruling opinion follows what is, in Germany, called the "Theory of Dowry" [Mitgifttheorie]. See § 7, subsection 2.1.1

1.4.2. Other approaches

While agreeing with the ruling opinion that human dignity is grounded in inherent features of the human being, *Aldunate* does not regard these as necessarily following from a transcendental order. In addition, he suggests that the practical meaning of human dignity lies in mutual human respect,[218] describing the social dimension of dignity as a claim to respect.[219]

Conversely, *Undurraga* seems to affirm that the foundation of dignity does not lie in inherent potentialities but in the individual's capacity to act autonomously.[220] *Contreras*, in turn, expressly rejects the ruling opinion, which he asserts is grounded in the theory of natural law. *Contreras* may thus be the only Chilean scholar to propose a contingent and communicative legitimation of dignity by suggesting the latter is not based on inherent human features but on the reciprocal recognition between members of the polity.[221]

2. The jurisprudence of the Chilean Constitutional Tribunal

2.1. Legal form

The CCT has repeatedly characterized dignity as a value or principle via various statements emphasizing its juridical importance.[222] It initially qualifies Art. 1, par. 1 CPR, as the "capital" principle,[223] and "matrix principle of the current institutional system."[224] Moreover, it refers to dignity as the "fundamental principle,"[225] the "pinnacle" of the national constitutional or-

218 Aldunate Lizana, *Derechos Fundamentales* (n 8) 98–99.

219 In this sense, the opinion of Aldunate is also connected with the "Theory of Recognition" [Anerkennungstheorie]. See § 7, subsection 2.1.3.

220 Verónica Undurraga, 'Derecho a la autonomía personal y libre desarrollo de la personalidad' in Pablo Contreras and Constanza Salgado Muñoz (eds), *Curso de Derechos Fundamentales* (2021) 46, who, however, then suggests that the right to personal autonomy is an implicit right that can be deduced from human dignity.

221 Contreras Vásquez, 'Titularidad de Derechos Fundamentales (n 196) 121–122

222 See, e.g., CCT Rol 943-2007, par. 16; CCT Rol 389-2003, par 27; CCT 740-2007, par. 46; CCT 1185-08, par. 11.

223 CCT Rol 389-2003, par. 17. [principio capital]

224 CCT Rol 1287-2008, par. 16; CCT Rol 976-2007, par. 22. [matriz del sistema institucional vigente]

225 CCT Rol 433-2005, par. 24. [principio fundamental]

der,[226] the "supreme value,"[227] and "guiding principle of the entire juridical order."[228] In this sense, the legal system must be understood as a "set of instruments" at the service of human dignity.[229]

Finally, the CCT has also defined dignity as a rule or norm, "notwithstanding its legal description as a principle," at least in the Chilean constitution.[230] As a result, dignity doubly influences the remaining clauses of the Constitution, both as a principle and a positive norm.[231]

2.2. Concept and content of human dignity

The CCT has developed its own approach to dignity, defining it as:

> (...) the quality of the human being that makes him always deserving of respect because dignity is the source of the essential rights and the guarantees aimed to obtain their protection.[232]

And as the quality:

> (...) of a legal subject, so of every human being as such.[233]

In addition to affirming this unconditionality of human dignity, the CCT has meticulously described the difference between dignity as enshrined in Art. 1, par. 1 CPR and the dignity of public office.[234] The universal human

226 CCT Rol 1348–2009, par. 27. [cúspide]
227 CCT Rol 1340–2009, par. 20. [valor supremo]
228 CCT Rol 3364–2017, par. 17. [principio rector de todo el ordenamiento jurídico]
229 CCT Rol 8892–2020, par. 30. [conjunto de instrumentos]
230 CCT Rol 1348–2009, par. 30:"On the other hand, in the well-known distinction of Dworkin between norms and principles, it is possible to place a person's dignity among the 'norms' because, though it has a legal description of a principle, the dignity of the person is a juridical norm, at least in the Chilean juridical order." [Por otra parte, en la conocida distinción de Dworkin entre "normas y principios" es dable ubicar a la dignidad de la persona entre las "normas," pues, aun teniendo un contenido típico de principio, la dignidad de la persona es una norma jurídica, por lo menos en el ordenamiento jurídico chileno (...).]
231 CCT Rol 1348–2009, par. 31.
232 CCT Rol 389–2003, par. 17; definition used again on other judgments, such as CCT Rol 3729–2017, par. 132. [(..) la cualidad del ser humano que lo hace siempre digno de respeto, porque ella es la fuente de los derechos esenciales y de las garantías destinadas a obtener su protección.]
233 CCT Rol 3062–2016, par. 2. [sujeto de derecho de todo hombre como tal]
234 See CCT 3421–2017, pars. 9–14.

quality may be deduced directly from Art. 1,[235] which additionally prohibits the instrumentalization of any human being.[236] In other words, dignity implies that the "human being must always be respected as such, simply by virtue of his humanity, without taking into consideration other attributes or personal capacities."[237] A person's dignity further implies that the rights to which he or she is entitled are precedent to positive law, "since they are manifestations of [his or her] own nature (...)."[238]

According to the CCT, dignity is also linked to the "nature of the human being," which is a spiritual-corporeal being with a transcendent meaning in the constitutional order. Therefore, the human being is "superior and precedent to the state and society."[239] Furthermore, human dignity is what raises people above any other entity, be that alive or inanimate.[240]

2.3. Holders of human dignity

In several decisions, the CCT has stated that every human being, without distinction or exclusion, is gifted with dignity, as can be "deduced from Art. 1, par. 1" CPR.[241] Accordingly, the unborn holds dignity as well.[242] However, in a more recent decision, the CCT has judged, without expressly saying that the unborn child lacks dignity, that it is not a legal person, and therefore has no rights, including the right to life.[243] Nevertheless, the

235 CCT Rol 1287-2008, par. 16.

236 CCT Rol 3729-2017, par. 132.

237 CCT Rol 433-2005, par. 24. [ha de ser siempre respetado en sí mismo por el sólo hecho de serlo, con total independencia de sus atributos o capacidades personales.]

238 CCT Rol 740-2007, par. 68. [manifestaciones de su propia naturaleza]

239 CCT Rol 3364-2017, par. 17.

240 CCT Rol 3364-2017, par. 17. No concurring or dissenting opinions have provided a different conceptualization of dignity. However, one concurring opinion has sketched further elements that complement the jurisprudence of the CCT. Justice Mariano Fernández, concurring opinion, Rol 740-2007, affirmed that "[h]uman dignity encompasses the dignity of the person enshrined in Article 1 of the Constitution, but exceeds it both in its positive and natural juridical meaning. (...) The juridical dimension of dignity rests in the positive enshrinement of the fundamental rights (...)."

241 CCT Rol 976-07, par. 22. Quoting the latter decision, e.g., CCT Rol 1287-2008, par. 16; CCT Rol 1348-2009, par. 27.

242 CCT Rol 740-2007, pars. 40-60.

243 CCT Rol 3729-2017, pars. 40 and 62-78.

dignity of the woman, the CCT confusingly suggests later, may limit the right to life of the unborn, as when a pregnancy is terminated.[244]

2.4. Effects of human dignity on the legal doctrine of fundamental rights

The CCT has regularly highlighted two normative areas where human dignity influences the general theory of fundamental rights: first and most frequently, dignity as the foundation of basic rights and the juridical order,[245] and second, dignity as both a limitation to fundamental rights and to certain restrictions on these rights.[246]

In addition, the CCT sees dignity as a fundamental source of interpretation for constitutional precepts, remarking on the central interpretative role of Art. 1 CPR since it came into effect. As early as 1983, the court stated that this norm "orients the interpreter in its mission of declaring and explaining the true meaning and scope"[247] of constitutional norms.[248] Furthermore, any general reference made to the values and principles expressed in the constitution's first chapter ("Institutional Foundations")[249] to interpret the CPR includes dignity, as the CCT has asserted on several occasions.[250] Nevertheless, beside the deduction of some implicit rights[251] and broad references to the concept, there are few concrete applications of dignity as a decisive interpretative means in CCT case law.

3. *Summary*

Chilean constitutional scholarship and case law have developed several approaches to dignity. Most commonly, these include theories that ground dignity in inherent human qualities or as a transcendental gift. Such approaches view human dignity as the most crucial constitutional value or

244 CCT Rol 3729–2017, par. 49.
245 See § 4.
246 See § 6.
247 CCT Rol 19–1983, par. 9.
248 In almost identical language, Rol 53–1988, par. 12.
249 See *supra* subsection 1.4.
250 See, e.g., Rol 46–1987, par. 19; Rol 245–1996.
251 See § 4.

principle, which every individual holds,[252] an understanding highlighted by the CCT's own conceptualization.[253]

Against this background, the dimensions of dignity as described by case law and in scholarship may be classified into four major groups.

a) The superiority of the human being before the state, as well as before any other living being.[254]
b) The respect for autonomy,[255] free moral capacity,[256] self-determination,[257] free development of personality,[258] or everyone's (equal) capacity of pursuing a life project,[259] which includes the definition of the means to achieve the latter.[260]
c) The protection of basic equality between human beings,[261] including between nationals and foreigners.[262]
d) The protection of human subjectivity,[263] personal identity, and individuality,[264] as well as the guarantee of intimacy,[265] which includes a protected area of family and private life,[266] and the possibility of conscientious objection.[267]

---

252 Fernández González concurs with this view (n 142) 26–27.
253 See *supra* subsection 2.2.
254 Rodríguez Collao (n 184) 12.
255 ibid; Vivanco Martínez, *Curso de Derecho Constitucional. Vol.II* (n 195) 44.
256 Contreras Vazquez, 'Titularidad de Derechos Fundamentales' (n 196) 122.
257 Aldunate Lizana, *Derechos Fundamentales* (n 8) 162.
258 Nogueira Alcalá, 'Dignidad de La Persona y Bloque Constitucional de Derechos' (n 145) 224; CCT Rol 1683–2010, par. 51; CCT Rol 398–2003, par. 21; CCT Rol 433–2005, par. 27.
259 Evans de la Cuadra (n 136) 24.
260 Ponce de León Solís (n 150) 55.
261 Cea Egaña, *Derecho Constitucional Chileno Tomo II. Derechos, Deberes y Garantías* (n 144) 50; Rodríguez Collao (n 184) 12; Contreras Vazquez, 'Titularidad de Los Derechos Fundamentales ["Ownership of Fundamental Rights"]' (n 196) 122.
262 Ruiz-Tagle Vial (n 33) 103.
263 Rodríguez Collao (n 184) 12.
264 CCT Rol 1340–2009, par. 10.
265 CCT Rol 398–2003, par. 27; CCT Rol 433–2005, par. 34.
266 A concretization of this dimension was achieved by the CCT's declaration of the confidentiality of private communications; see CCT Rol 389–2003, par. 27.
267 CCT Rol 3729–2017, par. 131.

4. Evaluation and criticism

4.1. General remarks

Only limited normative consequences of dignity have been inferred from the approaches described above. Apart from providing a basis for basic fundamental rights, other functions of dignity in the legal doctrine of basic rights have not been systematically deployed, as shown below. Moreover, there is a clear lack of a doctrinal consensus on how the CPR's dignity clause should be treated.

4.2. Indistinct characterization of the term as a principle or value

Chilean scholarship and case law have used the terms "principle" and "value" indistinctly when defining the legal form of dignity. But this should not obscure the possible normative differences between a constitutional value versus a constitutional principle.[268] Furthermore, since the Chilean Constitution does not itself define the legal form of such crucial yet highly interpretable notions,[269] these must ultimately await clarification by legal practitioners. The CCT has only intensified the problem, when, while failing to differentiate between dignity as a value or as a principle within its case law, it has made characterizations of the concept that more appropriately belong to legal theory, thereby unnecessarily complicating the doctrinal understanding of dignity.[270]

268 For an exception, see Verdugo Marinkovic, Pfeffer Urquiaga and Nogueira Alcalá (n 144) 80, who differentiate between the concepts of values and principles. However, the authors also use both the terms "value" and "principle" to describe dignity.

269 For example, the Constitution of Spain itself states that freedom, justice, equality, and political pluralism are the superior *values* of the juridical order (Art. 1.1.), while legality, and normative hierarchy, among others, are presented as *principles* (Art. 9.3; emphasis added).

270 See Rol 1348–2009, par. 30: "Certainly, among the so-called general principles of the law, those labeled as positive principles of the law are distinguished (...), within them, it is possible to locate the dignity of the person. In contrast, in the well-known distinction by Dworkin between norms and principles, it is possible to locate dignity of the person within the 'norms' because, while its legal description is that of a principle, the dignity of the person is a juridical norm, at least in the Chilean juridical order." [Por otra parte, en la conocida distinción de Dworkin entre "normas y principios" es dable ubicar a la dignidad de la persona entre las "normas," pues, aun teniendo un contenido típico de principio, la dignidad de la persona es una norma

4.3. Indistinct substrate of dignity

Different terms allow different interpretations of normative wordings, which may entail profoundly divergent legal consequences. While a philosophical, moral, or religious viewpoint might permit the terms "human being" and "person" to be used interchangeably, this is not the case in law, where the word "person" has a specific technical meaning, as the very legal notion of a "juridical person" [corporative legal entity] shows. The current study found that both Chilean scholarship and case law tend, with some exceptions, to implement these terms interchangeably when dealing with dignity. This suggests the link between dignity and the concept of person has not been considered in sufficient depth, particularly regarding the role that dignity plays as a criterion for attributing legal personhood.[271]

4.4. Connection to the positive constitutional text

In general, the ambiguity of some language in the concrete conceptualizations reviewed weakens their link to the CPR's clause on dignity. Too frequently, discussions and conclusions from other constitutions – even those featuring dignity clauses with quite different wordings – have been somewhat uncritically applied to the Chilean case.[272] Although the treatment of dignity in other jurisdictions must be considered, it is crucial to focus on the unique features of the CPR's positive text on dignity when proposing a particular content, legal form, and normative consequences for this clause.

---

jurídica, por lo menos en el ordenamiento jurídico chileno (...).] In this context, it is not clear what is the content of the doctrinal statement that the court is trying to do with this quotation. See also *supra* subsection 2.2.

271 For an exception, see the exposition given in Aldunate Lizana, *Derechos Fundamentales* (n 8) 96–100, § 5.

272 Making the same observation, Aldunate Lizana ibid 349 particularly criticizes how scholars have freighted dignity with the role of the foundation of basic rights without further relation to Art. 1, par. 1 CPR.

5. Open questions – construction of an operative concept supported by the positive text

As already suggested,[273] to maintain the view that human dignity is the foundation of fundamental rights in a given constitutional order and that it plays an outstanding normative role in it requires the development of a functional concept defining clearly what human dignity protects and how it does so. While Chilean scholarship and case law have repeatedly affirmed the former, they have not successfully realized the latter. In order to benefit fully from the potentialities of human dignity and avoid its risks, this task must be accomplished.

273 ibid 99.

§ 4 Foundation of basic rights

1. Scholarship

Scholars of the Chilean Constitution overwhelmingly view dignity as the foundation or source of fundamental rights. One leading jurist in this regard is *Nogueira*, who has repeatedly emphasized the grounding function of human dignity. Hence, dignity represents a "supra-positive and supra-constitutional" grounding of basic rights,[274] whose fundamentality rests on the fact that they are the immediate and positive expression of dignity.[275] Moreover, each individual basic right contributes to developing a particular ambit of dignity.[276] The extralegal character of dignity also provides a source for all legal and moral duties, such as those that demand respect for human rights.[277] Consequently, the CPR does not create the value of dignity but merely recognises and guarantees it.[278] Thus, no constitutional reform may "ignore, delete, reduce or denaturalize" dignity,[279] which also serves as the foundation of the entire constitutional order.[280]

Comparably, *Cea* maintains that fundamental rights are inherent to human dignity and emanate therefrom.[281] In other words, dignity is the "axiological substratum" of human rights and their correlative duties,[282] and functions as the moral and anthropological grounding of basic rights.[283]

274 Nogueira Alcalá, *Dogmática Constitucional* (n 43) 107.
275 ibid 130.
276 Nogueira Alcalá, 'Dignidad de La Persona, Derechos Fundamentales y Bloque Constitucional de Derechos: Una Aproximación Desde Chile y América Latina' (n 160) 86.
277 Nogueira Alcalá, *Dogmática Constitucional* (n 43) 109.
278 Nogueira Alcalá, 'Dignidad de La Persona y Bloque Constitucional de Derechos' (n 145) 70.
279 Nogueira Alcalá, *Lineamientos de Interpretación Constitucional y del Bloque Constitucional de Derechos* (n 150) 225.
280 Nogueira Alcalá, *Dogmática Constitucional* (n 43) 113.
281 José Luis Cea Egaña, *El Sistema Constitucional Chileno: Síntesis Crítica* (1999) 90.
282 Cea Egaña (n 176) 21.
283 Cea Egaña, *Derecho Constitucional Chileno Tomo II. Derechos, Deberes y Garantías* (n 144) 49.

Similar claims are advanced in most of the Chilean doctrine.[284] Here, human dignity has been described as the essential value of the CPR, on which all other constitutional values and rights are founded,[285] or as the unique and noblest source from which they all emanate.[286] Dignity has also been conceptualized as the source of all rights due to its key role in supporting the right to life.[287]

2. Case law

There are three different ways that the CCT concurs with the current scholarship on the crucial role played by dignity in grounding basic rights. First, the CCT has continuously emphasized that dignity justifies all rights in a general sense; second, human dignity grounds particular positive constitutional rights to which it is linked particularly closely; and finally, the CCT has deduced some implicit rights from the dignity clause itself.

2.1. Foundation of all rights in general

In a few judgments, the court has ruled that dignity is the "cornerstone of the whole edifice of fundamental rights,"[288] "the source of the essential rights and the guarantees aimed to obtain their protection,"[289] and, in particular, of those rights enshrined in the CPR's Bill of Rights (Art. 19).[290] The CCT has also said that basic rights "emanate"[291] from, are "consubstan-

284 In this sense, also Ibaceta Medina (n 157) 150; Rosales Rigol (n 139) 119; Soto Kloss (n 148) 52; Tapia Rodríguez (n 145) 40; Bulnes Aldunate (n 145) 127; Williams Benavente (n 148) 31.

285 Emilio Pfeffer Urquiaga, 'Algunos Criterios que Permiten Solucionar el Conflicto Derivado de la Colisión de Derechos' (1998) Número Especial, Revista de Derecho 225, 227.

286 Molina Guaita (n 72) 60.

287 Vivanco Martínez, 'El Derecho a la Vida y a la Integridad Física y Psíquica en la Carta Fundamental de 1980' (n 194) 143–146.

288 CCT Rol 834–2007, par. 25; similarly, CCT Rol 1340–2009, par. 9.

289 CCT Rol 389–2003, par. 17; statement repeated in several later judgments. See, e.g., CCT Rol 3729–2017, par. 132.

290 CCT Rol 976–2007, par. 22; CCT 1287–2008, par. 16.

291 CCT Rol 976–2007, par. 33; CCT Rol 1287–2008 pars. 33 and 41.

tial"[292] with or "inherent"[293] to human dignity. The CCT further elucidated this in detail, when it affirmed that from human dignity:

> [A] cluster of attributes is derived, with which the person is born and that is preserved throughout his life. Between those attributes, there are subjective public rights or faculties that the juridical order guarantees to the person. These faculties are inalienable, inviolable, and irrevocable at any moment, in any place or circumstance.[294]

The CCT has therefore concluded that basic rights enable the most extensive deployment of human dignity.[295] It has provided some universal recommendations, speaking about dignity in a prescriptive form and stating that on dignity "must rest the existence of any juridical order."[296]

2.2. Foundation of concrete rights

2.2.1. The legal doctrine of strictly personal rights

The CCT has also suggested that there are some positive constitutional rights within the CPR that are more closely linked to dignity or that emanate more directly from it than others. The CCT has called these "strictly personal rights," as "belonging to the moral patrimony of every individual," or of "moral and spiritual essence."[297] In this sense, these rights:

> (...) form the moral patrimony of each individual, which emanates from personal dignity (...) and are [the strictly personal rights], as intimate to

292 CCT Rol 976–2007, pars. 34, 36, 38 and 39; CCT Rol 1287–2008, pars. 35, 37, 39 and 40.

293 CCT Rol 976–2007, par. 40; CCT Rol 1287–2008, par. 41.

294 Rol 976–2007, par 23.[(...) un conjunto de atributos, con los cuales la persona nace y conserva a lo largo de su vida. Entre estos atributos, están los derechos públicos subjetivos o facultades que el orden jurídico garantiza a la persona. Estas facultades son inalienables, inviolables e irrenunciables en todo lugar o circunstancia.] Compare the similarity to the description in Cea Egaña, *Derecho Constitucional Chileno Tomo I* (n 16) 207.

295 CCT Rol 8452–2020, par. 25.

296 CCT Rol 1348–09, par. 38.

297 Settled CCT case law. See CCT Rol 389–2003, par. 20; CCT Rol 943–2009, pars. 25, 27 and 36; CCT Rol 1185–2008, par. 16; CCT Rol 5278–2018, par. 8.

> any subject, those that are closer to this unique and distinctive characteristic [dignity] of the human being.[298]

This proximity charachterizes strictly personal rights as deserving "categorical exceptional recognition and protection," not only from the state but also from any act of authority, the conduct of an individual, or stipulations entered into between them.[299] Specifically, the CCT has included in this category the right to a private life (Art. 19, no. 4 CPR),[300] the inviolability of private communications (Art. 19, no. 5),[301] and the right to honor (Art. 19, no. 4).[302]

2.2.2. Implicit rights derived from dignity

2.2.2.1. Right to personal identity

First, either in conjunction with Art. 5, par. 2 CPR,[303] or solely as a direct aspect of dignity,[304] the CCT has affirmed the existence of an implicit basic right to personal identity under the Chilean Constitution. More concretely, it has identified a close relationship between this right and human dignity, since the latter "is only firmly stated when the person knows with certainty his origins, and from that base, aspires to be acknowledged as such by society."[305] The right to personal identity, as an emanation of human dignity, the CCT continues, "implies the possibility that each person can be himself

298 CCT Rol 398–2003, par. 20. [Que la privacidad, en los variados rubros descritos, integra los derechos personalísimos o del patrimonio moral de cada individuo, los cuales emanan de la dignidad personal, como se ha dicho, y son, por su cualidad de íntimos de cada sujeto, los más cercanos o próximo a esta característica, única y distintiva del ser humano]

299 CCT Rol 398–2003, par. 20. [Por tal razón, ellos merecen reconocimiento y protección excepcionalmente categóricos tanto por la ley, como por los actos de autoridad y las conductas de particulares o las estipulaciones celebradas entre éstos.] Similarly, in CCT Rol 521–2006, par. 20.

300 CCT Rol 389–2003, par. 18, and similarly in CCT Rol 521–2006, par. 19.

301 CCT Rol 389–2003, par. 18, and similarly in CCT Rol 521–2006, par. 19.

302 CCT Rol 1185–2008, par. 16; CCT Rol 943–2009, par. 25.

303 CCT Rol 1340–2009, par. 10. This claim is also a strict personal right.

304 CCT Rol 3364–17, par. 17.

305 CCT Rol 834–2007, par. 25. Similarly, CCT Rol 1340–2009, par. 10.

and not another (...)."[306] This claim includes the right to a name,[307] which should correspond when possible with that bestowed by an individual's biological parents.[308] Indeed, to know this origin is itself a dimension of the right to personal identity.[309] Finally, the right to gender identity manifests another dimension of the right to personal identity, and must be considered an offspring of human dignity.[310]

2.2.2.2. Right to conscientious objection

The CCT held that a right to conscientious objection created by statutory law must be understood as covered by the constitutional dignity clause.[311] The tribunal reasoned, based on its own conceptualization of dignity,[312] that:

> (...) no law may use persons as means up to a point even including the obligation of the persons, as if they were just human resources, to dispose of the convictions that define them as such, in order to satisfy the wishes, appetites, or needs of others. Such an alienation implies, then, to deprive the addressees of the norm of their inherent quality as persons (...).[313]

Thereupon, the CCT held that the right to conscientious objection is also a manifestation of the right to freedom of conscience, ensured by Art. 19, no. 6 CPR.[314] This right, added the CCT, when stated in favor of natural

306 CCT Rol 1340-2009, par. 10.
307 CCT Rol 1340-2009, par. 10.
308 CCT Rol 3364-2017, par. 18.
309 CCT Rol 3364-2017, par. 11.
310 CCT Rol 7620-2020, par. 13.
311 CCT Rol 3729-2017, par. 131.
312 See § 3, subsection 2.2.
313 CCT Rol 3729-2017, par. 132. [De esta forma, ninguna ley puede disponer de las personas como un medio; a un punto tal que incluso a costa de tener que enajenar las propias convicciones que la definen como persona, cual recurso humano, sea puesta a satisfacer los deseos, apetencia o necesidad de otros. Tal alienación tal implica, entonces, despojar a los destinatarios de la norma de misma calidad de personas (...).]
314 CCT Rol 3729-2017, par. 133.

persons in a relevant case, may be extended to institutions as juridical persons, but then rather in accordance with Art. 1, par. 3 CPR.[315]

2.2.2.3. Right to free development of personality

Finally, the CCT, while affirming that the right to personal freedom (Art. 19, no. 17 CPR) may not be understood in a broader sense than mere freedom of movement,[316] maintained that this understanding:

> [does] not mean to ignore that the free development of personality constitutes an expression of the dignity of each person, a dignity that is emphatically affirmed in Art. 1, par. 1 of the Constitution.[317]

Accordingly, the free development of personality is obtained from dignity in conjunction with the right to life and communication.[318] However, both rulings lack precision. It is not entirely clear whether the CCT is constructing a fundamental right implicit in the constitution's dignity clause, or just affirming values.

3. *Evaluation, criticism, and open questions*

3.1. Lack of strong positive-legal text support for dignity as the foundation of rights in general

Aldunate is one of the few scholars who has relativized the otherwise absolutely dominant perspective that dignity is the foundation of basic rights in general. While cautioning that the majoritarian position is based on doctrine developed in the Spanish or German contexts, he asserts that, unlike those constitutional texts, Art. 1, par. 1 CPR does not enshrine an equivalent relation between rights and dignity. Accordingly, at least on first view, it would be untenable to frame dignity as a basis of fundamental rights in the

---

315 CCT Rol 3729–2017, par. 136 ff. Therefore, the constitutional basis for this right of legal entities is the autonomy of civil society organizations and freedom of association. See also CCT Rol 5527–2018, par. 24.

316 CCT Rol 1683–2010, pars. 50 and 51, which reflect on the right to the free development of personality in relation to dignity, not personal freedom (Art. 19 no. 7 CPR).

317 CCT Rol 1683–2010, par. 51.

318 CCT Rol 398–2003, par. 21; Rol 433–2005, par. 27.

Chilean case.[319] However, *Aldunate* does not appear to entirely deny this possibility, but to demand more sophisticated and profound support for the point. Hence, a deeper justification of that sort of statement is still required.

3.2. Theory of strictly personal rights: not sufficiently convincing

As described above, the CCT has characterized some rights as "strictly personal" because they are intimately connected with human dignity, utilizing a concept from civil law.[320] These rights, claims the tribunal, deserve particular protection. However, if dignity is the foundation of all fundamental rights, to suggest – without stating convincing doctrinal reasons – that some rights enjoy a privileged bond with dignity and must therefore benefit from greater protection, implies the presence of arbitrary hierarchies within fundamental rights. While predetermining that some rights will always outweigh others when they conflict, this characterization also encroaches on the constitutional design of competences. If the CPR has established equality between fundamental rights, they may not then be ranked by the CCT.

3.3. Implicit rights – risk of arbitrariness

The CCT and the ruling opinion have affirmed that, according to Art 5, par. 2 CPR, the Bill of Rights is not exhaustive. Accordingly, the CPR contains some implicit rights, including those that may originate in the dignity clause.[321] However, neither scholarship nor case law has supplied enough doctrinal criteria to pursue this line of argument with sufficient clarity. There has been some scholarly reaction to this situation. *Contreras*, for one, utterly rejects that possibility, insisting that, under the current doctrinal

319 Aldunate Lizana, *Derechos Fundamentales* (n 8) 349.

320 Jorge Eduardo Aillapán Quinteros, 'El Derecho a la Propia Imagen: ¿Derecho Personalísimo?, ¿Derecho Fundamental? Precisiones terminológicas para el ordenamiento jurídico chileno' (2016) 43 Revista chilena de derecho 433.

321 See *supra* § 2.2.2 and § 2.5; see also Pfeffer Urquiaga, 'Breves Reflexiones y Algunas Propuestas en Torno a los Derechos, Garantías y Deberes Constitucionales' (n 135) 171; Silva Bascuñan (n 73) 26–27; Vivanco Martínez, 'La Importancia del Concepto Constitucional de Persona y la Protección de la Vida en la Carta Fundamental de 1980' (n 77) 328.

state, any subjective claim presumed to fall under the scope of dignity could be recognized as a fundamental right: "In other words, if arguing that one has a fundamental right only and exclusively because it shall be understood that it forms part of human dignity, then the work of redacting a Bill of Rights and specifying its guarantees becomes futile."[322]

All things considered, it remains to be tested whether a more sophisticated legal doctrine on dignity might open a new path that avoids the undesirable effects of the majority position without abandoning the affordances of dignity for resolving juridical conflicts. In that sense, *Candia* has affirmed that, confronted by broad norms such as the dignity clause, the constitutional judge be permitted to recognize the implicit rights in an act that should be characterized as a normative construction rather than an interpretative act. However, explains *Candia,* in this formulation, the judge is limited by several factors, including the principles of the rule of law and those rights that are expressly recognized by the constitution.[323] In this context, a reconstruction of the CPR's dignity clause probably demands not only a detailed approach to the norm worded in Art. 1, par. 1 but also in Art. 5, par. 2 CPR. The latter may help with disciplined interpretations of the phrase "essential rights that emanate from human nature."

322 Contreras Vásquez, '¿Derechos Implícitos? Notas sobre la Identificación de Normas de Derecho Fundamental' (n 141) 172–173.

323 Gonzalo Candia Falcón, 'Analizando la Tesis de los Derechos Implícitos: Comentario a la Sentencia del Tribunal Constitucional Recaída sobre el Requerimimiento de Inaplicabilidad Rol N°2408–2013' (2014) 21 Revista de Derecho (Universidad Católica del Norte) 497, 498.

§ 5 Ownership of basic rights

1. Description of sources

As previously mentioned, the ownership of basic rights is a topic that, generally speaking, has been inadequately covered by treatises and handbooks of constitutional law.[324] In this sense, the Chilean scholarship has scarcely dealt with this subject, which, in addition, is the central theme of only a small number of articles.[325] What remains is covered in works devoted to the right to life[326] and is mostly the reactive product of discussions around other regulations. Specifically, more than as an independent general element of legal doctrine, the ownership of fundamental rights has been addressed in the course of debates concerning the right to life of the unborn. It has particularly arisen as a reaction to norms regulating the distribution of the morning-after pill (2007) and the termination of pregnancy (2016).[327]

---

324 See § 2, subsection 2 ff.

325 Manuel A Núñez Poblete, 'Titularidad y Sujetos Pasivos de los Derechos Fundamentales' (2001) 63 Revista de Derecho Público 200; Contreras Vásquez, 'Titularidad de Derechos Fundamentales' (n 196); Eduardo Aldunate Lizana, 'La Titularidad de los Derechos Fundamentales' (2003) 1 Estudios Constitucionales 187.

326 See, e.g., Humberto Nogueira, 'El Derecho a la Vida en el Ordenamiento Jurídico Chileno' [1997] Gaceta Jurídica; Hernán Corral Talciani, 'El Concepto Jurídico de Persona y su Relevancia para la Protección del Derecho a la Vida' (2005) 11 Ius et Praxis 37; Patricio Zapata Larraín, 'Persona y Embrión Humano Nuevos Problemas Legales y su Solución en el Derecho Chileno' (1998) 15 Revista Chilena de Derecho; Vivanco Martínez, 'El Derecho a la Vida y a la Integridad Física y Psíquica en la Carta Fundamental de 1980' (n 194); Vivanco Martínez, *Disposición Sobre La Vida Humana y Principios Constitucionales* (n 35); Vivanco Martínez, 'La Importancia del Concepto Constitucional de Persona y la Protección de la Vida en la Carta Fundamental de 1980' (n 77).

327 See, e.g., Antonio Bascuñan Rodríguez, 'Simposio Aborto y Derechos Humanos' (2015) 11 Anuario de Derechos Humanos 58; Antonio Bascuñan Rodríguez, 'Después de la Píldora' [2006] Anuario de Derechos Humanos 2006 235; Angela Vivanco Martínez, 'La Pildora del Día Después' (2008) 35 Revista Chilena de Derecho 543; Rodolfo Figueroa García Huidobro, 'Concepto de Persona, Titularidad del Derecho a la Vida y Aborto' (2007) 20 Revista de derecho (Valdivia) 95.

2. Scholarship

The concept of ownership answers the question of who holds fundamental rights.[328] In Chilean constitutional scholarship, this question has primarily focused on a single criterion: the concept of a person. Although some have remarked that this concept must be read in accordance with Art. 1, par. 1 CPR,[329] this reasoning stems from the wording of the first phrase of Art. 19 CPR, which has been recognized as the crucial constitutional rule on ownership. Art. 19 CPR comprises the catalog of constitutional rights, covering 26 numbered sections, as follows:

> Article 19. The Constitution guarantees all *persons*:[330]
> 1.The right to life and to the physical and mental integrity of the person.
> The law protects the life of the unborn.
> The death penalty may only be instituted for a crime established in a law approved by a qualified quorum.
> The application of any illegitimate force [*apremio*] is forbidden.

(...)

> 2.Equality before the law (...)
> (...) [26 further numbered sections]

Since the CPR does not explicitly define who is considered a person, this has been discussed from two opposing perspectives: civil law and non-civil law-based conceptualizations. While these perspectives are sharply divergent, both have been supported by the CCT at different times and they share points of confusion that expose them to criticism.

2.1. The civil law-based concept of a constitutional person

The central thesis of this position is that the constitutional silence on the meaning of the concept of a person should be filled by Articles 55 and 74 of the Civil Code. The former states that:

---

328 Contreras Vazquez, 'Titularidad de Derechos Fundamentales' (n 196) 119
329 See, e.g., ibid 133
330 Emphasis added.

> [A]ll individuals of the human species are persons, regardless of age, sex, lineage, or condition. They shall be grouped into Chileans and foreigners.[331]

And Art. 74, par. 1 of the same code, that:

> [T]he legal existence of every person begins at birth, i.e. upon complete separation from one's mother.[332]

This position claims that holders of fundamental rights are those individuals of the human species (Art. 55 of the Civil Code) that have achieved the requirement stated in Art. 74. par. 1 of the Civil Code. This is the point of view of several authors.[333] The unborn, therefore, is not considered to hold fundamental rights. For its proponents, this thesis is strongly supported by the structure of Art. 19 no. 1 CPR.[334] Indeed, they affirm that two features of the crime of abortion in the Chilean Criminal Code legally support this perspective, bestowing coherence on the complete set of norms. First, abortion is not mentioned in the chapter on crimes against persons ("Crimes and Ordinary Offences against Persons").[335] Second, punishments for crimes committed against already born human beings are substantively more severe.[336]

2.2. Non-civil-law-based concepts of a constitutional person

2.2.1. Approaches not based on positive law

The ruling opinion believes that it is possible to grasp the notion of a person for constitutional goals independently of the civil-law rules. This approach, however, has rarely grounded its position in other constitutional norms as its key argumentative point, instead searching for extra-legal inspiration. In other words, this view claims, the "person" to whom the constitution refers is rather a pre-juridical fact.

---

331 [Son personas todos los individuos de la especie humana, cualquiera que sea su edad, sexo, estirpe y condición.]

332 [La existencia legal de toda persona comienza al nacer, esto es, al separarse completamente de su madre.]

333 See, e.g., Contreras Vásquez, 'Titularidad de Los Derechos Fundamentales' (n 196) 133; Figueroa García Huidobro (n 327) 117.

334 Figueroa García Huidobro (n 327) 117 ff.

335 ibid 117.

336 ibid.

Thus, *Alvear*, commenting on the latter, states that:

> [T]he term 'person' does not only refer, from a metaphysical point of view, to the reality of who the human being is but also, from the state's activity, a juridical institutional principle, which orients the goals of the state (…).[337]

Similarly, *Diez* commenting on Art 4, par. 4 CPR, points out that:

> [I]n the occidental metaphysical tradition, a person is characterized by his independence, as a reality subsisting in a spiritual form constitutes by itself a universe (…). The individual and the person are different realities but coexistent in the being. Completely myself, I am an individual on the grounds of what I possess because of matter, and a person due to the spirit (…).[338]

This extra-legal approximation of the notion of a *person* is coherent with the natural law approach to constitutional rights that these scholars hold. Accordingly, the support of the explicit wording of a statute or the affirmation of a constitutional rule is not required to be a holder of fundamental rights. A good summary of this view is advanced by *Molina Guaita*, who indicates that:

> Persons are born equal in rights. With the same rights that stem from human nature (...). The State neither creates rights nor does it concede them but only recognizes and regulates them (…).[339]

---

337 Alvear Téllez (n 200) 58. [El vocablo "persona" no sólo designa, desde el punto de vista metafísico, la realidad de quién es el hombre, sino también, desde el punto de vista de la organización y actividad del Estado, un principio jurídico institucional que orienta la identificación de los fines de éste, la elección de los medios gubernativos, y el sentido regulativo de la normatividad estatal.]

338 Diez Urzúa (n 186) 74. [En esta tradición metafísica occidental se caracteriza a la persona por su independencia, como una realidad que, subsistiendo espiritualmente, constituye un universo aparte (...). El individuo y la persona son realidades distintas, pero coexistentes en el ser. Todo yo soy individuo en razón de los que poseo por la materia, y todo entero, persona, por lo que poseo además por el espíritu.]

339 Molina Guaita (n 72) 60–61. [Las personas nacen con igualdad de derechos. Con los mismos derechos que emanan de la naturaleza humana (...). Porque estos derechos son anteriores al Estado y superiores a él; no los crea ni los concede; los reconoce, los regula en vistas al bien común y los garantiza.]

Moreover, generally, to refute the position based on civil law rules, no other positive law rules are provided as support. Thus, *Soto Kloss,* while recognizing that the CPR does not define the term *person*, nevertheless declares that the unborn clearly *is* a person in the constitution's own description.[340] *Nuñez,* although arriving at the same conclusion by similar means, provides a more sophisticated approach to the issue. He affirms that it is necessary to distinguish between the different categories of subjects that are behind the term "persons,"[341] enshrined in the first sentence of Art. 19 CPR. He contends this term should not be understood as a legal one. Hence, "moral" or "collective" persons are, in general, to be considered holders of fundamental rights. Thus, juridical personhood, clarifies *Nuñez,* is merely an "external manifestation of a material reality of a higher entity, namely the existence of an association. In other words, there is personhood since there is an association and not vice versa."[342]

Using the same logic, *Nuñez* explains that:

> (...) constitutionalism (...) champions the rights of the natural person or, synonymously, of the human being. Therefore, utilizing the remarkably precise language of the Civil Code, any individual member of the human race is considered a natural person.[343]

Next, *Nuñez* claims, in a footnote, that, in constitutional matters, Art. 74 of the Civil Code regarding the "legal existence" of a person is not valid.[344]

340 Eduardo Soto Kloss, 'La Noción de Persona en la Constitución' (1991) 50 Revista de Derecho Público 139.

341 Núñez Poblete (n 325) 201.

342 ibid.

343 ibid. [No cabe duda que el constitucionalismo, como parte de la filosofía política moderna, es un movimiento de reivindicación de los derechos de la persona natural o, lo que es idéntico decir, del ser humano. Se comprende aquí entonces, utilizando el lenguaje tan preciso de nuestro Código Civil, a todo individuo que pertenezca a la especie humana.]

344 ibid.

2.2.2. Approaches based on constitutional norms

2.2.2.1. Vivanco's approach

Vivanco has been one of the few to claim that civil law rules should not be used to fill the absence of constitutional norms in this matter while also attempting to back her position in other positive rules and principles. In this sense, she affirms that the civil law rules would lend the constitutional notion of a person a discriminatory character, should they not treat the unborn child and the born human being in the same way.[345]

Instead, she interprets Art. 19 CPR through the lens of the first constitutional chapter, especially its reference to dignity in Art. 1 CPR. The task is to unravel what the term *person* means here, as this provides the content of the word throughout the constitution. Preliminarily, claims *Vivanco,* human dignity is related to a conception of the person that demands the most "favorable and inclusive criterion of human being's protection."[346] Thereby, the term "are born" of Art. 1 CPR is not to be connected to biological birth, but to the idea of onset, since:

> [T]he person in essence, from his beginning, is not subjected to any act of authority and is free and equal to others in dignity and rights. In other words, [the person] is generated with those features, which are intrinsic and not acquired.[347]

From this, she concludes that the constitutional protection of the human being and the recognition of his or her dignity can neither be limited by civil law, nor by a textual reading of the CPR. It is the opposite, believes this scholar: only a completely inclusive reading of the CPR, considering all human beings as persons, would be correct.[348] Thus, the CPR understands the terms *person* and *human being* in relation to identity.[349]

345 Vivanco Martínez, 'La Importancia del Concepto Constitucional de Persona y la Protección de la Vida en la Carta Fundamental de 1980' (n 77) 137.

346 ibid 136.

347 ibid 139. [En efecto, la persona en esencia, desde un inicio que no está sujeto a acto de autoridad alguno, es libre e igual a las demás en dignidad y en derechos. En otras palabras, es generada con dichas catacterísticas, le son intrínsecas y no adquiridas.]

348 ibid.

349 *Vivanco* ends by recommending two reforms to the CPR: (1) deleting par. 2 of Art. 19 no. 1 and (2) adding the following second paragraph to Art. 1: "All individuals of the human species are persons since their conception, regardless of race, sex, lineage, or condition." See ibid 163.

2.2.2.2. Aldunate and the confusing wording of the CPR

Aldunate contends that two norms should be considered to construct the doctrinal category of ownership: Art. 19. par. 1., and Art. 1. par. 1 CPR. For these parameters, he notes the fact that from a historical perspective, fundamental rights belong to every individual. Before the emergence of fundamental rights, recalls this scholar, there were rights and freedoms as well but these were only attributed to certain strata or statuses. On this account, *Aldunate* criticizes the wording of Art. 1 CPR, asserting that while its original version directly connected the entitlement of rights to any human being,[350] the current one introduced the term "person" confusingly because the attribution of personhood always corresponds to law. Thereby, claims *Aldunate,* in order to gain a universal understanding of Art. 1 it is now necessary to:

> [r]esort to an additional argumentation, possibly through Art. 5., par. 2's first sentence, to connect the idea of an individual of the human race with the one of a person, with the goal of, only then, shelter [the right above mentioned] under Art. 1, par. 1, and Art. 19.

Be that as it may, *Aldunate* excludes the unborn from this universality. However, he does not affix his opinion primarily to the Civil Code rules but to the structure of Art. 19, no. 1 CPR.[351] *Aldunate* indicates that this structure means the unborn is constitutionally excluded from the category of a person – the express enshrinement of a legal duty to protect the unborn differs from the right to life guaranteed to persons.

3. *Case law*

3.1. Rulings not based on civil law norms

The CCT, commenting on Art. 5, par. 2 CPR, affirmed in 1995 that:

> [i]t [the latter norm] means that men are holders of rights as such, [therefore] it is not necessary their constitutional assurance [positive

350 See § 2, subsection 4.
351 Although he states that Art. 19 no. 1 CPR coincides with the Civil Code statute.

> enshrinement] for them [those rights] to enjoy constitutional protection (...).[352]

However, in subsequent judgments the CCT has consistently held the general rule on ownership to be provided by Art. 19, par. 1 CPR.[353] Thereby, as with the scholarship, the CCT has needed to define who is covered by the term "person." In a later decision (2007), the tribunal recognized that, according to the constitution, the entitlement to rights is dependent on this term. In that sense, the CCT maintained that, in Art. 1 CPR, the constitution has both typified the person in a humanistic way and has registered his or her primary attributes.[354] The CCT infers from the sole reading of the first paragraph of this article that, on the one hand, "any human being, regardless of age, sex or special condition is always creditor of a respectful treatment." On the other hand, humans possess dignity and are free, equal, and inherently sociable beings. Hence, the "person," explained the CCT, is "matter and spirit" according to the CPR.[355] From the latter, the CCT concludes that when the constitution "guarantees" some rights to all "persons," it only recognizes attributes that are part of a person's nature. In other words, the CCT asserted, "the constitution has not created those rights but merely has recognized, regulated, and guaranteed their exercise (...)."[356]

On this account, the court next analyzes whether the unborn can be classified under the constitutional concept of a person and hence whether they can be considered a holder of fundamental rights.[357] After quoting the scholarship, the CCT provides biological data to affirm the latter fact, asserting that:

> [i]f from the moment of conception an individual with all the genetic information required for his development emerges (...) it is possible to conclude that we are faced with a person, as a subject of law (...).[358] He

352 CCT Rol 226–1995, par. 25. [Los hombres son titulares de derechos por ser tales, sin que sea menester que se aseguren constitucionalmente para que gocen de protección constitucional.]

353 CCT Rol 740–2007, par. 19; CCT Rol 2273–2012 par. 27; CCT Rol 3729–2017, par. 40.

354 CCT Rol 740–2007, par. 45.

355 CCT Rol 740–2007, par. 46.

356 CCT Rol 740–2007, par. 47.

357 CCT Rol 740–2007, par. 48.

358 CCT Rol 740–2007, par. 50.

> [the embryo] could not be merely subsumed in another entity not to say manipulated, without affecting the substantial dignity that he [the embryo] already enjoys as a person.[359]

3.2. Change of criterion

In 2017, apropos of reviewing a law bill that legalized abortion in three cases,[360] the CCT adopted the civil-law-based criterion. Here, the CCT claimed that the CPR does not grant the unborn the status of a person.[361] The genealogy of the norm contained in Art. 19, no. 1, par. 2 CPR, must be found in the Civil Code rules.[362] In this sense, the Civil Code only considers the already born as persons. Also, from Art. 1, par. 1 CPR, the CCT concludes that the condition of personhood starts at birth and cannot be lost so it holds "forever." Therefore, after birth, the condition of being a person becomes inherent: "all persons have the feature of being a person" ends the CCT, redundantly.

4. Analysis and criticism

4.1. Criticism of the non-civil-law-based conceptualization of a person

As Figueroa points out, a legal concept of the person is yet to be truly established by the ruling position.[363] In this position, positive norms (both constitutional rules and legal statutes) seem to play no vital role in defining the concept of a person. The position thereby infers its concept of personhood from extra-legal sources, including religious ones, which produces a moral perspective on the person rather than a doctrinal approach. This former perspective typically consists of a moral line of reasoning that seeks to justify the adoption of some philosophical conception of a person by the legal order. However, one objection might be that scholarship and case law

359 CCT Rol 740–2007, par. 50. The CCT recalls as a subsidiary argument Art. 4.1 of the American Convention on Human Rights: "Every person has the right to have his life respected. This right shall be protected by law and, in general, from the moment of conception. No one shall be arbitrarily deprived of his life."

360 Rol 3729–2017.

361 Rol 3729–2017, par. 40.

362 Rol 3729–2017, par. 44.

363 Figueroa García Huidobro (n 327) 97.

should attend more closely to existing positive norms when developing a constitutional concept of a person.

4.2. Criticism of the civil law-based conceptualization of a person

Notwithstanding its greater fidelity to positive law, the civil law-based conceptualization of the person is similarly unconvincing. It shares the reactivity of the opposing view discussed in the previous subsection. For example, it first appears to take a moral stance on the worth of the unborn child and only then builds a general theory of ownership. Its crucial weakness is its inadequate systematic assertion of the constitutional norms involved. Indeed, from the structure of the norms that regulate the right to life (Art. 19, no. 1 CPR), it concludes the general meaning of the term "persons" enshrined in the title of Art. 19 CPR. Besides, the civil law approach does not seek meanings for the term in other constitutional norms without stating sufficient reasons. Therefore, the resort to the rules of civil law seems precipitate and preconceived, at the very least. In fact, *Contreras*, one of its main supporters, commenting on the rationality that underpins the rules of civil law, claims that "fetuses and embryos are not able to perform a significant role in juridical life, and the political community has decided that they are not persons regarding the law."[364] Conversely, it depends on the political community whether embryos will play a significant role in juridical life.

5. Open questions: the role of dignity as a criterion for the attribution of legal personhood

Scholars have tackled the question of who holds dignity. However, dignity's role in the ownership of rights remains under researched, despite being of equal if not greater doctrinal relevance. As the Chilean scholarship demonstrates, debates over the ownership of fundamental rights have centered on how to conceptualize the legal person that claims these rights. Yet the two most influential positions reviewed above rarely highlight the link between dignity and legal personhood.

---

364 Contreras Vásquez, 'Titularidad de Derechos Fundamentales' (n 196) 180.

§ 6 Restrictions on basic rights

1. Introduction

Chilean scholarship and case law lack the shared doctrinal tools to address possible impairments to basic rights.[365] Accordingly, it is hard to find consistent doctrinal proposals to review impacts on dignity beyond general statements about its inviolability.[366] Nevertheless, the scholarship repeatedly highlights the major role of dignity when defining restrictions and limits to restrictions on fundamental rights, although commonly without further development.[367] In turn, the CCT has concretized these doctrinal statements in several judgments, emphasizing human dignity as a limiting factor on restrictions to basic rights.

2. The case law of the CCT

First, the CCT has suggested that dignity may restrict the right to equality before the law.[368] Chilean criminal law considered consensual sexual intercourse between a male of 18 years or above with another male aged between 14 and 17 years old to be a punishable act,[369] but not when the 14–17 year-old partner was female, nor when the partner aged 18+ was female and the younger partner was either male or female. The applicant – who was facing a criminal prosecution for violating the above rule – submitted his claim arguing that the norm was against the CPR, as it infringed dignity, the principle of equality under the law and the prohibition of arbitrary discrimination, the right to a private life, privacy, and freedom, and the essential content of the aforementioned rights. Apropos of the applicant's claim,[370] the CCT reviewed the norm and reaffirmed its constitutionality,

365 See § 2, subsections 2 and 3.

366 See, in general, § 3.

367 See, in general, § 3.

368 See CCT Rol N° 1683–2010, pars. 31–33.

369 This statute is the former Art. 365 Criminal Code, which was abolished in 2022 by Act no. 21.483.

370 For more on the remedy of inapplicability, see § 2, subsection 3.

arguing that the legislator acted constitutionally by concluding that the "passive role in a sodomite relation" configures a type of relationship that, in the case of the adolescent, is "harmful for his dignity as a person," given his still incomplete sexual and psychic development.[371]

Second, the CCT has affirmed that human dignity restricts the right to life, but also, that it limits possible restrictions on that right. In 2007, reviewing the constitutionality of a governmental decree that allowed the public distribution of an oral contraceptive (the "morning-after" pill), the CCT held that there was "reasonable doubt" that the pill might terminate the embryo in some cases, implying a possible effect on the latter's right to life. Summing up, the CCT emphasized that the existence of reasonable doubt obligated it to pursue "that interpretation that favors the right to life of the person before any other interpretation that implies the annulation of that right." Any other reasoning entailed ignoring "the substantial dignity of every person."[372] Ten years later, however, the CCT argued from the opposite side. Reviewing a bill legalizing the termination of pregnancy in three exceptional cases, the court asserted that dignity (of the pregnant woman) restricted the right to life of the unborn in those cases. Human dignity, added the court, also justifies the restriction on the right to life of the attacker in cases of self-defense and the death penalty.[373]

In addition, the case law of the CCT found that dignity limits restrictions on the right to privacy and confidentiality in personal communications,[374] and on the right to free speech; specifically, it is incompatible with human dignity to legally force the individual to express a given statement.[375] Finally, the CCT has most frequently reiterated that human dignity is the ultimate grounding of several norms and principles – many explicitly enshrined in the constitution – that set boundaries to the state's *ius puniendi.*

---

371 CCT Rol 1683–2010, par. 31. The dissident opinion, nevertheless, severely criticized the decision but its argument was not expressly based on the norm of dignity. This dissident opinion was correctly implemented over time as recognized by the legislature when it abolished Art. 365 of the Criminal Code.

372 CCT Rol 740–2007, par. 68.

373 CCT Rol 3729–2017, par. 49.

374 CCT Rol 398–2003, par. 27; similarly, CCT Rol N 433–2005, par. 34.

375 CCT Rol 5527–2018, pars. 59–60. However, the CCT does not expressly state that the affected right is that of freedom of speech but rather reasons that freedom of conscience is primarily at stake.

Such is the case with the principles of *nen bis in idem,*[376] of criminal law liability,[377] and of proportionality.[378]

Accordingly, the state's authority to restrict some basic freedoms has several concrete limits. Overall, imprisonment must be applied only in the cases of the most serious crimes.[379] In its first ruling on this matter, the CCT also held that human dignity implies restrictions on the ways in which imprisonment may be carried out[380] – particularly that the punishment must respect the personality of the individual.[381] On the other hand, the CCT also stated that:

> (...) only the imposition of a sanction that effectively promotes the applicant's resocialization, that is less harmful to his human dignity and that balances the functions and objectives of the penalties is consistent with the petitioner's essential rights.[382]

However, it would have been more consistent to affirm that when the aforementioned principles are respected, human dignity remains unharmed – as the CCT itself did on another occasion, when stating that:

> (...) since there has been no violation of thc guarantees of due process or equality before the law, it cannot be considered that the dignity of the petitioner has been harmed.[383]

376 See, e.g., CCT Rol 6462–2019, par. 7.
377 See, e.g., CCT Rol 3329–2017, par. 28.
378 See, e.g., CCT Rol 4384–2018 par. 22.
379 CCT Rol 3581–2017, pars. 2–5, settled case law, confirmed in hundreds of cases. For a recent example, see CCT Rol 11428–2021. In another concrete instance of this case law, the CCT affirmed that a minor that is subjected to a disciplinary process before a family court may not be referred to as the "accused" [*imputado*], see CCT Rol 6294–2019, par. 9.
380 CCT Rol 3062–2016, pars. 2–5.
381 CCT Rol 3062–2016, par. 2.
382 CCT Rol 3062–2016, par. 31. [(...) solo se aviene con los derechos esenciales del requirente la imposición de una sanción que efectivamente propenda a su resocialización, *menos lesiva de su dignidad humana* y que equilibra las funciones y objetivos de las penas (...).]
383 CCT Rol 3372–2017, par. 43. [(...) por lo mismo, al no haber transgresión a las garantías de un debido proceso o de igualdad ante la ley, no puede estimarse que se ha lesionado la dignidad de la requirente, en los términos por esta (sic) planteada.]

3. Summary and open questions

In the abstract, if dignity is considered the supreme value of the constitutional order, as is the case in Chilean scholarship and case law, it should play a crucial role in concrete cases as a determinant doctrinal criterion for resolving juridical conflicts. While the scholarship has mostly restricted itself simply to formulating dignity's possible role when reviewing cases of restrictions on basic rights, the CCT has produced several concretized rulings. However correct the results of such concretizations may be, the CCT has not provided sufficient doctrinal reasoning to explain how it reached the outcome in each case. This deficiency can be explained both by the lack of an outlined content of human dignity and the absence of shared doctrinal methods to treat cases of basic rights. Thus in this context, the CCT could do nothing but intuitively arrive at a conclusion without describing how it got there.

III
Human Dignity in Germany

§ 7 Content of human dignity

1. Introduction

1.1. Preliminary

In comparison to France or England, the history of guaranteed fundamental rights started somewhat late in Germany.[384] The Basic Law [*Grundgesetz*][385] was the first German constitution to recognize constitutional rights as human rights.[386] In line with the previous Geman constitutional tradition, the GG's antecessor, the Imperial Constitution of Weimar [*Weimarer Reichsverfassung*][387] (1918), in the chapter devoted to the basic rights and duties of the individual, instead mentioned only the "rights of Germans"

384 Jörn Ipsen, *Staatsrecht II* (2019) 8. These statements should, however, be qualified. Basic rights in the modern sense of "defensive rights of the citizen against the state," were present in the constitutional history of Germany long before the Basic Law or the Imperial Constitution of Weimar. Indeed, in *Verfassungsgeschichte* (2019) 138, Rn. 288, Werner Frotscher and Bodo Pieroth identify basic rights in some German state [*Länder*] constitutions at the start of the period that German legal historians call "Constitutionalism" [*Konstitutionalismus*], e.g., in § 21 and § 24 of the Constitution of the Kingdom of Württemberg (1819). The authors claim that, unlike the American and French traditions, basic rights were not conceived as rights that precede the state but as state-citizen freedoms conceded by the sovereign, ibid 142, Rn. 292. In addition, they were not in fact "guaranteed," as they were almost entirely unprotected from legislative restrictions and were not supported by any means of juridical defense before the courts. Later, the Constitution of St. Paul's Church (1849) [*Paulskirchenverfassung*] had a more extensive and democratic Bill of Rights but this was not ultimately put into force (ibid 172–175).

385 Hereafter also referred to as "GG."

386 Hasso Hofmann, 'Die Grundrechte 1789 – 1949 – 1989' [1989] Neue Juristische Wochenschrift 3177, 3177.

387 Hereafter also referred to as "WRV."

[*Deutschenrechte*]. In this context, the concept of "human being" or "man" [*Mensch*] is only used once (Art. 151 WRV),[388] and then in the adjectival form [*menschenwürdiges Dasein*].[389]

However, since 1949, when the GG came into effect, German constitutional legal doctrine and case law on fundamental rights have achieved a leading position in constitutional law, thereby enjoying great international resonance.[390] Furthermore, they have significantly influenced a number of developments in international public law.[391] The transfer of concepts elsewhere that were first developed in Germany, such as the principle of proportionality[392] or fundamental rights as an objective order of values, is well known.[393]

388 Hofmann, 'Die Grundrechte 1789 – 1949 – 1989' (n 386) 3179.

389 Art. 151 WRV: Die Ordnung des Wirtschaftslebens muss den Grundsätzen der Gerechtigkeit mit dem Ziel der Gewährleistung eines menschenwürdigen Daseins für alle entsprechen. [The organization of economic life must conform to the principles of justice with the aim of ensuring to all an existence according to human dignity.]

390 See an overview of this phenomenon in András Jakab, 'The Fading International Influence of German Constitutional Thinking' (2020) 2020–43 MPIL Research Paper Series 27. Although affirming the decline of the German constitutional law influence for the last two decades, Jakab asserts that "Germany is still the most influential constitutional culture" (ibid 29) and lavishes superlative praise on German constitutional development after World War Two (ibid 27). The combination of the case law of the German Federal Constitutional Court with traditional German "dogmatics" resulted in what Jakab calls "the most sophisticated legal doctrine of fundamental rights in human history (…)."

391 See, e.g., Armin Bogdandy, 'German Legal Hegemony?' (2020) 2020–43 MPIL Research Paper Series 2, where the author describes the tensions produced by the supposedly far-reaching influence of German juridical science in European legal doctrine.

392 A detailed history can be found in Alec Stone Sweet and Jud Mathews, 'Proportionality Balancing and Global Constitutionalism' (2008) 47 Columbia Journal of Transnational Law 68, 97–159. See also Bernhard Schlink, 'Proportionality in Constitutional Law: Why Everywhere But Here?' (2012) 22 Duke Journal of Comparative and International Law 291, where the author relativizes the idea that the principle of proportionality is a "German" principle. Rather, according to him, the principle of proportionality offers a universal, methodical solution to a universal legal problem.

393 Michaela Hailbronner, 'Rethinking the rise of the German Constitutional Court: From anti-Nazism to value formalism' (2012) 12 International Journal of Constitutional Law 626, 626–627: "The Basic Law and many of the Court's jurisprudential innovations have become export models in many foreign countries. For some liberal American scholars, the German Constitutional Court has even come to define the positive counter-model to the US Supreme Court."

In this respect, the case of human dignity is particularly remarkable. The former Chief Justice of the Supreme Court of Israel, Aaron Barak, in a well-documented book analyzing the role of human dignity in several constitutional jurisdictions, affirms that "[h]uman dignity (...) has been the subject of impressive and unprecedented development in the Constitutional Court of Germany and in German legal scholarship."[394] Other scholarly voices have echoed this claim.[395]

Be that as it may, such bold statements cannot be fully comprehended without considering at least two particularities of human dignity in the German jurisdiction. The first key aspect is that the norm on dignity is unanimously considered the most important constitutional clause and is widely viewed as both a principle and constitutional right. Additionally, this development has occurred in a legal environment historically characterized by its formalism and systematicity.[396]

One can comprehend this framework by observing the treatment of possible restrictions on fundamental rights and its analysis through the so-called Three-Step Test [*Drei-Schritte-Prüfung*]. This method requires distinguishing between the scope of protection of a right [*Schutzbereich*], an interference with it [*Eingriff*], and a constitutional justification or basis for the latter [*Rechtfertigung*]. The Three-Step Test is based on the terminology used by the German Federal Constitutional Court [*Bundesverfassungs-*

394 Aharon Barak, *Human Dignity. The Constitutional Value and the Constitutional Right* (2015) 240.

395 See, inter alia, Henk Botha, 'Human Dignity in Comparative Perspective' (2009) 20 Stellenbosch Law Review 171; Matthias Mahlmann, 'The Basic Law at 60 – Human Dignity and the Culture of Republicanism' (2010) 11 German Law Journal 9.

396 An interesting account of developments in BVerfG and German Constitutional scholarship since the GG came into effect can be found in Michaela Hailbronner (n 393), who describes the BVerfG's approach as "value formalism." However, even as early as the 1990s, Bernhard Schlink in 'German Constitutional Culture in Transition' (1992) 14 Cardozo Law Review 711, 729, observed that the BVerfG's jurisprudence was increasingly considering fundamental rights as principles. This had led to more manifest judicial activism, in turn causing a loss of "consistent legal methodology": "While methodologically convincing decisions still occur every now and again, there are many others that simply arise from the Courts' feel for what is indicated by social and political life – for what is accepted and 'fits' into the social and political landscape. Decisions thus encompass only the individual cases subjudice, and are expressed and handed down as such. They are also taught to students as such, which is perhaps the best indication that German Constitutional law is changing from code-oriented, systematic law to case law."

gericht],[397] and has been further developed by legal scholars.[398] It is widely used by juridical practitioners and is a key part of the undergraduate curriculum in German law faculties;[399] it provides a helpful tool for analyzing the vast quantity of material on this topic in German law.[400] The approach to human dignity as a right in the German jurisdiction should not be set apart from this juridical context when conducting comparative legal research.

An overwhelming quantity of literature on constitutional human dignity exists in the German context, ranging from articles of diverse length to dense sections of constitutional commentaries [*Grundgesetz Kommentare*] and detailed post-doctoral works [*Habilitationen*]. There is also an extensive body of relevant case law. Consequently, the sections of this work devoted to dignity in Germany are not the product of an exhaustive review of the literature but focus on particularly influential scholarly contributions and case law relevant to each point of discussion.

However, the depth and quantity of the existing doctrinal work on human dignity can cause problems. The over-theorization of legal doctrine may be problematic, for example, if it overloads the study of fundamental rights with issues of a philosophical nature.[401] This risk is especially pertinent to the concept of human dignity, which had been discussed for many centuries by philosophers and theologians before entering the legal world. Moreover, the doctrinal use of dignity requires establishing the most universally accepted definition of its content or scope of protection.[402]

---

397 Hereafter also referred to as "BVerfG."

398 Ipsen, *Staatsrecht II* (n 384) 37.

399 This curriculum follows, inter alia, course books on fundamental rights written by Thorsten Kingreen and Ralf Poscher, *Grundrechte Staatsrecht II* (2016); Friedhelm Hufen, *Staatsrecht II. Grundrechte* (2020); Volker Epping, *Grundrechte* (2019); and Rolf Schmidt, *Grundrechte* (2019). An alternative is proposed by Ipsen in *Staatsrecht II* (n 384).

400 For a detailed description of the Three-Step Test, see § 10, subsection 2.

401 Ipsen, *Staatsrecht II* (n 384) 1. Klaus Stern, *Das Staatsrecht der Bundesrepublik Deutschland, Band IV/1* (2006) 60, has described this situation as follows: "Thanks to its inclusion in Article 1 (1) GG, human dignity has been lifted out of the meta-legal, philosophical, ethical, or theological sphere and has become part of the constitutional legal order." [Durch die Aufnahme der Würde des Menschen in die Verfassungsrechtsnorm des Art. 1 Abs. 1 GG ist diese aus der Sphäre des Metarechtlichen, Philosophischen, Ethischen oder Theologischen herausgehoben und Teil der Verfassungsrechtsordnung geworden.]

402 Hufen, *Staatsrecht II. Grundrechte* (n 399) 136.

Despite such difficulties, German legal practitioners have managed to find a functional and delimited use of the term. Some standard practices help to explain this achievement. Although, in Germany, there is no formal commitment to *stare decisis*, the "leading" decisions of the BVerfG remain the most important source for determining the content of basic rights.[403] Next, the scholarship, both critical and supportive, further shapes the doctrinal contours of the topic on basic rights addressed by the BVerfG[404]. One author, discussing a somewhat theoretical element of dignity, summarizes the situation as follows: "What does Karlsruhe say about it? This question – as we know – is always obligatory for a German constitutionalist."[405]

1.2. Historical semblance

The enshrinement of human dignity at the beginning of the GG responds to two major causes. First, it is a reaction to the National Socialist dictatorship and its heinous crimes (1933–1945).[406] The proceedings of the

403 Ipsen, *Staatsrecht II* (n 384) 39.

404 In this regard, see, e.g., Schlink, 'German Constitutional Culture in Transition' (n 396) 730: "Constitutional scholarship thus thinks and works in the wake of the *Bundesverfassungsgericht*, rather than ahead of it. The *Bundesverfassungsgericht* develops the central tenets of Germany's Constitutional doctrine more or less on the spot, and scholarship then elaborates on them."

405 Hasso Hofmann, 'Die versprochene Menschenwürde' (1993) 118 Archiv des Öffentlichen Rechts 253, 359. [Es bleib die Frage: Was sagt Karlsruhe dazu? Diese Frage ist – wie wir wissen – für einen deutschen Verfassungsrechtler allemal obligatorisch]. (The city of Karlsruhe, located in the federal state of Baden-Württemberg, is the seat of the BVerfG).

406 Cf., e.g., ibid 356; Ernst-Wolfang Böckenförde, 'Menschenwürde als normatives Prinzip. Die Grundrechte in der bioetische Debatte' (2003) 58 Juristenzeitung 809, 809; Ralf Poscher, 'Die Würde des Menschen ist unantastbar' (2004) 59 Juristenzeitung 756, 759; Martin Nettesheim, 'Leben in Würde' (2019) 74 Juristenzeitung 1, 1; Epping (n 399) 265; Horst Dreier, 'Art. 1 Abs. 1' in Horst Dreier (ed), *Grundgesetz, Band I (Art. 1 – 19)* (2013) Rn. 49; Hans Jarass, 'Art. 1' in Hans Jarass and Bodo Pieroth (eds), *Grundgesetz für die Bundesrepublik Deutschland* (2020) Rn. 1; Stern (n 401) 60 'Die Gründe sind evident und vor allem aus den Jahren der deustchen Dämonie von 1933 bis 1945 zu erklären'; Christian Starck, 'Art. 1 Abs. 1' in Hermann von Mangoldt, Friedrich Klein and Christian Starck (eds), *Kommentar zum Grundgesetz* (2018) Rn. 17. Jarass, 'Art. 1.' Rn. 1, describes the change of paradigm with precision: "with that [i.e., the incorporation of human dignity] it becomes clear that in the order of the GG the human being comes first and only then the state, in contrast with the Nazi guiding principle; namely, that the individual is nothing; the state (or the community) is everything." [Damit wird deutlich gemacht, dass in der

Parliamentary Council [*Parlamentarischer Rat*] clearly testify to this fact.[407] Second, these documents show that the legal recognition of dignity was based on the cultural heritage of the drafters, particularly the Christian teaching of the value of the person and the Enlightenment tradition of inalienable human rights.[408] Against this background, the new dignity clause represented both a rejection of the darkest period of Germany and the horizon of a new time yet to come: the strengthening of the German state under the rule of law [*Rechtsstaat*] that would prevent such a catastrophe from ever recurring.[409]

Surpassing its modest role in the Weimar Constitution,[410] drafted previously,[411] and already considered in several federal state constitutions [*Länderverfassungen*],[412] the central role of dignity in the new German federal constitutional order was soon confirmed by the BVerfG. As early as 1956, the court affirmed that "human dignity is the supreme value of liberal

---

Ordnung des GG zuerst der Mensch kommt und erst dann der Staat, in Umkehrung des nationalsozialistischen Leitsatzes, der Einzelne sei nichts, der Staat (oder die Gemeinschaft) alles.]

407 See Eberhard Pikard and Wolfram Werner, 'Nr. 5 Vierte Sitzung des Ausschusses für Grundsatzfragen 23. September 1948' in Eberhard Pikard and Wolfram Werner (eds), *Der Parlamentarische Rat 1948 – 1949. Akten und Protokolle. Band 5. Ausschuß für Grundsatzfragen* (1993).

408 Hufen, *Staatsrecht II. Grundrechte* (n 399) 132 Rn. 4.

409 Manfred Baldus, *Kämpfe um die Menschenwürde. Die Debatten seit 1949* (2016) 26. Baldus remarks how several members of the commission pointed out that the dignity clause also represented the rejection of other totalitarian phenomena, such as the Soviet dictatorship.

410 Art. 151 WRV. See *supra* subsection 1.1.

411 Before the Parliamentary Council met, the minister-presidents of the German states [*Länder*] selected a group of constitutional experts to prepare a draft constitution to be later used by the Parliamentary Council as a starting point for its mission – later informally called the "Herrenchiemsee Constitutional Convention" [*Der Herrenchiemseer Verfassungskonvent*]. On this, see *Frotscher and Pieroth* (n 384) 383–385. This group suggested the following norm on dignity: "The dignity of the human personality shall be inviolable. The public power, in all its forms, shall respect and protect human dignity." [Die Würde der menschlichen Persönlichkeit ist unantastbar. Die öffentliche Gewalt ist in allen Erscheinungsformen verpflichtet, die Menschenwürde zu achten und zu schützen].

412 Before the GG was written, some state constitutions had already enshrined a norm on human dignity, e.g., Art. 100 of the Constitution of Bavaria [2.12.46]; Art. 3 of the Constitution of Bremen [1. 12. 46]; Arts. 1 and 2 of the Constitution of Baden-Württemberg [28.11.46]. See overview in Peter Häberle, 'Die Menschenwürde als Grundlage der staatlichen Gemeinschaft', *Handbuch des Staatsrechts der Bundesrepublik Deutschland* (2004) 319 ff, Rn. 3 ff.

democracy."[413] This declaration, which may be interpreted as simply a constituent statement, soon achieved a substantive doctrinal meaning within the jurisprudence of basic rights as values that required development by the court over the ensuing years.

1.3. Basic rights as elements of an "objective order of values" and the place of dignity within this order

With doctrinal roots that can be traced back to the work of *Smend* at least,[414] and since its landmark decision in the *Lüth* Case (1958), the BVerfG has affirmed that the GG's bill of basic rights erected an "objective order of value."[415] In 1951, the court had remarked on the internal coherence of the GG, stating that "no single constitutional provision may be taken out of its context and interpreted by itself" and that "every constitutional provision must always be interpreted in such a way as to render it compatible with the fundamental principles of the constitution and the intentions of its authors."[416] One year later, the court characterized the grounding order of the liberal democracy referred to in the GG as a "value-bound order."[417] Accordingly, the BVerfG soon rejected "value-free legal positivism" (in 1953).[418] Against this background, the court has consistently characterized human dignity as the highest value of the constitution.[419]

413 BVerfGE 5, 85 (204) – *KPD-Verbot* (1956) [In der freiheitlichen Demokratie ist die Würde des Menschen der oberste Wert].

414 See Rudolph Smend, *Verfassung und Verfassungsrecht* (1928).

415 BVerfGE 7, 198, (205) - *Lüth* (1958).

416 BVerfGE 1, 14, (32) - *Neugliederung* (1951). Translation of excerpts from Donald P. Kommers and Russell A. Miller, *The Constitutional Jurisprudence of the Federal Republic of Germany* (2012) 56.

417 BVerfGE 2, 1, (12) - *SRP-Verbot* (1952) [Wertgebundene Ordnung].

418 BVerfGE 3, 225, (232) - *Gleichberechtigung* (1953).

419 Cf. "supreme value" [*Oberster Wert*], BVerfGE 5, 85, (204) - *KPD-Verbot* (1956); "highest legal value" [*Höchster Rechtswert*], BVerfGE 45, 187, (204) - *Lebenslange Freiheitstrafe* (1977). More examples are provided *infra* in subsection 3. In BVerfGE 30, 173 (193) – *Mephisto* (1965), where it is possible to find an explicit reference of the dominion of dignity over the remaining fundamental rights. [Als Teil des grundrechtlichen Wertsystems ist die Kunstfreiheit insbesondere der in Art. 1 GG garantierten Würde des Menschen zugeordnet, die als oberster Wert das ganze grundrechtliche Wertsystem beherrscht (...). Dennoch kann die Kunstfreiheitsgarantie mit dem ebenfalls verfassungsrechtlich geschützten Persönlichkeitsbereich in Konflikt geraten, weil ein Kunstwerk auch auf der sozialen Ebene Wirkungen

This conception, however, has not been free of critique.[420] Some scholars have highlighted the risk that it might promote a hierarchy of basic rights, which the GG does not indicate, except to note the supreme importance of dignity.[421] Indeed, affirming such a hierarchy would endanger the subjective contents of basic rights which protect individual autonomy, for the freedoms they comprise are not to be directed towards supposedly higher goals.[422]

Either as a reaction to this criticism, or for other reasons, the BVerfG almost entirely jettisoned substantive phrases such as "fundamental rights as a system of values" or "constitutional order as objective order of values" over a number of years.[423] However, the consequences of the underlying conception were, and remain, the object of a significant body of scholarly work. Ultimately, the central meaning of this conceptualization of basic rights has been widely adopted by practitioners. Indeed, throughout its history of adjudication, the objective meaning of basic rights as values or principles has become increasingly important for the BVerfG.[424]

Essentially, this conception holds that the state must also view the content of each basic right as an objective value, independent of its legal

---

entfalten kann.] Before the GG entered into force, the Constitutional Court of Bavaria had already conceptualized dignity as a "value" in the context of its state constitution. For details, see Baldus (n 409) 78 ff.

420 For a comprehensive critique, see Ernst-Wolfgang Böckenförde, 'Kritik der Wertbegründung des Rechts [1976]', *Recht, Staat, Freiheit: Studien zur Rechtsphilosophie, Staatstheorie und Verfassungsgeschichte* (1991). Its developed normative consequences are later discussed in Ernst-Wolfgang Böckenförde, 'Grundrechte als Grundsatznormen: Zur gegenwärtigen Lage der Grundrechtsdogmatik' (1990) 29 Der Staat 1. Following Dürig, Ernst-Wolfang Böckenförde, 'Die Würde des Menschen war unantastbar' *Frankfurter Allgemeine Zeitung* (2003) 33, only recognizes Art. 1 (1) GG as having an (indirect) "irradiating" effect on private law.

421 Hufen, *Staatsrecht II. Grundrechte* (n 399) 42 Rn. 6

422 Ipsen, *Staatsrecht II* (n 384) 31. In contrast, Luhmann, *Grundrechte als Institution* (1974) 74, fn 57 argues that such a possibility (order without ranking) is impossible: values can only be understood as a system when they represent a hierarchy of rules of preference for deciding conflicts.

423 See Dominik Rennert, 'Die verdrängte Werttheorie und ihre Historisierung' (2014) 53 Der Staat 31.

424 Schlink, 'German Constitutional Culture in Transition' (n 396) 717. Affirming this development, Schlink also explains that the "cases themselves speak of fundamental rights as values and value decisions, as fundamental value determining norms, objective fundamental norms, objective legal principles and the like. However, the same thing is always meant – the objective principle, as opposed to the subjective right."

meaning to the individual.[425] This has normative consequences in several legal areas, two of which are linked particularly closely to the dignity norm. First, the discussion on the application and interpretation of ordinary law in conformity with the constitution [*grundrechtskonforme Auslegung*] is linked to dignity. This particularly applies to the debate about interpreting the "general clauses" and "indeterminate legal concepts" of ordinary law. The scope of these interpretations has prompted lengthy discussion about the third-party effect of basic rights [*Drittwirkung*], which, at least in its indirect form, is widely accepted.[426] Second, the debate on the concrete content of state obligations of protection in relation to basic rights, *vis à vis* third parties, as well as the possibility of protecting individuals even from themselves, has ramifications for dignity.[427]

To reiterate, human dignity is affirmed without contradiction as the highest value of the GG, both by the BVerfG and the constitutional scholarship: not only do the attributed objective-law effects of the dignity clause considerably influence the legal system but also human dignity is the primary source for interpreting both constitutional and infra-constitutional norms. Hence, it is the supreme measure used when interpreting general clauses and indeterminate legal concepts. Thus, besides its significance as a basic individual right, giving the dignity clause a certain content is, most of all, a doctrinal task of great importance.

2. The legitimation of human dignity

On this subject, the main challenge is to assign functional and broadly accepted juridical content to the dignity clause such that it is applicable to a wide variety of cases. This is perhaps one of the most challenging questions regarding constitutional dignity in Germany.

The dilemma is that, from one viewpoint, interpreting the dignity clause depends more than any other basic right or constitutional principle on its

---

425 Schmidt (n 399) 25.

426 ibid 61 ff.: it seems, however, that in its most recent case law, the BVerfG has tended not to use the concept of "indirect" third-party effects, either. Existing critiques of the theory of direct third-party effects are summarized by Jan Schapp, 'Grundrechte als Wertordnung' (1998) 53 Juristenzeitung 913, 913.

427 Schmidt (n 399) 26.

treatment throughout the history of ideas.[428] Yet from a different perspective, the interpretation of the concept should reach the degree of neutrality required in a secular state under the rule of law.[429] A further difficulty arises because at least some dimensions of the meaning of dignity are indissolubly attached to the changes that a society experiences over the years.[430] The march of technology posits several challenges for law – even the self-representation of the human being as capable of exercising autonomy is now questionable, which also problematizes the meaning of dignity.[431] Amid such challenges, a certain pessimism about the possibility of determining the content of dignity is understandable.[432]

In this complex context, the challenge is to accommodate these competing considerations as far as possible without sacrificing the potential juridical force of dignity. In this vein, from the outset, some commentators have suggested that no positively formulated definition (later referred to as "positive definition") of dignity is possible: one can only identify what constitutes a violation of it.[433]

In this search for neutrality, a phrase from one of the GG's drafters is often quoted: "In my proposal, the dignity of the human being stands as an uninterpreted thesis" [*nicht interpretierte These*]."[434] This statement by *Theodor Heuß*, however, does not mean that human dignity lacks content, as *Böckenförde* informs us. *Böckenförde*, when amending an incorrect quotation of the phrase as "uninterpretable thesis" [*nicht-interpretierbare*], states that *Heuß's* intention was to prevent an overly specific foundation of dignity.[435] Art. 1 (1) GG may be considered an open-ended clause but not an empty one.[436]

Indeed, with the recognition of dignity in Art. 1 (1) GG, the centuries-old discussion of its meaning and foundations became a key feature of German

428 Hufen labels the dignity clause, emphasizing its dependency on the history of ideas, as a "an ethic that became a basic right" [*Grundrechtsgewordene Ethik*]. See Hufen, *Staatsrecht II. Grundrechte* (n 399) 130.

429 ibid 131 Rn. 1.

430 Kingreen and Poscher (n 399) 91.

431 Nettesheim (n 406) 7.

432 Cf., e.g., Baldus (n 409) 11, who affirms that the different existing approaches are almost incompatible.

433 From a doctrinal viewpoint, these attempts are rather reflections on how to identify interferences with dignity, and are treated in § 10, subsection 4.

434 Pikard and Werner (n 407) 72.

435 Ernst-Wolfang Böckenförde, 'Menschenwürde als normatives Prinzip. Die Grundrechte in der bioetische Debatte' (n 406) 811, fn 12.

constitutional scholarship and case law, seeking to tackle dignity's normative consequences. Dignity's historical roots, its prominent position at the opening of the constitution, its unique wording, and its non-reformable character has made identifying and analyzing its normative consequences a matter of great doctrinal interest.

The practical aim of law (that judges must ultimately reach decisions) makes the task here harder than in any other field or discipline. For where philosophy or ethics theorize, the law must provide concrete answers – "what the jurist cannot define, he cannot use either."[437] Furthermore, such difficulties do not end there but continue to circulate through other fields. In post-war Germany, the meaning of legal human dignity does not solely concern legal practitioners, with members of other disciplines participating intensively in its interpretation.[438] Indeed, legal scholars, such as *Häberle,* have provided theoretical grounds for this phenomenon – "everyone may participate in the open society of constitutional interpreters,"[439] and the structure and location of the norm invites every citizen to provide his own interpretation.[440] This complexity manifests itself in the extensive literature on the issue, which extends well beyond the legal domain.[441]

The wide diversity of scholarly attempts to ground dignity in the German doctrine can, in fact, be classified into several groups. Though other proposals deserve attention, a useful starting point is that of *Kingreen and Poscher* in their well-known course book.[442] This distinguishes between three main approaches: firstly, the Theory of Dowry [*Mitgifttheorie*], which, in all its variances, considers dignity as a quality present in the human

436 Josef Isensee, 'Würde des Menschen' in Detlef Merten and Hans-Jürgen Papier (eds), *Handbuch der Grundrechte in Deutschland und Europa Band IV Grundrechte in Deutschland:Einzelgrundrechte* (2011) 36, Rn. 47.

437 Josef Isensee, 'Menschenwürde: die säkulare Gesellschaft auf der Suche nach dem Absoluten' (2006) 131 Archiv des Öffentlichen Rechts 173, 182.

438 Baldus (n 409) 13.

439 Isensee, 'Menschenwürde: Die säkulare Gesellschaft auf der Suche nach dem Absoluten' (n 437) 179.

440 Isensee, 'Würde des Menschen' (n 436) 7, Rn. 6.

441 Dreier (n 406) Rn. 52, correctly states that "there is no generally accepted and doctrinally precise legal concept of human dignity that would be able to go beyond general declarations regarding meaning, legal character, and rank." [Einen allgemein akzeptierten, dogmatisch präzisen Rechtsbegriff der Menschenwürde, der über die allgemeinen Aussagen zu Bedeutung, Rechtscharakter und Rang hinausginge, gibt es nicht.]

442 Kingreen and Poscher (n 399) 92 ff.

being. Secondly, the Theory of Performance or Capacity [*Leistungstheory*], which views dignity as something to be achieved in accordance with one's accomplishments in communicative processes. Finally, the Theory of Recognition [*Annerkennungstheorie*], in which dignity is conceptualized as emerging from a reciprocal process of recognition between members of a society.[443]

2.1. Theories on the legitimation of human dignity

2.1.1. Theory of Dowry

2.1.1.1. Transcendental versions of the Theory of Dowry

This approach departs from the methodological postulate that the conceptual origins and development of human dignity are inextricable from the influence of Christianity on the formation of modern law, and must be studied accordingly.[444] It also seems to suggest that modern law cannot depart from these roots without damaging the law itself.[445] In this sense, the reference to God in the constitutions of several *Länder* and the GG would evidence the non-secular prerequisites of the existence of dignity.[446]

The Declaration of Independence of the United States of America resonates with this theory, even if it does not mention dignity.[447] The main related statement of the Christian religious tradition is clear: dignity – as a right – is a "grace of God."[448] Indeed, influenced by classical thought, Christianity very soon understood dignity as inhering in the human being,

443 Dreier (n 406) Rn. 56 fn 273 states that the division in these three main groups has indeed become"canonical." For a "cultural" foundation of dignity, an approach that cannot be completely integrated in one of the three groups will be exposed, cf. the proposal of Häberle (n 412) 344 ff, Rn. 46 ff.

444 Christian Starck, 'Menschenwürde als Verfassungsgarantie im modernen Staat' (1981) 36 Juristenzeitung 457, 457.

445 ibid.

446 Josef Isensee, 'Menschenwürde: Die säkulare Gesellschaft auf der Suche nach dem Absoluten' (n 437) 178.

447 US, 'The Declaration of Independence' par. 2. "We hold these truths to be self-evident, that all men are created equal, that they are endowed by their Creator with certain unalienable Rights, that among these are Life, Liberty and the pursuit of Happiness."

448 Epping (n 399) 271 [*Gnadenerweis Gottes*].

as granted by God.[449] In the German constitution, dignity thus represents "positivized supra-positive law."[450] In this interpretation, the absoluteness of the human dignity clause is then a reflection of religion[451] – the roots of dignity are deeper than the constitution and the secular state.[452]

Isensee, for one, explains that the Christian grounding of dignity is the biblical revelation that God created humankind in his own image, separate from the rest of creation. The content of constitutional dignity could only be deduced within this cosmological hierarchy.[453] He explains that biblical teachings on the relationship between God and humankind led to the postulation of the Western view of the relationships between people, and then between individuals and the state.

The normative consequences of the Christian doctrine of the creation and redemption, according to *Isensee*, form human dignity in the everyday sense: the person's indispensability to others, a claim and duty of respect regarding others and oneself, freedom in moral responsibility, equality between people, and love of one's neighbor.[454] As can be seen, the Christian understanding of dignity comes with duties, which constitutes one of its remarkable traits.[455]

Stark, in turn, remarks that the Christian understanding is not postulated against modernity but is rather a prerequisite for its development. Modern individualism emerges from the Christian teaching that claims a direct relationship between the human being and God.[456] The transcendental or metaphysical grounding of dignity is the basis of the Enlightenment triad of freedom, equality, and fraternity; for all men and women are in the same measure the image of God.[457] The German constitutional doctrine that understands dignity as a subjective right is rooted in the Christian postulate

---

449 Nikolaus Knoepffler, *Würde und Freiheit. Vier Konzeptionen im Vergleich* (2018) 62 ff.

450 Josef Isensee, 'Menschenwürde: Die säkulare Gesellschaft auf der Suche nach dem Absoluten' (n 437) 175.

451 ibid 209.

452 Josef Isensee, 'Der grundrechtliche Konnex von Menschenleben und Menschenwürde' (2009) 18 Zeitschrift für Lebensrecht 114, 119.

453 Isensee, 'Menschenwürde: Die säkulare Gesellschaft auf der Suche nach dem Absoluten' (n 437) 205.

454 ibid 207.

455 Knoepffler (n 449) 66 ff.

456 Starck, 'Menschenwürde als Verfassungsgarantie im modernen Staat' (n 444) 460.

457 ibid.

that dignity is possessed by every human being.[458] The image of man in the GG, *Stark* adds, also speaks in favor of this interpretation: the human being exists prior to the state, and the latter's power is therefore only relative.

2.1.1.2. Immanentist versions of the Theory of Dowry

Though it does not invoke divinity to justify them, immanentist approaches to the Theory of Dowry also assume that the human being possesses some unique qualities that place him or her at the pinnacle of existence. Here, the foundational document of human rights is the French Declaration of Rights of the Man and the Citizen, which, like the Theory of Dowry, sees rights as natural, though not expressly as given by God.[459]

The roots of this position are found in classical antiquity, with some ideas traceable to *Aristotle*, who suggested that people's unique capacities equip them to live their own lives independently.[460] *Cicero* utilized the concept of dignity in this sense as well.[461] Later, *Aquinas* spoke of humans as being an end in themselves.[462] In modernity, the work of *Kant* stands out. His ideas were influenced by several authors who had previously developed an innovative approach to human freedom, such as *Pico della Mirandola*, *Rosseau*, and *Wolff*.[463] Kant's most influential paragraph on dignity reads:

> In the kingdom of ends, everything has either *a price* or a *dignity*. What has a price can be replaced by something else as its *equivalent*, what on the other hand is raised above all price and therefore admits of no equivalent has a dignity. What is related to general human inclinations and needs has a *market price*, that which, even without presupposing a need, conforms with a certain taste, that is, with a delight in the mere purposeless play of our mental powers, has a *fancy price;* but that which constitutes the condition under which alone something can be an end in

458 ibid 462.

459 Hofmann, 'Die Grundrechte 1789 – 1949 – 1989' (n 386) 3180 ff. describes the historical developments of this tradition.

460 Knoepffler (n 449) 63.

461 ibid 64.

462 ibid 69.

463 ibid 121–122.

> itself has not merely a relative worth, that is, a price, but an inner worth, that is, *dignity.*[464]

From this conceptualization, *Kant* derives the following obligation for action: "For, all rational beings stand under the *law* that each of them is to treat himself and all others *never merely as means* but always *at the same time as ends in themselves.*"[465] Following *Kant,* the prohibition of instrumentalization is based both on human rationality and on the capacity for self-determination.[466]

Kant conceives the holder of dignity not to be the human being as a biological fact but, in the strictest sense, his or her moral-practical rationale; namely, the ability to self-legislate.[467] The grounding of dignity is thus autonomy: the human being's capacity to make laws of action for him or herself.[468] Hence, dignity is related to the obligations between fellow human beings and to one's own duties to oneself. Consequently, self-instrumentalization is forbidden and dignity means respecting the humanity present in everyone.[469]

Kant's understanding was influentially applied to Art. 1 (1) GG by *Dürig* in the 1950s.[470] *Dürig* affirmed that "every human being is such by virtue of his spirit, which elevates him aside from the impersonal nature, and enables him to become conscious, to determine and to shape himself and his envi-

---

464 Immanuel Kant, *Groundwork of the Metaphysics of Morals* (1997) 42. [Im Reiche der Zwecke hat alles entweder einen *Preis*, oder eine *Würde.* Was einen Preis hat, an dessen Stelle kann auch etwas anderes als *Äquivalent* gesetzt werden; was dagegen über allen Preis erhaben ist, mithin kein Äquivalent verstattet, das hat Würde. Was sich auf die allgemeinen menschlichen Neigungen und Bedürfnisse bezieht, hat einen *Marktpreis*; das, was, auch ohne ein Bedürfnisse voraussetzen, einem gewissen Geschmacke, d.i. einem Wohlgeffallen am bloßen zwecklosen Spiel unsere Gemüthskräfte, gemäß ist, einen *Affectionpreis;* das aber, was die Bedingung ausmacht, unter der allein etwas Zweck an sich selbst sein kann, hat nicht bloß einen relativen Werth, d.i. einen Preis, sondern einen inneren Werth, d.i. *Würde.*]

465 ibid 41. [Denn vernünftige Wesen stehen alle unter dem *Gesetz*, daß jedes derselben sich selbst und alle andere *niemals bloß als Mittel*, sondern jederzeit *zugleich als Zweck an sich selbst* behandeln solle.]

466 Friedhelm Hufen, 'Erosion der Menschenwürde?' (2004) 59 Juristen Zeitung 313, 316.

467 Knoepffler (n 449) 125.

468 ibid 133.

469 ibid 123.

470 Baldus (n 409) 74 ff.

ronment by his own judgment."[471] From this conception, *Dürig* deduced the following consequences. Firstly, the human being is free; secondly, all human beings share this freedom; and, finally, they are equal among each other. Dignity, then, as an inherent value, resides in every human being as an "abstract possibility of execution."[472]

2.1.1.3. Reception and critique of the Theory of Dowry

A historical interpretation of Art. 1 (1) GG shows that the majority of the Parliamentary Council accepted the foundation of dignity, either as provided by God or by nature.[473] A natural law approach, in the sense of considering that human dignity and basic rights precede the state, predominated among the authors of the GG.[474]

The religious motivation of several constitutional drafters becomes manifest when examining the relevant proceedings. Indeed, the first draft of the norm on dignity even contained the word "sacred."[475] Moreover, *Süsterhenn*, a member of the commission that discussed the norm of dignity, directly requested the phrase "given by God" be included after the words "human rights" in Art. 1 (2) GG. Only when human rights are understood as God-given can they make a person free, *Süsterhenn* argued, since this clarifies that fundamental rights precede the state.[476] In this sense, the "Christian background" of the GG at least represents a part of the "norma-

471 Günter Dürig, 'Der Grundrechtssatz von der Menschenwürde. Entwurf eines praktikablen Wertsystems der Grundrechte aus Art. 1 Abs. I in Verbindung mit Art. 19 Abs. II des Grundgesetz' (1956) 81 Archiv des Öffentlichen Rechts 117, 125. [Jeder Mensch ist Mensch kraft seines Geistes, der ihn abhebt von der unpersönlichen Natur und ihn aus eigener Entscheidung dazu befähig, seiner selbst bewußt zu werden, sich selbst zu bestimmen und sich und die Umwelt zu gestalten.]

472 ibid.

473 Hofmann, 'Die versprochene Menschenwürde' (n 405) 361. A different conclusion, however, has been defended by Baldus (n 409) 79.

474 Isensee, 'Würde des Menschen' (n 436) 18, Rn. 19.

475 See Isensee, 'Menschenwürde: Die säkulare Gesellschaft auf der Suche nach dem Absoluten' (n 437) 177, fn 17: "Respecting and protecting human dignity is the sacred obligation of all state power" [*heilige Verpflichtung aller staatlichen Gewalt.*]

476 Parlamentarischer Rat, Verhandlungen des Hauptausschusses Bonn 1948/1949, 42. Sitzung v. 19.01 1949, 529–531. The proposal was narrowly rejected (11 v 10). [von Gott gegeben] [Menschenrechte]

tive program" of the constitution.[477] On the other hand, scholars such as *Bergsträsser* and *Mangoldt*, similarly commented that Art. 1 GG established the pre-state character of rights, but as a natural rather than a divine endowment.[478] The essential distinction between both approaches is that Kant's position is constructed in a universal sense whereas the Christian interpretation is based on transcendentalist reasoning.[479]

Despite such differences, the central normative teaching in both the theological and Enlightenment models is that dignity concerns the intrinsic value of the human being.[480] Each justification of dignity, and thus of human rights, is traceable in the GG.[481] Indeed, the BVerfG soon considered that man, owing to his intrinsic value, is located in a privileged space in the world: "in the order of the creation, the human being possesses his own independent value."[482] Dignity, as the court stated elsewhere, is inherent to one's condition as a person.[483] This means that dignity is allocated to each human being without any consideration of one's particular case and situation.[484] This idea that rights attend the human being due to his or her inherent value and are not conceded but only recognized by that state, has been confirmed by the court in several decisions.[485] Some scholars

477 Hufen, 'Erosion der Menschenwürde?' (n 466) 314. [So stellt der christliche Hintergrund des Grundgesetzes zwar einen Teil des Normprogramms der Verfassung dar, aber eben nicht den einzigen.]

478 Pikard and Werner (n 407) 63–64.

479 Knoepffler (n 449) 135.

480 Epping (n 399) 271.

481 Hofmann, 'Die Grundrechte 1789 - 1949 - 1989' (n 386) 3184.

482 BVerfGE 2, 1, (12) - *SRP-Verbot* (1952). [Dieser Grundordnung liegt letztlich nach der im Grundgesetz getroffenen verfassungspolitischen Entscheidung die Vorstellung zugrunde, dass der Mensch in der Schöpfungsordnung einen eigenen selbständigen Wert besitzt und Freiheit und Gleichheit dauernde Grundwerte der staatlichen Einheit sind.]

483 BVerfGE 30, 1, (2) - *Abhörurteil* (1970). [Die Behandlung des Menschen durch die öffentliche Hand, die das Gesetz vollzieht, muß, wenn sie die Menschenwürde berühren soll, Ausdruck der Verachthung des Wertes, der dem Mensch kraft seines Personseins zukommt, sein.]

484 BVerfGE 96, 375, (399) – *Kind als Schaden* (1997). [Jedem Mensch ist sie eigen ohne Rücksicht auf seine Eigenschaften, seine Leistungen und seine sozialen Status.]

485 See e.g., BVerfGE 5, 85, (205) – *KPD-Verbot* (1956). [Da Menschenwürde und Freiheit jedem Menschen zukommen, die Menschen insoweit gleich sind, ist das Prinzip der Gleichbehandlung aller für die freiheitliche Demokratie ein selbstverständliches Postulat. Das Recht auf Freiheit und Gleichbehandlung durch den Staat schließt jede wirkliche Unterdrückung des Bürgers durch den Staat aus, weil alle staatliche Entscheidung den Eigenwert der Person achten und die Spannung zwischen Person

even consider this continuity as the basis of the BVerfG's case law on the matter.[486]

Nevertheless, the BVerfG has frequently remarked that the human being must always remain an "end-in-himself"[487] affirming that "the constitutional order bases the representation of a human as being a moral-spiritual being, which was created to self-determine and to unfold himself in freedom."[488] From these ideas, and following the Kantian thought developed by *Dürig*, the BVerfG has applied the so-called "object formula" to review when a state action might violate dignity, that is, when making "the human being a mere object of the state or treat[ing] him in such a way that his quality as a subject is in principle set in question."[489]

As strong as this approach to dignity appears, it has nonetheless attracted criticism. Constitutional drafters such as *Schmid* or *Heuss* were skeptical of this grounding.[490] *Badura* subsequently remarked in the 1960s that the GG provides no evidence that through its Art. 1 (1), it intended to consider material ethics as the basis of the constitutional order.[491] *Dreier* admonishes

---

und Gemeinschaft im Rahmen des auch dem Einzelnen zumutbaren ausgleichen soll.]; 6, 32, (41) – *Elfes* (1957). [Demgegenüber hat das Grundgesetz eine wertgebundene Ordnung aufgerichtet, die die öffentliche Gewalt begrenzt. Durch diese Ordnung soll die Eigenständigkeit, die Selbstverantwortlichkeit und die Würde des Menschen in der staatlichen Gemeinschaft gesichert werden (...). Die obersten Prinzipien dieser Wertordnung sind gegen Verfassungsänderungen geschützt (Art. 1, 20, 79 Abs. 3 GG)]; 45, 187, (229) – *Lebenslange Freiheitsstrafe* (1977). [Bei alledem darf nicht aus den Augen verloren werden: Die Würde des Menschen ist etwas Unverfügbares. Die Erkenntnis dessen, was das Gebot, sie zu achten, erfordert, ist jedoch nicht von der historischen Entwicklung zu trennen.]

486 Nettesheim (n 406) 2.

487 See, e.g., BVerfGE 45, 187, (228) – *Lebenslange Freiheitsstrafe* (1977). [Der Satz, "der Mensch muß immer Zweck an sich selbst bleiben," gilt uneingeschränkt für alle Rechtsgebiete; denn die unverlierbare Würde des Menschen als Person besteht gerade darin, daß er als selbstverantwortliche Persönlichkeit anerkannt bleibt.]

488 BVerfGE 45, 187, (227) – *Lebenslange Freiheitsstrafe* (1977). [Dem liegt die Vorstellung vom Menschen als einem geistig-sittlichen Wesen zugrunde, das darauf angelegt ist, in Freiheit sich selbst zu bestimmen und sich zu entfalten.]

489 BVerfGE 50, 166 (175) – *Ausweisung I* (1979). [Dem Menschen kommt in der Gemeinschaft ein sozialer Wert- und Achtungsanspruch zu; deshalb widerspricht es der menschlichen Würde, den Menschen zum bloßen Objekt des Staates zu machen oder ihn einer Behandlung aussetzen, die seine Subjektqualität prinzipiell in Frage stellt.] The object formula will be reviewed in detail later in § 10, subsection 4.

490 Pikard and Werner (n 407) 62 ff.

491 Peter Badura, 'Generalprävention und Würde des Menschen' (1964) 19 Juristenzeitung 337, 340 argued that the problematic consequences of considering dignity as the basis of an order of values could be avoided if the dignity clause were subjected

that this conception is not imaginable without theology or metaphysics.[492] By the same token, *Stöcker* asks how secular content for the norm could be derived from a religious understanding of the concept of dignity.[493] Similarly, other jurists emphasize the unacceptability of grounding any constitutional norm of a secular state in theological models.[494] *Hoffmann* remarks that the "Theory of Dowry" group of approaches remains highly abstract: to justify dignity, one must resort to the mere potential human capacity of reason.[495] In addition, treating dignity as absolute can have no basis in actual human properties, *Hörle* suggests.[496]

Others go further and reject the normative presuppositions of the Theory of Dowry. *Nettesheim*, for one, affirms that the old certainties of humanity's exalted place in nature have been lost, and thus the interpretations of dignity that resort to that image are no longer valid,[497] leaving no pre-legal basis for the constitutional order.[498] In today's context, any aim of re-sacralization is doomed to fail.[499] *Luhmann* condenses this critique by commenting "whether we should continue to consider the essence of the human being in distinction from that of animals has become questionable since Heidegger."[500]

Of greater doctrinal importance, however, is work that acknowledges the Theory of Dowry's contribution to understanding dignity in the GG, while critiquing the normative consequences deriving from it. Firstly, both the

---

to a teleological interpretation and was thus intended to ensure the legal content of dignity through a "casuistic of clear cases of infringement" [Verletzungtatbestände]. See ibid 341.

492 Dreier (n 406) Rn. 57.

493 Hans A. Stöcker, 'Menschliche Würde und kritische Jurisprudenz' (1988) 23 Juristenzeitung 685, 686.

494 Cf., e.g., Tatjana Hörle, 'Menschenwürde und Lebenschutz' (2003) 89 Archiv für Rechts- und Sozialphilosophie 318, 323; Ulfrid Neumann, 'Die Tyrannei der Würde: Argumentationstheoretische Erwägungen zum Menschenwürdeprinzip' (1998) 84 Archiv für Rechts- und Sozialphilosophie 153, 158; Hofmann, 'Die versprochene Menschenwürde' (n 405) 361.

495 Hofmann, 'Die versprochene Menschenwürde' (n 405) 361.

496 Hörle (n 494) 20.

497 Nettesheim (n 406) 2.

498 ibid 3.

499 ibid. [Eine empirische angelegte Suche nach einem spezifischen Wesen des Menschen, das ihn aus der Natur heraushebt, droht in der Moderne ins Leere zu laufen.]

500 Luhmann, *Grundrechte als Institution* (n 422) 58, fn 13. [Ob wir aber fortfahren sollen, das Wesen des Menschen in seinem Abstand zum Tier zu erblicken, ist seit Heidegger fragwürdig geworden.]

Christian and Kantian approaches follow an "ought to" as a "duty" dimension of dignity.[501] Therefore, "undignified" activities would violate dignity, and would be prohibited, even against the will of the affected. In this context, cases involving accusations of paternalism have received particular attention, because they may represent the imposition of a particularistic morality.[502] Secondly, this group of theories cannot delimit the concept of dignity from that of freedom; namely, from the contents of Arts. 1 (1) and 2 (1) GG.[503] Finally, when understood as a value, Art. 1 (1) GG does not achieve its goal: the possibility remains for the state to drive a human being to self-degradation.[504]

2.1.2. Theory of Performance

According to the Theory of Performance, dignity is not inherent to a human being but something to be achieved through communicative processes. The theory's leading proponent is *Niklas Luhmann*, [505] whose "Grundrechte als Institution" (1965) is its foundational text.[506]

Luhmann's theoretical vision was that fundamental rights prevent the dedifferentiation of functional subsystems.[507] Broadly, he theorized how social development obstructs the individual's generalization of (self-)representation.[508] *Luhmann* criticizes the traditional understanding of dignity and freedom in constitutional doctrine: "it has remained Aristotelian."[509] This means, above all, that "the human personality is, as always, under-

501 Knoepffler (n 449) 150.

502 Hufen, *Staatsrecht II. Grundrechte* (n 399) 133. Archetypal example: BVerwGE 64, 274 – *Peep Show* (1981). See § 10, subsection 5.

503 Luhmann, *Grundrechte als Institution* (n 422) 77.

504 ibid 68, fn 44.

505 Cf. Dreier (n 406) Rn. 58 fn 276.

506 Luhmann, *Grundrechte als Institution* (n 422).

507 ibid 23–24; further explained at 71–72: "They do not refer to the production of differentiation in relatively autonomic communicative structures, but to the preservation of the overall order of constituted differentiations from hazards that emerge from system separations and connected mutual dependencies." [Sie bezieht sich nicht auf die Herstellung der Differenzierung in relativ autonome Kommunikationsstrukturen, sondern auf die Erhaltung der die Gesamtordnung konstituierenden Differenzierung gegenüber Gefährdungen, die aus den Systemtrennungen und den damit verbundenen wechselseitigen Abhängigkeiten entstehen.]

508 Luhmann, *Grundrechte als Institution* (n 422) 56.

509 ibid. [Sie ist aristotelisch geblieben]

stood as a substance."[510] What is required, argues *Luhmann,* is a rethinking of the main questions of human ontology itself.[511]

According to *Luhmann*, basic rights guarantee neither freedom nor dignity.[512] Rather they "denote basic conditions for the success of the self-representation of a human being as an individual personality." Constitutional rights lay the groundwork for the possibility of individualization through social contact. Processes of self-representation are, however, very fragile, and therefore require the institutionalization of certain limits to communication, to protect the intimate sphere.[513] For Luhmann, while self-representation does not depend on independence from external causes but upon one's own performance,[514] it presupposes freedom from manifest coercion and external social causes.

From the functionalist viewpoint, *Luhmann* explains, the social order requires the preservation of individual sociability.[515] Here, the challenge of dignity corresponds to the difficulties involved in maintaining a "consistent and convincing self-representation," as the individual is ultimately responsible for the accomplishment of this goal. However, this in turn presupposes that the state will act to allow self-representation. The state must balance maintaining peace (which requires the maintenance of bodily integrity)[516] with ensuring some additional conditions for freedom, under which individuals are responsible for their own dignity.[517] For this reason, the constitution protects the individual from the state.[518] In summary:

> [t]he fundamental rights of dignity and freedom have the crucial function of protecting personal and individual representation of one's self from state interferences, which could paralyze the expressive potential of personality's symbolic communication decisively.[519]

510 Luhmann, *Grundrechte als Institution* (n 422) 58.

511 ibid 60. [Die Unterscheidung von Sein und Schein – ebenfalls ein ontologisches Denkschema – ist für das Verständnis dieses Vorgangs ungeeignet. Der Mensch wird die Persönlichkeit, als welche er sich darstellt.]

512 ibid 72.

513 ibid 67.

514 ibid 61.

515 ibid 70.

516 ibid 71.

517 ibid 73.

518 ibid 75. Moreover, Luhmann expressly rejects third parties' duties of respect. See ibid 76–77, fn 60.

519 Luhmann, *Grundrechte als Institution* (n 422) 82. [Die Grundrechte der Freiheit und Würde haben eine wichtige Funktion des Schutzes dieser Sphäre gegen staat-

As can be seen, dignity is, in this functionalist approach, neither a natural property nor a value, but a "desirable" concept, which denotes success in self-representation. Hence, it must be constructed: the failure to self-represent also entails the loss of dignity.[520]

Reception and critique of the Theory of Performance

This theory differs manifestly not only from other theories on the legitimation of dignity, but also from conventional methods of approaching basic rights. Nonetheless, some of its tenets have been adopted by jurists working on the problem, and there is broad agreement that one dimension of dignity is the possibility of a protected and free self-representation. This claim can be found in the so-called "general right of personality," constructed by the BVerfG from Art. 2 (1) in conjunction with Art. 1 (1).[521] Indeed, the BVerfG emphasized that Art. 1 (1) GG:

> [P]rotects the dignity of the human being, as he understands himself in his own individuality and self-awareness. Part of the latter is that the human being is both under his own command and can shape his destiny on his own responsibility. Art. 2. (1) GG in connection to Art. 1 (1) GG guarantees the free development of the capacities and powers invested in the human being.[522]

---

liche Eingriffe, welche das symbolisch kommunikative Ausdruckspotential der Persönlichkeit entscheidend lähmen könnten.]

520 ibid 69. Luhmann praises his own theory for its ability to delimit the content of dignity and freedom (ibid 77): "While dignity refers to the internal ones, freedom refers to the external conditions and problems of self-representation of the individual personality." [Die Würde bezieht sich auf die inneren, die Freiheit auf die äußeren Bedingungen und Probleme der Selbstdarstellung als individuelle Persönlichkeit.] An overview of scholars that at least partially follow the approach of Luhmann on dignity can be found in Dreier (n 406) Rn. 58, footnote 276.

521 This right will be treated in detail below in § 8, subsection 3.2.

522 BVerfGE 49, 286, (289) – *Transexuelle I* (1978). [Art. 1 Abs. 1 GG schützt die Würde des Menschen, wie er sich in seiner Individualität selbst begreift und seiner selbst bewußt wird. Hierzu gehört, daß der Mensch über sich selbst verfügen und sein Schicksal eigenverantwortlich gestalten kann. Art. 2 Abs. 1 GG in Verbindung mit Art. 1 Abs. 1 GG gewährleistet die freie Entfaltung der im Menschen angelegten Fähigkeiten und Kräfte.]

And in another place, that the:

> [I]ndividual should have the freedom to decide for himself - without any restrictions on his private sphere - how to portray himself to third parties or the public, as well as whether and to what extent third parties may have access to his personality.[523]

This approach has also been used by scholars to criticize some judicial decisions. *Höfling*, for one, referring to the *Peep Show* case, stated that:

> Dignity and freedom are basic conditions for the success of self-representation of a human being as an individual personality. The human being primarily has to be responsible for his own dignity. Indeed, dignity is this responsibility.[524]

The concrete differences between this and the Theory of Dowry are clear. According to the Theory of Performance, not only was the *Peep Show* ruling incorrect, but in principle, participating in "undignified" activities, such as 24-hour reality shows, are not a violation of dignity. On the contrary, such activities constitute a legitimate and effective way to achieve personal success thanks to the broad avenues for self-representation they offer.[525] The favorable consequences of this approach to dignity are now apparent: it is free of metaphysical assumptions[526] and therefore protects

523 BVerfGE 54, 148, (155) - *Eppler* (1980). English translation taken from Kommers and Miller (n 416) 407. [Der Einzelne soll - ohne Beschränkung auf seine Privatsphäre - grundsätzlich selbst entscheiden können, wie er sich Dritten oder der Öffentlichkeit gegenüber darstellen will, ob und inwieweit von Dritten über seine Persönlichkeit verfügt werden kann.]

524 Wolfram Höfling, 'Menschenwürde und gute Sitten' (1983) 36 Neue Juristische Wocheschrift 1582, 1583. [Würde und Freiheit bezeichnen Grundbedingungen des Gelingens der Selbstdarstellung eines Menschen als individuelle Persönlichkeit. Seine Würde hat der Mensch - nach dem hier vertreten grundrechtsdogmatischen Ansatz - primär selbst zu verantworten, gerade diese Verantwortung ist die Würde.]. The link between cases such as the *Peep-Show* and dignity will be reviewed in § 10, subsection 5.

525 Stefan Huster, 'Individuelle Menschenwürde oder öffentliche Ordnung? Ein Diskussionsbeitrag anlässlich "Big Brother"' [2000] Neue Juristische Wocheschrift 3477, 2478. In this context, Huster affirms that a *Reality Show* indeed provides "what (almost) everyone wants in an anonymous mass society based on performance: to be rich and famous." [was in einer Leistungs- und anonymen Massengesellschaft (fast) alle wollen: reich und berühmt zu sein.] The author, however, does not provide any evidence of this presumption of a common desire.

526 Stephan Kirste, 'A legal concept of dignity as a foundation of law' in Kirste, Stephan; Brugger, Winfried (ed), *Human dignity as a foundation of law: proceedings of the*

the individual against external conceptions of dignity, thereby assuring the moral neutrality of the state.[527]

Despite such benefits, the Theory of Performance has been subject to several criticisms. First of all, its grounding does not appear in the proceedings of the Parliamentary Council,[528] and therefore did not play a role in the original intention of the drafters when interpreting the norm.[529] Much stronger than this reproach, however, are several critiques that reject several normative outcomes of this theory.

Firstly, as *Hufen* affirms, focusing on performance excludes anyone who lacks the required capacities for self-representation.[530] In other words, the theory does not assist those who may suffer from one or more "human abnormalities" to form their identity.[531] And as *Kirste* claims, the concept of dignity was introduced into law precisely to prevent the exclusion of such people.[532] The "comprehensive concept of protection" of the GG as a reaction to the National Socialist dictatorship opposes the idea that dignity is something to be earned, affirms *Epping.*[533] Besides, adds *Isensee,* if dignity is to be considered self-produced, there remains the question of who decides whether it has been achieved – and according to what criteria.[534] In contrast to the GG's intention, dignity as conceptualized in the Theory of Performance reflects the differences but not the basic equality between human beings.[535] *Luhmann's* conception produces consequences that neglect the normative kernel of human dignity, argues *Mahlmann.*[536] The view of *Enders* is that *Luhmann's* approach explains through a functionalist design

special workshop held at the 24th world congress of the International Association for Philosophy of Law and Social Philosophy in Beijing, 2009 (2013) 72.

527 Hofmann, 'Die versprochene Menschenwürde' (n 405) 362.

528 Pikard and Werner (n 407).

529 Baldus (n 409) 96.

530 Hufen, *Staatsrecht II. Grundrechte* (n 399) 133.

531 Hofmann, 'Die versprochene Menschenwürde' (n 405) 362. [menschlicher Abnormalitäten]

532 Kirste, 'A Legal Concept of Dignity as a Foundation of Law' (n 526) 72, affirms that "if dignity is relative to achievements, this right is unable to address a problem for whose solution the concept was introduced; namely, the dignity of those persons who are, because of mental or other handicaps, incapable of acting or articulating themselves."

533 Epping (n 399) 271.

534 Starck, 'Menschenwürde als Verfassungsgarantie im modernen Staat' (n 444) 463.

535 Isensee, 'Würde des Menschen' (n 436) 39, Rn. 87.

536 Matthias Mahlmann, *Elemente einer etischen Grundrechtstheorie* (2008) 275.

"what personality is but dissolves it [the personality] in that scheme."[537] In line with this critique, the BVerfG has insisted on the inherent character of dignity and its inalienability.[538]

2.1.3. Theory of Recognition

Against the background of social contracts,[539] the Theory of Recognition also rests on communicative human constructions.[540] However, it does not consider dignity as achievable, but as recognized by concrete communities. Hence, dignity should not be located in the individual, but in the interaction between people, as a relational concept.[541] Therefore, according to this approach, dignity protects human solidarity and sociability, in particular.[542]

Hoffmann is an important proponent of this approach in the doctrinal field.[543] He contends that the Theories of Dowry and Performance share a basic defect: they are grounded in the subjectivity of the individual. Dignity is, therefore, incorrectly affirmed as either a quality or an outcome of the individual. In contrast, dignity must be understood as constructed in interpersonal recognition through affirmations of social claims of respect.[544]

---

537 Christoph Enders, *Die Menschenwürde in der Verfassungsordnung: Zur Dogmatik des Art. 1 GG* (1997) 507.

538 BVerfGE 87, 207, (228) – *Tanz der Teufel* (1992): "Everyone possesses dignity, regardless of his particularities, achievements, or social status. It is also intrinsic to those who, in virtue of their corporal or mental states, are not able to act rationally. Not even through undignified behavior can dignity be lost. It cannot be taken from any human being. However, the claim of respect that arises from it is violable." [Jeder besitzt sie, ohne Rücksicht auf seine Eigenschaften, seine Leistungen und seinen sozialen Status. Sie ist auch dem eigen, der aufgrund seines körperlichen oder geistigen Zustands nicht sinnhaft handeln kann. Selbst durch unwürdiges Verhalten geht nicht verloren, Sie kann keinem Menschen genommen werden. Verletzbar ist aber der Achtungsanspruch, der sich aus ihr ergibt.]

539 Hörle (n 494) 324.

540 Hufen, *Staatsrecht II. Grundrechte* (n 399) 134.

541 Neumann (n 494) 165.

542 Hufen, *Staatsrecht II. Grundrechte* (n 399) 134.

543 See Hofmann, 'Die versprochene Menschenwürde' (n 405).

544 Similarly, Jürgen Habermas, *Die Zukunft der menschlichen Natur. Auf dem Weg zu einer liberalen Eugenik?* (2002) 68, who holds that human dignity "is not a quality that one can "possess" by nature, like intelligence or blue eyes; rather, it denotes an "inviolability", which can only have meaning within interpersonal relations of reciprocal recognition, in the egalitarian interaction of persons with one another". [Sie ist nicht eine Eigenschaft, die man von Natur aus „besitzen" kann wie Intelligenz

The protected interest of human dignity, *Hoffmann* goes on to explain, is the fraternal solidarity of a relevant human group. Dignity is more than a subjective right: it entails reciprocal recognition of others with all their particularities, cannot be detached from a concrete human community of recognition,[545] and therefore differs in content in Germany and among other polities.[546] Indeed, one must distinguish between the universal idea of dignity as an ethical impulse for constitutional clauses on the one hand; and dignity in the GG as the concrete grounding norm of the German state on the other.[547]

From this perspective, *Neumann* adds, one should ask "which actions imply an undignified treatment" of others in order to determine the scope of protection of dignity. *Hörnle* phrases this idea similarly: the dignity clause demands "minimal requirements of human solidarity," which do not permit certain types of treatment of fellow human beings.[548] Concrete cases that are classified as inadmissible by consensus are those that indicate social contempt and humiliation.[549] The theory thus implies a negative approach to the determination of the content of dignity, in which the object formula is a useful tool.[550]

Reception and critique of the Theory of Recognition

Nettesheim suggests that the Theory of Recognition cannot predict concrete consequences for the state.[551] According to *Isensee*, it also obscures the view that the GG refers to the self-worth of the human being, according to which dignity is the measure for a possible social contract, and not the inverse.[552] With this reversal, dignity loses its unconditionality[553] and its recognition in particular cases comes to depend on the discretion of whoever holds

oder blaue Augen; sie markiert vielmehr diejenige „Unantastbarkeit," die allein in den interpersonalen Beziehungen reziproker Anerkennung, im egalitären Umgang von Personen miteinander eine Bedeutung haben kann.]

545 Hofmann, 'Die versprochene Menschenwürde' (n 405) 364.

546 ibid 375.

547 ibid 368. [*Staatsgründungsfunktion*]

548 Hörle (n 494) 324.

549 Neumann (n 494) 166.

550 Hörle (n 494) 324–325.

551 Nettesheim (n 406) 3.

552 Isensee, 'Menschenwürde: Die säkulare Gesellschaft auf der Suche nach dem Absoluten' (n 437) 205.

553 ibid 197.

the power.[554] This may result in legal doctrine being approached through the methods of a particular constitutional theory – in this way, *Isensee* warns, "the interpretation of positive constitutional law is replaced by an act of fictive creation of a constitution."[555] Moreover, the social human emphasized in these kinds of theories could endanger the inherent value of the individual human being.[556]

However, the contributions made by the Theory of Recognition should also be acknowledged. First, it grasps the communitarian dimension of dignity correctly – dignity not only concerns the individual, but also the solidarity between fellow human beings. Indeed, in the 1970s, the BVerfG affirmed that human dignity is a "constitutionally protected social claim to respect and value."[557] The community is responsible for ensuring that every member receives the minimum resources necessary to live a decent human life. From a legal point of view, this means that the individual has a claim on these resources. This rationale can be found behind some decisions by the BVerfG, such as those referring to the right to minimal conditions for a decent life.[558] In addition, as this solidarity endures even after death, the Theory of Recognition can explain the posthumous protection of dignity.[559]

3. *Legal form of dignity*

There is almost total unanimity in the German scholarship concerning the normativity of dignity in the GG.[560] Dignity is not a programmatic phrase, but rather the highest norm of the German legal order.[561] The clearest reasons for this are enshrined in the constitutional text. On the one

554 Isensee, 'Würde des Menschen' (n 436) 26, Rn. 31. [Die Interpretation des positiven Verfassungsrechts wird substituiert durch den Akt einer fiktiven Verfassungsgebung.]

555 ibid 27, Rn. 32.

556 Hufen, *Staatsrecht II. Grundrechte* (n 399) 134.

557 BVerfGE 28, 386, (391) – *Kurzzeitige Freiheitstrafe* (1970). [(...) verfassungsrechtlich geschützten sozialen Wert- und Achtungsanspruchs (...).]

558 See § 8, subsection 3.1.

559 Dreier (n 406) Rn. 77. On the posthumous protection of dignity, see § 9, subsection 3.2.

560 Stern (n 401) 60.

561 Cf. Hufen, *Staatsrecht II. Grundrechte* (n 399) 134; Hofmann, 'Die versprochene Menschenwürde' (n 405) 355; Knoepffler (n 449) 156. An exception can be found in Enders (n 537) 501. See *infra* subsection 3.1.4.

hand, only a legal norm can directly command the public power that the second section of Art. 1 (1) does.[562] On the other hand, the human dignity clause is not only covered by the "eternity guarantee" [*Ewigkeitsgarantie*] provided by Art. 79 (3) but is also inviolable [*unantastbar*], i.e., it is a claim of absolute character.[563]

The importance attached to dignity is supported by various statements: "[dignity] is a norm of the superlatives."[564] For instance, it has been labeled as the "fundamental constitutional principle,"[565] the "supreme value"[566] or "supreme constitutional principle,"[567] and the "highest juridical value"[568] by the BVerfG. The literature is also very generous in ranking dignity, *inter alia,* as the "state's norm of legitimation,"[569] the "most important decision of value of the GG,"[570] the "highest value-adding constitutional principle,"[571] and even as the "highest positivized juridical source concerning the position of the human being in state and society."[572]

Conversely, there is no such agreement as to the legal form or nature of this norm.[573] While a minority of powerful voices regard it only as a principle, the majoritarian opinion, following the corresponding case law of the BVerfG, sees it as a subjective right.[574]

562 Dreier (n 406) Rn. 44.

563 ibid Rn. 45–46.

564 Baldus (n 409) 11. Similarly, Dreier (n 406) Rn. 42. [Die herausgehobene Stellung, der leitmotivische Charakter und die feierlich knappe, gerade deswegen so eindringliche Formulierung haben der Bestimmung vielfältige Umschreibungen eingetragen, die zumeist in Modus des Superlativs operieren.]

565 BVerfGE 6, 32 (36) – *Elfes* (1957); 45, 187 (227) – *Lebenslange Freiheitsstrafe* (1977). [tragendes Konstitutionsprinzip]

566 BVerfGE 5, 85, (204) – *KPD-Verbot* (1956); 27, 1, (6) – *Microzensus* (1969); 30, 173, (193) – *Mephisto* (1971); 32, 98, (108) – *Gesundbeter* (1971); 50, 166, (175) – *Ausweisung I* (1979). [oberster Wert]

567 BVerfGE 54, 341, (357) – *Wirtschaftsasyl* (1980). [oberstes Verfassungsprinzip]

568 BVerfGE 45, 187, (204) – *Lebenslange Freiheitsstrafe* (1977). [höchster Rechtswert]

569 Wolfram Höfling, 'Art. 1' in Michael Sachs (ed), *Grundgesetz Kommentar* (2021) Rn. 53 [Staatslegitimationsnorm].

570 Jarass, 'Art. 1' (n 406) Rn. 3 [wichtigste Wertentscheidung des GG].

571 Stern (n 401) 60 [höchstes wertsetzendes Verfassungsprinzip].

572 Starck, 'Menschenwürde als Verfassungsgarantie im modernen Staat' (n 444) 457 [höchste positivierte Rechtsquelle über die Stellung des Menschen in Staat und Gemeinschaft].

573 Stern (n 401) 61.

574 For this position, see, e.g, Knoepffler (n 449) 157, Dreier (n 406) Rn. 121.

3.1. Human dignity as a principle

Formally, the position affirming that the clause on dignity consists only of a principle has been supported by two arguments. The first of these refers to the wording of the norm, which can be characterized by its "proclamatory indeterminacy".[575] The second argument departs from the location of Art. 1 (1) within the GG, i.e., before Art. 1 (3). The latter talks about the "following" basic rights, meaning only the rules that come afterwards may be considered basic rights, thereby excluding Art. 1 (1) from that category of norms.[576]

These formal arguments have been rejected convincingly. Proclamatory indeterminacy characterizes the grammar of other basic rights as well.[577] Neither does the "location" argument stand up to closer inspection: the clause on dignity belongs to the chapter entitled "Basic Rights."[578] Moreover, the location of a norm does not define its legal form, as the existence of subjective rights in the GG beyond chapter one definitively shows.[579] So, the answer to this question is neither provided by the wording nor by the location of the norm.[580]

The most crucial remaining point is to review the opinions based on substantive reasons. *Kingreen and Poscher* summarize these opinions as ones that reject, in principle, the possibility of a right with an absolute scope of protection.[581] *Hufen* centers them on the view that the quality of dignity is the highest constitutional value, and the principle would be devalued if it were also considered to be a right.[582] *Dreier* points out that dignity's absoluteness distinguishes it from all fundamental rights, and that classifying it as a basic right could result in its relativization and balancing, thereby weakening it.[583] In addition, he also argues that the normative structure of dignity differs considerably from the usual basic rights since it

---

575 As described by Kingreen and Poscher (n 399) 91.
576 Cf. Epping (n 399) 267. Similarly, Isensee, 'Würde des Menschen' (n 436) 69–70, Rn. 104.
577 Kingreen and Poscher (n 399) 91.
578 ibid; Stern (n 401) 62 [Grundrechte].
579 Hufen, *Staatsrecht II. Grundrechte* (n 399) 135.
580 Dreier (n 406) Rn. 122.
581 Kingreen and Poscher (n 399) 91.
582 Hufen, *Staatsrecht II. Grundrechte* (n 399) 135.
583 Dreier (n 406) Rn. 124.

is difficult to discuss the scope of protection of dignity.[584] *Epping* suggests that since the BVerfG has defined basic rights as concretizations of dignity, it is difficult to see how the scope of protection of a supposed right to dignity could be defined independently of these rights.[585]

3.1.1. Dürig's seminal position of dignity as a principle

During the GG's early years, the ruling opinion – particularly as proposed by *Günther Dürig* – denied that the guarantee of human dignity was a basic right.[586] *Dürig's* main argument was that the far-reaching scope of basic rights enshrined in the GG's Bill of Rights made it unnecessary to consider Art. 1 (1) GG as a fundamental right. Any attack on human dignity would already have violated one of those rights, at least the catch-all right contained in Art. 2 (1) GG, *Dürig* affirmed.[587]

Dürig characterized Art. 1 (1) GG as a "supreme constitutional principle of all objective law," which "then gradually is implemented in favor of the individual holder of rights."[588] In this position, the dignity clause has essentially two functions. First, it represents the principal standard for any state action, thereby elevating the individual above the state. Furthermore, as a legal representation of the human being, it provides "substantive value" to formal concepts, such as the "essential content" of basic rights, allowing Arts. 19 (2) and 79 (3) GG to be fulfilled. Second, it demands protection against third-party attacks on dignity. Consequently, the state must configure the entire legal order, particularly civil law, in a way that prevents those attacks. Juridical actors shall therefore interpret the norms accordingly.

---

584 ibid.

585 Epping (n 399) 267. For an exhaustive review of German scholarship opposed to recognizing a subjective law content in Art. 1 (1) GG, see Dreier (n 406) Rn. 121, fn 513; also, Isensee, 'Würde des Menschen' (n 436) 69, Rn. 103 (n 333), who additionally lists scholars that favor considering dignity as a subjective right.

586 Dürig (n 471) 119. On the doctrinal importance and significance of Dürig's work on dignity, see Ernst-Wolfang Böckenförde, 'Die Würde des Menschen war Unantastbar' (n 420).

587 Dürig (n 471) 122.

588 ibid 119. [Vollends hat im Grundgesetz nach Wortlaut und Systematik der Art. 1 I GG den Charakter eines obersten Konstitutionsprinzip allen objektiven Rechts erhalten, welches schrittweise zu Gunsten des einzelnen Rechtsträgers realisiert wird.]

3.1.2. Böckenförde's extension of Dürig's approach

Taking a historical view, *Böckenförde* sees Art. 1 (1) GG primarily as the normative foundation of the state order. Similar to *Dürig*, the command of respect and protection of dignity is understood as the recognition that the normative consequences derived from it – the recognition of human subjectivity, ownership of basic rights, and freedom to undertake responsible actions – also precede the state. Dignity, according to this scholar, is also the foundation of basic rights, and should therefore inform their interpretation and use.[589] Furthermore, the attribution of basic rights depends on the attribution of dignity.[590] Dignity, *Böckenförde* concludes, should not be understood as a basic right but as a guarantee: every human being enjoys basic rights and thus has the legal status of a subject.[591]

3.1.3. Dreier – drawing the doctrinal consequences

Dreier also identifies dignity as a principle, and explains the functions that dignity performs as such. First, owing to its position as the highest-ranking clause in the GG, dignity is the supreme measure to judge acts of public power. It thereby functions as a "limit to restrictions,"[592] elevating the standard of justification for state action. In addition, it can demand some positive action from the public power, including beneficial measures. Second, it informs interpretations of both basic rights and the entire constitutional order.[593] Third, for *Dreier*, even when denying its subjective law content, the concrete effects of dignity may be analyzed as legal doctrine has done with basic rights, distinguishing between impacts that are defensive, protective, welfare-focused, and that radiate to the rest of the legal order.[594]

---

589 Ernst-Wolfang Böckenförde, 'Menschenwürde als normatives Prinzip. Die Grundrechte in der bioetische Debatte' (n 406) 810.

590 ibid.

591 In a similar vein, Isensee, 'Würde des Menschen' (n 436) 66, Rn. 99 affirms that dignity as a principle expresses itself through concretizations – fundamentally, via basic rights. These concretizations, though based on dignity, do not share dignity's absoluteness.

592 For further detail, see § 10, subsection 6.

593 Dreier (n 406) Rn. 125.

594 ibid Rn. 127, presenting relevant examples at Rn. 138–155, which predominately correspond to the dimensions of dignity as a right presented *infra* in section 3.2.

3.1.4. Enders and Kirste: dignity as the right to have rights

One of *Böckenförde's* main claims is more profoundly described by *Enders*, who remarks that Art. 1 (1) GG has an (irrevocable) pre-state significance: human subjectivity.[595] More precisely, this means that any human being has a pre-state "right to have rights."[596] This vision requires, however, that the dignity clause lacks legal content. Given its "abstraction," *Enders* maintains, the clause does not concede any "executable claim:" neither a subjective right nor a "value-fulfilling interpretative measure."[597] In the face of this reduction, the question emerges as to the proper meaning of dignity. *Enders* answers that human dignity constitutes a principle operative as "reason, criterion and justification" but in the sense of the "most general declaration on the legal capacity of the human being."[598] In this minimal character, *Enders* recognizes that what dignity means in a constitutional state could just have been presupposed.[599]

Kirste, for his part, follows a similar line of reasoning, but rejects the negation of the juridical content of the dignity clause. In contrast, he considers dignity to be a subjective right and specifically the right "to be a legal person."[600] The concept of "legal persons," *Kirste* explains, must be understood technically according to its function in the legal system, where it expresses the human "ability of being addressed by rights and duties." As a right, dignity therefore serves as the criterion for attributing legal personhood in the form of an enforceable individual right, which under the GG is "proclaimed and fulfilled at the same time."[601]

Similarly, based on the typology developed by Jellinek (status negativus, positivus, activus, etc.), Isensee, 'Würde des Menschen' (n 436) 111 ff., Rn 181 ff.

595 Enders (n 537) 501.

596 ibid 503 [Recht auf Rechte].

597 ibid [wertausfüllender Interpretationsmaßstab].

598 ibid [Grund, Kriterium und Rechtfertigung].

599 ibid 507, where Enders argues, however, that this formal guarantee is far from superfluous: "After the recognition of his dignity, the [external] freedom of the human being is no longer something accidental, but is strengthened to become a principle, from which, in turn, the subjective rights of the individual are also to be understood and interpreted." [Nach der Anerkennung seiner Würde ist die [äußere] Freiheit des Menschen nichts Zufälliges mehr, sondern erstarkt zum Prinzip, aus welchem umgekehrt auch die subjektiven Rechte der einzelnen zu begreifen und auszulegen sind.]

600 Kirste, 'A Legal Concept of Dignity as a Foundation of Law' (n 526) 75.

601 ibid 78. While Enders and Kirste present dignity as a right, its effects are more comparable with those of a principle, in both cases. On the one hand, Enders's

3.2. Dignity as a subjective right

In the 1950s, *Nipperday* was one of the first to interpret Art. 1 (1) GG as a public subjective right, and *Dürig* claims he was the most prominent supporter of this interpretation during the period,[602] ensuring it became established in the ruling opinion over time.[603] Even in a recent edition of *Dürig's* classic GG commentary, the section devoted to Art (1) – this time authored by *Herdegen* – accorded dignity the form of a right,[604] though with some features sharply critiqued by *Böckenförde*.[605]

This approach finds it unreasonable that the supreme norm of the GG only protects the individual indirectly, without also providing him or her with a subjective legal status.[606] Regarding personal interests, an objective principle is weaker than a subjective right.[607] In other words, a constitutional principle is most powerful when it also includes a subjective right for the individual.[608] Moreover, the detachment of dignity from the concrete individual could mean that dignity as a principle might be used against the dignity of the concrete holder of basic rights.[609] In addition, even when dignity is considered as the foremost norm, namely as a pre-legal or pre-state principle that takes precedence over basic rights, this abstract elevation diminishes its normative force to resolve concrete juridical conflicts.[610]

---

position attributes no legal consequences to dignity. On the other, according to *Kirste*, the content of dignity serves as a criterion for attributing basic legal capacity, and can thus also be understood as a principle.

602 Dürig (n 471) 119.

603 Stern (n 401) 61.

604 See Matthias Herdegen, 'Art. 1. Abs. 1' in Theodor Maunz and Günther Dürig (eds), *Kommentar zum Grundgesetz* (CH Beck 2020).

605 Ernst-Wolfang Böckenförde, 'Die Würde des Menschen war unantastbar' (n 420), labelled Herdegen's new commentary an 'epochal rupture' [*Epochenbruch*], given the importance of Dürig's work in Germany's postwar constitutional law on dignity, since Herdegen's proposal left dignity open to balancing. For a well-grounded and summarized defense of human dignity as a subjective right, see Ralf Poscher, '§ 17 Menschenwürde' in Matthias Herdegen and others (eds), *Handbuch des Verfassungsrechts* (2021).

606 Ipsen, *Staatsrecht II* (n 384) 61 Rn 234. Even Luhmann, with all his skepticism on constitutional dignity and his somehow unique interpretation of dignity's content, sees Art. 1 (1) GG as a basic right.

607 Kirste, 'A Legal Concept of Dignity as a Foundation of Law' (n 526) 70.

608 Hufen, *Staatsrecht II. Grundrechte* (n 399) 136.

609 Hufen, 'Erosion der Menschenwürde?' (n 466) 314, who remarks this regarding the role of dignity in the context of bio-ethical discussions.

610 ibid.

This subjective law attribution also fits the wording of the norm, which clearly prescribes the obligations of the state.[611] The two commands correspond to the subjective and objective law contents of the norm, respectively. In general, the obligation of respect consists primarily of the individual's defensive right against any intervention or encroachment from the state into dignity's scope of protection. However, the duty of protection demands from the public power active measures to safeguard dignity.[612] Finally, according to a historical and teleological interpretation, the first chapter of the GG guarantees basic rights.[613]

According to *Herdegen*, this understanding honors the fact that including dignity in the GG was primarily a reaction to a specific historical time, for:

> [I]t is precisely the light of the intellectual-historical background of the guarantee of human dignity that argues against its reduction to an objective principle or only a mere idea of order. According to current constitutional standards, it appears unbearable, for instance, to deny to the victims of the Holocaust the violation of their own claim to dignity and to classify state terror only as an encroachment of an objective principle of dignity.[614]

The BVerfG has always accepted the possibility of reviewing constitutional complaints based on encroachments on dignity.[615] Moreover, it has expressly affirmed that Art. 1 (1) includes a basic right,[616] though it has never resolved a constitutional complaint only based on a supposed violation of

611 Cf. Kingreen and Poscher (n 399) 91; Ipsen, *Staatsrecht II* (n 384) 61.

612 In this sense Kingreen and Poscher (n 399) 91.

613 Stern (n 401) 62.

614 Herdegen, 'Art. 1. Abs. 1' (n 604) Rn. 29. [Gerade der geistesgeschichtliche Hintergrund der Würdegarantie streitet gegen deren Reduktion auf ein objektives Prinzip oder gar eine bloße Ordnungsidee. Es scheint schlechthin unerträglich, etwa den Opfern des Holocaust nach heutigen Verfassungsstandards die Verletzung in ihrem eigenen Würdeanspruch abzusprechen und den staatlichen Terror nur als Verstoß gegen ein objektives Würdeprinzip einzustufen.]

615 According to Hufen, *Staatsrecht II. Grundrechte* (n 399) 135 Rn. 11, this jurisprudence has been settled in case law since BVerfGE 1, 322, (343) – *Erzwungene Staatsangehörigkeit* (1952). Isensee, 'Würde des Menschen' (n 436) 70, Rn. 104 concurs, but notes that the BVerfG has never provided arguments supporting this position.

616 See BVerfGE 140, 317 (318) – *Identitätskontrolle* (1995) The 1st point of the ruling [Entscheidungsformel] states that the decision of the relevant lower court "violates the complainant in his right of Art. 1.1 (...)." [Der Beschluss des Oberlandesgerichts (...) verletzt den Beschwerdeführer in seinem Grundrecht aus Artikel 1 Absatz 1 des Grundgesetzes (...).] According to Stern (n 401) 62, the BVerfG's implicit-because-

dignity, but always in conjunction with one another basic right.[617] Besides, the court has often affirmed that dignity "is due to any human being."[618]

The dual legal form of the dignity clause as a principle and fundamental right, alongside its accepted status as the highest-ranking constitutional norm and the source of constitutional rights, endows dignity with a unique character within the Bill of Rights.[619] As a subjective right, dignity guarantees the individual respect for his or her personal sphere, and in its objective effects, operates as the "basis and foundation" of the state.[620] In this fashion, the right to dignity is neither a catch-all nor a special right. Therefore, in the case of concurrence with other rights, the corresponding specific right should first be applied.[621]

3.2.1. Respect for dignity

The content of dignity became somewhat easier to define following the BVerfG's rulings. The systematization of those decisions, and the relevant scholarship, has meant that dimensions derived from various theories of legitimation (the aforementioned gift, performance, and recognition theories) have been incorporated into its scope of protection.[622] This technique,

evident [selbstverständlich] consideration of dignity as a fundamental right exists in a large number of cases. See the reference to cases in ibid 62, fn 280.

617 Stern (n 401) 62. For Dreier (n 406) Rn. 126, this also supports the viewpoint that dignity is only a principle. The main strategy of the court for dealing with this ambiguity has been to apply the formula "in conjunction with." See § 8, subsection 3 for more on this formula.

618 BVerfGE 87, 209, (228) – *Tanz der Teufel* (1992); 88, 203, (251) – *Schwangerschaftsabbruch II* (1993) [komme jedermann zu].

619 See Jarass, 'Art. 1' (n 406) Rn. 3. While Jarass believes that Art. 1 (1) GG contains a subjective right, he considers the discussion on whether or not dignity has substantive law content of "limited significance" because the protection of dignity is to a large extent guaranteed by the "subsequent" basic rights. Similarly, Stern (n 401) 64 suggests that the most important legal effects of dignity are those in objective law.

620 Stern (n 401) 63.

621 Hufen, *Staatsrecht II. Grundrechte* (n 399) 143. Jarass, 'Art. 1' (n 406) Rn. 5, comes to similar conclusions. While the doctrinal outcome is similar, Stern (n 401) 73 suggests that, given the particular characteristics of dignity, it is better to qualify dignity's overlap with another basic right – not by making use of the common categories (e.g., concurrence) [Konkurrenz] but rather as an "atypical" doctrinal category.

622 C.f. Häberle (n 412) 338, Rn. 31, who says that "constitutional adjudication has processed the different approaches towards grounding dignity according to the

however, has inevitable drawbacks. For instance, in concrete cases, different theories might provide different responses which tend to conflict rather than complement each other.[623] Unsurprisingly, this is particularly common in those concrete cases that are most discussed in law and ethics,[624] when any observer is ultimately obliged to choose between the competing interpretations. More importantly, the BVerfG must resort to one of the theories, at least implicitly.

Meanwhile, numerous German scholars that have analyzed the competing theories tend to agree on the fact that, notwithstanding its differences, constitutional law can use them complementarily to determine the main content or scope of protection of the dignity clause. *Kingreen and Poscher*, for one, hold that each theory contributes a valuable response to the central problem of what is to be understood as "inviolable" with respect to dignity.[625] Similarly, *Hufen* affirms they all contribute to the legal understanding of dignity, and belong to intellectual traditions coherent with the formation of the GG.[626] As *Dreier* argues, the distinct approaches are not mutually exclusive alternatives.[627]

---

maxim of 'pragmatic integration of theoretical elements'." [Sie wurden dann von der Verfassungsgerichtbarkeit nach der Devise „pragmatischer Integration von Theorieelementen" verarbeitet.] This chapter, and section 2.1 in particular, deals with what in Germany is called the material or substantive scope of protection [sachlicher Schutzbereich] of human dignity. For more details on the meaning and treatment of the material scope of protection of fundamental rights in general, see § 9.1 and § 10.2.1. For the personal scope of protection of both fundamental rights in general and human dignity in particular, see § 9. Traditionally, when examining the general legal doctrine of fundamental rights or a particular right, German legal doctrine treats these two areas (the material and the personal scope of protection) together as the two steps necessary to define the scope of protection of a particular right. The present study differentiates these two more sharply since this is how Chilean jurisprudence deals with this topic: as *content* (substantive scope of protection) [sachlicher Schutzbereich] and *ownership* (personal scope of protection) [persönlicher Schutzbereich] of fundamental rights.

623 Nowadays, this incompatibility seems particularly likely to emerge in the context of bioethical debates. Knoepffler (n 449) 15–16 describes how four different bills proposed by the *Bundestag* with the aim of regulating assisted suicide [2015] were all based on human dignity but reached different solutions. For the latest judgement on assisted suicide in the German jurisdiction, see BVerfGE 153, 182–310 – *Suizidhilfe* (2020)

624 Friedhelm Hufen, 'Die Menschenwürde, Art. 1 I GG' [2020] Juristische Schulung 1, 2.

625 Kingreen and Poscher (n 399) 92.

626 Hufen, *Staatsrecht II. Grundrechte* (n 399) 134.

627 Dreier (n 406) Rn. 60.

Furthermore, *Böckenförde* believes all these features are derived from *Kant's* thinking, specifically of his formula that defines the human being as an "end-in-himself."[628] As will be seen, this could explain the BVerfG's adoption of the object-formula to identify interferences with dignity in several cases.[629] In this context, one can summarize the dimensions included in the scope of dignity as follows:

A first dimension of the scope of dignity demands the respect and protection of human identity and singularity as well as physical and psychic integrity,[630] alongside the assurance of legal equality.[631] The roots of this dimension are to be found in the Theory of Dowry, which holds that dignity corresponds to an unconditional equal and inherent value or attribute of any human being, independent of any particular condition.[632]. Additionally, archetypal encroachments on dignity can be classified, *inter alia,* as torture, breaking of the will, medical manipulation for research aims, slavery, serfdom and human trafficking, cruel punishments, and systematic discriminations or degradations. Acts such as categorizing the existence of a child with a disability as an "injury" to its mother;[633] the rejection by the relevant authorities of a transsexual's desire to change his or her gender in the state register of birth;[634] cruel punishments in general[635] and, specifically, the full

628 Ernst-Wolfang Böckenförde, 'Menschenwürde als normatives Prinzip. Die Grundrechte in der bioetische Debatte' (n 406) 812 [*Zweck an sich selbst*].

629 See § 10.

630 Hufen, *Staatsrecht II. Grundrechte* (n 399) 136.

631 Kingreen and Poscher (n 399) 92, point out that most of these features are present in BVerfGE 144, 20, (21) – *NPD-Verbotsverfahren* (2017), Headnote 3a: "In particular, the human dignity guarantee encompasses the protection of personal individuality, identity, and integrity, as well as basic legal equality." [Die Garantie der Menschenwürde umfasst insbesondere die Wahrung personaler Individualität, Identität und Integrität sowie die elementare Rechtsgleichheit.]

632 Hufen, *Staatsrecht II. Grundrechte* (n 399) 134.

633 BVerfGE 88, 203, (296) – *Schwangerschaftabbruch II* (1992). "In contrast, to legally qualify the very existence of a child as a source of damage is constitutionally excluded by Art. 1 (1) GG. The obligation on all state powers to respect every human being in his existence for his own sake (...) forbids understanding the duty to support a child as damage." [Eine rechtliche Qualifikation des Daseins eines Kindes als Schadensquelle kommt hingegen von Verfassungs wegen (Art. 1 Abs. 1 GG) nicht in Betracht. Die Verpflichtung aller staatlichen Gewalt, jeden Menschen in seinem Dasein um seiner selbst willen zu achten (...), verbietet es, die Unterhaltspflicht für ein Kind als Schaden zu begreifen.]

634 BVerfGE 49, 286 (298) – *Transsexuelle I* (1978): "Human dignity and the basic right to development of one's personality therefore demand classifying the civil status of the person to the sex to which he belongs, according to his psychological

application of life imprisonment;[636] carrying out the death penalty;[637] and longer-term solitary confinement in a small space;[638] and the execution of a criminal judgment without establishing individual blameworthiness.[639]

A second dimension of dignity is linked to the guarantee of self-determination and self-representation, the respect of personal honor, and an inviolable core of private intimacy. Encroachments on this dimension are linked to the aspect of dignity defined under the Theory of Performance, whose main normative claim is that no external conceptualization of dignity can be imposed on individuals regarding how they wish to live their life.[640] Examples of typical encroachments from this perspective of human dignity are actions such as the destruction of human intimacy, severe offences or defamations, intrusion into the core of one's private sphere,[641] and the

---

and physical constitution." [Die Menschenwürde und das Grundrecht auf freie Persönlichkeitsentfaltung gebieten daher, den Personenstand des Menschen dem Geschlecht zuzuordnen, dem er nach seiner psychischen und physischen Konstitution zugehört.]

635 BVerfGE 45, 187, (228) – *Lebenslange Freiheitsstrafe* (1977): "The obligation to respect human dignity means, in particular, that cruel, inhuman, and degrading punishments are forbidden." [Das Gebot zur Achtung der Menschenwürde bedeutet insbesondere, daß grausame, unmenschliche und erniedrigende Strafen verboten sind.]

636 BVerfGE 45, 187, (228–229) – *Lebenslange Freiheitsstrafe* (1977): "Therefore, from Art. 1 (1) GG in conjunction with the social state principle – and this applies in particular to the execution of a sentence – it is the obligation of the state to guarantee that minimum subsistence level, which is the basic constituent of humane existence. It would be incompatible with human dignity, understood in this way, for the state to claim for itself the right to forcibly deprive the individual of his freedom, without at least giving him the chance to eventually regain his freedom." [Aus Art. 1 I GG in Verbindung mit dem Sozialstaatsprinzip ist daher – und das gilt insbesondere für den Strafvollzug – die Verpflichtung des Staates herzuleiten, jenes Existenzminimum zu gewähren, das ein menschenwürdiges Dasein überhaupt erst ausmacht. Mit einer so verstandenen Menschenwürde wäre es unvereinbar, wenn der Staat für sich in Anspruch nehmen würde, den Menschen zwangsweise seiner Freiheit zu entkleiden, ohne daß zumindest die Chance für ihn besteht, je wieder der Freiheit teilhaftig werden zu können.]

637 BVerfG, Judgment of the 1st Chamber of the Second Senate of 04 May 2018 – 2 BvR 632/18 – Rn. 1–70, (47).

638 BVerfG, Judgment of the 3rd Chamber of the First Senate of 14. July 2015 – 1 BvR 1127/14 -, Rn. 18.

639 BVerfGE 140, 317, (342) – *Identitätskontrolle* (2015). [Vorwerfbarkeit]

640 Kingreen and Poscher (n 399) 92.

641 See BVerfGE 109, 279 (314) *Großer Lauschangriff* (2003): "The private dwelling is a means to safeguard human dignity as a 'last refuge'. Although this does not demand absolute protection of the rooms of a private dwelling, it implies the abso-

denial of the legal conditions necessary to develop one's self-representation. Accordingly, the BVerfG has considered the following incompatible with the dignity clause: the use of lie detectors;[642] the acoustic surveillance of dwellings with criminal prosecution aims when the nucleus of privacy is not respected;[643] self-incrimination in criminal prosecution;[644] and defamations or affirmations that damage an individual's reputation.[645]

Finally, it can be understood that the Theory of Recognition, which claims that dignity also "lives by recognition" and therefore involves a "claim to recognition,"[646] particularly contributes to our understanding of this basic right with its assertion that dignity involves the responsibility of a specific, actual community to provide all its members with certain standards, for without them, a human's potential cannot be fully realized. The typical encroachment on this dimension consists of a denial of the necessary conditions for a decent human life.[647] In the protective sphere of dignity, however, according to the BVerfG in connection with the constitutional principle of the social state, this aspect of dignity includes the guarantee of minimal cultural, social, and economic resources.[648] Thus, according to the relevant case law of the BVerfG, the subjective law content

---

lute protection of the conduct within this space, as far as it represents individual development in the core area of the private life." [Die Privatwohnung ist als „letztes Refugium" ein Mittel zur Wahrung der Menschenwürde. Dies verlangt zwar nicht einen absoluten Schutz der Räume der Privatwohnung, wohl aber absoluten Schutz des Verhaltens in diesen Räumen, soweit es sich als individuelle Entfaltung im Kernbereich privater Lebensgestaltung darstellt.]

642 BVerfGE 2 BvR 166/81 – *Lügendetektor* (1981).

643 BVerfGE 109, 279, (279) – *Großer Lauschangriff* (2003), 2nd Headnote: "According to Art. 1 (1), the recognition of an absolute protected core area of private life belongs to the inviolability of human dignity. In this area, the acoustic surveillance of the dwelling with the aim of criminal prosecution (Art. 13 (3)) is prohibited." [2. Zur Unantastbarkeit der Menschenwürde gemäß Art. 1 Abs. 1 GG gehört die Anerkennung eines absolut geschützten Kernbereichs privater Lebensgestaltung. In diesen Bereich darf die akustische Überwachung von Wohnraum zu Zwecken der Strafverfolgung (Art. 13 Abs. 3 GG) nicht eingreifen.]

644 BVerfG, Judgment of the 2nd Chamber of the Second Senate of 06 September 2016 – 2 BvR 890/16 -, Rn. 35

645 BVerfGE 30, 173 (194) – *Mephisto* (1971).

646 Kingreen and Poscher (n 399) 92.

647 ibid 94. Consequently, the BVerfG prohibited the taxation of the minimum income required for a decent existence. See BVerfGE 82, 60, (85) – *Steuerfreie Existenzminimum* (1983). Details in § 8, subsection 3.1.

648 Cf. Hufen, *Staatsrecht II. Grundrechte* (n 399) 136; Kingreen and Poscher (n 399) 92; Epping (n 399) 311; Ipsen, *Staatsrecht II* (n 384) 63; Schmidt (n 399) 122.

of the dignity clause is both a right of liberty and also includes a welfare right.[649] A detailed jurisprudential history and the characteristics of this subject in Germany are provided below.[650]

3.2.2. Protection of dignity

Primarily, respect for dignity is ensured by its quality as a defensive right, i.e., one that rejects interferences by the state in its sphere of protection.[651] This feature corresponds to the original roots of basic rights, as the BVerfG has also stated.[652] Constitutional rights are primarily intended to "guarantee the sphere of freedom of the individual from interventions by the public power."[653]

However, Art. 1 (1) GG also contains a duty to protect [*Schutzpflicht*], which is individually actionable against the state in the event of attacks by third parties.[654] In other words, the state is obliged to prevent the violation of dignity in the context of relations between private parties.[655] The third-party effect of the dignity guarantee comes to the fore here.[656] The overall ramifications are that the state must produce norms directly aimed at protecting dignity at the infra-constitutional level. In addition, all infra-constitutional law (particularly its open-ended clauses) must be interpreted in accordance with dignity.

This obligation is to be fulfilled primarily through criminal law and complementarily through civil law,[657] with the state allotted a margin of appreciation for choosing the measures to be taken.[658] Some scholars affirm that the state's measures are also subject to constitutional review.[659] Indeed,

649 Stern (n 401) 64 [Leistungsrecht].
650 See § 8, subsection 3.1.
651 See BVerfGE 115, 118 (153) – *Luftsicherheitsgesetz* (2006) [Abwehrecht].
652 BVerfGE 7, 198, (198) – *Lüth* (1958): "Primarily, fundamental rights are the citizen's rights of defense against the state" [Die Grundrechte sind in erster Linie Abwehrrechte des Bürgers gegen den Staat.]
653 BVerfGE 7, 198, (204) – *Lüth* (1958).
654 Ipsen, *Staatsrecht II* (n 384) 62.
655 Hufen, *Staatsrecht II. Grundrechte* (n 399) 148.
656 Stern (n 401) 64.
657 Ipsen, *Staatsrecht II* (n 384) 62.
658 Hufen, *Staatsrecht II. Grundrechte* (n 399) 148.
659 Stern (n 401) 65. Of importance here is the contested legal doctrine on the prohibition of insufficient means [Untermaßverbot], which holds that state protective

the BVerfG has derived some concrete duties in a few cases, such as the protection of unborn life by criminal law.[660] Especially problematic, however, is the doctrinal discussion regarding the protection of dignity against the will of the affected.[661]

3.3. Other objective-law effects of dignity

Two objective-law effects of dignity have received particular scholarly attention. According to *Stern*, the strongest repercussion has been its function as a standard for interpreting basic rights, several of which have been protected more extensively as a result.[662] Secondly, as *Isensee* remarks, dignity protects not only the concrete individual, but also humanity as a whole. This entails the duty of each human being not to offend the dignity of the human race in general.[663]

4. Conclusions and open questions

4.1. Functional use of the human dignity clause

German legal practitioners have managed to operationalize Art. 1 (1) GG in a delimited fashion. This is because, first, as the doctrine itself recognizes, (although in Germany there is formally no *stare decisis*), the most important source for determining the content of basic rights is the record of decisions made by the BVerfG.[664] Secondly, despite the extensive literature

---

measures that do not reach a sufficient level are unconstitutional. On this, see Lars Peter Störring, *Das Untermaßverbot in der Diskussion. Untersuchung einer umstrittenen Rechtsfigur* (2009).

660 BVerfGE 39, 1, (45 ff) – *Schwangerschaftabbruch* I; 88, 203 – *Schwangerschaftabbruch* II (1993). See also a recent decision of the court on climate, human dignity and the protection of human life, BVerfGE 157, 30 – *Klimaschutz* (2021).

661 See § 10, subsection 5.

662 Stern (n 401) 66.

663 Isensee, 'Würde des Menschen' (n 436) 65, Rn. 97. In contrast, scholars such as Dreier (n 406) Rn. 115 ff; Hufen, 'Die Menschenwürde, Art. 1 I GG' (n 624) 5; and Häberle (n 412) 329, Rn. 15, fn 95, are critical of this dimension of dignity.

664 For further detail, see § 10, subsection 2. Schlink, 'German Constitutional Culture in Transition' (n 396) 730, describes this practice clearly, stating that "[scholarship] obtains its material, ideas, and confirmation from the Court's decision, and attempts to harmonize these decisions into a coherent doctrinal corpus". Moreover, ibid 735

on the topic, dignity is conceptualized functionally in the literature. As German course books on fundamental rights show, this is especially evident in the treatment of dignity as a subjective right. In these works, dignity is systematized according to the Three-Step Test, with similar results and conclusions.[665]

4.2. Theories of the legitimation of dignity

The systematization of dignity according to the Three-Step Test has been achieved through a combination of BVerfG rulings and the prevailing scholarly opinion. This process has entailed extracting distinct aspects or dimensions from each of the three theories on the legitimation of dignity, labeled and discussed above as the Theories of Dowry, Performance and Recognition. Together, these dimensions form dignity's content and scope of protection.[666]

4.3. Compatibility within limits

Despite the aforementioned benefits of amalgamating the three theories, this has been problematic when they provide different solutions to a given conflict.[667] Notably, this issue has been manifested in extremely controversial cases such as those touching on the beginning or end of human life and the limits of personal freedom, for example. In legal terms, the theories provide different answers to highly relevant doctrinal questions, such as who has the capacity to hold basic rights and whether a right can be waived. This means, finally, that in several cases, the courts have had to resort to one theory, and disregard the others, in order to resolve a conflict based on the dignity clause.

"the scholarship reads and interprets these decisions, and their reasoning, as though they were codified law."

665 Namely, that no restriction on the right to dignity is justifiable. See § 10, subsection 4.

666 Dederer 'Die Garantie der Menschenwürde (Art. 1 Abs. 1 GG) Dogmatische Grundfragen auf dem Stand der Wissenschaft' (2009) 57 Jahrbuch des öffentlichen Rechts der Gegenwart Neue Folge (JöR) 89, 107, argues that in any case – although without expressly admitting it – the BVerfG has followed the Theory of Dowry (which he prefers to call the "Theory of Value" [Werttheorie]).

667 Dreier (n 406) Rn. 52 even says that one might find consensus only at a "highly abstract level."

4.4. Indigenous thought

The debates within Germany over the foundations of dignity have determined its current legal content and scope of protection. They have also covered the question of the universality versus the specificity of dignity. An interesting related research question is whether the content of the dignity clause in the Chilean Constitution should be determined only by referring to the three theories that have played such a prominent role in Germany, or whether Chile's distinct sources must also be taken into consideration. The current study holds that it is advisable to consider the thoughts of Chile's indigenous peoples on dignity, or its equivalent, when determining the content of legal dignity in Chile.[668]

4.5. Inclusion v. exclusion

As the German debate on dignity has developed from the country's historical roots, the Chilean debate should also be shaped by its own unique history. This history seems to be marked by the substantive exclusion of numerous subjects from the benefit of rights, notwithstanding what is formally enshrined in the constitution and the laws. The prerequisites for the dignity clause to become both a formal and substantive criterion for inclusion are therefore especially interesting when researching the Chilean case. The German experience is nonetheless relevant from this perspective, as demonstrated by the BVerfG's recognition of a right to a minimum subsistence level derived from the dignity clause in connection with the constitutional principle of the social state [*Sozialstaatsprinzip*] – a topic that will be reviewed in the next chapter.

668 See § 13, subsection 1.4.2.2.

§ 8 Foundation of basic rights

1. Introduction

In Germany, there is a broad-ranging agreement that dignity is the foundation of all basic rights in the GG. In addition, the role of dignity as the specific basis of particular constitutional rights has been developed through BverfG case law. The BVerfG, using the formula of "Art. 1 (1) in conjunction with" [*in Verbindung mit – i.V.m*] either another specific right in the Bill of Rights, or with a constitutional principle, public good, or an interest of the GG, has deduced, recognized, or created – depending on the preferred nomenclature – at least two unwritten or implicit rights.

2. Human dignity as the foundation of basic rights in the general sense

Based on the constitutional innovations incorporated in the GG,[669] both scholarship and case law see human dignity in general as – in the words of *Stern* – the "foundation of basic rights."[670] The first reason is already in the written text: dignity is recognized as the "grounding of basic rights."[671] As the supreme constitutional principle or value of the GG, this is one of the main functions attributed to dignity in the general theory of basic rights. The key word that backs the GG, both in positivist and non-positivist constitutional approaches, is the adverb "therefore" [*darum*] in Art. 1 (2) GG.[672]

---

669 See § 7, subsection 1.

670 Stern (n 401) 9 [Fundament der Grundrechte].

671 Ernst-Wolfang Böckenförde, 'Menschenwürde als normatives Prinzip. Die Grundrechte in der bioetische Debatte' (n 406) 810. It is noteworthy that the Constitution of the Free State of Saxony establishes this relationship even more explicitly. While its Art. 14 (1) is identical to Art. 1 (1) GG, the Art. 14 (2) of the former prescribes that the "inviolability of human dignity is the source of all basic rights" [Die Unantastbarkeit der Würde des Menschen ist Quelle aller Grundrechte.]

672 Art. 1 (2) GG: "The German people therefore acknowledge inviolable and inalienable human rights as the basis of every community, of peace, and of justice in the world." All translation of the Basic Law quoted in this work are taken from the official translation of the Basic Law into English, German Office of Justice <https:/

Starck, while clarifying that human and basic rights are not identical, believes that human rights are the "consequence and expression of dignity's guarantee" from that word [*darum*].[673] Others remark that its foundational function connects dignity directly with the written rights expressed in the GG.[674] In this sense, *Dreier* says that dignity stands in "a founding relation" with basic rights.[675] *Herdegen* speaks of the "respect for human dignity as the basis of a system of value conformed by basic rights;" namely, a material foundation as an "Archimedean point."[676] Moreover, *Hufen* says that dignity is the fundamental norm concerning basic rights as well as the state principles enshrined in Art 20 GG.[677] Even more generously, *Häberle* affirms that human dignity is the basis of the constitutional state and its branches.[678]

Meanwhile, the BVerfG has not only supported such views,[679] but has also spoken of dignity as the "root" [*Wurzel*] of basic rights,[680] a term also

---

/www.gesetze-im-internet.de/gg/BJNR000010949.html> accessed 9 March 2021. [Das Deutsche Volk bekennt sich darum zu unverletzlichen und unveräußerlichen Menschenrechten als Grundlage jeder menschlichen Gemeinschaft, des Friedens und der Gerechtigkeit in der Welt.] Isensee, 'Würde des Menschen' (n 436) 20 affirms that, while the GG recognizes the supra-positive basis of the positive human dignity clause, the positive constitutional text does not connect this recognition directly with a natural-law grounding of dignity. Thus, ibid 22, Art. 1 (1) GG contains supra-positive content on the one hand while acting as the positive-law basis of the subsequent basic rights prescribed by the GG on the other. A similar approach to dignity as a positive norm of supra-positive origin is seen in Ernst-Wolfang Böckenförde, 'Die Würde des Menschen war Unantastbar' (n 420).

673 Christian Starck, 'Art. 1. Abs. 2' in Hermann von Mangoldt, Friedrich Klein and Christian Starck (eds), *Kommentar zum Grundgesetz* (2018) Rn. 124.

674 Cf. Davor Susnjar and Johannes Greiser, 'Zur dogmatischen Einordnung des Grundrechts auf ein menschenwürdiges Existenzminimum' (2018) 20 Deutsches Verwaltungsblatt 1329, 1330.

675 Dreier (n 406) Rn. 160 [Fundierungsverhältnis].

676 Herdegen, 'Art. 1. Abs. 1' (n 604) Rn. 21 [Die Achtung der Menschenwürde als Grundlage eines grundrechtlichen Wertsystems].

677 Hufen, *Staatsrecht II. Grundrechte* (n 399) 143.

678 Häberle (n 412) 358. Similarly, Isensee, 'Würde des Menschen' (n 436) 65, comments that dignity is the "foundation of the constitutional order" [Fundament der Verfassungsordnung].

679 See, e.g., BVerfGE 21, 362 (369) – *Sozialversicherungsträger* (1967): "The value system of basic rights is based on the dignity and freedom of the individual as a natural person." [Das Wertsystem der Grundrechte geht von der Würde und Freiheit des einzelnen Menschen als natürlicher Person aus.]; BVerfGE 48, 127, (164) – *Wehrpflichtnovelle* (1977): "Article 4 (3) GG directly guarantees, as a basic right, the right to refuse military service (...). The Basic Law is founded on the dignity of the

adopted by some scholars.[681] However, others, such as *Dreier*, criticize this characterization for historical reasons—as most classical declarations of human rights show, basic rights developed before constitutional dignity.[682] Therefore, from a chronological viewpoint, describing dignity as the "root" of basic rights is an inaccurate extension of its link with such rights.[683] *Herdegen* shares a similar point of view, as well as commenting that some doctrinal repercussions of this approach could distance the German understanding of basic rights from its interpretation in other jurisdictions.[684]

---

free, self-determining human personality as the highest legal interest." [Art. 4 Abs. 3 GG gewährleistet als Grundrecht unmittelbar das Recht, aus Gewissensgründen den Kriegsdienst mit der Waffe zu verweigern (...). Das Grundgesetz geht von der Würde der freien, sich selbst bestimmenden menschlichen Persönlichkeit als höchstem Rechtswert aus.]

680 BVerfGE 93, 266 (293) - *Soldaten-sind-Mörder* (1995): "(...) because human dignity as the root of all basic rights cannot be weighed up against any individual basic right. However, since not only some but all basic rights are concretizations of the principle of human dignity, a detailed justification is always required if it is to be considered that the use of a basic right affects inviolable human dignity." [(...) denn die Menschenwürde als Wurzel aller Grundrechte ist mit keinem Einzelgrundrecht abwägungsfähig. Da aber nicht nur einzelne, sondern sämtliche Grundrechte Konkretisierungen des Prinzips der Menschenwürde sind, bedarf es stets einer sorgfältigen Begründung, wenn angenommen werden soll, daß der Gebrauch eines Grundrechts auf die unantastbare Menschenwürde durchschlägt.] Interestingly, the BVerfG quotes the latter paragraph in a later case, but replaces the concept of "root" for "foundation" and "all the basic rights" for "basic rights as a whole": BVerfGE 107, 275, (284) - *Schockwerbung* II (2003): "Human dignity as the foundation of all basic rights cannot be weighed up against any individual basic right. However, since basic rights as a whole are concretizations of the principle of human dignity, a detailed justification is always required if it is to be considered that the use of a basic right affects inviolable human dignity (...)." [Die Menschenwürde als Fundament aller Grundrechte ist mit keinem Einzelgrundrecht abwägungsfähig. Da aber die Grundrechte insgesamt Konkretisierungen des Prinzips der Menschenwürde sind, bedarf es stets einer sorgfältigen Begründung, wenn angenommen werden soll, dass der Gebrauch eines Grundrechts die unantastbare Menschenwürde verletzt (...).] However, later the BVerfG again uses the concepts expressed in *Soldaten-sind-Mörder*. See BVerfG, Judgment of the First Chamber of the First Senate of 4 February 2010 - 1 BvR 369/04 - Rn. 29.

681 For instance, Jarass, 'Art. 1' (n 406) Rn. 5. Apparently, the expression was first used by the scholar Hans Karl Nipperday, and, following the BVerfG, by a few other authors. See Dreier (n 406) Rn. 161.

682 Dreier (n 406) Rn. 161. Similarly, Hufen, *Staatsrecht II. Grundrechte* (n 399) 152.

683 Dreier (n 406) Rn. 162.

684 Herdegen, 'Art. 1. Abs. 1' (n 604) Rn. 22–24.

Thus, these divergent approaches are not superfluous; they highlight vital differences in the assessment of the theory of the human dignity content or core of fundamental rights.[685] Moreover, if other basic rights represent concretizations of dignity, when a supposed interference with a fundamental right is examined, the right to dignity is also to be tested, since the other rights represent concretizations of dignity.[686] Simply by considering dignity as the foundation or root of all basic rights, the BVerfG has affirmed that dignity will resist being balanced against another basic right.[687]

Be that as it may, *Stern* remarks that, at least, the character of Art. 1 (1) GG as the:

> basic and guiding norm for the general understanding of the basic rights and the orientation of state power in a liberal democratic order, based on the principles of the social state and the rule of law; namely, the complete constitution

is out of the discussion.[688]

3. Human dignity as the foundation of specific rights: Art. 1 (1) GG "in conjunction with"

Constitutional doctrine identifies several overlapping configurations of constitutional norms.[689] In this context, the BVerfG has developed a methodological category to cover some overlaps between two constitutional norms. Through the linguistic formula *in conjunction with* [*in Verbindung mit*], the BVerfG has developed associations between two basic rights, as well as between a specific basic right and a constitutional principle.[690] As a

---

685 See § 10, subsection 6.

686 Jarass, 'Art. 1' (n 406) Rn. 5.

687 BVerfGE 93, 266 (293) – *Soldaten-sind-Mörder* (1995); BVerfGE 107, 275, (284) – *Schockwerbung II* Case (2003); BVerfG, Judgment of the First Chamber of the First Senate of 4 February 2010 – 1 BvR 369/04 – Rn. 29.

688 Stern (n 401) 9. [Grund- und Leitnorm für das Gesamtverständnis der Grundrechte und die Orientierung der Staatsgewalt in einer freiheitlichen demokratischen, rechts- und sozialstaatlichen Ordnung, also der Verfassung insgesamt.]

689 On this, see Monika M. Meinke, *In Verbindug mit* (2006) 23 ff.

690 For a detailed description and analysis of this doctrinal development, see Meinke (n 689).

result, it has derived some independent unwritten or implicit fundamental rights in addition to those expressly set out in the GG text.

Specifically, the BVerfG has derived at least two independent basic rights.[691] First, in conjunction with Art 2 (1) GG, the BVerfG recognized a general right of personality.[692] Second, in conjunction with the social state principle (Art 20 (1) GG), the BVerfG created the right to a minimum subsistence income in accordance with human dignity.[693]

3.1. Right to a subsistence income according to human dignity

The jurisprudential history of this right is fascinating for several reasons: over the years, after first denying that the state has any concrete social duty, the BVerfG increasingly recognized that the protective dimension of Art. 1 (1) GG also includes subjective law claims on basic social security. The human dignity clause is one of the few basic rights from which the BVerfG has – in connection with another constitutional norm – derived an individual entitlement to social benefits. Indeed, this recognition did not come exclusively from Art. 1 (1) GG but by postulating a concrete doctrinal association with the social state principle. This connection requires a brief examination of the doctrinal meaning of this principle in Germany before reviewing the MSI.

3.1.1. The principle of the social state

Although one of its initial drafts proposed a constitutional right to a minimal amount of food, clothing, and housing,[694] the GG does not explicitly

691 However, not without criticism. Isensee, ‘Der Grundrechtliche Konnex von Menschenleben und Menschenwürde’ (n 452) 121 recalls that all basic rights are, to a greater or lesser extent, “in conjunction with” human dignity. Therefore, if this is expressly stated in only some cases, it can easily create the impression that the remaining basic rights do not share this connection.

692 Hereafter also referred to as “GRoP.” [Allgemeine Persönlichkeitsrecht]

693 Hereafter also referred to as “MSI”. [Grundrecht auf Gewährleistung eines menschenwürdigen Existenzminimums.]

694 Draft according to the 1st reading of the Principal Commission of the Parliamentary Council. [Entwurf nach der 1. Lesung des Hauptausschusses des Parlamentarischen Rats] (10.12.1948) <http://www.verfassungen.de/de49/grundgesetz-entwurf2-48-i.htm> accessed 16 April 2021.

contain social rights. Instead, it prescribes the principle of the social state in two articles.[695] The intention was to leave the lawmaker able to freely design and implement the social law according to the country's financial possibilities. While the social state principle appears only as an adjective, it is fundamental to the GG, and as such, benefits from the guarantee of eternity enshrined in Art 79 (3).[696] Hence, as the BVerfG soon declared,[697] the social state principle extends beyond a mere programmatic sentence and has direct juridical force.[698]

The principle has several functions.[699] It must be considered by the courts and the administration when interpreting both constitutional and infra-constitutional law. It can justify restrictions on basic rights and function as a standard of interpretation for them. It means objective law for the legislative branch, in the sense of an order or commission to pursue social equality and security. This task encompasses numerous areas of human life that demand special protection by the state which is, accordingly, manifested in multiple ways. The specific rights prescribed in law and any state's social action manifest the social state in the broad sense.[700] Nonetheless, both case law and scholarship tend to affirm that it is fundamentally impos-

---

Article 2 [Artikel 2.]
(1) Everyone shall have the right to life, to freedom and to the security of the person. [Jeder hat das Recht auf Leben, auf Freiheit und auf Sicherheit der Person.]
(2) Every person shall have the right to free development of his personality insofar as he does not violate the rights of others or offend against the Constitutional order or the moral law. [Jeder hat das Recht auf die freie Entfaltung seiner Persönlichkeit, soweit er nicht die Rechte anderer verletzt und nicht gegen die verfassungsmäßige Ordnung oder das Sittengesetz verstößt.]
(3) This freedom may only be interfered within the boundaries of the legal order. *Under no circumstances may a person be denied the minimum level of food, clothing and housing necessary for life.* [In diese Freiheit darf nur im Rahmen der Rechtsordnung eingegriffen werden. Keinesfalls darf das Mindestmaß der zum Leben notwendigen Nahrung, Kleidung und Wohnung verweigert werden] (Emphasis added).
(4) (...).

695 Art. 20 (1) and Art. 28 (1), first sentence GG.

696 Hans Jarass, 'Art. 20' in Hans D. Jarass and Bodo Pieroth (eds), *Grundgesetz für die Bundesrepublik Deutschland* (2020) Rn. 153.

697 BVerfGE 1, 97, (105) – *Hinterbliebenenrente I* (1951).

698 Andreas Voßkuhle and Thomas Wischmeyer, 'Grundwissen – Öffentliches Recht: Das Sozialstaatsprinzip' [2015] Juristische Schulung 693, 693.

699 The functions of the social state (ibid 693–694) are described in this paragraph.

700 Jörn Ipsen, *Staatsrecht I. Staatsorganisationsrecht* (2015) 269.

sible to derive immediately subjective rights from the principle of the social state:[701] the exception is the MSI.

The progressive strengthening of the welfare state in postwar Germany shows that the responsibility of executing the social state principle has been consistently assumed by German lawmakers over the decades.[702] In the modern sense, however, social security started with *Bismarck's* reforms in the 1880s.[703] During the Weimar Republic, social security continued its expansion through infra-constitutional law. However, Germany's first democratic constitution did not mention the principle of the social state, but only the aim of achieving decent conditions of life [*menschenwürdiges Dasein*] for the entire population (in Art. 151 WRV).[704]

As a concept, the social state is thus to be understood as opposing the view that the state only guarantees defensive rights to its citizens. A social state is not only required to protect freedom and property, but also to achieve a balance between freedom and equality.[705] Consequently, one of the state's social objectives is to create the prerequisites necessary for exercising freedom.[706] Yet compared to the other organizational principles enshrined in Art 20 (1) GG,[707] the social state principle is specified less by the GG's other norms.[708] First, the GG contains no (written) social rights. It only allows federal lawmakers to develop legislation in spheres such as social security, social welfare or assistance, the protection of work, educational support, or the economic security of hospitals.[709] Such concretizations of the social state principle largely depend on the legislator, who enjoys a broad leeway to design them.

701 Cf. Jarass, 'Art. 20' (n 696) Rn. 167.

702 Stern (n 401) 51. Stern not only affirms that since the enforcement of the GG "the social security system has been expanded formidably under the auspices of the social state" but also that "at present the question is increasingly being raised whether it [the social state] should not be scaled back." [Seither ist das System der sozialen Sicherheit unter den Auspizien des Sozialstaates in Deutschland formidabel ausgebaut worden, so dass gegenwärtig mehr und mehr die Frage aufgeworfen wird, ob es nicht zurückgeführt werden muss.]

703 Voßkuhle and Wischmeyer (n 698) 693.

704 ibid.

705 Ipsen, *Staatsrecht I. Staatsorganisationsrecht* (n 700) 269.

706 Jarass, 'Art. 20' (n 696) Rn. 159.

707 Art 20 (1) GG: "The Federal Republic of Germany is a democratic and social federal state. [Die Bundesrepublik Deutschland ist ein demokratischer und sozialer Bundesstaat.]

708 Voßkuhle and Wischmeyer (n 698) 693.

709 See Art. 74 (1) GG.

In this context, some views emphasize the "liberal" character of the principle, finding that the GG's backing for individual dignity and freedom is incompatible with the state's centralized social provision [*Versorgungstaat*] and individuals are primarily responsible for their own well-being.[710] In contrast, others remark that social equality is an ineludible precondition of freedom.[711] On balance, the concrete meaning of the social state is disputed and represents various ideological and political positions, "different concepts of the social state satisfy the constitutional demands equally if they guarantee a minimal measure of social balance."[712] In light of this, the constitutional bases of the welfare state have required development by the courts.[713] Indeed, analyzing the BVerfG's recent decisions on social law, its former vice-president *Ferdinand Kirchhof* affirmed:

> Systematically, the decisions have dealt with the question of how a coherent and consistent system of social law can be produced from abundant laws, how rationality and continuity are to be introduced into legislation that is at times somewhat hectic, and how typification and generalization must find their limits because social law must assist and protect the individual human being adequately.[714]

---

710 See, e.g., Jarass, 'Art. 20' (n 696) Rn. 159. This rather liberal interpretation is, however, subsequently qualified by the author, who adds, "the social state principle is not limited by the market economy system, since the latter does not represent a constitutional principle" [Dagegen wird das Sozialstaatsprinzip nicht durch das System der Marktwirtschaft begrenzt, da dieses kein Verfassungsprinzip darstellt], ibid Rn. 164, backed by BVerfGE 4, 7 (17 ff) – *Investitionshilfe* (1954). Here, the BVerfG discusses the "economic (policy) neutrality" of the GG [Die „wirtschaftspolitische Neutralität" des Grundgesetzes.]

711 Dieter Suhr, 'Gleiche Freiheit. Allgemeine Grundlage und Reziprozitätsdefizite in der Geldwirtschaft' [2001] Fragen der Freiheit 5, 68 ff.

712 Ipsen, *Staatsrecht I. Staatsorganisationsrecht* (n 700) 270. [Folgerichtig genügen verschiedene sozialstaatliche Konzeptionen gleichermaßen den verfassungsrechtlichen Anforderungen, wenn sie das Mindestmaß sozialen Ausgleichs garantieren.] For a somewhat skeptical view of the attributed meaning of the social state principle, see, e.g., Walter Leisner, 'Darf der Staat gütig sein? – Förderung und Hilfe zwischen Sozialstaat und Rechtstaat' [2001] Neue Juristische Wocheschrift 1329.

713 Ferdinand Kirchhof, 'Die Entwicklung des Sozialverfassungsrechts' [2015] Neue Zeitschrift für Sozialrecht 1, 1.

714 ibid. [Systemisch haben die Urteile sich den Fragen gewidmet, wie aus zahllosen Einzelgesetzen eine in sich stimmige und konsistente Sozialrechtsordnung hergestellt werden kann, wie Rationalität und Kontinuität in eine zuweilen etwas hektische Gesetzgebung einzubringen ist und wo Typisierung und Pauschalierung ihr Ende finden müssen, weil Sozialrecht den individuellen Menschen sachgerecht schützen und versorgen muss.]

The BVerfG has dealt with the social state principle in several judgments that specify its structure. These decisions have been praised for their cautious spirit, since the BVerfG has generally avoided deducing specific rules or concrete claims, instead limiting itself to checking whether the pertinent laws comply with the social state principle. Indeed, the BVerfG has deduced only a single social right from the principle and did so when examining current social laws. This conforms with the ruling opinion in the literature "as, in principle, original claims to grant individual social benefits can be derived neither from the social state clause nor from its connection with individual basic rights."[715]

There are some remarkably long-lasting tendencies in BVerfG case law on this matter. First, as mentioned previously, the court has always held that the social state principle consists of a general command to the legislative branch, which enjoys considerable leeway in its implementation. Thus, it is mainly for the legislature to determine what is necessary to implement the principle.[716] Art 20 (1) only determines *what* the purpose is, but allows the legislature leeway in deciding *how* to do it.[717] The social state principle binds all state organs, but requires lawmakers to actualize it.[718] In other words, while the principle establishes the state's duty to construct a just social order, lawmakers have a great deal of freedom when fulfilling this duty. The social state principle sets the task, but says little about how it should be executed. Furthermore, the BVerfG has indicated that, were it to differ, the principle would contradict the principle of democracy.[719]

---

715 Voßkuhle and Wischmeyer (n 698) 694. [Aus der Sozialstaatsklausel sowie aus ihrer Verbindung mit einzelnen Grundrechten lassen sich grundsätzlich keine originären Ansprüche auf die Gewährung individueller sozialer Leistungen ableiten.]

716 BVerfGE 1, 97, (105) – *Hinterbliebenenrente I* (1951). [Das Wesentliche zur Verwirklichung des Sozialstaates aber kann nur der Gesetzgeber tun.]

717 BVerfGE 22, 180, (204) – *Jugendhilfe* (1967). [Keineswegs folgt aus dem Sozialstaatsprinzip, daß der Gesetzgeber für die Verwirklichung dieses Ziels nur behördliche Maßnahmen vorsehen darf. Art. 20 Abs. 1 GG bestimmt nur das "Was," das Ziel, die gerechte Sozialordnung. Er läßt aber für das "Wie," d. h. für die Entstehung des Ziels, alle Wege offen.]

718 BVerfG, Judgment of the First Senate of 5 November 2019 – 1 BvL 7/16, par. 125. [Die Staatszielbestimmung verpflichtet alle Staatsorgane unmittelbar, bedarf aber zu ihrer Verwirklichung in hohem Maße der Konkretisierung vor allem durch den Gesetzgeber (...)]

719 BVerfGE 59, 231, (262–263) – *Freie Mitarbeiter* (1951). [Das Sozialstaatsprinzip stellt also dem Staat eine Aufgabe, sagt aber nichts darüber, wie diese Aufgabe im Einzelnen zu verwirklichen ist – wäre es anders, dann würde das Prinzip mit dem Prinzip der Demokratie in Widerspruch geraten: Die demokratische Ordnung des

It is reasonable to claim that the BVerfG interprets the social state principle as a mandate to protect the weak.[720] But the court has also emphasized that the freedom to apply the principle is only limited by the obligation of guaranteeing to every human being a minimal existence in accordance with dignity.[721] For example, the BVerfG has indicated some duties pursuant to the social state principle, such as assistance for people in need, which includes the care of citizens whose physical or mental afflictions have hindered their personal and social development.[722]

3.1.2. Jurisprudential history of the MSI

At the beginning of its jurisdiction (in 1951), the BVerfG rejected the idea that the human dignity clause guaranteed a minimum subsistence income for each individual.[723] Although the court had already acknowledged that the protective sphere of the dignity clause demands positive action by the state, it held that this did not include protection against material urgency or

Grundgesetzes würde als Ordnung eines freien politischen Prozesses entscheidend eingeschränkt und verkürzt, wenn der politischen Willensbildung eine so und nicht anders einzulösende verfassungsrechtliche Verpflichtung vorgegeben wäre.]

720 Meinke (n 689) 39.

721 BVerfGE 125, 175 (222) – *Hartz IV* (2010).

722 BVerfGE 44, 353, (375) – *Durchsuchung Drogenberatungsstelle* (1977).

723 BVerfGE 1, 97 (97) – *Hinterbliebenenrente* I (1951). Headnote no 4: "Neither Art. 1 (1) nor Art. 2 (2) of the GG establishes a basic right of the individual to legal regulation of entitlements to an adequate social care through the state." [Weder Art. 1 Abs. 1 noch Art. 2 Abs. 2 Satz 2 GG begründet ein Grundrecht des Einzelnen auf gesetzliche Regelung von Ansprüchen auf angemessene Versorgung durch den Staat]. Interestingly, the BVerfG had already started to consider dignity as a basic right at this point. See BVerfGE 1, 97 (106) *Hinterbliebenenrente* I (1951): "Therefore, the assessment of pensions neither violates the basic right of Art. 1 nor the basic rights of Arts. 2 and 6 GG." [Die Bemessung der Renten verstößt also weder gegen das Grundrecht des Art. 1 noch gegen die Grundrechte der Art. 2 und 6 GG.]. A few years later, however, the BVerwG took a different approach when considering a similar issue. In the so-called "public assistance" decision [Fürsoge-Entscheidung] of 1954, the highest administrative court in Germany affirmed, for the first time, that individuals have an enforceable claim to public benefits if required to achieve minimum living conditions. This decision is seen as a turning point in the relationship between the state and the individual regarding welfare in Germany: from a traditional, paternalistic view that regarded assistance to the needy as a means of averting threats to public order to one that frames the individual as a citizen with enforceable social claims against the state. See Katharina M. Hauer, *Die Fürsorgeentscheidung des Bundesverwaltungsgerichts (BVerwGE 1, 159) aus rechtshistorischer Sicht* (2020).

need, but only against attacks on dignity from third parties.[724] Furthermore, the BVerfG confirmed that the lawmaker's duty to implement the principle of the social state involves great freedom of design. A constitutional complaint could be presented before the BVerfG only if the legislator had arbitrarily executed this obligation.[725]

25 years later (1977), the BVerfG tackled the same issue when assessing the constitutionality of life imprisonment.[726] It declared for the first time the existence of duties derived from Art. 1 (1) GG in conjunction with the principle of the social state.[727] Accordingly, the state had to provide conditions to the individual that would allow him or her a dignified existence.[728]

---

724 BVerfGE 1, 97, (104) – *Hinterbliebenenrente I* (1951): "When Art. 1 (1) GG states that 'human dignity is inviolable', it only wants to protect dignity against attacks (...). Although the second sentence, that to 'respect and protect it [human dignity] shall be the duty of the entiry authority of the state' obligates the state to carry out the positive act of 'protecting', this does not mean the protection of material needs, but protection against attacks on human dignity by others, such as humiliation, branding, persecution, marginalization, etc." [Wenn Art. 1 Abs. 1 GG sagt: „Die Würde des Menschen ist unantastbar," so will er sie nur negativ gegen Angriffe abschirmen. Der zweite Satz: „... Sie zu achten und zu schützen ist Verpflichtung aller staatlichen Gewalt" verpflichtet den Staat zwar zu dem positiven Tun des „Schützens," doch ist dabei nicht Schutz vor materieller Not, sondern Schutz gegen Angriffe auf die Menschenwürde durch andere, wie Erniedrigung, Brandmarkung, Verfolgung, Ächtung usw. gemeint.]

725 BVerfGE 1, 97, (105) – *Hinterbliebenenrente I* (1951). [Aber nur wenn der Gesetzgeber diese Pflicht willkürlich, d. h. ohne sachlichen Grund versäumte, könnte möglicherweise dem Einzelnen hieraus ein mit der Verfassungsbeschwerde verfolgbarer Anspruch erwachsen.]

726 BVerfGE 45, 187 – *Lebenslange-Freiheitsstrafe* (1977). For settled case law afterwards, see, e.g., BVerfGE 64, 261 (272–281) – *Hafturlaub* (1983); BVerfGE 86, 288 (312) – *Strafaussetzung bei lebenslanger Freiheitsstrafe* (1992).

727 Meinke (n 689) 34.

728 BVerfGE 45, 187, (245) – *Lebenslange-Freiheitsstrafe* (1977): "[even when the punishment of life imprisonment is applied] the basic preconditions of the individual and social existence of the human being must remain. Therefore, from Article 1 (1) of the GG in conjunction with the principle of the social state, it is the obligation of the state – and this particularly applies to the execution of a sentence – to guarantee the minimum subsistence that constitutes an existence according to human dignity in first place. It would be incompatible with such an understanding of human dignity if the state were to claim the right to forcefully deprive the human being of his freedom without at least giving him the chance to regain it again." [Die grundlegenden Voraussetzungen individueller und sozialer Existenz des Menschen müssen erhalten bleiben. Aus Art. 1 Abs. 1 GG in Verbindung mit dem Sozialstaatsprinzip ist daher – und das gilt insbesondere für den Strafvollzug – die Verpflichtung des Staates herzuleiten, jenes Existenzminimum zu gewähren, das ein menschenwürdiges Da-

In that case, the BVerfG considered that life imprisonment is constitutional only insofar as the possibility of eventually regaining freedom remains open to the convicted. However, this condition did not yet equate to a claimable basic right, but was merely a constitutional principle.[729] It would take longer for the right to be recognized.

The first step in this direction was the decision in a case concerning a minimal basic tax-free income (1983), where the BVerfG recognized, based on Art. 1 (1) GG in conjunction with the social state principle, a defensive right against state taxation.[730] The BVerfG judged that the state "must leave the taxpayer's income free of taxes as far as this is necessary to guarantee the minimal preconditions for an existence according to human dignity,"[731] just as the state also had an obligation to ensure these minimal preconditions by providing social benefits.[732] This latter duty, however, was not viewed as an actionable entitlement at that time. [733]

This obligation of the state, the BVerfG added in the *Familienlastenausgleich II* case (1998), must also reflect the objective conditions of families, including each member, and in particular, the minimum income that parents need in order to provide for their children. Also, taxation must reflect the fact that parents' need to care for their children typically affects their economic productivity.[734]

---

sein überhaupt erst ausmacht. Mit einer so verstandenen Menschenwürde wäre es unvereinbar, wenn der Staat für sich in Anspruch nehmen würde, den Menschen zwangsweise seiner Freiheit zu entkleiden, ohne dass zumindest die Chance für ihn besteht, je wieder der Freiheit teilhaftig werden zu können.]

729 Meinke (n 689) 37.

730 Christian Seiler, 'Das Grundrecht auf ein menschenwürdiges Existenzminimum' (2010) 10 Juristenzeitung 500, 503.

731 BVerfGE 82, 60, (85) – *Steuerfreies Existenzminimum* (1983). [Ausgangspunkt der verfassungsrechtlichen Beurteilung ist der Grundsatz, daß der Staat dem Steuerpflichtigen sein Einkommen insoweit steuerfrei belassen muß, als es zur Schaffung der Mindestvoraussetzungen für ein menschenwürdiges Dasein benötigt wird.]

732 BVerfGE 82, 60 (85) – *Steuerfreies Existenzminimum* (1983) [Ebenso wie der Staat nach diesen Verfassungsnormen verpflichtet ist, dem mittellosen Bürger diese Mindestvoraussetzungen erforderlichenfalls durch Sozialleistungen zu sichern, darf er dem Bürger das selbst erzielte Einkommen bis zu diesem Betrag – der im Folgenden als Existenzminimum bezeichnet wird – nicht entziehen.]

733 BVerfGE 82, 60 (80) – *Steuerfreies Existenzminimum* (1983).

734 BVerfGE 99, 216 (233 ff) – *Familienlastenausgleich II* (1998) (233). [Die Leistungsfähigkeit von Eltern wird demnach, über den existentiellen Sachbedarf und den erwerbsbedingten Betreuungsbedarf des Kindes hinaus, generell durch den Betreuungsbedarf gemindert. Dieser Betreuungsbedarf ist als Bestandteil des kindbedingten Existenzminimums steuerlich zu verschonen. Steuerpflichtige mit Kindern sind

The right's positive dimension would only come almost 30 years later, in the *Hartz IV* case (2010).[735] A few years earlier, a new "book" had been inserted into the German Code of Social Law [*Sozialgesetzbuch*], regulating welfare for long-term unemployed people.[736] The BVerfG found that some of the book's clauses were incompatible with the GG and gave the legislature around ten months to replace them.[737] The main doctrinal claim of this judgment was that the norms were incompatible with the basic right to a guaranteed minimal income in accordance with human dignity, as deduced from Art. 1 (1) in conjunction with Art 20 (1) GG. This right, affirmed the BVerfG, guarantees "to any individual in need those material preconditions which are imperative for his physical existence as well as for a minimum level of participation in social, political, and cultural life."[738]

The BVerfG clarified that this right must be understood as coming from the protective dimension of dignity and the obligation to apply the principle of the social state.[739] This right has an "independent meaning alongside the 'absolute validity' of Art. 1 (1)." As such, though essentially indispensable, it requires "concretization and permanent actualization through the lawgiver," who "has to organize the services to be provided according to the relevant stage of development of the polity and the existing living conditions. In doing that, it has discretion."[740]

---

wegen ihrer Betreuungspflichten, die ihre Arbeitskraft oder ihre Zahlungsfähigkeit beanspruchen, im Vergleich zu Steuerpflichtigen ohne Kinder steuerlich weniger leistungsfähig.]

735 BVerfGE 125, 175 – *Hartz IV* (2010).

736 For a summary of the legal situation at the time, see Seiler (n 730).

737 ibid.

738 BVerfGE 125, 175, (175) – *Hartz IV* (2010), headnote 1 [Das Grundrecht auf Gewährleistung eines menschenwürdigen Existenzminimums aus Art. 1 Abs. 1 GG in Verbindung mit dem Sozialstaatsprinzip des Art. 20 Abs. 1 GG sichert jedem Hilfebedürftigen diejenigen materiellen Voraussetzungen zu, die für seine physische Existenz und für ein Mindestmaß an Teilhabe am gesellschaftlichen, kulturellen und politischen Leben unerlässlich sind.]

739 BVerfGE 125, 175, (222) – *Hartz IV* (2010).

740 BVerfGE 125, 175, (222) – *Hartz IV* (2010) [Dieses Grundrecht aus Art. 1 Abs. 1 GG hat als Gewährleistungsrecht in seiner Verbindung mit Art. 20 Abs. 1 GG neben dem absolut wirkenden Anspruch aus Art. 1 Abs. 1 GG auf Achtung der Würde jedes Einzelnen eigenständige Bedeutung. Es ist dem Grunde nach unverfügbar und muss eingelöst werden, bedarf aber der Konkretisierung und stetigen Aktualisierung durch den Gesetzgeber, der die zu erbringenden Leistungen an dem jeweiligen Entwicklungsstand des Gemeinwesens und den bestehenden Lebensbedingungen auszurichten hat. Dabei steht ihm ein Gestaltungsspielraum zu.]

In subsequent decisions, the BVerfG elaborated upon the new right. According to Art. 1 (1) GG, all residents of Germany (not only citizens) are entitled to benefit from it.[741] Moreover, in determining the minimum level of existence, the legislator is not allowed to differentiate based on residential status, but only on the actual, proven need for benefit payments.[742] Besides, benefits are not only to be calculated according to abstract consumption statistics but also to a "basket" of the necessary goods and services. What is crucial is that the minimum necessary amount is covered.[743] In another important decision, the BVerfG held that the norms requiring benefit recipients to meet certain obligations to provide for themselves were constitutional[744] and must comply with the principle of proportionality.[745]

The BVerfG also analyzed whether norms establishing sanctions on recipients who do not fulfill their obligations were compatible with the GG.[746] The court held that these sanctions must be strictly proportionate since they are in significant tension with the state's duty to guarantee the means of subsistence for any individual.[747] The sanctions reduced the benefit amount substantively:[748] indeed, the BVerfG – applying the principle of proportionality to each norm under its review – found that most of these sanctions and their temporal requirements infringed the right to a guaranteed income in accordance with human dignity.[749] Accordingly, the BVerfG struck down most sanctions and ordered the legislature to change most of them, along with some transitionary rules.[750]

---

741 BVerfGE 132, 134 (159) – *Asylbewerberleistungsgesetz* (2012).

742 BVerfGE 132, 134 (164) – *Asylbewerberleistungsgesetz* (2012). [Falls der Gesetzgeber bei der Festlegung des menschenwürdigen Existenzminimums die Besonderheiten bestimmter Personengruppen berücksichtigen will, darf er bei der konkreten Ausgestaltung existenzsichernder Leistungen nicht pauschal nach dem Aufenthaltsstatus differenzieren. Eine Differenzierung ist nur möglich, sofern deren Bedarf an existenznotwendigen Leistungen von dem anderen Bedürftigem signifikant abweicht und dies folgerichtig in einem inhaltlich transparenten Verfahren anhand des tatsächlichen Bedarfs gerade dieser Gruppe belegt werden kann.]

743 BVerfGE 137, 34 (76) – *Existenzsichernder Regelbedarf* (2014).

744 BVerfG, Judgment of the First Senate of 5 November 2019 – 1 BvL 7/16 –, par. 126.

745 ibid, par. 128.

746 BVerfG, Judgment of the First Senate of 5 November 2019 – 1 BvL 7/16 –, par. 130.

747 ibid, pars. 132–133.

748 ibid, pars. 136–210.

749 ibid.

750 ibid, pars. 211–222.

Excursus: the context of the Hartz IV decision – the "Hartz Reforms"

At the beginning of 2003, the Federal Chancellor of Germany, *Gerhard Schröder,* announced "Agenda 2010," a set of reforms to the national welfare system and labor market. Initially, the chancellor explained that Germany had to:

> struggle with weak growth, which also has structural causes. Non-wage labor costs have reached a level that has become an almost unbearable burden for employees and obstructs employers from creating more jobs. Investment and spending on consumption have fallen drastically (...).[751]

The government statement listed a number of measures to overcome the situation described by the chancellor. *Schröder* emphasized that it was necessary to "reduce state benefits, promote personal responsibility and demand more personal contribution from each individual."[752] Some reforms implied a profound reorganization of the unemployment security system.

Behind the government statement stood the recommendations of the "Committee for Modern Services in the Labor Market" [*Kommission für moderne Dienstleistungen am Arbeitsmarkt*] convened by the German Federal Government in February 2002[753] and known colloquially as the *Hartz-Kommission*[754] after its leader, Peter Hartz.[755] In August 2002, the com-

751 Gerhard Schröder, 'Mut zum Frieden und zur Veränderung' [2003] Regierungserklärung des Bundeskanzlers – 14.03.2003 [Deutschland hat darüber hinaus – das gilt es ebenfalls zu sehen – mit einer Wachstumsschwäche zu kämpfen, die auch strukturelle Ursachen hat. Die Lohnnebenkosten haben eine Höhe erreicht, die für die Arbeitnehmer zu einer kaum mehr tragbaren Belastung geworden ist und die auf der Arbeitgeberseite als Hindernis wirkt, mehr Beschäftigung zu schaffen. Investitionen und Ausgaben für den Konsum sind drastisch zurückgegangen (...).] <http://www.documentarchiv.de/brd/2003/rede_schroeder_03-14.html> accessed 11 July 2022.

752 ibid. [Wir werden Leistungen des Staates kürzen, Eigenverantwortung fördern und mehr Eigenleistung von jedem Einzelnen abfordern müssen.]

753 See Bundesministerium für Arbeit und Sozialordnung, 'Zweistufenplan der Bundesregierung für kunden- und wettbewerbsorientierte Dienstleistungen am Arbeitsmarkt' [2002] Pressemitteilung, 22. February 2002 <http://www.portal-sozialpolitik.de/index.php?page=zweistufenplan> accessed 13 July 2022.

754 ibid.

755 For example, in official documents, see Bruno Kaltenborn, Petra Knerr and Sylvia Kurth-Laatsch, 'Hartz-Evaluierung: Ausgangslage' [2004] Erster Zwischenbericht im Auftrag des Bundesministeriums für Wirtschaft und Arbeit (BMWA), Dezember 2004 80, 78.

mittee presented its report to the Federal Government.[756] The measures proposed by the committee[757] were ratified by four federal acts – the First, Second, Third, and Fourth Acts for Modern Services in the Labor Market [*Erstes, Zweites, Drittes und Viertes Gesetz für moderne Dienstleistungen am Arbeitsmarkt*] – unofficially named after the leader of the committee and the corresponding number.[758]

The *Hartz IV Act* was enacted by the end of 2003 but only entered into force from 2005 onwards.[759] Essentially, it merged unemployment [*Arbeitslosehilfe*] and social benefits [*Sozialhilfe*] for people fit for work into one basic social security benefit called "Unemployment Benefit II" [*Arbeitslosengeld II*],[760] to be financed by general taxes. This benefit is claimable when a person is ineligible for other social security programs, such as regular unemployment insurance,[761] and cannot reach a minimal standard of living via his or her own means, i.e., through savings, property, or assistance by relatives. Although in most practical cases it is classified as a minimal social benefit for long-term unemployed people who are fit to work, this is not invariably true. However, compared with the social benefits that could be claimed before the *Hartz IV* reforms, Unemployment Benefit II provides substantially fewer benefits, in most cases.

---

756 See Peter Hartz and others, 'Moderne Dienstleistungen am Arbeitsmarkt' [2002] Bericht der Kommission zum Abbau der Arbeitslosigkeit und zur Umstrukturierung der Bundesanstalt für Arbeit, 16 August 2002 343.

757 See ibid 19–36 for a summary of the proposals of the committee.

758 See, for example, official documents like Kaltenborn, Knerr and Kurth-Laatsch (n 755) 78. The timeline of this process is summarized in ibid 10–16.

759 The Hartz IV reforms summarized here are fully documented in Landeszentrale für politische Bildung Baden-Württemberg <https://www.lpb-bw.de/hartz-gesetze> accessed 14 July 22.

760 Kaltenborn, Knerr, and Kurth-Laatsch (n 755) 15.

761 Thus, "Unemployment Benefit I" [Arbeitslosengeld I] acts as traditional unemployment insurance in the following ways: it is funded by employee and employer contributions; it is paid to unemployed people who have previously contributed to it for a number of months; the amount paid corresponds to a percentage of the claimant's previous net salary, with a cap; and the payments are restricted to a period of time. The Hartz IV reforms stipulated that if the person remains unemployed, he or she may only claim Unemployment Benefit II, which pays substantially lower benefits than I in most cases, although the payments are not restricted to a period of time.

3.1.3. Scope of protection of the MSI

Nevertheless, the new right was accompanied by doctrinal challenges.[762] As seen, its scope of protection has been progressively refined through successive decisions and it now has several particular features. First, the right represents a substantial extension of what the BVerfG traditionally understood as the protective dimension of dignity.[763] Second, it is an autonomous basic right.[764] As such, it must receive different doctrinal treatment from the right to human dignity.[765] Thus on the one hand, the entitlement to benefits finds its basis in Art (1) GG but not its scope; and on the other, the purpose of Art 20 (1) GG within this doctrinal construction is to indicate the legislature's leeway in shaping the social state. In this way, the BVerfG can avoid any relativization of the absolutely protected content of Art. 1 (1) GG.[766]

However, since the right is derived from human dignity, it can be held by any human being resident in the country, whether German or foreign. Although its scope of protection can be determined by law according to the personal circumstances of the subject,[767] any difference between groups would need to pass strict scrutining. It would be necessary to demonstrate the reasons for any group receiving fewer benefits to achieve the minimal conditions for an existence according to human dignity.[768]

762 For a critical approach to this right, see e.g., Spellbrinck, 'Zur Bedeutung der Menschenwürde für das Recht der Sozialleistungen' (2011) 126 Deutsches Verwaltungsblatt 661–663, where the author warns against converting human dignity into "little coins" in the area of social law, along with considering that there are better constitutional provisions than human dignity on which to ground a basic right to social security.

763 Seiler (n 730) 503.

764 Ipsen, *Staatsrecht II* (n 384) 63; BVerfGE 125, 175, (222) – *Hartz IV* (2010): "(...)this fundamental right from Article 1 (1) takes on autonomous significance, in its conjunction with Article 20 (1) of the Basic Law, in addition to the right from Article 1 (1) of the Basic Law to respect for the dignity of each individual, which has an absolute effect." Official translation by BVerfG staff <http://www.bverfg.de/e/ls20100209_1bvl000109en.html> accessed 19 April 2021. [Dieses Grundrecht aus Art. 1 Abs. 1 GG hat als Gewährleistungsrecht in seiner Verbindung mit Art. 20 Abs. 1 GG neben dem absolut wirkenden Anspruch aus Art. 1 Abs. 1 GG auf Achtung der Würde jedes Einzelnen eigenständige Bedeutung.]

765 Kirchhof (n 713) 4.

766 Seiler (n 730) 504.

767 Kingreen and Poscher (n 399) 93.

768 BVerfGE 132, 134 (164) – *Asylbewerberleistungsgesetz* (2012).

Indeed, the most remarkable characteristic of this right is that its substantive content is left almost entirely to the discretion of the lawmaker, who has considerable freedom to design a statutory regime of minimal protection.[769] The legislature has a constitutional duty to construct a benefits system that complies with the requirement of ensuring a minimum income to claimants in accordance with human dignity,[770] subject to constitutional review.[771] The BVerfG would then deliver the minimal criteria for the legal design of the right to the legislature.[772]

A justice that participated in the decision summarized the situation as follows:

> Since, on the one hand, the Basic Law itself does not quantify the benefits, and, on the other, the lawgiver decides according to current economic circumstances, the first senate resorted to an assistance standard. Thus, considering that material control of the claim's scope is not possible, it is replaced by a formal test. In this test, the legislature must prove that it has assessed – through a transparent and appropriate procedure – realistically, comprehensibly, and based on reliable figures and conclusive calculation procedures, all the existentially necessary expenses.[773]

At the constitutional level,[774] that is, directly from the right deduced from Arts. 1 (1) in conjunction with Art. 20 (1) GG, some criteria emerge for the system of calculating benefits. The system is not fully generalizable but must leave room for consideration of the recipients' individual situations. Further, the criteria must consider both the requirements for mere physical subsistence and what is required for minimal participation in social, cultural, and political life.[775]

---

769 BVerfGE 125, 175, (224–225) – *Hartz IV* (2010).

770 BVerfGE 125, 175, (225–226 ff) – *Hartz IV* (2010).

771 BVerfGE 125, 175, (226 ff) – *Hartz IV* (2010).

772 ibid.

773 Kirchhof (n 713) 5. [Weil das Grundgesetz selbst die Leistung nicht quantifiziert und der Gesetzgeber nach aktuellen wirtschaftlichen Umständen entscheidet, griff der Erste Senat zu einem Hilfsmaßstab. Die nicht mögliche materielle Kontrolle des Umfangs des Anspruchs wird durch eine formelle Prüfung ersetzt, in der der Gesetzgeber belegen muss, dass er alle existenznotwendigen Aufwendungen in einem transparenten, sachgerechten Verfahren realitätsgerecht, nachvollziehbar und auf der Grundlage verlässlicher Zahlen und schlüssiger Berechnungsverfahren bemessen hat].

774 For a detailed analysis, see Seiler (n 730) 501 ff.

775 BVerfGE 125, 175, (223) – *Hartz IV* (2010).

A second important issue is whether and how it may be justifiable to restrict the right, not least because it is supported by Art. 1 GG. This question has emerged primarily in relation to legal sanctions implying the lowering or suspension of benefits and the doctrinal character of these sanctions. The first possible response is that sanctions can shape the right at the legislative level, representing no interference. The second is that sanctions are conceived as restrictions, but since the right is unwritten, one could not expect written authorization for interferences.[776] In this context, the BVerfG held that the question of whether a restriction may be justified is a matter of strict proportionality,[777] also noting limitations on the discretion of the lawmaker owing to the burden that it imposes on the affected.[778]

3.2. The general right of personality

3.2.1. Jurisprudential history of the general right of personality

"Every person shall have the right to free development of his personality insofar as he does not violate the rights of others or offend against the constitutional order or the moral law," reads Art 2 (1) GG.[779] For several decades, the BVerfG has interpreted this norm both as comprising a general freedom of action [*allgemeine Handlungsfreiheit*] and, in conjunction with Art. 1 (1) GG, a general right of personality [*allgemeines Persönlichkeitsrecht*].[780] This conception has been followed by most of the scholarship.[781]

This approach commenced with the *Elfes* case (1957),[782] which involved one of the BVerfG's most groundbreaking doctrinal decisions.[783] Firstly,

776 Susnjar and Greiser (n 674) 1335.

777 ibid.

778 BVerfG, Judgment of the First Senate of 5 November 2019 – 1 BvL 7/16 –, pars. 1–225, summary in headnote 3.

779 [Jeder hat das Recht auf die freie Entfaltung seiner Persönlichkeit, soweit er nicht die Rechte anderer verletzt und nicht gegen die verfassungsmäßige Ordnung oder das Sittengesetz verstößt.]

780 Hereafter also "GRoP." "APR" is the abbreviation generally used in Germany.

781 Kingreen and Poscher (n 399) 97–98.

782 BVerfGE 6, 32 (32) – *Elfes* (1957).

783 The opinion can only be fully understood when locating it in the context of the Cold War and the specific antecedents of the complainant, Mr. Wilhelm Elfes. For a full account, see Stefan Lenz, 'Das Elfes-Urteil des Bundesverfassungsgericht von 1957' (2016) 2 Rechtswissenschft 149.

the BVerfG refuted that the freedom to leave the country [*Ausreisefreiheit*] was protected by the freedom of movement [*Freizügigkeit*] enshrined in Art. 11 (1) GG.[784] Then, in a somewhat counter-intuitive move, the BVerfG also rejected the view that Art 2 (1) GG only protects the "core area of personality." Instead, it held that the clause protects freedom of action in an "all-encompassing" [*umfassend*] sense.[785] The provision of Art 2 (1) GG thus became "a general clause of all the guarantees of freedom of the Basic Law."[786]

In *Elfes*, then, the BVerfG's main achievement was to develop the grounds for a doctrinal understanding of general freedom of action. However, it had already remarked on the existence, in the light of human dignity, "of an inviolable space of human personal freedom and personality,"[787] affirming:

> [A]bove all, laws shall not violate human dignity, which is the supreme value of the Basic Law. Besides, they must not restrict intellectual, political and economic freedom in such a way that they would be affected in their essence (Article 19 (2), Article 1 (3), Article 2 (1) GG). It follows from this that a sphere of private life is constitutionally reserved for the individual citizen. This means that there exists a final inviolable sphere of human freedom, which must remain free from any influence of any public authority.[788]

The explicit reference to an independent general right of personality derived from Art 2 (1) in conjunction with Art. 1 (1) GG would only appear more than a decade later, in the *Ehescheidungsakten* case (1970). Before then, the BVerfG had continued developing the doctrinal ideas first ex-

---

784 BVerfGE 6, 32, (35–36) – *Elfes* (1957).

785 BVerfGE 6, 32, (36) – *Elfes* (1957).

786 Hans D. Jarass, 'Das Allgemeine Persönlichkeitsrecht im Grundgesetz' [1989] Neue Juristische Wocheschrift 857, 857. [Zur Generalklausel aller Freiheitsverbürgungen GG.]

787 Hufen, *Staatsrecht II. Grundrechte* (n 399) 175.

788 BVerfGE 6, 32, (41) – *Elfes* (1957) [Vor allem dürfen die Gesetze daher die Würde des Menschen nicht verletzen, die im Grundgesetz der oberste Wert ist, aber auch die geistige, politische und wirtschaftliche Freiheit des Menschen nicht so einschränken, daß sie in ihrem Wesensgehalt angetastet würde (Art. 19 Abs. 2, Art. 1 Abs. 3, Art. 2 Abs. 1 GG). Hieraus ergibt sich, daß dem einzelnen Bürger eine Sphäre privater Lebensgestaltung verfassungskräftig vorbehalten ist, also ein letzter unantastbarer Bereich menschlicher Freiheit besteht, der der Einwirkung der gesamten öffentlichen Gewalt entzogen ist].

pressed in *Elfes*. In *Mikrozensus* (1969), the BVerfG clarified some important links between Arts. 1 (1) and 2 (1) GG. It firstly recalled the relevant paragraph of *Elfes*, affirming that, according to human dignity, "the Basic Law guarantees the individual an inviolable space of freedom to shape his private life, which is therefore removed from the influence of public power."[789] Then, the BVerfG applied the object formula to government surveys, with an impressive outcome, stating that "it would not be compatible with human dignity, if the state were allowed, even in the anonymity of a statistical gathering, to register and catalogue the person in his complete personality, and, with that, to treat him as a thing or object (...)."[790]

As mentioned, in the *Ehescheidungsakten* case, for the first time, the BVerfG declared the existence of an independent right deduced from Art 2 (1) in conjunction with Art. 1 (1) GG.[791] Although this opinion did recognize a "general right of personality" with a constitutional basis, it did so only when repeating the nomenclature used by the Federal Minister of Justice in the relevant proceedings.[792] When presenting its reasons for accepting the constitutional complaint, the BVerfG did not use the expression itself. Instead, quoting its previous case law on the matter, it first recalled that the GG guaranteed an inviolable space for the private life of every citizen. This guarantee is grounded in Art 2 (1) GG, whose contents and scope must be defined taking Art. 1 (1) GG into consideration, in particular. Finally, the BVerfG noted the obligation to consider the inviolability of the right's essence, according to Art. 19 (2) GG.

Nevertheless, the BVerfG remarked that absolute protection is not granted to every area of private life. For instance, although the records of divorce proceedings come under this protection, such an "absolutely inviolable space" does not mean that previous access to the records by third parties in advance would be inadmissible. Next, the BVerfG found that access

789 BVerfGE 27, 1, (6) – *Mikrozensus* (1969). [Damit gewährt das Grundgesetz dem einzelnen Bürger einen unantastbaren Bereich privater Lebensgestaltung, der der Einwirkung der öffentlichen Gewalt entzogen ist.]

790 BVerfGE 27, 1, (6) – *Mikrozensus* Case (1969). [Mit der Menschenwürde wäre es nicht zu vereinbaren, wenn der Staat das Recht für sich in Anspruch nehmen könnte, den Menschen zwangsweise in seiner ganzen Persönlichkeit zu registrieren und zu katalogisieren, sei es auch in der Anonymität einer statistischen Erhebung, und ihn damit wie eine Sache zu behandeln, die einer Bestandsaufnahme in jeder Beziehung zugänglich ist]. On the object-formula, see § 10, subsection 4.2.1.1.

791 BVerfGE 27, 344, (344–345) – *Ehescheidungsakten* (1970).

792 BVerfGE 27, 344, (347) – *Ehescheidungsakten* (1970).

to divorce proceedings outside the trial would encroach on the affected couple's entitlement to privacy, unless they provide their consent. Without consent, sending the records of the divorce proceedings to a third party would constitute an intervention into the couples' "right to personality" [*Persönlichkeitsrecht*], which would only be justified if it met the proportionality test. Ultimately, the BVerfG accepted the constitutional complaint because the lower court involved had not applied the principle correctly.[793]

Overall, the BVerfG seems to suggest that, in some way, the divorce proceedings are part of the inviolable area of private life. However, it does not clarify the boundaries of that space. It affirms that even if this space is accessed without the affected person's consent, the inviolable area is not affected, provided that the principle of proportionality is respected. However, "inviolability" means that no intervention can be justified, as the BVerfG's case law on dignity has constantly held.[794]

Similarly, the decision in the *Tonbandaufnahme* case (1973) represents doctrinal progress in the treatment of the right.[795] Here, the BVerfG reconstructed its previous decisions on the matter while clarifying the aforementioned and confusing phrases contained in the *Scheidungsakten* case. First, the BVerfG elucidated that only an interference outside the absolutely protected area of the right could be justified by a predominant public interest.[796] But it also went on to state that whether an interference affects the absolutely protected area could only be decided on a case-by-case basis.[797] The BVerfG opinion is ambiguous since it refers to the right as if it were one and the same as the written "right to free development of personality" and as an implicit independent right from Art 2 (1) in conjunction with Art. 1 (1) GG.[798]

A clearer signal would come just a few months later. In the *Soraya* case, the BVerfG declared some case law of the Supreme Court of Justice [*Bundesgerichtshof*] constitutional.[799] The BGH had recognized an implicit

---

793 BVerfGE 27, 344, (355) – *Mikrozensus* (1969).

794 See § 10, subsection 4.

795 BVerfGE 34, 228, (224) – *Tonbandaufnahme* (1973). Here, the BVerfG reasserted the existence of a right deduced from Art. 2 (1) in conjunction with 1 (1) GG. It is again the Minister of Justice who describes a "general right to personality," rather than the BVerfG itself.

796 BVerfGE 34, 238, (246) – *Tonbandaufnahme* (1973).

797 BVerfGE 34, 238, (248–251) – *Tonbandaufnahme* (1973).

798 ibid.

799 Hereafter also referred to as "BGH."

general civil right to personality when interpreting some civil norms (§ 823 German Civil Code [*Bürgerliches Gesetzbuch*]) in the light of Arts. 1 and 2 GG, while affirming that this also operated as a plausible limitation on the basic right to free speech and press[800] as established by BGH case law.[801] Furthermore, it served as a basis for the explicit constitutional recognition of the GRoP by the BVerfG.[802]

The complete concretization of that recognition would arrive a few years later with the *Eppler* case,[803] whose first headnote states that a "general right of personality" is constitutionally guaranteed.[804] The headnote represents the core of the most important doctrinal section of the opinion, in which the BVerfG proceeds to clarify and systematize what was unclear from its previous case law.

For decades, the BVerfG had conceptualized the right deriving from Art. 2 (1) in conjunction with Art. 1 (1) as a "general right of personality," before finally adopting the BGH's terminology. Indeed, after denying that the relevant complaint could be grounded in any special right from the GG's Bill of Rights, the BVerfG affirmed:

> The general right to personality, constitutionally guaranteed by Art. 2 (1) in conjunction with Art. 1 (1), remains a benchmark. This right, as an unexpressed right to freedom, complements the special enumerated freedoms, such as freedom of conscience and freedom of speech, which also protect the constitutive elements of personality. Its task is to guarantee the intimate personal sphere and its prerequisites, which are not fully covered by the traditional and concrete guarantees of freedom in

800 BVerfGE 34, 269, (279–282) – *Soraya* (1973).

801 BGHZ 13, 334 – *Veröffentlichung von Briefen* (1954).

802 Cf. Martin Eifert, 'Das Allgemeine Persönlichkeitsrecht des Art. 2 Abs. 1 GG' (2015) 11 Juristische Ausbildung 1181, 1181; Hufen, *Staatsrecht II. Grundrechte* (n 399) 174. However, it must be emphasized that the content, function, and possibility of limitations on both rights should not be confused. Importantly, the constitutional right does not elicit a "direct third-party effect". See Jarass, 'Das Allgemeine Persönlichkeitsrecht im Grundgesetz' (n 786) 861 ff.

803 BVerfGE 54, 148 – *Eppler* (1980).

804 BVerfGE 54, 148, (148) – *Eppler* (1980), headnote 1: "The general right of personality, constitutionally guaranteed by Art. 2 (1) in conjunction with Art. 1 (1) GG, also protects against wrongly attributed statements that impair someone's self-defined claim to social recognition." [Das durch Art. 2 Abs. 1 i.V.m. Art. 1 Abs. 1 GG verfassungsrechtlich gewährleistete allgemeine Persönlichkeitsrecht schützt auch dagegen, daß jemandem Äußerungen in den Mund gelegt werden, die er nicht getan hat und die seinen von ihm selbst definierten sozialen Geltungsanspruch beeinträchtigen.]

> accordance with the supreme constitutional principle of human dignity (Art. 1 (1)). This guarantee is a necessity particularly with a view to modern developments and the related new dangers for the protection of human personality.[805]

Second, the paragraph defines the doctrinal relationship of the GRoP with the general freedom of action as its negative dimension, explaining:

> As its link with Art. 1 (1) shows, the general right of personality in Art. 2 (1) contains an element of the right to the free development of personality. As a defensive right included in its protected area, this element stands out from the "active" element of the right, namely, the general right to freedom. Consequently, the factual prerequisites of the general right of personality must also be narrowly extracted from those of the general right to freedom.[806]

Third, the section also explains that the case law of the BVerfG and the BGH has not conclusively defined the scope of protection of the general right of personality, but instead proceeded to different concretizations on a case-by-case basis:

805 BVerfGE 54, 148, (153) – *Eppler* (1980). [Kommt hiernach eine Verletzung von Einzelgrundrechten nicht in Betracht, so bleibt als Prüfungsmaßstab nur das durch Art. 2 Abs. 1 i.V.m. Art. 1 Abs. 1 GG verfassungsrechtlich gewährleistete allgemeine Persönlichkeitsrecht. Dieses ergänzt als „unbenanntes" Freiheitsrecht die speziellen („benannten") Freiheitsrechte, die, wie etwa die Gewissensfreiheit oder die Meinungsfreiheit, ebenfalls konstituierende Elemente der Persönlichkeit schützen. Seine Aufgabe ist es, im Sinne des obersten Konstitutionsprinzips der „Würde des Menschen" (Art. 1 Abs. 1 GG) die engere persönliche Lebenssphäre und die Erhaltung ihrer Grundbedingungen zu gewährleisten, die sich durch die traditionellen konkreten Freiheitsgarantien nicht abschließend erfassen lassen; diese Notwendigkeit besteht namentlich auch im Blick auf moderne Entwicklungen und die mit ihnen verbundenen neuen Gefährdungen für den Schutz der menschlichen Persönlichkeit.]

806 BVerfGE 54, 148, (153) – *Eppler* (1980). [Wie der Zusammenhang mit Art. 1 Abs. 1 GG zeigt, enthält das allgemeine Persönlichkeitsrecht des Art. 2 Abs. 1 GG ein Element der „freien Entfaltung der Persönlichkeit," das sich als Recht auf Respektierung des geschützten Bereichs von dem „aktiven" Element dieser Entfaltung, der allgemeinen Handlungsfreiheit (vgl. BVerfGE 6, 32), abhebt. Demgemäß müssen auch die tatbestandlichen Voraussetzungen des allgemeinen Persönlichkeitsrechts enger gezogen werden als diejenigen der allgemeinen Handlungsfreiheit: Es erstreckt sich nur auf Eingriffe, die geeignet sind, die engere Persönlichkeitssphäre zu beeinträchtigen.]

> Due to the already exposed singularity of the general right of personality, the case law of the BVerfG, as well as that of the BGH, has not described the content of the protected right conclusively, but worked out its manifestations, respectively, on a case-by-case basis.[807]

The BVerfG then refers to different concretizations of the right from its previous case law, quoting the corresponding cases[808] and thereby consolidating its main doctrinal outline. Accordingly, the BVerfG's additional case law on the general right of personality will, based on the doctrinal characteristics described above, consist largely of providing new concretizations of the right; i.e., to indicate ongoing cases that are covered by its scope of protection, as presented in the following subsection.

However, what remains relatively obscure is the content of the absolutely protected area of the GRoP. First, in *Volkszählung* (1983), the BVerfG seemed to change its doctrinal approach to this issue, "avoiding" any mention of this area[809] and only demanding that any restriction be authorized by restriction clauses and the requisites for their implementation, such as the principle of proportionality.[810] Nevertheless, this change of direction did not last long. In many subsequent decisions on the constitutionality of intrusive measures aimed at gathering evidence in criminal processes, the BVerfG has continued to resort to its conceptualization of the spheres as the decisive criterion for resolving the corresponding cases.

In the *Tagebuch* (1989) case,[811] the BVerfG again recalled its case law on the absolutely protected area of the GRoP,[812] whose inviolability followed

807 BVerfGE 54, 148, (153–154) – *Eppler* (1980). [Wegen der dargelegten Eigenart des allgemeinen Persönlichkeitsrechts hat die Rechtsprechung des Bundesverfassungsgerichts, ebenso wie die des Bundesgerichtshofs, den Inhalt des geschützten Rechts nicht abschließend umschrieben, sondern seine Ausprägungen jeweils anhand des zu entscheidenden Falles herausgearbeitet.]

808 BVerfGE 54, 148, (154) – *Eppler* (1980).

809 Max-Emanuel Geis, 'Der Kernbereich des Persönlichkeitsrechts' 46 Juristenzeitung 112, 116. Others believe that even this decision saw the BVerfG uphold the existence of a core area; e.g., Ralf Poscher, 'Meschenwürde und Kernbereichsschutz' (2009) 64 Juristenzeitung 269, 271, fn 24.

810 BVerfGE 65, 1, (43 ff) – *Volkszählung* (1983). Bernd Wölfl, 'Sphärentheorie und Vorbehalt des Gesetzes' [2002] NVwZ 49 praises this supposed change of direction and makes a claim for its definitive adoption.

811 BVerfGE 80, 367 – *Tagebuch* (1989).

812 On the spheres theory, see Bernd Wölfl (n 810).

from the guarantee of the essence of basic rights and from the protection that dignity provides to the core of personality,[813] while also remarking:

> [W]hether some facts can be assigned to the core area depends on whether its content is of a highly personal character and on the nature and intensity with which they affect others' spheres or the community's interests.[814]

Accordingly, a diary or similar record is not automatically excluded from being used in criminal trials but this would depend on the relevant content:

> [F]or example, if such records contain information on the planning of impending criminal acts or reports on already committed ones, that is, if they are thus directly related to specific criminal acts, they do not belong to the inviolable sphere of private life.[815]

When this is the case, the utilization of these records must be justified in virtue of the general public's preponderant interest.[816] In the concrete case reviewed, the judges were tied in their decision, which, by the court's rules, meant the constitutional complaint was rejected.[817] Interestingly, the judges opposing the complaint suggested that the written form of the communication – despite its content – excluded it from the core area of private life.[818] However, the remaining judges held that the contents of the diary, by their nature, belonged to this area. Furthermore, not recognizing this would in

813 BVerfGE 80, 367, (373–374) – *Tagebuch* (1989).

814 BVerfGE 80, 367, (374) – *Tagebuch* (1989). [b) Ob ein Sachverhalt dem Kernbereich zugeordnet werden kann, hängt ferner davon ab, ob er nach seinem Inhalt höchstpersönlichen Charakters ist und in welcher Art und Intensität er aus sich heraus die Sphäre anderer oder die Belange der Gemeinschaft berührt.]

815 BVerfGE 80, 367, (375) – *Tagebuch* (1989). [Enthalten solche Aufzeichnungen etwa Angaben über die Planung bevorstehender oder Berichte über begangene Straftaten, stehen sie also in einem unmittelbaren Bezug zu konkreten strafbaren Handlungen, so gehören sie dem unantastbaren Bereich privater Lebensgestaltung nicht an.]

816 ibid.

817 § 15 (3), last section, Act on the Federal Constitutional Court [BVerfGG] [Bei Stimmengleichheit kann ein Verstoß gegen das Grundgesetz oder sonstiges Bundesrecht nicht festgestellt werden.]

818 BVerfGE 80, 367, (374) – *Tagebuch* (1989). [Die Aufzeichnungen gehören nicht dem absolut geschützten Bereich persönlicher Lebensgestaltung an. Eine solche Zuordnung ist schon deshalb in Frage gestellt, weil der Beschwerdeführer seine Gedanken schriftlich niedergelegt hat. Er hat sie damit aus dem von ihm beherrschbaren Innenbereich entlassen und der Gefahr eines Zugriffs preisgegeben.]

practice imply abolishing the distinction between the core area of the right and the rest of its scope of protection, which the state may restrict.[819]

In later cases such as *Großer Lauschangriff* (2003), the BVerfG continued in the direction set by *Tagebuch.* It reviewed the constitutionality of a reform that added a third section to Art. 13 GG [inviolability of the home].[820] First affirming that the essence of a basic right differs from its human dignity content, the BVerfG stated that the constituent power is only subject to the latter. The BVerfG's principal statement was that "acoustic surveillance of the dwelling with aim of criminal persecution does not violate, in general, the human dignity content of Art. 13 (1) and Art. 2 (1) in conjunction with Art. 1 (1) GG." However, some modalities of surveillance could lead to a violation of human dignity. Therefore, the problem could only arise in the legal regulation of what had been authorized by the constitutional amendment.[821] The BVerfG then proceeded to summarize its jurisprudence on human dignity.[822]

Next, the BVerfG analyzed how the basic right of Art. 13 (1) also protects human dignity. Diverging from *Tagebuch*, it concluded that both highly personal matters (e.g. feelings, emotions, reflections, and experiences) and their confidential expression belong to the core of the private design of life, including their communication to persons of special trust,[823] and that they thus enjoy absolute protection.[824] Nevertheless, the definitive criterion for deciding whether these matters and their communication warrant absolute protection depends on their content – namely, whether they qualify as

---

819 BVerfGE 80, 367, (381 ff). *Tagebuch* (1989). [... so wäre die Unterscheidung zwischen Kernbereich und Abwägungsbereich für das Strafverfahren praktisch aufgehoben] 382.

820 Art. 13 (1). The home is inviolable.
(2) ...
(3) If particular facts justify the suspicion that any person has committed an especially serious crime specifically defined by a law, technical means of acoustical surveillance of any home in which the suspect is supposedly staying may be employed pursuant to judicial order for the purpose of prosecuting the offence, provided that alternative methods of investigating the matter would be disproportionately difficult or unproductive. The authorization shall be for a limited time. The order shall be issued by a panel composed of three judges. When time is of the essence, it may also be issued by a single judge.
(4)...

821 BVerfGE 109, 279, (311) – *Großer Lauschangriff* (2003).

822 BVerfGE 109, 279, (312 ff) – *Großer Lauschangriff* (2003).

823 BVerfGE 109, 279, (222) – *Großer Lauschangriff* (2003).

824 BVerfGE 109, 279, (313–314) – *Großer Lauschangriff* (2003).

"highly personal" [*höchstpersönlich*] – a question that, in turn, depends on "in which way and intensity they [these matters] directly affect the sphere of others or the interest of the community."[825]

In addition, the BVerfG demanded that the law, which reflects in detail what has basically been authorized by the constitutional amendment (13 (3) GG), must exclude interventions that could penetrate the inviolable area of private lifestyle.[826] It then enunciated in the corresponding headnotes what this would involve and how it might be achieved.[827] Essentially, the state must avoid any interference with, and collection of, highly personal matters pertaining to one's character. However, when this occurs unintentionally, the interference must immediately stop and the information must be immediately deleted. The state may only use information that does not involve highly personal content. The protection of the core area is thus divided into two spheres: (i) the collection and (ii) the utilization of data. In the main, later cases have confirmed these criteria.[828]

3.2.2. Scope of protection of the GRoP

The GRoP was formed by combining two constitutional norms and has been summarized in the following way: on the one hand, the right has

825 BVerfGE 109, 279, (314) – *Großer Lauschangriff* (2003). [Ob ein Sachverhalt dem unantastbaren Kernbereich zuzuordnen ist, hängt davon ab, ob er nach seinem Inhalt höchstpersönlichen Charakters ist, also auch in welcher Art und Intensität er aus sich heraus die Sphäre anderer oder Belange der Gemeinschaft berührt.]

826 BVerfGE 109, 279, (318) – *Großer Lauschangriff* (2003).

827 BVerfGE 109, 279, (318 ff) – *Großer Lauschangriff* (2003).

828 See BVerfGE 113, 348, (391) – *Vorbeugende-Telekommunikationsüberwachung* (2005); BVerfGE 119, 1, (23) – *Roman Esra* (2007); BVerfGE 124, 43, (69–70) – *Beschlagnahme von E-Mails* (2009); BVerfGE 141, 220, (276) *Bundeskriminalamtsgesetz* (2016). Nevertheless, each of these cases presents some particularities worth mentioning here. For instance, in BVerfGE 113, 348, (391), the BVerfG did not resort to the concept of the "human dignity content" of the relevant basic right [Art. 10 GG (Privacy of correspondence, mail and telecommunications)]; in BVerfGE 119, 1, (23), the court refers rather to the "human dignity core" [Menschenwürdekern] of the relevant rights; in BVerfGE 124, 43, (69–70), the court suggests that the nuclear area of the private design of life is also derived from an understanding of the protected area of Art. 10 interpreted according to Art. 1 (1) GG; finally, in BVerfGE 141, 220, (276), the court goes further, suggesting that the protection of the core area of the private design of life is not restricted to the general right of personality, but of additional rights in connection to human dignity, as the human dignity core of those rights.

its "roots" in Art 2 (1) GG because it covers all areas of human life; on the other, it is related to the dignity clause because this right primarily concerns the person as an "autonomous subject."[829] In this last sense, the basic content of the GRoP represents "the pioneering concretization of human dignity."[830] In other words, the GRoP protects the "preconditions" that allow the active development of personality or its "inner side."[831]

Against this background, the GRoP operates in the BVerfG's case law as a "general clause," to which the latter resorts whenever it intends to protect the intimate sphere of the individual.[832] However, as has been affirmed, this is no easy task since no comprehensive model exists from which to deduce the preconditions for the development of one's personality.[833] For this reason, defining the right has become a permanent challenge for the BVerfG. The open-ended character of the GRoP, however, also enables the GRoP to deal with new threats to the individual.[834] Accordingly, there is abundant BVerfG case law declaring various expressions of the GRoP, which scholars have classified in a number of ways.

For example, *Di Fabio* distinguishes between (a) the protection of the private and intimate sphere, (b) the right to personal representation of one's self, which includes the rights to informational self-determination, to one's own image and to one's own word, (c) further protection of personal autonomy, which encompasses, *inter alia,* the rights to sexual self-determination and to one's own name, and (d) the protection of the basic conditions of the more intimate sphere of life, which also includes the right to know one's own origins and the right to resocialization.[835] *Hufen,* in turn, differentiates between (a) an inviolable core space or the core of the private sphere, (b) the self-determination of one's personality, (c) the right to self- representation or portrayal, and (d) the protection of personal hon-or. An original approach is presented by *Eifert,* who distinguishes between those interferences with the GRoP that come from the state and those that

829 Kingreen and Poscher (n 399) 116.

830 Udo Di Fabio, 'Art. 2 Abs. 1' in Theodor Maunz and Günter Dürig (eds), *Kommentar zum Grundgesetz* (2020) Rn. 3. [Das Recht auf freie Entfaltung der Persönlichkeit ist von seinem grundsätzlichen Gehalt her die wegweisende Konkretisierung der Menschenwürde.]

831 Eifert (n 802) 1181.

832 Ipsen, *Staatsrecht II* (n 384) 87 Rn. 315.

833 Eifert (n 802) 1181.

834 Epping (n 399) 320.

835 Di Fabio (n 830) Rn. 147–222.

come from private individuals before remarking on the relevant areas of protection.[836]

The aforementioned categorizations of the protected area can be reduced following *Kingreen and Poscher* to just three main dimensions or "daughter-rights": (a) self-determination, (b) self-preservation, and (c) self-representation.[837] First, the self-determination dimension of the GRoP underwrites the conditions that the individual needs to construct or consistently define his or her own identity. For instance, the right to know one's own origin [*Recht auf Kenntnis der eigenen Abstammung*],[838] the right to sexual self-determination [*Recht auf sexuelle Selbstbestimmung*],[839] the right to informa-

---

836 Eifert (n 802) 1184 ff. For an alternative classification, see Isensee, 'Würde des Menschen' (n 436) 115.

837 Kingreen and Poscher (n 399) 116. Here, the present study summarizes the authors' classifications for each group, not necessarily the relevant concretizations.

838 BVerfGE 79, 256, (269) – *Kenntnis der eigenen Abstammung* (1989): "As an individualizing characteristic, parentage belongs to personality. Regardless of the extent of scientific results, the knowledge of parentage offers the individual important points of reference for the understanding and development of his own individuality. Therefore, the right of personality also includes the knowledge of one's own ancestry." [Als Individualisierungsmerkmal gehört die Abstammung zur Persönlichkeit, und die Kenntnis der Herkunft bietet dem Einzelnen unabhängig vom Ausmaß wissenschaftlicher Ergebnisse wichtige Anknüpfungspunkte für das Verständnis und die Entfaltung der eigenen Individualität. Daher umfaßt das Persönlichkeitsrecht auch die Kenntnis der eigenen Abstammung.]

839 BVerfGE 47, 46, (73) – *Sexualkundeunterricht* (1977): "The Basic Law has placed the human intimate and sexual sphere, as part of the private sphere of the individual, under the constitutional protection of Article 2 (1) in conjunction with Article 1 (1) of the Basic Law. These provisions of the Basic Law guarantee the person's right to determine his own view regarding sexuality." [Das Grundgesetz hat den Intim- und Sexualbereich des Menschen als Teil seiner Privatsphäre unter den verfassungsrechtlichen Schutz des Art. 2 Abs. 1 in Verbindung mit Art. 1 Abs. 1 GG gestellt. Diese Vorschriften des Grundgesetzes sichern dem Menschen das Recht zu, seine Einstellung zum Geschlechtlichen selbst zu bestimmen.]; BVerfGE 121, 175, (190) – *Transsexuelle* (2008): "Article 2 (1) in conjunction with Article 1 (1) of the Basic Law provides protection for the narrower personal sphere of life, to which the sexual sphere also belongs. The sexual sphere includes the sexual self-determination of the individual and thereby the finding and recognizing of one's own gender identity as well as one's own sexual orientation." [Art. 2 Abs. 1 in Verbindung mit Art. 1 Abs. 1 GG bietet der engeren persönlichen Lebenssphäre Schutz, zu der auch der Sexualbereich gehört, der die sexuelle Selbstbestimmung des Menschen und damit das Finden und Erkennen der eigenen geschlechtlichen Identität sowie der eigenen sexuellen Orientierung umfasst].

tional self-determination [*Recht auf informelle Selbstbestimmung*],[840] and the right to a self-determined death [*Recht auf selbstbestimmtes Sterben*].[841] Second, the self-portrayal dimension fundamentally protects the individual against false or distorting representations of him/herself in public.[842] Therefore, *inter alia,* the individual has the right to his or her own word [*Recht auf das eigene Wort*][843] image [*Recht auf das eigene Bild*],[844] and to the protection of his or her honor.[845]

840 BVerfGE 65, 1, (43) – *Volkszählung* (1983): "It follows from this: under the modern conditions of data processing, the free development of personality presupposes the protection of the individual against the unlimited collection, storage, use, and disclosure of his personal data. This protection is therefore covered by the fundamental right of Article 2 (1) in conjunction with Article 1 (1) of the Basic Law. The Basic Right thus guarantees the individual's authority to determine for himself the disclosure and use of his personal data. This right to 'informational self-determination' (...)" [Hieraus folgt: Freie Entfaltung der Persönlichkeit setzt unter den modernen Bedingungen der Datenverarbeitung den Schutz des Einzelnen gegen unbegrenzte Erhebung, Speicherung, Verwendung und Weitergabe seiner persönlichen Daten voraus. Dieser Schutz ist daher von dem Grundrecht des Art. 2 Abs. 1 in Verbindung mit Art. 1 Abs. 1 GG umfaßt. Das Grundrecht gewährleistet insoweit die Befugnis des Einzelnen, grundsätzlich selbst über die Preisgabe und Verwendung seiner persönlichen Daten zu bestimmen. (...) Dieses Recht auf „informationelle Selbstbestimmung (...).]

841 BVerfG, Judgment of the Second Senate of 26 February 2020 – 2 BvR 2347/15 –, pars. 1–343, Headnote 1. a: "As an expression of personal autonomy, the general right of personality (Art. 2 (1) in conjunction with Art. 1 (1) of the Basic Law) encompasses a right to a self-determined death." (official translation by BVerfG staff <http://www.bverfg.de/e/rs20200226_2bvr234715en.html> accessed 20 April 2021). [a) Das allgemeine Persönlichkeitsrecht (Art. 2 Abs. 1 i.V.m. Art. 1 Abs. 1 GG) umfasst als Ausdruck persönlicher Autonomie ein Recht auf selbstbestimmtes Sterben.]

842 Hufen, *Staatsrecht II. Grundrecht8e* (n 399) 179.

843 BVerfGE 54, 148, (155) – *Eppler* (1980); 54, 208, 217 – *Böll* (1980): "This [the GRoP] includes, among other things, the personal honor and the right to one's own word; it also protects the holder of the basic right from statements being wrongly attributed to him, and which affect his self-defined claim to social validity." [...dass verfassungsrechtlich gewährleistete allgemeine Persönlichkeitsrecht des Beschwerdeführers zu beeinträchtigen. Dieses umfaßt unter anderem die persönliche Ehre und das Recht am eigenen Wort; es schützt den Grundrechtsträger auch dagegen, daß ihm Äußerungen in den Mund gelegt werde, die er nicht getan hat und die seinen von ihm selbst definierten sozialen Geltungsanspruch beeinträchtigen.]

844 BVerfGE 101, 361, (381) – *Caroline von Monaco II* (2000): "bb) The right to one's own image (...) guarantees the individual possibilities of control and decision-making as far as the making and use of photographs or recordings of his person by others is concerned. Whether these photographs and recordings show the individual in private or public contexts is in principle irrelevant." [bb) Das Recht am eigenen Bild (...) gewährleistet dem Einzelnen Einfluß- und Entscheidungsmöglichkeiten, soweit

The third and final dimension of the GRoP deals with the protection of the private or intimate sphere of the individual as a right to self-preservation. As such, this provides the individual with the right to withdraw socially and spatially[846] and the right not to be disturbed in some personal areas,[847] thus protecting his or her communications with people of trust,[848] whatever the means used.[849] On the other hand, within this space, the BVerfG has since affirmed the existence of an absolutely protected core area,[850] which, therefore, enjoys the same absolute protection as human dignity:[851] "A core area of private lifestyle, in virtue of its proximity to human dignity, is protected as absolutely inviolable."[852] As shown above, this has been settled case law since *Elfes*.

To identify what should enjoy absolute protection, the BVerfG has developed what has been described as the "theory of the spheres."[853] Like the GRoP itself, this theory originates from the BGH's civil case law.[854] It primarily distinguishes between an absolutely protected intimate area and a private area. While no interference with the absolutely protected area can be justified, the private area can be restricted when the proportionality principle is strictly applied[855] and the public interest prevails.[856]

---

es um die Anfertigung und Verwendung von Fotografien oder Aufzeichnungen seiner Person durch andere geht. Ob diese den Einzelnen in privaten oder öffentlichen Zusammenhängen zeigen, spielt dabei grundsätzlich keine Rolle.]

845 BVerfGE 54, 208, (217) – *Böll* (1980).

846 Kingreen and Poscher (n 399) 100.

847 Di Fabio (n 830) Rn. 149.

848 BVerfGE 32, 373, (378 ff) – *Ärztliche Schweigepflicht* (1980).

849 Including a "right to the guarantee of the confidentiality and integrity of technical-informative systems. [Recht auf Gewährleistung der Vertraulichkeit und Integrität informationstechnischer Systeme]. See BVerfGE 120, 274, (274) – *Online-Durchsuchungen* (2008), headnote 1.

850 Already in BVerfGE 6, 34, (41) – *Elfes* (1957).

851 Kingreen and Poscher (n 399) 100.

852 BVerfGE 119, 1, (29) – *Roman Esra* (2007). [Das Bundesverfassungsgericht geht in ständiger Rechtsprechung davon aus, dass wegen der besonderen Nähe zur Menschenwürde ein Kernbereich privater Lebensgestaltung als absolut unantastbar geschützt ist.]

853 At least since BVerfGE 34, 238, 245 – *Tonbandaufnahme* (1973), although already seminal in BVerfGE 27, 1 (6 ff) – *Mikrozensus* (1969).

854 Geis (n 809) 112. The criminal case law of the BGH, however, did not always follow the same path. See ibid 113.

855 Kingreen and Poscher (n 399) 123.

856 See, e.g., BVerfGE 34, 238, (248) – *Tonbandaufnahme* (1973).

However, its proposed distinctions are not entirely defined and have consequently been criticized. The BVerfG, it is suggested, has not yet defined the content of this intimate sphere aside from "acts that do not affect someone else or the general public," the examples of which include "expressions of sexuality"[857] or "the possibility of expressing inner processes such as impressions and feelings, as well as reflections, views, and experiences of a highly personal nature," along with their communication, in general, with trusted persons.[858] Moreover, it is not clear how to differentiate between that area of the GRoP, which is protected as inviolable, and the right to human dignity, which is always inviolable: the BVerfG sometimes seems to refer to both interchangeably.

One way to resolve the ambiguity is to view the absolutely protected area of the GRoP as its human dignity content,[859] which all rights, in any case, share.[860] Nevertheless, this does not explain what could be the distinctive effect of grounding the GRoP in dignity rather than in any other right to freedom while maintaining its independence as a right. If human dignity is the shared content of all basic rights, the right to a general freedom of action also has this content, although the BVerfG does not ground it directly in dignity.

Ever since the particular link between the GRoP and dignity was established, some have ranked it above the other liberties,[861] or have at least granted it a stronger protective effect than general freedom of action.[862] It is also necessary to consider which role should be attributed to the essence of the GRoP, which, in itself, is hard to define, for that essence has been mentioned repeatedly by the BVerfG in its case law.

For considerations like these, some have argued that the theory of the spheres is of limited use. On the one hand, the theory merely tests the proportionality of a given interference in the private area, but must not

---

857 BVerfGE 119, 1, 30 – *Roman Esra* (2007).

858 BVerfGE 141, 220, (276) – *Bundeskriminalamtsgesetz* (2016) [official translation by BVerfG staff <http://www.bverfg.de/e/rs20160420_1bvr096609en.html> accessed 12 March 2021.] [Zur Entfaltung der Persönlichkeit im Kernbereich privater Lebensgestaltung gehört die Möglichkeit, innere Vorgänge wie Empfindungen und Gefühle sowie Überlegungen, Ansichten und Erlebnisse höchstpersönlicher Art zum Ausdruck zu bringen.]

859 See, e.g., BVerfGE 109, 279, (313 ff) – *Großer Lauschangriff* (2003).

860 Kingreen and Poscher (n 399) 118.

861 Di Fabio (n 830) Rn. 127.

862 Jarass, 'Das Allgemeine Persönlichkeitsrecht im Grundgesetz' (n 786) 857.

replace the interference's required justification on a legal basis.[863] On the other, when the BVerfG tried to define what is specifically protected by the intimate sphere, no manageable criterion remained besides a balancing test, which also belongs to the principle of proportionality, in any case.[864] Additionally, since the special connection affirmed between the GRoP and dignity is no more than a proportionality test of both the private and intimate spheres, the theory could lead to the relativization of the very right to human dignity.[865] Moreover, the BVerfG has not coherently differentiated between spheres[866] nor been consistent in assuming the existence of an absolutely protected area.[867] Finally, the theory of the spheres prompts a "spatial" conception of a basic right's protection, which is ill-suited to properly understand how protection operates,[868] resulting in contradictions. The situation is summarized by *Poscher* as follows:

> [B]ut if the core area, as it seems to correspond to its derivation from the guarantee of human dignity, is absolutely protected as an ideal space, how then can measures be justified for which the intrusion into the core

863 Wölfl (n 810) 50–51.

864 ibid.

865 ibid 51. To prevent this relativization, the author suggests removing dignity from the construction of the GRoP. The core area should instead be connected only to the guarantee of the essential content of the GRoP. Indeed, Michael Kloepfer, 'Humangentechnik als Verfassungsfrage' (2002) 57 Juristen Zeitung 417, 423, uses the GRoP, a doctrinal creation of the BVerfG from 2 (1) *i.V.m.* 1 (1) GG, as a supporting reason for its view that human dignity is a limitable right.

866 See, e.g., BVerfGE 80, 367, (375) – *Tagebuch* (1989); BVerfGE 109, 279, (314) – *Großer Lauschangriff* (2003).

867 BVerfGE 65, 1 – *Volkszählung* (1983). Here the BVerfG does not resort to the theory of the spheres but demands, on the one hand, compliance with the proviso of legality for the constitutionality of interferences in the right, and, on the other, that the content of the collected data must, in general, have social interest. Consequently, the BVerfG seems also to deny the existence of an absolutely protected area, in 65, 1, (43): "The individual does not have a right in the sense of an absolute, unrestricted dominion over 'his' data; rather, he is a personality dependent upon communications unfolding within a community (...). In principle, therefore, the individual must accept restrictions on his right to informational self-determination in the overriding public interest (...)" [Der Einzelne hat nicht ein Recht in Sinne einer absoluten, uneinschränkbaren Herrschaft über „seine" Daten; er ist vielmehr eine sich innerhalb der sozialen Gemeinschaft entfaltende, auf Kommunikation angewiesen Persönlichkeit ... Grundsätzlich muß daher der Einzelne Einschränkungen seines Rechts auf informationelle Selbstbestimmung im überwiegenden Allgemeininteresse hinnehmen...]

868 Poscher (n 809) 273.

area is "practically unavoidable"? How is the absolute protection of the core area guaranteed in the evaluation phase if "an (...) impact on human dignity (...) is basically present at the moment of evaluation"?[869]

Despite such criticisms, the theory of the spheres does not lack supporters. First, it allows the GRoP to be handled beyond a "merely" case-by-case jurisdiction.[870] Second, the delimitation of the core area of the GRoP is challenging in itself and neither case law nor the scholarship has provided enough criteria to define it. However, there are no acceptable excuses to stop searching for coherent doctrinal paths since the protection of inviolable dignity must trump all other concerns.[871]

In this vein, some have suggested that a solution can only be reached by diverging from BVerfG case law. The absolutely protected content should not be restricted to certain personal matters but should also contain the communication thereof when carried out with confidential aims, and independently of the communicated content.[872] Therefore, the latter should not be submitted to the balancing process against the general interest to define only then whether it is absolutely protected.[873]

869 ibid. [Wenn aber der Kernbereich, wie es seiner Ableitung aus der Menschenwürdegarantie zu entsprechen scheint, als ideeller Raum absolut geschützt ist, wie können dann Maßnahmen gerechtfertigt sein, bei denen ein Eindringen in dem Kernbereich „praktisch unvermeidbar" ist? Wie soll in der Auswertungsphase der absolute Schutz des Kernbereichs gewährleitet sein, wenn doch „eine ... Berührung der Menschenwürde ... bei „Kenntnisnahme" grundsätzlich gegeben ist?]

870 Hufen, *Staatsrecht II. Grundrechte* (n 399) 176. Equally, Geis (n 809) 113.

871 Geis (n 809) 115.

872 ibid. This kind of approach, however, has also been criticized: cf. Claus Dieter Classen, 'Die Menschenwürde ist – und bleibt – unantastbar' (2009) 2009 Die Öffentliche Verwaltung 689, 693, who suggests that the relevant interference cannot be evaluated separately from the content of what has been encroached upon by the state. [Ein so enges Verständnis aber überzeugt nicht, weil die Bewertung des Zugriffes nicht davon abgekoppelt werden kann, was inhaltlich dem staatlichen Zugriff unterzogen wurde.]

873 See Geis (n 809) 116–117. See also ibid 117 for his multilayered doctrinal proposal to treat the GRoP based on the theory of spheres.

4. Conclusions and open questions

4.1. Right to a subsistence income in accordance with human dignity – absolute and relative

There are good reasons to suppose that the decision of the BVerfG to recognize a basic right to a subsistence income was not only grounded in doctrinal considerations. Therefore, grasping its relevance to a comparative law perspective also requires a contextual view that extends beyond doctrine alone.

Accordingly, it is probable that the BVerfG thought the country was well-resourced enough to constitutionally guarantee this dimension of the right when it recognized it, having analyzed an already existing strong body of infra-constitutional social law. Indeed, the court encountered the issue late: for decades, statutory law had provided for a regime of basic subsistence grants that would clearly exceed any potential minimal threshold prescribed by the constitution. Most state expenditure on supporting the created right had long been assigned to this policy field. This development is compatible with the view, for instance, that the social state does not involve concrete duties for lawmakers, on the one hand, and that the latter has to consider this constitutionally defined goal regarding new benefits, on the other.[874]

A subsistence income is a promise of intra-community solidarity.[875] The BVerfG's decision affirmed that this promise becomes constitutionally enforceable when the community has the resources to comply with it. From a doctrinal point of view, at this point, objective law – the command of the social state – must be interpreted as subjective law. That is to say, in conjunction with dignity, this command becomes subjective law to an extent corresponding with a minimal state subsidy. The doctrinal particularities of this right only confirm the difficulties of subjectivizing the objective law content of a basic right.[876]

874 Jarass, 'Art. 20' (n 696) Rn. 168.

875 Following Isensee, 'Würde des Menschen' (n 436) 107, this dimension of dignity is incompatible with the theory of performance: "Since dignity does not depend on any individual performance, but is a feature of the species, it also forms the grounding of solidarity." [Da Würde keine individuelle Leistung ist, sondern Merkmal der Gattung, bildet sie auch das Fundament der Solidarität].

876 Stern (n 401) 65.

In other words, the subjective law content of the dignity clause stands alongside its objective law content. It has been affirmed that this objective law content has even weightier juridical effects involving the duty to protect dignity.[877] This duty of protection requires the lawmaker to guarantee minimal conditions for a decent life. Recognizing the basic right to minimal subsidized income in accordance with human dignity constructed from Art. 1 (1) GG in conjunction with the social state principle, the BVerfG decided it needed to subjectivize the core of the constitutional order of constructing social protection for the lawmaker; namely, to provide everyone with the minimal conditions for a decent life. Thus, the BVerfG, when creating the new right, enacted the promise at the start of the dignity clause in the GG, as well as that included in the old Art. 151 of the Weimar Constitution.

While poorer societies could advance substantively in respect of dignity and the formal recognition of everyone as a legal person, the effective protection of dignity requires a certain level of economic development. Not every society can guarantee a minimal existence that would allow the subjective exercise or enjoyment of basic rights, and, objectively, participation in the differentiated subsystems that form modern society. The latter is also related to the level of implementation of the principle of the social state.[878]

4.2. GRoP – particularities

4.2.1. Independent doctrinal development of general freedom of action and the GRoP

Following the BVerfG's rulings, the legal doctrine developed independently. The consequences of the court's seminal opinion in *Elfes,* – that general freedom of action is included in Art 2 (1) but not the second sentence of 2 (2) GG – were at that time unforeseeable. Most of the BVerfG's doctrinal treatment of basic rights could be analyzed similarly, independent of whether the given constitutional complaint was successful or not. Several cases were ultimately decided based on the balancing test (the principle of proportionality in the narrow sense), and are now remembered thanks to the doctrinal developments involved in the corresponding decisions.

877 Stern (n 401) 64.
878 About this, see § 13.

4.2.2. Doctrinal difficulties of the inviolable core area of private lifestyle

The GRoP condenses some of the most complex doctrinal themes on the role of dignity into the general theory of basic rights.[879] Since dignity is considered the foundation of all basic rights in general, the effect of grounding an implicit basic right directly in dignity through the formula "in conjunction with" is unclear. Initially, the main effect of its partial grounding in Art. 1 (1) GG is to provide the GRoP with an absolutely protected space. However, using the formula "in conjunction with" is not justified by considering this space as either the human dignity or essential content of the GroP.

On the other hand, when the BVerfG finally considered what is concretely protected by this area, it applied flexible standards to determine its absolute protected content. In this sense, as *Poscher* correctly states, the inconsistencies around the topic in the BVerfG's case law have generated two undesirably polarized theories to resolve them. While some scholars argue that every communication from some spaces or within certain relationships should be absolutely protected, others claim that the jurisprudential treatment of the right by the BVerfG ultimately shows that dignity is not excluded from balancing.[880]

Against this background, since dignity is itself considered a basic right, it would be advisable to leave the core area of private lifestyle as just one dimension of the right to dignity, without confounding it with the GRoP.[881] In this sense, *Stern* suggests that here dignity plays the role – in its objective law content – of a "principle for the interpretation of basic rights, expanding the protected area of Art 2." This role, he adds, is not restricted to Art. 2 (1) GG, but relate to other basic rights as well. Accordingly, the BVerfG's utilization of the formula Art. 1. (1) in conjunction with 2 (1) produces

879 Cf. e.g., *Stern* affirms that "whether the invocation of Article 1 (1) GG was necessary in view of the explicit mention of 'personality' in Article 2 (1) GG, may be left undecided" [Ob die Berufung auf Art. 1 Abs. 1 GG in Anbetracht der ausdrücklichen Erwähnung der „Persönlichkeit" in Art. 2 Abs. 1 GG nötig war, mag dahingestellt sein.] See Stern (n 401) 76.

880 Poscher (n 809) 273 ff. Poscher himself proposes an interesting solution, which, using other doctrinal and most consistent arguments, arrives at practical consequences not so far from those suggested by the case law of the BVerfG. See ibid 274 ff.

881 Cf. also, Martin Nettesheim, 'Die Garantie der Menschenwürde Zwischen metaphysischer Überhöhung und bloßem Abwägungstopos' (2005) 130 Archiv des Öffentlichen Rechts 71, 104, fn 128.

more questions than solutions.[882] Be that as it may, these considerations show that the direct grounding of implicit constitutional rights in dignity is replete with doctrinal challenges – some of which still await a consistent solution.[883]

882 Stern (n 401) 75–76.

883 Dreier (n 406) Rn. 137 explains this problem clearly: "The amalgamation of norms creates a major problem, i.e., according to the generally hardly answerable question: which part is attributed to the absolute and inviolable human dignity, which to the limitable and thus relative basic right or constitutional principle? The recourse to the idea of a fixed core of human dignity does not solve the problem (...)." [Normamalgamierungen schaffen ein gewichtiges Folgenproblem: Welcher Anteil, so die allgemein kaum lösbare Frage, kommt dabei der absoluten und unantastbaren Menschenwürde, welcher dem einschränkbaren und insofern relativen Grundrecht oder sonstigem Verfassungsprinzip zu? Der Rekurs auf die Vorstellung eines festen Menschenwürde-Kern löst das Problem nicht (...).]

§ 9 Ownership of basic rights

1. Introduction

Traditionally, in the German general theory of basic rights [*allgemeine Grundrechtslehre*], the scope of protection of a right has two dimensions.[884] On the one hand, its substantive dimension must be determined; namely, which human activities or attributes belong to the protected content of a given right.[885] On the other, it is necessary to define who is protected by the norm, a personal dimension that requires the attribution of the content of a relevant constitutional right to a particular individual.[886]

In the GG, the division between fundamental rights granted to any human being ("everyone's rights" [*Jedermannrechte*]) and those bestowed only on Germans ("Germans' rights" [*Deutschenrechte*])[887] substantiates the final point made in the previous paragraph.[888] In general, the wording of

884 Hufen, *Staatsrecht II. Grundrechte* (n 399) 79.

885 See § 10, subsection 2.1 for further detail. [sachlicher Schutzbereich] For the material scope of protection of human dignity in particular, see § 7.

886 Hufen, *Staatsrecht II. Grundrechte* (n 399) 79. [personelle Schutzbereich, Grundrechtsberechtigung, or Grundrechtsträgerschaft]

887 A list of these rights, including some harder-to-classify cases, can be found in Kingreen and Poscher (n 399) 37. Article 116 (1) GG, in turn, defines who is considered a German.

888 While "everyone's rights" are also labeled as "human rights" [Menschenrechte] – see Horst Dreier, 'Vorbemerkungen vor Art. 1 GG' in Horst Dreier (ed), *Grundgesetz, Band I (Art. 1 – 19)* (2013) Rn. 72, who argues against this identification – some prefer to call the rights reserved for Germans "citizens' rights" [Bürgerrechte] – see Ipsen, *Staatsrecht II* (n 384) 19. Kingreen and Poscher (n 399) 38 recall that the restriction of some rights to Germans has been rejected, *inter alia*, on the grounds of supposed incompatibility with the theory of the human dignity content of every basic right, including the rights of Germans. Accordingly, in what corresponds to its human dignity content, the rights of Germans must also benefit foreigners. The authors, nonetheless, state that even if the protection of Art. 1 (1) GG overlapped with the protection of a right of Germans in certain areas, this does not turn that right of Germans into everyone's right. For more on the theory of the human dignity content of basic rights, see § 10, subsection 6.1. In any case, as mentioned by Hans Jarass, 'Art. 19' in Hans Jarass and Bodo Pieroth (eds), *Grundgesetz für die Bundesrepublik Deutschland* (2020) Rn. 11 ff, it is generally recognized that foreigners have recourse to Art. 2 (1) GG [general freedom of action] or to another right that is applicable to everyone; moreover, foreign citizens of a member state of the

each right indicates its type. Usually, the rights of Germans are either positively attributed to "all Germans" [*alle Deuschen*],[889] "every German" [*jeder Deutsche*],[890] or in cases of negative framing, "no German" [*kein Deutscher*].[891] In contrast, everyone's rights refer either positively to "everyone" [*jeder – jedermann*],[892] "all human beings" [*alle Menschen*],[893] or negatively to "nobody" [*niemand*][894]. Alternatively, they prescribe a guarantee without a direct reference to a subject.[895]

However, the question of who is protected by a concrete right presupposes first identifying who, in the abstract, is capable of holding basic rights at all [*Grundrechtsfähigkeit*].[896] This issue is closely related to the guarantee of human dignity, and is explored below.[897]

European Union enjoy a privileged position, and must be treated as Germans in the relevant cases prescribed by EU law.

889 Cf. Art. 8 (1) GG Freedom of assembly [Versammlungsfreiheit]: "All Germans shall have the right to assemble peacefully and unarmed without prior notification or permission" [Alle Deutschen haben das Recht, sich ohne Anmeldung oder Erlaubnis friedlich und ohne Waffen zu versammeln]. See also Art. 9 (1) GG Freedom of association [Vereinigungs- und Koalitionsfreiheit], Art. 11 (1) GG Freedom of movement [Freizügigkeit], Art. 12 (1) Occupational freedom [Berufsfreiheit], 20 (4) GG Right of resistance [Widerstandrecht].

890 See Art. 33 (1) GG Equal citizenship [Gleichstellung als Staatsbürger]: "Every German shall have in every *Lande* the same political rights and duties." [Jeder Deutsche hat in jedem Lande die gleichen staatsbürgerlichen Rechte und Pflichten.]

891 Cf. 16 (2) first sentence GG on extradition [Auslieferung]: "No German may be extradited to a foreign country." [Kein Deutscher darf an das Ausland ausgeliefert werden.]

892 See, e.g., Article 2 (2) GG on personal freedoms [Persönliche Freiheitsrechte] (In the official translation of the GG, this was noted as "every person" – see fn 909): "Every person shall have the right to life and physical integrity." [Jeder hat das Recht auf Leben und körperliche Unversehrtheit.] See also e.g., Art. 5 (1) GG Freedom of expression [Freiheit der Meinung]; Art. 17 GG, Right of Petition [Petitionsrecht].

893 See, Art. 3 (1) GG Equality before the law [Gleichheit vor dem Gesetz] (In the official translation of the GG, this was noted as "all persons" – see fn 909): "All persons shall be equal before the law." [Alle Menschen sind vor dem Gesetz gleich.]

894 Cf. Art. 3 (3) GG Equality before the law [Gleichheit vor dem Gesetz] (In the official translation of the GG, this was noted as "no person" – see fn 909): "No person shall be favored or disfavored because of sex, parentage (...)." [Niemand darf wegen seines Geschlechtes, seiner Abstammung (...).]

895 See Art. 4. (1) Freedom of faith and conscience [Glaubens- und Gewissensfreiheit]: "Freedom of faith and conscience and freedom to profess a religious or philosophical creed shall be inviolable" [Die Freiheit des Glaubens, des Gewissens und die Freiheit des religiösen und weltanschaulichen Bekenntnisses sind unverletzlich.]

896 Hufen, *Staatsrecht II. Grundrechte* (n 399) 79 summarizes this matter thus: "In contrast [to ownership], basic legal capacity refers to the fundamental possibility of

2. Basic legal capacity and human dignity

At the infra-constitutional level, the initial boundary of legal capacity is defined by § 1 of the BGB,[898] which establishes that the "legal capacity of a human being begins on the completion of birth."[899] While lacking equivalent clarity, the final boundary is also determined by ordinary law as death, the precise moment of which is "when the brain has irreversibly become incapable of functioning."[900]

Although some have suggested also utilizing this infra-constitutional law criterion for attributing basic legal capacity in constitutional law,[901] the

being a bearer of fundamental rights. It corresponds to legal capacity in the sense of § 1 of the German Civil Code (…)." [Mit „Grundrechtsfähigkeit" wird demgegenüber die grundsätzliche Möglichkeit bezeichnet, Träger von Grundrechten zu sein. Sie entspricht der Rechtfähigkeit im Sinne von § 1 BGB (…)]. Similarly, Michael Sachs, 'Vorbemerkungen zu Abschnitt I' in Michael Sachs (ed), *Grundgesetz Kommentar* (8th edn, Beck-online 2018) 70 believes that the "personal precondition of any entitlement to a basic right is basic legal capacity." [Personelle Voraussetzung jeder Grundrechtsberechtigung ist die Grundrechtsfähigkeit]. Nevertheless, some scholars use the aforementioned different conceptualizations [Grundrechtsberechtigung, Grundrechtsträgerschaft, Grundrechtfähigkeit or Grundrechtssubjetivität] rather like synonyms in the sense of personal scope of protection [personeller Schutzbereich] without providing, at least explicitly, much doctrinal meaning to this distinction. See Dreier (n 888) Rn. 109; Jarass, 'Art. 19' (n 888) Rn. 10; also, Schmidt (n 399) Rn. 41 ff. The position that will be presented and described here affirms that the differentiation of these two levels (basic legal capacity and ownership) is important not only for understanding the role of dignity in the doctrinal category of ownership of fundamental rights, but as a category itself.

897 The following pages deal with the role of dignity regarding natural persons (human beings) as holders of fundamental rights. It is indisputable that juridical persons (entities) are not entitled to dignity. Therefore, the issue of legal entities as holders of fundamental rights or the justification of their basic legal capacity is not reviewed here.

898 Hereafter also referred to as "BGB."

899 Translation provided by the Langenscheidt Translation Service for the German Federal Ministry of Justice, available at https://www.gesetze-im-internet.de/englisch_bgb/englisch_bgb.html#p0030 accessed 22 April 2021. [Die Rechtsfähigkeit des Meschens beginnt mit der Vollendung der Geburt.]

900 Kingreen and Poscher (n 399) 40 [wenn das Hirn irreversibel funktionsunfähig geworden ist.] However, according to Jarass, 'Art. 1' (n 406) Rn. 10, at a scholarly level, the discussion switches between those that affirm that, from a constitutional perspective, death requires the complete collapse of the human organism, and those that only demand the extinction of all cerebral activity.

901 This criterion follows Häberle (n 412), at least implicitly, when it comes to attributing dignity. He suggests that before birth and after death, there are only pre-effects [Vorwirkungen] and post-effects [Nachwirkungen] of dignity.

dominant opinion favors a more extensive standard. The question of who possesses basic legal capacity has been principally addressed when the BVerfG has made its corresponding decisions about who holds dignity. This can be seen from how commentaries, handbooks, and course books on the GG describe the ownership of basic rights in their sections on general theory. Commonly, these sections merely state that, according to the case law of the BVerfG, the ownership of dignity starts before birth and continues after death. For further details, they tend to refer readers to the sections where the right to dignity is individually reviewed.[902]

3. *Ownership of human dignity*

There is widespread agreement that everyone is a holder of human dignity, irrespective of personal conditions.[903] This is a major consequence derived from the wording of Art. 1 (1) GG, which speaks about the "dignity of the human being." *Stern* provides a good criterion for identifying human beings: "only those living beings which have been procreated by human beings can be subsumed under the term 'human being'."[904] By this token, scholarship and case law have emphasized the comprehensive scope of dignity by including concrete examples of some human groups (e.g., criminals, children, foreigners, and mentally ill people),[905] whose subjectivity has historically been once and again denied. However, this basic agreement

902 See Kingreen and Poscher (n 399) 56–57; Dreier (n 888) Rn. 111; Jarass, 'Art. 19' (n 888) Rn. 10, who only recognizes 'Folgewirkungen' regarding postmortal dignity; Christian Starck, 'Art. 1 Abs. 3' in Hermann von Mangoldt, Friedrich Klein and Christian Starck (eds), *Kommentar zum Grundgesetz* (2018) Rn. 211; Matthias Herdegen, 'Art. 1. Abs. 3' in Theodor Maunz and Günter Dürig (eds), *Kommentar zum Grundgesetz* (CH Beck 2020) Rn. 51, mostly referring to the relevant right involved; Hufen, *Staatsrecht II. Grundrechte* (n 399) 81; Sachs (n 896) Rn. 70, while more ambiguous, described it similarly to the above; Sebastian Müller-Franken, 'Vormerkung vor Art.1 Allgemeine Grundrechtslehren', *Kommentar zum Grundgesetz* (2017) Rn. 28–30; Klaus Stern, 'Einleitung. Die Hauptprinzipien des Grundrechtssystems des Grundgesetzes' in Klaus Stern and Florian Becker (eds), *Grundrechte Kommentar* (2019) Rn. 114 – 120; Uwe Volkmann, '§ 16 Allgemeine Grundrechtslehre' in Matthias Herdegen and others (eds), *Handbuch des Verfassungsrechts* (2021) Rn. 22; Schmidt (n 399) Rn. 50 ff.

903 Ipsen, *Staatsrecht II* (n 384) 59.

904 Stern (n 401) 70. [Sicher ist, dass unter den Begriff Mensch nur solche Lebewesen subsumiert werden können, die vom Menschen gezeugt worden sind.]

905 See Dreier (n 406) Rn. 64; Jarass, 'Art. 1' (n 406) Rn. 7; BVerfGE 109, 133, (150) – *Langfristige Sicherheitsverwahrung* (2003): "For the administration of criminal

has not prevented the emergence of highly controversial debates around the corresponding timeframe.

3.1. Initial boundary

3.1.1. Prenatal ownership of human dignity

The prevailing view affirms that dignity already applies to the unborn[906], as supported by the jurisprudence of the BVerfG in both of its decisions on abortion,[907] when it affirmed that the unborn is, at minimum, entitled to the objective-law protection of the right to life and holds dignity from the moment it is implanted.[908]

In the first abortion case (1972), the BVerfG spent several paragraphs explaining why the word "everyone" [*jeder*], with which the wording of the right to life starts,[909] also includes the unborn.[910] Then, after affirming that

justice, the imperative of respecting human dignity means, in particular, that cruel, inhuman and degrading punishments are banned. The offender must not be made a mere object of the fight against crime (...)." [Für die Strafrechtspflege bedeutet das Gebot zur Achtung der Menschenwürde insbesondere, dass grausame, unmenschliche und erniedrigende Strafen verboten sind. Der Täter darf nicht zum bloßen Objekt der Verbrechensbekämpfung unter Verletzung seines verfassungsrechtlich geschützten sozialen Wert- und Achtungsanspruchs gemacht werden.]

906 For a detailed enumeration of the supporters of this position, see Dreier (n 406) Rn. 68, at fn 302.

907 BVerfGE 39, 1 – *Schwangerschaftsabbruch I* (1972); BVerfGE 88, 203 – *Schwangerschaftsabbruch II* (1993).

908 There is scholarly agreement regarding this interpretation (if not always the content) of the corresponding BVerfG case law. Cf. Christian Starck, 'Verfassungsrechtliche Grenzen der Biowissenschaft und Fortpflanzungsmedizin' (2002) 57 Juristen Zeitung 1065, 1067.

909 Art. 2 (2) GG: „Jeder hat das Recht auf Leben und körperliche Unversehrtheit." The official translation of the GG to English translates "Jeder" as "every person": "Every person shall have the right to life and physical integrity." Although this translation corresponds to English legalese conventions, it is unable to explain the reflections of the BVerfG on this point. In its judgment, the BVerfG analyzed the meaning of the word *Jeder* (everyone), which is not loaded with the juridical, moral, and philosophical controversies and complexities that surround the concept of a "person." Prof. Donald P. Kommers, who is one of the authors of the above-mentioned translation, seems to have been aware of this. In his book, with Russell A. Miller, (n 416), when reviewing this case, he utilizes both expressions: when quoting directly Art. 2 (2) GG, ibid 373, he sticks to the official translation. But when he proceeds to translate the corresponding paragraphs of the decision from the original German

individual human life exists in any case from implantation onwards,[911] it asserted that:

> The right to life is guaranteed to everyone who "lives"; here, no distinction can be drawn between the individual stages of the developing life before birth or between unborn and born life. Within the meaning of Article 2 (2) sentence 1 GG, 'everyone' is 'everyone alive'. In other words: every human individual possessing life; therefore, 'everyone' is also the yet unborn human being.[912]

Next, the BVerfG recalled the traditional understanding of basic rights as defensive rights. Accordingly, in the sense of protecting human existence from attacks by the state, the right to life would be incomplete if it did not include unborn life.[913] Besides, the BVerfG stated that this view corresponds with recognized principles of constitutional interpretation,[914] including the history of the provision itself.[915] Furthermore, the protection of every human life is not confined to Art 2 (2) GG, but is also covered by the guarantee of human dignity.[916] Human dignity and human life are therefore inextricably connected, as the BVerfG posited somewhat "apodictically":[917]

> *Wherever human life exists, it merits human dignity*; whether the subject of this dignity is conscious of it and knows how to safeguard it is not important. The potential capabilities inherent in human existence from its inception are adequate to merit human dignity.[918]

---

where the BVerfG is quoting this article, ibid 375, he translates *Jeder* as *everyone*: "b. In interpreting Article. 2 (2) [1] of the Basic Law, one must proceed from its wording: 'Everyone shall have the right to life (...). Life in the sense of (...)'."

910 BVerfGE 39, 1, (37) – *Schwangerschaftsabbruch I* (1972).

911 ibid.

912 BVerfGE 39, 1, (37) – *Schwangerschaftsabbruch I* (1972). [Das Recht auf Leben wird jedem gewährleistet, der „lebt"; zwischen einzelnen Abschnitten des sich entwickelnden Lebens vor der Geburt oder zwischen ungeborenem und geborenem Leben kann hier kein Unterschied gemacht werden. „Jeder" im Sinne des Art. 2 Abs. 2 Satz 1 GG ist „jeder Lebende," anders ausgedrückt: jedes Leben besitzende menschliche Individuum; „jeder" ist daher auch das noch ungeborene menschliche Wesen.]

913 ibid.

914 ibid.

915 BVerfGE 39, 1, (38–41) – *Schwangerschaftsabbruch I* (1972).

916 BVerfGE 39, 1, (41) – *Schwangerschaftsabbruch I* (1972).

917 See Ipsen, *Staatsrecht II* (n 384) 59.

918 ibid (emphasis added). Translation from Kommers and Miller (n 416) 376. [Wo menschliches Leben existiert, kommt ihm Menschenwürde zu; es ist nicht entschei-

Nevertheless, while affirming that the unborn merits the objective law protection of (some) basic rights, the BVerfG explicitly left open the question of whether the unborn is capable of holding basic rights.[919] This was despite speaking at several points of the unborn as having the right to life.[920]

Later, in the second abortion case (1993), the BVerfG confirmed most of these normative traits.[921] However, some subtle yet significant differences between both opinions are worth mentioning. The prospect of an individual's right to life and thus of the unborn's basic legal capacity is more strongly affirmed in the second decision, from the headnotes of the judgment onwards.[922] Also, the possibility of individual human life since fecundation – and therefore of a correspondingly earlier attribution of dignity – is explicitly not excluded by the court, but was not analyzed on the grounds of the merits of the proceedings.[923] The BVerfG also deployed its apodictic

---

dend, ob der Träger sich dieser Würde bewußt und sie selbst zu wahren weiß. Die von Anfang an im menschlichen Sein angelegten potentiellen Fähigkeiten genügen, um die Menschenwürde zu begründen.]

919 BVerfGE 39, 1, (41) – *Schwangerschaftsabbruch I* (1972).

920 BVerfGE 39, 1, (37) – *Schwangerschaftsabbruch I* (1972). [Already quoted above in the main text: "The right to life is guaranteed to everyone (…)."]

921 BVerfGE 88, 203 – *Schwangerschaftsabbruch II* (1993): a) the unborn enjoys dignity from at least implantation onwards [See 88, 203, (251)]; b) at minimum, the unborn enjoys the objective-law protection of the respective constitutional norms [See 88, 203, (252).]

922 BVerfGE 88, 203 (203) – *Schwangerschaftsabbruch II* (1993): Already the 1st headnote: "(...) The legal system must create the statutory prerequisites for its development by granting the unborn its independent right to life (…)." [Die Rechtsordnung muß die rechtlichen Voraussetzungen seiner Entfaltung im Sinne eines eigenen Lebensrechts des Ungeborenen gewährleisten.] In addition, at 88, 203, (252), this idea is developed in detail regarding its connection with dignity; at 88, 203, (254), "Right to life of the unborn" [Lebensrecht des Ungeborenen]; at 88, 203, (255), "The right to life of the nasciturus" [Lebensrecht des Nasciturus]; at 88, 203, 256, the "right of the unborn life" [Das Recht des ungeborenen Lebens]; at, 88, 203, (267), "(…) the unborn has its own right to life vis-à-vis her [the pregnant woman]"[(…) daß das Ungeborene insbesondere auch ihr gegenüber ein eigenes Recht auf Leben hat (…).] Official translation into English by BVerfG staff <http://www.bverfg.de/e/fs19930528_2bvf000290en.html> accessed 30 June 2021.

923 BVerfGE 88, 203, (251) – *Schwangerschaftsabbruch II* (1993). The argumentation of the BVerfG on this point can be summarized as follows: any individual human life merits dignity. However, whether or not individual human life exists before implantation does not concern this proceeding, which deals with the termination of pregnancy, which starts with implantation. From implantation onwards the embryo represents, in any case, an individual human life with its corresponding dignity. In this sense, Werner Heun, 'Embryonenforschung und Verfassung – Lebensrecht und Menschenwürde des Embryos' (2002) 57 Juristen Zeitung 517, 519, argues that

talent here when stating that, from implantation onwards, the growing and unfolding embryo:

> (...) does not just develop *into a* human being, but develops *as a* human being.[924]

Several scholars follow the BVerfG's criterion. *Jarass*, for one, remarks that, since multiple pregnancies are still possible before implantation, it is only possible to distinguish an entirely individual human identity from implantation onwards.[925] *Schroth* concurs, adding that the embryo has a complete set of genes at the point it is implanted.[926] Therefore, it is correct to affirm continuity between the unborn and the born human being from that moment onwards.[927]

Dederer, in turn, comes to similar results, but disagrees with the premises of *Jarass* and *Schroth*. He suggests that individual, singular, and unique human life already exists before implantation, since the fact that twins have identical genes does not mean that they do not merit human dignity. Furthermore, genetic division remains possible after implantation, as science can clone an already-born human being.[928] However, *Dederer* concedes that it is correct to attribute dignity only from the point of implantation, with the key being the BVerfG's statement affirming that the embryo develops *as* a human being from implantation. In other words, the "developmen-

---

the BVerfG at least showed "sympathy" for the position that human life starts with fecundation. For a similar interpretation, see Matthias Herdegen, 'Die Menschenwürde im Fluß des bioetischen Diskurses' (2001) 56 Juristen Zeitung 773, 774.

924 BVerfGE 88, 203, (251–252) – *Schwangerschaftsabbruch II* (1993): "In any case, during (...) pregnancy what we are dealing with in the case of the unborn is an individual life, with a genetically determined identity, which is thus unique, unmistakable and inseparable. As it grows and unfolds, such life does not just develop into a human being, but develops as a human being." Official translation by BVerfG staff <http://www.bverfg.de/e/fs19930528_2bvf000290en.html> accessed 30 June 2021. [Jedenfalls in der so bestimmten Zeit der Schwangerschaft handelt es sich bei dem Ungeborenen um individuelles, in seiner genetischen Identität und damit in seiner Einmaligkeit und Unverwechselbarkeit bereits festgelegtes, nicht mehr teilbares Leben, das im Prozeß des Wachsens und Sich-Entfaltens sich nicht erst zum Menschen, sondern als Mensch entwickelt.] (emphasis added)

925 Jarass, 'Art. 1' (n 406) Rn. 8.

926 Ulrich Schroth, 'Forschung mit embryonalen Stammzellen und Preimplantationsdiagnostik im Lichte des Rechts' (2002) 57 Juristen Zeitung 170, 175.

927 ibid 176.

928 Hans-Georg Dederer, 'Menschenwürde des Embryo in vitro?' (2002) 127 Archiv des Öffentlichen Rechts 2, 9.

tal program" of the embryo is only completed with implantation.[929] From this fact, several significant normative consequences may be drawn:

> While human life is an "organic" physical fact, personhood forms, hereto, an "emergent" (...) personal fact. As an "organic," physical circumstance, human life is a phenomenon of the reality of life, which is accessible to scientific evidence. In contrast, personhood, as an "emergent," personal fact, constitutes a status which gives an individual the general ability to be a subject of rights and duties. The status of personhood is independent of the development of the human life that forms its "substrate."[930]

This "development as a human being," *Dederer* claims, allows individual personhood and human dignity to be extended from the born human being to the implanted embryo.[931] This extension in turn provides the anticipated effects [*Vorwirkungen*] of Art. 1 (1) GG, as the born human being is the "normal case" to which the GG refers.[932]

3.1.1.1. Critique of the prenatal ownership of human dignity

Viewing implantation as the starting point of dignity has received some scholarly criticism. *Dreier*, for one, argues that the crucial position defended by the BVerfG constitutes a naturalistic fallacy, for "the fact that something represents human life in the biological-scientific sense does not necessarily make it a bearer of human dignity."[933] *Heun* believes that the outcome of the BVerfG's case law on this matter is incompatible with its

---

929 ibid 15.

930 ibid 13–14. [Während das menschliche Leben einen „organischen" physischen Sachverhalt darstellt, bildet das Menschsein einen hierzu „emergenten" (...), personalen Tatbestand. Als „organischer" physischer Sachverhalt ist menschliches Leben eine Erscheinung der dem naturwissenschaftlichen Beweis zugänglichen Lebenswirklichkeit. Demgegenüber bildet das Menschsein als „emergenter," personaler Tatbestand, einen Status, welcher einem Individuum die allgemeine Fähigkeit, Zurechnungssubjekt von Rechten und Pflichten zu sein, verleiht. Der Status des Menschseins ist unabhängig von der Entwicklung des sein „Substrat" bildenden menschlichen Lebens.]

931 ibid 9.

932 ibid 9–11.

933 Dreier (n 406) Rn. 68. [Dass etwas im biologisch-naturwissenschaften Sinne menschliches Leben darstellt, macht dieses noch nicht zwingend zum Träger der Menschenwürde.]

premises.[934] Should inviolable dignity be assigned to the unborn, doctrinal coherence is only achievable if medical grounds are the sole criterion for legally permitted abortion.[935] Besides, it is not doctrinally plausible to claim that basic rights can protect an entity that is unattributed with basic legal capacity.[936] Therefore, for this group of scholars, it is hard to justify an unborn child's ownership of dignity.[937]

3.1.1.2. Protection of human dignity from the moment of fertilization

The prevailing position argues that the protection of human dignity is to be afforded from the moment of fertilization.[938] Because dignity depends only on belonging to the human species,[939] there is no human life without human dignity.[940] Although dignity is neither ontological nor biological, the starting point of human life must be defined in correspondence with

934 Heun (n 923) 177.

935 Cf. Ipsen, *Staatsrecht II* (n 384) 59: "Moreover, the BVerfG becomes caught up in an irresolvable contradiction when, on the one hand, it considers the killing of unborn life to be permissible even beyond medical indication and, on the other hand, it grants the same life 'inviolable' human dignity." [Überdies verstrickt sich das BVerfG in einen unauflöslichen Widerspruch, wenn es einerseits die Tötung ungeborenen Lebens auch jenseits der medizinischen Indikation für zulässig hält, andererseits demselben Leben „unantastbare" Menschenwürde zuspricht.]

936 Heun (n 923) 519.

937 Similarly, Dreier (n 406) Rn. 72, though he accepts it would be more plausible from implantation onward than from fertilization. See ibid 73.

938 Stern (n 401) 72, providing several references at fn 334; also, Heun (n 923) 517, who supports granting the protection of dignity only from the differentiation of the brain onward, recognizes the state of the art; Jörn Ipsen, "Der 'verfassungsrechtliche Status' des Embryos in vitro" (2001) 56 Juristen Zeitung 989, 995 demands birth as the starting point. The prevalent opinion also proposes that the unborn has a right to life from fertilization onward, see Hörle (n 494) 335, providing references at fn 103.

939 See Starck, 'Verfassungsrechtliche Grenzen der Biowissenschaft und Fortpflanzungsmedizin' (n 908) 1067; Isensee, 'Der grundrechtliche Konnex von Menschenleben und Menschenwürde' (n 452) 119; Stern (n 401) 72; Matthias Mahlmann, *Rechtstheorie und Rechtsphilosophie* (6th edn, Nomos 2021) 348; also, Ernst Benda, 'Verständigungsversuche über die Würde des Meschen' [2001] Neue Juristische Wocheschrift 2147.

940 This position is also well summarized by Kloepfer (n 865) 419 [(...) weil es menschliches Leben ohne Menschenwürde nicht gebe.]

the reality of its normative character.[941] Hence, if human dignity is to be respected, its recognition must start at the onset of human life.[942]

Starck therefore claims that the BVerfG's reluctance to declare dignity a property earlier in the developmental process arises from the nature of the cases decided. Each of these dealt with protecting embryos procreated *in vivo*. Whereas the preimplanted existence of these is almost impossible to probe, the protection of the embryo's dignity before implantation has importance for *in vitro* fertilization where there are far fewer difficulties involved in probing the presence of life.[943] Besides, it confirms that the BVerfG's point of departure for attributing dignity should be the existence of individual human life.[944] According to the relevant biological information, this sort of existence indeed starts with fertilization.[945] From this point onwards, the fertilized egg is already an individual with potentially every characteristic of a grown human being.[946] Hence, while in principle a "purely biological process," fertilization is "also the legal starting point for the emergence of human life."[947]

Similarly, *Isensee* affirms that this approach is the one that is most coherent with the protective purpose of constitutional rights.[948] Accordingly, the GG itself does not contain any "categorical" difference between unborn and born human beings.[949] Supporters of a different position necessarily resort to some arbitrary threshold, whereas the "basic idea of human rights is that

941 Isensee, 'Der grundrechtliche Konnex von Menschenleben und Menschenwürde' (n 452) 119.

942 Ernst-Wolfgang Böckenförde, 'Einspruch im Namen der Menschenwürde' *Frankfurter Allgemeine Zeitung* (2011).

943 Starck, 'Verfassungsrechtliche Grenzen der Biowissenschaft und Fortpflanzungsmedizin' (n 908) 1067.

944 ibid.

945 ibid.

946 A detailed exposition of this argument can be found in Mahlmann, *Rechtstheorie und Rechtsphilosophie* (n 939) 348 ff.

947 Stern (n 401) 72. [Mit der Verschmelzung von Samenzelle und Ei ist bereits der genetische Code und damit ein sich entwickelnder Mensch vorhanden. Mit diesem Vorgang ist biologisch der Mensch – bei eineiigen Zwillingen zwei Menschen – entstanden, deren Individualität determiniert ist. (...). Diese Konjugation von Ei und Samenzelle ist als zunächst rein biologischer Vorgang auch juristischer Anknüpfungspunkt für die Entstehung des menschlichen Lebens.]

948 Isensee, 'Der grundrechtliche Konnex von Menschenleben und Menschenwürde' (n 452) 122.

949 ibid.

one *has* rights; not that they *are* conceded" by the political power.[950] Any other approach could lead to unacceptable discrimination against members of our species who could be labelled as not "real" human beings, in some sense.[951]

The juridical consequences of this perspective become evident at the beginning and end of life, when the human being is most weak and defenseless, states *Isensee*.[952] The protective outcome of this position for the embryo, especially for those fertilized *in vitro*, is indeed robust. This perspective entails that some practices concerning, *inter alia*, assisted reproduction or embryo research should be widely restricted.[953]

3.1.1.3. Critique of protection from the point of fertilization

Although highly prevalent, this position has been critiqued for its supposed inseparable attachment to some metaphysical or religious convictions.[954] As such, its grounding is only compatible with the Christian version of the theory of dowry,[955] and is thus irreconcilable with the modern secular state.[956] In addition, some argue that it treats the embryo *in vivo* – where abortion was allowed by the BVerfG in practice even after implantation[957]– differently from the embryo *in vitro* – where no such intervention would be possible.[958] In this sense, although the ruling opinion establishes the clearest point for deciding when human life begins, this advantage is severely

950 Starck, 'Verfassungsrechtliche Grenzen der Biowissenschaft und Fortpflanzungsmedizin' (n 908) 1070.
951 Mahlmann, *Rechtstheorie und Rechtsphilosophie* (n 939) 348.
952 Isensee, 'Der grundrechtliche Konnex von Menschenleben und Menschenwürde' (n 452) 122.
953 See Böckenförde, 'Einspruch im Namen der Menschenwürde' (n 942). Particularly problematic for this position is the fact that these techniques typically involve the parallel fertilization of several eggs, with only one eventually selected while the others are discarded.
954 Hufen, *Staatsrecht II. Grundrechte* (n 399) 139–140, Rn. 22.
955 Hufen, 'Erosion der Menschenwürde?' (n 466) 315. For additional detail on the traditional theories of the legitimation of dignity in German constitutional doctrine, see § 7, subsection 2.1.
956 Dreier (n 406) Rn. 85.
957 See BVerfGE 88, 203 – *Schwangerschaftsabbruch II* (1993).
958 Dreier (n 406) Rn. 87–88.

limited because the legal system already treats "the embryo, the *nasciturus* and the human being" [*Mensch*] differently.[959]

Moreover, it has been affirmed that neither the potentiality, nor the continuity, nor the identity argument endures. Ultimately, these arguments are either fallacies that derive from biological facts or normative conclusions, or are wrong in their premises.[960] To assume that the unborn has human dignity from fertilization onwards reduces the holder of dignity to "basic [human] biological functions."[961] Finally, the ruling opinion is primarily grounded in the BVerfG's two decisions on abortion. However, both of those decisions affirm dignity from the point of implantation, and, more importantly, are so full of contradictions that they do not help to deal with this matter.[962]

3.1.2. Ownership from birth

In contrast to the dominant view, the minority holds that when human life starts should not determine the attribution of dignity.[963] This view regards human life as necessary but insufficient for recognizing dignity,[964] which is instead a purely normative decision.

From the perspectives that hold this view, it can be concluded that the German legal order only considers those who have been born to hold dignity. Systematically considered, it is impossible to deny that the legal order treats the unborn and the born differently.[965] Theoretically approached, human dignity is a social claim to respect which necessarily presupposes birth.[966] Genealogically examined, it is impossible to affirm the relevance of the unborn, much least the unborn before implantation: this holds whether

959 Hufen, *Staatsrecht II. Grundrechte* (n 399) 140. [An zahlreichen Stellen wird vielmehr zwischen Embryo, Nasciturus und „Mensch" im vollen Rechtsinne unterschieden.]
960 For this, see Heun (n 923) 520 ff.
961 Hufen, 'Erosion der Menschenwürde?' (n 466) 315 [biologische Grundfunktionen].
962 Cf. Heun (n 923) 517, who also remarks that German scholars have barely considered the relevant discussion in the Anglo-American literature. Similarly, Hörle (n 494) 334.
963 Ipsen, 'Der "verfassungsrechtliche Status" des Embryos in Vitro' (n 938) 996.
964 Dreier (n 406) Rn. 69.
965 Kloepfer (n 865) 420.
966 Ipsen, 'Der "verfassungsrechtliche Status" des Embryos in Vitro' (n 938) 993.

one considers the history of the idea, its constitutional emergence, or the concrete crimes from which dignity should be protected.[967]

Besides, the utility of the relevant BVerfG case law is also disputed. *Dreier* claims that the decisions of the BVerfG are incoherent and so cannot provide definitive answers. In contrast to the regulatory outcome of the relevant case law, abortion (except for medical indications) is not coherent with the inviolability of the dignity of the unborn.[968]

Ipsen agrees that the relevant case law of the BVerfG is full of inconsistencies.[969] However, he affirms that their concrete outcomes reveal who holds dignity and basic rights.[970] The BVerfG established this constitutional standard when it declared some forms of interruption of pregnancy compatible with the GG.[971] In such cases, the embryo is entirely at its mother's disposal, a fact incompatible with legal subjectivity since one cannot simultaneously be a legal subject and wholly submitted to the discretion of a third party. Therefore, it should be concluded that the unborn is only protected by the objective law content of the guarantee of human dignity.[972]

The minority position that human dignity belongs to the individual from birth must also confront several objections from the scholarship. Firstly, it is based upon the mistaken idea that basic rights are granted.[973] Secondly, to claim the unborn lacks certain "constitutive" elements of dignity – such as reason or the capacity for self-determination – overlooks the fact that the newborn does not possess them either.[974] Indeed, there exist only minor biological differences between a viable fetus and a newborn baby.[975] Thirdly, by limiting the ownership of dignity to those able to reason or perform, constitutional protection is guaranteed only to those who need it less.[976] Finally, the argument that human life is necessary but insufficient to attribute

967 Dreier (n 406) 83.
968 ibid 71.
969 See Ipsen, 'Der "verfassungsrechtliche Status" des Embryos in Vitro' (n 938) 992 ff.
970 ibid 991.
971 ibid.
972 ibid 992.
973 Starck, 'Verfassungsrechtliche Grenzen der Biowissenschaft und Fortpflanzungsmedizin' (n 908) 1070.
974 Dederer (n 928) 9–10.
975 Hufen, *Staatsrecht II. Grundrechte* (n 399) 141, Rn. 25.
976 Isensee, 'Der grundrechtliche Konnex von Menschenleben und Menschenwürde' (n 452) 123.

dignity conflates two different doctrinal fields: determining the ownership of basic rights with the (posterior) question about their restriction.[977]

3.1.3. Other positions

Although most scholars support just one of the above perspectives, some aim for a compromise. These proposals aim to resolve the undeniable doctrinal complexities involved in BVerfG case law on the termination of pregnancy by justifying certain restrictions on dignity and the right to life of the unborn, while protecting the former to some extent.[978] However, as discussed below, this can only be achieved by renouncing settled standards regarding the doctrinal treatment of dignity in the German constitutional tradition.

3.1.3.1. Decoupling the right to life from human dignity

One doctrinal innovation proposes that the ownership of dignity and the right to life can begin at different moments. The right to life, which contains a restriction clause (unlike the right to dignity), starts first.[979] Because, under BVerfG case law, any restriction on the right to life of the unborn simultaneously represents a violation of its dignity,[980] *Heun's* novel and unique solution is to "decouple" the two. While the right to life starts with individualization,[981] furnishing the implanted embryo with basic legal capacity,[982] the ownership of dignity cannot begin before the differentiation of the fetal brain. This biological stage corresponds to the "theoretical basis" for the attribution of dignity, since it presupposes the existence of the conscious self and of self-determination.[983]

977 Kloepfer (n 865) 420.
978 For a piercing critique of such attempts, see Norbert Hoerster, 'Kompromisslösungen zum Menschenrecht des Embryos auf Leben' [2003] Juristische Schulung 529.
979 Similarly, cf. Dreier (n 406) Rn. 66. ff; Isensee, 'Würde des Menschen' (n 436) 87, strongly criticizes this approach.
980 Heun (n 923) 518.
981 ibid 522.
982 ibid 523.
983 ibid 518.

3.1.3.2. An increasing protection of human dignity

A different approach postulates increasing the protection of dignity in line with the developmental level of the unborn child.[984] Individual scholars have identified that protection starts with either fertilization, implantation, conscience, viability, or birth.[985] However, increasing the level of protection involves an unavoidable relativization of Art. 1 (1) GG regarding those biological stages where dignity has not yet achieved its full protective force. *Hufen* recognizes this fact, but insists this is the only way to solve concrete juridical conflicts regarding the unborn (i.e., interruption of pregnancy, IVF treatment, and pre-implantation diagnosis of a genetic disorder). Even if the "fertilization" thesis were clearer, it would be unable to deal with these conflicts successfully.[986]

Along these lines, *Kloepfer* believes that the constitutional protection of the unborn grows with time, starting at its weakest after fertilization and developing to its strongest shortly before birth.[987] However, this increasing protection is doctrinally only executable by recognizing possible restrictions on dignity. *Herdegen* adds that the very wording of Art. 1 (1) GG allows this interpretation, as it talks of the dignity of the human being [*Mensch*] and not of human life.[988] In this view, the intention or aim of the potential interference with human dignity is crucial to defining its compatibility with the GG.[989]

---

984 For a defense of the supposed benefits of this position, see Nettesheim (n 881) 96 ff.

985 Hufen, 'Erosion der Menschenwürde?' (n 466) 315, provides a list of those who support this approach in fn 32.

986 ibid 315.

987 Kloepfer (n 865) 420.

988 Herdegen, 'Die Menschenwürde im Fluß des bioetischen Diskurses' (n 923) 774.

989 ibid 775. This means that controversial cases in bioethics can only be resolved on a case-by-case basis; ibid 776 ff, utilizing the standard of the finality of the interference and balancing it with dignity would render the production of embryos only for research ends inadmissible, while the utilization of surplus embryos for the same end would probably be acceptable. Hufen, *Staatsrecht II. Grundrechte* (n 399) 142, also favors a "growing" protection of dignity.

3.2. Upper boundary

3.2.1. Protection of human dignity after death

German constitutional scholarship and case law have also discussed both when basic legal capacity ends and whether the effects of some basic rights remain even after death. Although this is a highly complex doctrinal matter, the majoritarian view holds that at least some effects of dignity do not end with the physical demise of its holder.[990] The judicial support for this position is traceable to the *Mephisto* case. Here, the BVerfG had to review the decisions of the competent civil courts in a legal conflict involving, on the one hand, the freedom of the arts and, on the other, the honor or reputation of the person affected by the corresponding artistic piece: in this case, a deceased person.[991]

Firstly, the BVerfG, after recalling that the first sentence of Art 5 (3) of the GG is a right without a restriction clause,[992] affirmed that restrictions may be applied to the freedom of the arts.[993] But in this case, the lack of a restriction clause meant that the limits of this provision had to be found within the constitution – in this concrete case, in Art. 1 (1) GG.[994] Against this background, the BVerfG held that death does not fundamentally affect a person's claim to respect because:

> [I]t would also be incompatible with the constitutional requirement that human dignity, a general claim to respect, shall be inviolable – a requirement that forms the basis of all basic rights – if the human being, to whom dignity is recognized in virtue of his personhood, could be degraded or demeaned after his death. Correspondingly, the order

990 The view held by Dreier (n 406) Rn. 74, with several references at fn 328. On the other hand, some scholarship has also postulated the existence of a posthumous protection of other basic rights, e.g., Diana Zacharias, 'Zur Abgrenzung von Menschenwürde und allgemeinem Persönlichkeitsrecht' [2001] Neue Juristische Wocheschrift 2950, 2951, regarding freedom of religion.

991 BVerfGE 30, 173 – *Mephisto* (1971). For an English summary of the circumstances of this case, see Kommers and Miller (n 416) 358.

992 Art. 5 (3) GG: "Art and science, research and teaching shall be free" [Kunst und Wissenschaft, Forschung und Lehre sind frei]. On restriction clauses in German legal doctrine, see § 10, subsection 2.3.1.

993 BVerfGE 30, 173, (192) – *Mephisto* (1971).

994 BVerfGE 30, 173, (193) – *Mephisto* (1971).

imposed on all state authorities in Art. 1 (1) GG to accord the individual protection against attacks on his dignity does not end with death.[995]

Nonetheless, the BVerfG – in contrast to the civil courts – rejected the view that the effects of the right of personality contained in Art. 2 (1) GG continued after death because:

> (...) only the living person is a bearer of this right; its protection expires with his death. The basic right of Art. 2 (1) GG indispensably presupposes the existence of a person capable of acting at least potentially or in the future.[996]

Based on the above considerations, the BVerfG then reviewed the case. In this context, another court's statements remained of decisive importance regarding the doctrinal treatment of posthumous dignity: the civil courts, when applying Art. 1 (1) GG to interpret civil law provisions, had correctly affirmed that:

> (...) the need for protection – and accordingly the [state's] obligation of protection – decreases to the extent that the memory of the deceased

995 ibid. [Es würde mit dem verfassungsverbürgten Gebot der Unverletzlichkeit der Menschenwürde, das allen Grundrechten zugrunde liegt, unvereinbar sein, wenn der Mensch, dem Würde kraft seines Personseins zukommt, in diesem allgemeinen Achtungsanspruch auch nach seinem Tode herabgewürdigt oder erniedrigt werden dürfte. Dementsprechend endet die in Art. 1 Abs. 1 GG aller staatlichen Gewalt auferlegte Verpflichtung, dem Einzelnen Schutz gegen Angriffe auf seine Menschenwürde zu gewähren, nicht mit dem Tode.]

996 BVerfGE 30, 173, (194) – *Mephisto* (1971). [Die Fortwirkung eines Persönlichkeitsrechts nach dem Tode ist jedoch zu verneinen, weil Träger dieses Grundrechts nur die lebende Person ist; mit ihrem Tode erlischt der Schutz aus diesem Grundrecht. Das Grundrecht aus Art. 2 Abs. 1 GG setzt die Existenz einer wenigstens potentiell oder zukünftig handlungsfähigen Person als unabdingbar voraus.] This criterion was confirmed in subsequent decisions, e.g., BVerfG, Judgment of the First Chamber of the First Senate of 22 August 2006 – 1 BvL 1168/04 [BVerfG NJW 2006, 3409 (3409)] – "Marlene Dietrich." Some constitutional scholarship, in contrast, supports the GRoP's posthumous continuity, e.g., Herdegen, 'Art. 1. Abs. 1' (n 604) Rn. 57. Several decades later, the BVerfG would invoke Art. 1 (1) GG when specifying that the protection of personality held by the living person in virtue of the GRoP does not equal that of the deceased. See BVerfG, Judgment of the First Chamber of the First Senate of 25 August 2000 – 1 BvL 2707/95 [BVerfG NJW 2001, 594 (594)] – "Willy Brandt"; BVerfG, Judgment of the First Chamber of the First Senate of 22 August 2006 – 1 BvL 1168/04 [BVerG NJW 2006, 3409 (3409)] – "Marlene Dietrich."

fades and, over time, the interest in preventing the falsification of his life's image also diminishes.[997]

Later, the BVerfG's judgments more strongly clarified that the posthumous protection that Art. 1 (1) GG provides is not the same as the GRoP gives to the living person. This is both because the posthumous protection of personality may not be submitted to balancing[998] and the protection of the personality of living persons is more extensive.[999]

In summary, the scholarship discusses two main normative consequences of the *post mortis* continuity of dignity protection. Firstly, Art. 1 (1) GG demands the protection of the image of the deceased from distortions.[1000] Secondly – although this dimension is mentioned neither in

997 BVerfGE 130, 173, (196) – *Mephisto* (1971). [Aufgrund dieser Feststellungen sind das Oberlandesgericht und der Bundesgerichtshof davon ausgegangen, daß der Schutz des Achtungsanspruchs des verstorbenen Gründgens im sozialen Raum noch fortdauere. Hierbei hat der Bundesgerichtshof zutreffend berücksichtigt, daß das Schutzbedürfnis – und entsprechend die Schutzverpflichtung – in dem Maße schwindet, in dem die Erinnerung an den Verstorbenen verblaßt und im Laufe der Zeit auch das Interesse an der Nichtverfälschung des Lebensbildes abnimmt.] About the general right of personality, see § 8, subsection 3.2.

998 Despite these normative statements, Heinz-Joachim Pabst, 'Der postmortale Persönlichkeitsschutz in der neueren Rechtsprechung des BVerfG' [2002] Neue Juristische Wocheschrift 999, 1001 ff, sees a relativization of the posthumous protection of dignity in BVerfG, Judgment of the First Chamber of the First Senate of 5 April 2001 – 1 BvL 932/94 [NJW 2001, 2957 (2958)] – 'Wilhelm Kaisen'. Indeed, some of the BVerfG's language in this judgment is, to say the least, confusing.

999 See BVerfG, Judgment of the First Chamber of the First Senate of 25 August 2000 – 1 BvL 2707/95 [BVerfG NJW, 2001, 594 (594–595)] – "Willy Brandt"; BVerfG, Judgment of the First Chamber of the First Senate of 5 April 2001 – 1 BvL 932/94 [NJW 2001, 2957 (2958)] – "Wilhelm Kaisen"; BVerfG, Judgment of the First Chamber of the First Senate of 22 August 2006 – 1 BvL 1168/04 [NJW 2006, 3409 (3409)] – "Marlene Dietrich." The latter describes the scope of protection effectively: "Posthumously protected is, firstly, the general claim to respect, which is assigned to the human being in virtue of his personhood; secondly, the moral, personal, and social value that the person gained by living his own life." [Postmortal geschützt wird zum einen der allgemeine Achtungsanspruch, der dem Menschen kraft seines Personseins zusteht, zum anderen der sittliche, personale uns soziale Geltungswert, den die Person durch ihre eigene Lebensleistung erworben hat]. Zacharias (n 109) 2950, sees, in the first aspect, a grounding on the *Mitgifttheorie*; in the second, on the *Leistungtheorie*. About these theories, see § 7 subsection 2.1.

1000 This dimension is particularly protected by Civil Law, cf. Bettina Spilker, 'Postmortaler Schutz durch das Grundgesetz' [2014] Die Öffentliche Verwaltung 637, 638–639.

Mephisto nor in other decisions[1001]– dignity entails some duties to properly treat the mortal remains.[1002] The literature concurs that the intensity of dignity's posthumous protection should decline over time.[1003]

However, it is disputed whether the BVerfG solely affirmed duties of protection or whether it also confirmed the existence of a subjective right of the deceased, to be claimed, in any case, by living relatives.[1004] Supporters of the former view think that, in principle, only living persons possess basic legal capacity.[1005] Therefore, posthumous dignity should be understood as a duty of protection for the state without subjective law content. This relates to protecting human dignity as the dignity of the species – protection exercised in the public interest.[1006] Others suggest that what remains after the death of its holder is dignity as a legal interest.[1007] When remarking on the deceased's lack of basic legal capacity, the expression "after-effects" [*Nachwirkungen*] is commonly used to define the kind of protection involved.[1008] The relevant duties are reflected in all spaces of infra-constitutional law,[1009] and the deceased's relatives are entitled to pursue their interests.[1010] Should the lower courts not fulfill the duties demanded by the GG, the relatives could then bring a constitutional complaint before the BVerfG.[1011]

In contrast, others contend that the decisions of the BVerfG imply the recognition of a basic posthumous legal capacity. The dignity clause entitles the deceased person to hold basic rights that are not necessarily bound to being alive.[1012] While personality during life is safeguarded by the

1001 Birgit Schmidt am Busch, 'Postmortaler Würdeschutz und gesetzgeberische Gestatltungsfreiheit' (2010) 49 Der Staat 211, 213.

1002 Relating to a dimension protected by criminal law, see Spilker (n 1000) 640.

1003 See Schmidt am Busch (n 1001) 224, which includes several references.

1004 Jarass, 'Art. 1' (n 406) Rn. 10.

1005 Cf. Spilker (n 1000) 638–639; Epping (n 399) Rn. 600; Ipsen, *Staatsrecht II* (n 384) Rn. 229; Pabst (n 998) 999.

1006 Spilker (n 1000) 638.

1007 See Ipsen, *Staatsrecht II* (n 384) Rn. 229.

1008 See Jarass, 'Art. 1' (n 406) Rn. 9–10; Herdegen, 'Art. 1. Abs. 1' (n 604) Rn. 57; Philip Kunig and Markus Kotzur, 'GG Art. 1' in Ingo von Münch and Philip Kunig (eds), *Grundgesetz-Kommentar* (2021) Rn. 28. ["weiterwirkende Würde."]

1009 See examples in Spilker (n 1000) 238 ff.

1010 Pabst (n 998) 1000.

1011 Epping (n 399) Rn. 600. This has occurred despite the outcomes of cases such as BVerfG, Judgment of the First Chamber of the First Senate of 25 August 2000 – 1 BvL 2707/95 [BVerfG NJW, 2001, 594 (594 ff)] – "Willy Brandt."

1012 Schmidt (n 399) Rn. 53, who is, however, critical vis-à-vis this perspective. See ibid Rn. 54–55.

GRoP, after death it is protected by Art. 1 (1) GG. Accordingly, no more than posthumous manifestations of the GRoP are protected after death.[1013] Nonetheless, as dignity provides this protection, any interference with the posthumous right to personality is unconstitutional.[1014] Finally, the medial position is that the posthumous protection of personality by Art. 1 (1) GG should be understood as a subjective right of each living human being to know that such protection exists – this certainty is part of dignity's scope of protection.[1015]

3.2.2. Critique of the protection of dignity after death

Criticism of the posthumous protection of dignity has centered on particular doctrinal statements issued by the BVerfG. Firstly, the court's decisions do not clarify how to differentiate between the living versus the posthumous right to personality.[1016] In this sense, the posthumous protection of some human attributes might have been better postulated as a subset of the GRoP.[1017] Furthermore, the GRoP of the deceased's relatives should have been protected by the court.[1018]

In addition, the posthumous attribution of dignity prevents a temporally graded approach to protecting the personality of the deceased.[1019] Indeed, to hold that the intensity of the protection decreases with time is incompatible with the inviolability of dignity (Art. 1 (1) GG) and its permanent validity (Art 79 (3) GG). Should the legal subjectivity of the deceased be accepted, the exercise of his or her rights would depend on the heirs, who would determine whether to resort to the civil courts to protect the interests of the deceased.[1020]

1013 Schmidt (n 399) Rn. 55. Pabst (n 998) 1001 sees this situation analogously, but regards posthumous manifestations as only objective-law effects; he also proposes criteria at 1004 to identify violations of the posthumous protection of dignity.

1014 Schmidt (n 399) Rn. 55. Nonetheless, Pabst (n 998) 1001 highlights some currents of relativization in the "Wilhelm Kaisen" case. See BVerfG, Judgment of the First Chamber of the First Senate of 5 April 2001 – 1 BvL 932/94 [NJW 2001, 2957].

1015 Pabst (n 998) 1000.

1016 Zacharias (n 990) 2950 ff, who also proposes some criteria for differentiating between the two.

1017 Dreier (n 888) Rn. 74, fn 328.

1018 Schmidt (n 399) Rn. 230.

1019 Dreier (n 406) Rn.76; Schmidt (n 399) 230.

1020 Schmidt (n 399) Rn. 34.

Some scholars have targeted the position that attributes dignity to mortal remains.[1021] The traditional grounding theories of human dignity cannot justify that view;[1022] neither can a negative approach to dignity.[1023] To apply the object formula is useless because the corpse is already an object.[1024] From this, it appears that this doctrinal category contains only representations and values on how those alive should deal with human mortal remains[1025] – dealing with the corpse is only a preoccupation of those still alive.[1026]

4. Conclusions and open questions

4.1. Human dignity and basic legal capacity

The main conclusion of this chapter is that the primary role of dignity – as merely a principle but even as a basic right – in the ownership of basic rights is to serve as the decisive criterion for attributing basic legal capacity.[1027] This approach is found in other disciplines, such as ethics, where the attribution of dignity is also conceived as the recognition of the human being as a person, i.e., as an entity able to hold rights and duties in the corresponding disciplinary subsystem.[1028] Worth remarking upon, however, is that German constitutional doctrine handles this matter by considering dignity a subjective right.

4.2. Human dignity as a basic right

German legal scholarship subjects human dignity to the same doctrinal categories as any other right. The first part of the traditional Three-Step Test

---

1021 Schmidt am Busch (n 1001) 213.
1022 ibid 224 ff. For more information on the traditional grounding theories, see § 7, subsection 2.1.
1023 ibid 226 ff.
1024 ibid 229.
1025 ibid 230. Also, Nettesheim (n 881) 94.
1026 Schmidt am Busch (n 1001) 230; similarly Dreier (n 406) Rn. 75.
1027 An exception can be found in the theory of the "decoupling." According to this theory the right to life starts before dignity. See *supra* subsection 3.1.3.1.
1028 See § 12, subsection 3.1.

requires defining the personal scope of protection [*personeller Schutzbereich*].[1029] Second, by answering this question, dignity also provides the criterion to attribute basic legal capacity as its objective law content: those who hold dignity also possess basic legal capacity.[1030]

4.3. Human dignity as a principle

While the prevailing view holds the double-headed character of dignity as a principle of objective law and as a subjective basic right, the minority position denies the latter.[1031] However, the minority position must refer to dignity in individual terms and enquire who may be considered a "holder" of dignity. Therefore, even when dignity is considered a principle, it remains the criterion for allocating basic legal capacity.[1032] Overall, when dignity is only considered a principle, it attributes basic legal capacity and the right to life, at minimum. When also considered a right, it attributes basic legal capacity and, minimally, ownership of the right to dignity and the right to life.

1029 See § 10, subsection 2.1. However, as shown below, the ruling opinion believes that no interference (the third step) with dignity may be justified.

1030 The reverse procedure can, nonetheless, produce the same outcome: the objective content of Art. 1 (1) GG is understood as the basic legal capacity of any human being; see § 12, subsection 3.2.1.

1031 See § 7, subsection 3.1.

1032 Cf. Isensee, 'Würde des Menschen' (n 436) 105, who believes that dignity is not a "legal interest like life and honor, freedom and property. Rather, human dignity forms the conditions that make the attribution of those legal interests possible for human beings. Dignity as such is not a subjective right, but it gives birth to the capacity of having rights: 'a right to have rights'. One's dignity allows everyone who belongs to the human species the possibility of having rights and duties, that is, dignity makes everyone a person." [Würde ist kein Rechtsgut wie Leben und Ehre, Freiheit und Eigentum. Vielmehr bildet sie die Voraussetzungen dafür, daß dem Menschen Rechtsgüter zukommen können. In seiner Würde konstituiert sich ein jeder, der zur menschlichen Gattung gehört, als möglicher Träger von Rechten und Pflichten, mithin als Person] Similarly, Ernst-Wolfang Böckenförde, 'Die Würde des Menschen war Unantastbar' (n 420).

4.4. Dignity – a clause of constitutional openness

Art 1 (1) GG is not a frozen norm. Despite initially reacting to specific crimes, its protective goal goes beyond those historical experiences. Consequently, the interpretation of its protected content may not be reduced to a negative test when faced with already familiar attacks against personhood. Conversely, when understood as a criterion for recognizing the basic legal capacity of any human being, dignity prevents new forms of exclusion from the community of legal persons.[1033] In this way, it enables the constitution to responsively protect persons from new challenges yet to come, especially working in favor of those who need it the most.

1033 Dignity is thus able to change, develop, and adapt only based on the stability of this core content: see § 12. This is important to remember since it has regularly been remarked that dignity is not a fixed norm, that it must evolve to confront new challenges, without noting at the same time what should *not* change. C.f. Hufen, 'Erosion der Menschenwürde?' (n 466) 313.

§ 10 Restrictions on basic rights

1. Introduction

The present chapter deals with the role of human dignity in the doctrinal category of restrictions on basic rights. Human dignity fulfills at least two crucial functions within this category thanks to its unique characteristics and status in the German constitutional order. The content of the dignity clause could both be appealed in order to justify restrictions on basic rights while also limiting such restrictions. However, understanding these functions requires specific knowledge of the relevant doctrinal practices of the German legal environment. Accordingly, before discussing these functions, it is advisable to review both the methodical treatment that a case of restriction on basic rights receives in the abstract, and how this treatment is applied specifically to the right to human dignity.

2. The Three-Step Test

As previously mentioned,[1034] German legal practitioners review possible impacts or effects on basic rights using a shared method – the Three-Step Test [*Drei-Schritte-Prüfung*].[1035] The task is to identify whether a state act that affects fundamental rights is constitutionally unobjectionable. The test consists of the successive determination of (1) the scope of protection [*Schutzbereich*] of the right in question; (2) whether the effects of an act that can be attributed to an addressee of basic rights obligations may be an interference, encroachment, or intrusion in that scope of protection [*Eingriff*]; and (3) whether there is a constitutional justification [*Rechtfertigung*] for that interference or encroachment.

1034 See § 7, subsection 1.1.

1035 Referring to this, Uwe Volkmann, 'Veränderung der Grundrechtsdogmatik' (2005) 60 Juristen Zeitung 261, argues that the main characteristic of this legal doctrine is the use of the "three-stage examination program." Indeed, this test has been described as "classical," see Andreas Voßkuhle and Anna-Bettina Kaiser, 'Grundwissen – Öffentliches Recht: Der Grundrechtseingriff' [2009] Juristische Schulung 313; and as "canonical," see Jörn Ipsen, 'Grundzüge einer Grundrechtsdogmatik' (2013) 52 Der Staat 266, 266.

Although some elements of this systematization also respond to previous historical developments in German public law,[1036] it was only with the Basic Law that they achieved canonicity, since this was when fundamental rights became directly enforceable juridical norms, thanks to Art. 1 (3) GG.[1037] Accordingly, legal practitioners had little experience of this legal challenge: the structure of constitutional rights diverges significantly from subjective rights in ordinary law that the judiciary had learned to enforce throughout the centuries.

In this sense, the Three-Step Test was the doctrinal response of German legal practitioners to deal with this complexity,[1038] First, the BVerfG developed its basic structure and terminology[1039] before the scholarship continually discussed and refined it over many years. Course books, handbooks, and commentaries on the GG tend to follow both the BVerfG's systematization and to describe the most critical academic discussions relating to the test.[1040] Taught from the most elementary stages of legal education

1036 Hufen, *Staatsrecht II. Grundrechte* (n 399) 25.

1037 Böckenförde, 'Grundrechte als Grundsatznormen: Zur gegenwärtigen Lage der Grundrechtsdogmatik' (n 420) 2. Art. 1 (3) [Legally binding force of basic rights]: The following basic rights shall bind the legislature, the executive, and the judiciary as directly applicable law. [Die nachfolgenden Grundrechte binden Gesetzgebung, vollziehende Gewalt und Rechtsprechung als unmittelbar geltendes Recht.]

1038 Sebastian Kielmansegg, 'Die Grundrechtsprüfung' [2008] Juristische Schulung 23, 23. Volkmann (n 1035) 261 ff describes how this legal doctrine won out over other competing proposals. See, e.g., Joachim Lege, 'Nochmals: Staatliche Warnungen' [1999] Deutsches Verwaltungsblatt 569, who analyzes two similar cases resolved by the Federal Administrative Court [hereafter also referred to as "BVerwG"] (BVerwGE 87, 37 – *Diethylenglykol* (1990) and BVerwGE 90, 112 – *Osho II* (1992)) where two different BVerwG senates applied two different doctrinal approaches (one, an older approach; the other, the Three-Step Test). Lege explains why the latter should be preferred; several years later, both opinions were reviewed by the BVerfG (see *infra* subsection 3).

1039 Ipsen, 'Grundzüge einer Grundrechtsdogmatik' (n 1035) 266.

1040 ibid. Ipsen explains that the test "appears in teaching books as if (…) prescribed by the Basic Law itself" […erscheint in Lehrbüchern geradezu als durch das Grundgesetz selbst vorgegeben]. Similarly, Ernst-Wolfang Böckenförde, 'Schutzbereich, Eingriff, verfassungsimmanente Schranken. Zur Kritik gegenwärtiger Grundrechtsdogmatik' (2003) 42 Der Staat 165, 166, highlights the outstanding role that Profs. Bodo Pieroth and Bernard Schlink's course book on basic rights ("Grundrechte. Staatrecht II," 1st edn, 1985, revised since 2013 by their former students, Profs. Thorsten Kingreen and Ralf Poscher) has had in the success of this terminology, among other achievements. Writing in 2003, Böckenförde notes that 17 editions of the course book had been published across the 18 years since it was first published, and emphasizes how it had shaped and still shapes thought on the onward,[1041] the test is used by legal practitioners everywhere to analyze cases of restrictions on basic rights.[1042]

While this legal doctrine reduces complexity, it does not entirely eliminate the difficulties of reviewing infringements of fundamental rights. First, even using the most canonical version of the method[1043] requires both sufficient knowledge of several technical terms and its appropriate application to concrete cases.[1044] Second, it only applies to encroachments on those guarantees that have the structure of a negative or subjective right to liberty (defensive rights or liberty rights) [*Abwehrrechte*]. In contrast, it is only partially - and then under significant adjustments - appropriate for reviewing equality rights [*Gleichheitsrechte*][1045] and is generally of no use when reviewing other functions of basic rights, such as duties of protection [*Schutz*] or provision [*Leistung*].[1046] Third, the BVerfG has not always followed or applied this method consistently; indeed, some of this court's innovations triggered a highly complex academic debate some years ago,

---

legal doctrine of basic rights among generations of young jurists and subsequently of public officials and judges." [Um dies zu erläutern, beziehe ich mich im Folgenden auf die Darstellung bei *Pieroth/Schlink; dies deshalb, weil der Pieroth/Schlink,* innerhalb von 18 Jahren in 17 Auflagen erschienen, das grundrechtsdogmatische Denken von Generationen junger Juristen und in der Folge dann von Beamten und Richtern geprägt hat und weiterhin prägt]. Indeed, Pieroth and Schlink's systematization is adopted with some changes by, inter alia, the course books written by Hufen, *Staatsrecht II. Grundrechte* (n 399); Epping (n 399); and Schmidt (n 399). Basic Law commentaries tend to follow this schema as well, cf. Hans Jarass, 'Vormerkungen vor Art. 1: Allgemeine Grundrechtslehren' in Hans Jarass and Bodo Pieroth (eds), *Grundgesetz für die Bundesrepublik Deutschland* (2020) Rn. 14 ff; Dreier (n 888).

1041 Kielmansegg (n 1038) 23, in Germany, and to be tested in the first final state examination [1. Staatsexamen].

1042 Voßkuhle and Kaiser (n 1035) 314.

1043 That is, the version that most closely follows the jurisprudence of the BVerfG on the matter.

1044 Along these lines, see Kielmansegg (n 1038).

1045 Some authors propose a two-level test here, while others remain true to the Three-Step Test. All, however, differ somewhat in the approach they use to review defensive rights. See, e.g., Jarass, 'Vormerkungen Vor Art. 1: Allgemeine Grundrechtslehren' (n 1040) Rn. 15; Dreier (n 888) Rn. 151–153; Kingreen and Poscher (n 399) 3–5.

1046 See Ulrich Jan Schröder, 'Der Schutzbereich der Grundrechte' [2016] Juristische Ausbildung 641, 641. Furthermore, scholars such as Voßkuhle and Kaiser (n 1035), suggest that in the case of rights of equality, this terminology is not useful at all. A different approach is proposed by Jarass, 'Vormerkungen Vor Art. 1: Allgemeine Grundrechtslehren' (n 1040) Rn. 15–15a.

birthing a doctrinal alternative that was well received by some scholars.[1047] The following section presents the traditional form of the test, along with information on the major controversies it has generated.[1048]

2.1. First step: determining the scope of protection

The goal of this step is to clarify both *what* is protected by a given basic right[1049] – the so-called material or substantive scope of protection [*sachlicher Schutzbereich*][1050] – and *who* is protected by the right [*personeller Schutzbereich*], i.e., whether the affected person is a holder or bearer of it.[1051] The treatment of this latter question has already been reviewed in the last chapter,[1052] leaving the material scope of protection to be described.

It has been suggested that, in general, defensive rights protect or guarantee behaviors [*Verhaltensweisen*] such as freedom of speech; relations [*Zuordnungen*] such as property; or states, conditions, and situations [*Zustände*] such as life.[1053] This protection could involve not only negative but also positive freedoms.[1054] Specifically, when defining the scope of protection of a specific right, initial guidance is found in the wording of the pro-

1047 See *infra* subsection 3.

1048 The following description essentially adheres to the general structure suggested by Kielmansegg (n 1038).

1049 ibid 24.

1050 The term "scope of protection" [Schutzbereich] has been criticized for its use of a "spatial" metaphor. Ipsen, *Staatsrecht II* (n 384) 39, Rn. 130, explains that basic "rights do not open up 'spaces' or 'areas'. Nor is the conventional spatializing notion of their quality appropriate. In basic rights cases, the question arises of which basic rights can be confronted by which state measures. (...) [R]ather, it is necessary to proceed with the relevant subsumption under constitutional concepts." [Grundrechte eröffnen weder „Räume" noch „Bereiche," noch ist überhaupt die gängige verräumlichende Vorstellung ihrer Qualität angemessen. In Grundrechtsfällen stellt sich stets die Frage, welche Grundrechte welchen staatlichen Maßnahmen entgegengesetzt werden können. (...) [G]efordet ist vielmehr die Subsumtion unter verfassungsrechtliche Begriffe]. The German legal doctrine also uses other terms to refer to the first step of the test – some of which do not imply a "spatial" metaphor. See, Schröder (n 1046) 641 [Normbereich, Grundrechtsinhalt/-gehalt, Gewährleistungsgehalt, Geltungs-, Anwendungs-, oder Wirkungsbereich].

1051 Kielmansegg (n 1038) 24.

1052 See § 9.

1053 Schröder (n 1046) 642.

1054 ibid.

vision.[1055] This commonly provides an indicative concept demonstrating which area of life [*Lebensbereich*] is referred to by the norm.[1056]

What constitutes an "area of life" is itself not entirely unproblematic,[1057] yet the real challenge is to define what is protected by the norm *within* the relevant area of life. There are two main approaches to this question: the traditional one has a more expansive conception of the freedoms potentially included in a particular area of life whereas other approaches have a more limited definition of the scope of protection.

In the traditional approach, basic rights should be understood as broads freedom to discretionary conduct within a given area of life.[1058] Because basic rights may be restricted, this does not mean absolute protection within the corresponding area of life; however, public power needs a constitutional justification to implement restrictions.[1059] According to its supporters, this understanding benefits both individual autonomy and democracy itself. Since any justifiable restriction requires the specific enactment of a statute [*Gesetzvorbehalt*], it strengthens the parliament and the concomitant separation of powers.[1060]

Against this background, *Schröder* proposes two steps to determine the protected area.[1061] Firstly, the scopes of protection of the various basic rights should be delimited [*Abgrenzung der Schutzbereiche*].[1062] In the first instance, this delimitation is achieved by applying the criterion of specialty. After this, the fundamental right to general freedom of action guaranteed by Art 2 (1) GG[1063] can act subsidiarily as a catch-all right.[1064]

Once the delimitation is completed, the scope of protection of the right in question is defined by traditional methods of interpretation (grammatical, historical-genealogical, teleological, and systematic).[1065] Importantly, in this traditional approach, each method is evaluated according to how much it favors the broadest interpretation of the scope of protec-

1055 Kielmansegg (n 1038).
1056 ibid 24.
1057 ibid.
1058 ibid.
1059 Schröder (n 1046) 641.
1060 ibid 642.
1061 ibid 642–644.
1062 ibid 642.
1063 On this right, see § 8, subsection 3.2., and *infra* subsection 3.1.
1064 Schröder (n 1046) 642.
1065 ibid 642 ff.

tion.[1066] Some other characteristic methods of constitutional interpretation should also be considered, for instance, the "norm-concretization" [*Normkonkretisierung*].[1067]

This approach corresponds to the jurisprudence of the BVerfG, which has been its "author and motor," and is followed by most scholars.[1068] Besides, the court regards general freedom of action as a comprehensive catch-all right when specific rights do not cover a concrete freedom.[1069] The result is an almost complete protection of freedoms by basic rights: the state must always have a constitutional justification for restricting them.[1070]

2.2. Second step: identifying the existence of an interference

After defining which basic right has been affected, the next step is to identify whether the effects of an act attributable to an addressee of the obligation of fundamental rights are potentially interfering with the right's scope of protection in a way that is not allowed by the constitution.[1071] In this sense, defining the impairment of a basic right as an *interference* depends,[1072] in principle, on two dimensions: the nature and the author of the act.[1073] In Germany, the answer to the second dimension is clear: only public power is considered to be directly bound by basic rights.[1074] By contrast, defining the first dimension is much more complex since it requires the fulfilment of criteria for both establishing a causal connection to an act of public power and for attributing responsibility.[1075] These criteria have been subject to considerable change over time, commonly described

---

1066 ibid 645.
1067 ibid 643.
1068 ibid 644.
1069 ibid 645.
1070 ibid.
1071 Voßkuhle and Kaiser (n 1035) 313.
1072 Jarass, 'Vormerkungen Vor Art. 1: Allgemeine Grundrechtslehren' (n 1040) Rn. 26, warns that the concept of interference or encroachment is not always used by case law and scholarship with the same meaning.
1073 Kielmansegg (n 1038) 24.
1074 Exceptionally, private parties may be considered addressees of basic rights when they are fulfilling a public task. In general, private persons are bound to basic rights only indirectly, according to the doctrine of the mediate effect on third parties. See Kingreen and Poscher (n 399) 52 ff.
1075 Kielmansegg Graf (n 1038) 25.

as the transition from the classical to the modern concept of interference [*moderner Grundrechtseingriffsbegriff*].[1076]

In this vein, *Voßkuhle and Kaiser* explain that the classical concept of interference required four preconditions: to be considered an interference, an impairment must be the consequence of a (i) direct, (ii) intentional act (iii) with a legal form, which is (iv) imposed through state command and coercion [*Befehl und Zwang*].[1077] In the transition from the liberal to the social state, this concept appeared too restrictive to adequately protect the individual. Consequently, the classical definitional criteria for interference were considerably loosened to comprise any act of the public power that could affect the scope of a right's protection, even without the concurrence of the other preconditions of the traditional approach.[1078]

Nevertheless, this highly comprehensive approach is, when revising a concrete case, somewhat limited. After all, classifying an act of the public power as an interference is an evaluative and normative process[1079] that has occasioned the development of a complex legal doctrine.[1080] Essentially, any act of public power will always be considered an interference if it displays all elements of the classical concept. In the remaining cases, *Kielmansegg* suggests that an act should be considered an interference depending on at least three criteria: (i) how many elements from the classical concept it combines; (ii) the characteristics of the causal chain; and (iii) how intensively the constitutionally protected interest is affected.[1081] However, despite the longstanding use of these criteria, several ambiguities remain when defining the contours of the modern concept of interference.[1082]

1076 Voßkuhle and Kaiser (n 1035) 312.

1077 ibid. Similarly, Dreier (n 888) 124 provides several references in fn 616, as well as indicating that many details remain unclear or disputed. See also BVerfGE 105, 279 (299) - Osho (2002).

1078 Voßkuhle and Kaiser (n 1035) 313.

1079 Kielmansegg (n 1038) 25.

1080 ibid. Some basic criteria to guide this process in Voßkuhle and Kaiser (n 1035) 313–315.

1081 Kielmansegg (n 1038) 25.

1082 Dreier (n 888) 127. [Insgesamt herrscht unverändert weder Klarheit noch Einigkeit über die genauen Konturen eines erweiterten Eingriffsbegriffs, dessen Kriterien für vielfältige Wertungen offenbleiben.]

2.3. Third step: justification of interferences

An affirmative assessment of the first two steps; namely, recognition that the scope of protection of a right has been indeed affected, and that this can be considered an interference, does not already mean that a fundamental right has been violated. This can only be established upon completing the third step, which determines whether the interference has a constitutional justification.

There are several standards for meeting such a justification. These standards are not expressly provided as such by the GG, but rather correspond to doctrinal constructions[1083] with varying names and configurations but whose main elements remain almost the same.[1084] The account below follows *Kielmannsegg*,[1085] who suggests splitting this level into two main steps: an initial check on whether a basic right may be restricted, and an additional check to confirm whether the relevant limits to restrictions have been respected.

2.3.1. Restriction clauses

Several of the GG's fundamental rights contain a clause that demands a statutory basis for interferences.[1086] These clauses prescribe that the given right may be interfered with only by a law or pursuant to a law [*durch Gesetz oder auf Grund eines Gesetzes*].[1087] Additionally, some rights[1088]

1083 Kielmansegg (n 1038) 25.

1084 Cf., e.g., Kingreen and Poscher (n 399) 85–99; Hufen, *Staatsrecht II. Grundrechte* (n 399) 107–128.

1085 See Kielmansegg Graf (n 1038) 25 ff. The content of each standard that will be described next also recurs in other sources.

1086 Kielmansegg (n 1038).

1087 See, e.g., Art. 10 [Privacy of correspondence, posts and telecommunications] (1) The privacy of correspondence, posts and telecommunications shall be inviolable. (2) *Restrictions may be ordered only pursuant to a law.* If the restriction serves to protect the free democratic basic order or the existence or security of the Federation or of a Land, the law may provide that the person affected shall not be informed of the restriction and that recourse to the courts shall be replaced by a review of the case by agencies and auxiliary agencies appointed by the legislature (emphasis added).

1088 See Article 13 [Inviolability of the home]: (7) Interferences and restrictions shall otherwise only be permissible to avert a danger to the public or to the life of an individual (…).

provide the possibility of restrictions directly in the constitution [*verfassungsunmittelbare Schranken*], without demanding a statutory basis for the corresponding interference.[1089]

2.3.2. Basic rights without restriction clauses [*vorbehaltlose Grundrechte*]

An increased doctrinal difficulty impacts rights that neither contain a clause demanding a statutory basis for restrictions [*Gesetzesvorbehalt*] nor foresee the possibility of restriction [*verfassungsunmittelbare Schranken*].[1090] At first glance, this omission appears to signify that no interference with these rights is justified.[1091] However, because such a constraint would make it impossible to manage conflicts between basic rights, case law and scholarship have developed a doctrinal construction suggesting that such rights have limits inherent in the constitution [*verfassungsimmanente Schranken*].[1092] According to a systematic interpretation of the constitution as a unity, these limits arise from other constitutional interests,[1093] especially the rights of third parties and the duties of protection they involve. Nonetheless, the implicit nature of these limits demands this concept be used restrictively.

While many criteria for applying limits inherent in the constitution remain under discussion, some have been widely adopted. One criterion is that a right must conflict with another constitutional interest, and the restriction must serve to protect the latter. Another is that a direct appeal to a limit inherent in the constitution to justify an interference is insufficient but requires a statutory basis in any case.

2.3.3. Limits to restrictions [*Schranken-Schranken*]

In any event, the protection of fundamental rights would be incomplete if it only demanded a statutory basis for restrictions, since this would not

1089 Kielmansegg (n 1038) 26.

1090 See, e.g., Article 4 [Freedom of faith and conscience]: (1) Freedom of faith and of conscience and freedom to profess a religious or philosophical creed shall be inviolable.

1091 Kielmansegg (n 1038) 26.

1092 ibid. The unique exception, as will be seen, is the right to dignity.

1093 ibid followed here and in the subsequent paragraphs of this subsection.

exclude even arbitrary acts of legislators or the executive acting in virtue of statutory empowerment.[1094] So there must be additional barriers which are commonly known as "limits to restrictions" [*Schranken-Schranken*].[1095] These correspond first to the provisions of Art. 19 (1) and (2) GG: the prohibition of statutes that only apply to a single case; the obligation to quote the affected basic right in the statute that interferes or authorizes an interference; and the guarantee that the essence of the fundamental right remains unaffected.[1096] The difficulties involved in complying with so many requirements are balanced by the general acceptance that it suffices if at least one interpretation of the law under examination can be considered compatible with the GG.[1097]

2.3.3.1. Additional controls for the intrusive state activity

In addition to those *Schranken-Schranken* that the GG expressly prescribes, others have been doctrinally constructed from the principle of the rule of law [*Rechtsstaat*].[1098] Within the jurisprudence of the BVerfG, the most important principle is that of proportionality [*Verhältmäßigkeitsgrundsatz – Übermaßverbot*].[1099] Along with these material principles, there are several formal ones linked to the GG's provisions for the law-making process.[1100]

2.3.3.2. The principle of proportionality

There is an overwhelming quantity of literature on the principle of proportionality in German law.[1101] While the principle traces developments

1094 ibid.
1095 ibid 27.
1096 ibid. For a condensed and didactic summary of the core meaning of these articles, see Kingreen and Poscher (n 399) 77–80.
1097 Kielmansegg (n 1038) 27.
1098 ibid 26. However, some scholars deduce them, or at least the principle of proportionality, from other sources; namely, the general principles of law or the essence of basic rights. See Dreier (n 888) 145, who also remarks that, in any case, the principle of proportionality is generally recognized as having constitutional status.
1099 Kingreen and Poscher (n 399) 73.
1100 Kielmansegg (n 1038) 27.
1101 A relevant bibliography can be found in Dreier (n 888) 145, at fn 207.

in German public law that predate the GG's entry into force,[1102] it has since played a crucial role in the BVerfG's jurisprudence.[1103] Sophisticated doctrinal discussions surround each element of the principle. Still, its core three-step analytical structure, consisting of appropriateness, necessity, and proportionality in a strict sense [*Geeignetheit, Erforderlichkeit und Verhältnismäßigkeit i.e.S*],[1104] has been widely accepted.

To explain these terms, the criterion of appropriateness demands that the chosen means is suitable for achieving a proposed (and legitimate) end, while complying with the necessity standard requires proving that no other less restrictive means can deliver the same effectiveness as the chosen one. Finally, proportionality in a strict sense demands careful analysis of the relevant means-end relationship: there must be a reasonable balance between the public interest supported by the proposed means and the resulting interference with basic rights.[1105]

3. *Alternative approaches*

Through its very existence, a majoritarian approach that supports the widest interpretation of the scope of protection implies the existence of other, more restrictive views. The latter range from those perspectives that reduce the protected content to a core area to those that suggest a functional understanding of basic rights, up to those that champion the

1102 Frotscher and Pieroth (n 384) 75, 441–443, recall that the first seeds of the principle already existed in the General State Laws for the Prussian States [Das Allgemeine Landrecht für die Preußischen Staaten] of 1794 with the intent of disciplining the use of violence by the police. However, it was not until almost a century later that the Supreme Administrative Court of Prussia developed the principle into its modern form.

1103 According to Frotscher and Pieroth (n 384), the BVerfG first used the principle in constitutional law in the *Elfes* case (BVerfG 6, 32) of 1957, where it also specified the principal criteria. For a list of important cases, see Dreier (n 888) Rn. 145, fn 709. This subsection primarily follows the exposition of the principle presented in ibid Rn.145–150.

1104 Dreier (n 888) Rn. 146.

1105 Because this last step unavoidably involves subjective value judgments, it has been severely criticized. Kingreen and Poscher (n 399) 75, for one, suggest that balancing lacks "rational and binding standards" [rationale und verbindliche Maßstäbe]. However, others, such as Dreier (n 888) Rn. 149, remark that while the latter issue arises, it can be controlled; furthermore, replacing or eliminating the final step would lead to worse consequences.

demarcation of the scope of protection according to general clauses.[1106] Among these, *Böckenförde's* "guaranteed content" is the most consistent and influential doctrine.[1107] In essence, this approach, when compared with its traditional counterparts, proposes that the area of life pertinent to a basic right should be differentiated more strictly from the protected content.

This alternative doctrinal approach is described below. In summary, it claims that the scope of protection of the GG's special basic rights must be conceived in a more limited way. It is also worth recounting the original dispute that occurred in the 1950s over whether the scope of protection of Art 2 (1) GG – the catch-all, subsidiary right of the Bill of Rights of the GG – should be understood narrowly or widely.

3.1. The scope of protection of Art 2 (1) GG

3.1.1. The *Elfes* Case

Since the *Elfes* case (1957),[1108] the BVerfG has affirmed that Art 2 (1) GG must be understood as a right to "general freedom of action" [*allgemeine Handlungsfreiheit*] in a broad sense.[1109] Although this was the most important doctrinal conclusion of the case, it was not the only one whose meaning was crucial. It is interesting to observe that neither the facts of the case nor the wording of Art 2 (1) GG would have helped predict the judgment which the BVerfG reached.

The case originated in the constitutional complaint made by *Wilhelm Elfes*. A politician of North Rhine-Westphalia, *Elfes* was also an active mem-

1106 A critical summary of descriptions of these perspectives can be found in Hufen, *Staatsrecht II. Grundrechte* (n 399) 71 ff. Sachs (n 896) Rn 77a, fn 228 provides a list of scholars justifying some of these variants.

1107 On this, see Wolfgang Kahl, 'Vom weiten Schutzbereich zum engen Gewährleistungsgehalt: Kritik einer neuen Richtung der deutschen Grundrechtsdogmatik' (2004) 43 Der Staat 167, 169. On Böckenförde's approach see *infra* subsection 3.2.

1108 BVerfGE 6, 32 – *Elfes* (1957). The basic consequences and the core meaning of this ruling are mentioned in § 8, subsection 3.2.1, when describing the origins of the GRoP.

1109 Art. 2 (1) GG. Every person shall have the right to free development of his personality insofar as he does not violate the rights of others or offend against the constitutional order or the moral law. [Jeder hat das Recht auf die freie Entfaltung seiner Persönlichkeit, soweit er nicht die Rechte anderer verletzt und nicht gegen die verfassungsmäßige Ordnung oder das Sittengesetz verstößt.]

ber of an organization that opposed the foreign policy of West Germany.[1110] *Elfes* had already presented his ideas within and beyond Germany when his application for a new passport was rejected based on a statute of ordinary law that permitted such denials when national security or interest was potentially at risk. Having failed before the respective administrative courts, *Elfes* brought the case before the BVerfG, claiming that this was a violation of Art. 11 (1) GG, which contains the right to freedom of movement.[1111] The headnotes of the judgment already contain the doctrinal innovations of the decision:

1. Article 11 of the Basic Law does not encompass the freedom to leave the country.
2. The freedom to leave the country is derived from the general freedom of action and thus guaranteed under Article 2 (1) of the Basic Law insofar as its exercise does not offend against the constitutional order.
3. The constitutional order within the meaning of Article 2 (1) of the Basic Law includes the entirety of legislation under the Constitution, i.e. all laws which are formally and substantively compatible with the Constitution.
4. Anyone may, by way of a constitutional complaint, assert that a legal provision restricting his general freedom of action is not part of the constitutional order.[1112]

First, the BVerfG denied that Art. 11 GG encompassed the freedom to leave the country based on the wording of Art. 11 GG, the proceedings of the Parliamentary Council, and a systematic analysis of the norm, in contrast

1110 Here and in the following, the facts of the case are described following BVerfGE 6, 32 (34) – *Elfes* (1957).

1111 Article 11 (1) [Freedom of movement]. All Germans shall have the right to move freely throughout the federal territory [Alle Deutschen genießen Freizügigkeit im ganzen Bundesgebiet].

1112 BVerfGE 6, 36 (36) – *Elfes* (1957). Translation by BVerfG staff https://www.bundesverfassungsgericht.de/SharedDocs/Entscheidungen/EN/1957/01/rs19570116_1bvr025356en.html accessed 26 July 2022. [1. Art. 11 GG betrifft nicht die Ausreisefreiheit. 2. Die Ausreisefreiheit ist als Ausfluß der allgemeinen Handlungsfreiheit durch Art. 2 Abs. 1 GG innerhalb der Schranken der verfassungsmäßigen Ordnung gewährleistet. 3. Verfassungsmäßige Ordnung im Sinne des Art. 2 Abs. 1 GG ist die verfassungsmäßige Rechtsordnung, d. h. die Gesamtheit der Normen, die formell und materiell der Verfassung gemäß sind. 4. Jedermann kann im Wege der Verfassungsbeschwerde geltend machen, eine seine Handlungsfreiheit beschränkende Rechtsnorm gehöre nicht zur verfassungsmäßigen Ordnung].

to what some scholarship had argued. Next, the BVerfG identified the main point that would need to be decided in this case:

> The BVerfG left open in its judgment of 20 July 1954, whether under the concept of free development of one's personality, human action is to be understood in a broad sense or whether Art. 2 (1) restricts itself to a minimal measure of protection of this freedom of action, without which the human being cannot at all develop his essence as a spiritual-moral person.[1113]

Until then, either position had been supported by the same scholars. In the next paragraph, the BVerfG chose a side:

> The Basic Law cannot have meant by the "free development of one's personality" only the development within that core area of personality – which constitutes the essence of man as a spiritual-moral person. For it would be incomprehensible how the development within this core area could violate the moral law, the rights of others or even the constitutional order of liberal democracy. Precisely these restrictions, imposed on the individual as a member of the community, show that the Basic Law, in Article 2 (1) GG, conceives freedom of action in a comprehensive sense.[1114]

The court then stated that the right to a general freedom of action functions as a subsidiary right when a given freedom is not protected by a special right of the GG. While each one of these rights enumerates how they may be constitutionally restricted by the public power, general freedom of action is limited by moral law, the rights of others, and the constitutional order.

1113 BVerfGE 6, 32 (36) – *Elfes* (1957). [Das Bundesverfassungsgericht hat in seinem Urteil vom 20. Juli 1954 (BVerfGE 4, 7 [15 f.]) offengelassen, ob unter den Begriff der freien Entfaltung der Persönlichkeit die menschliche Handlungsfreiheit im weitesten Sinne zu verstehen sei oder ob Art. 2 Abs. 1 GG sich auf den Schutz eines Mindestmaßes dieser Handlungsfreiheit beschränke, ohne dass der Mensch seine Wesensanlage als geistig-sittliche Person überhaupt nicht entfalten kann].

1114 ibid. [Das Grundgesetz kann mit der "freien Entfaltung der Persönlichkeit" nicht nur die Entfaltung innerhalb jenes Kernbereichs der Persönlichkeit gemeint haben, der das Wesen des Menschen als geistig-sittliche Person ausmacht, denn es wäre nicht verständlich, wie die Entfaltung innerhalb dieses Kernbereichs gegen das Sittengesetz, die Rechte anderer oder sogar gegen die verfassungsmäßige Ordnung einer freiheitlichen Demokratie sollte verstoßen können. Gerade diese, dem Individuum als Mitglied der Gemeinschaft auferlegten Beschränkungen zeigen vielmehr, daß das Grundgesetz in Art. 2 Abs. 1 GG die Handlungsfreiheit im umfassenden Sinne meint].

The court emphasized that the constitutional order must be understood within this clause as:

> (...) the general legal order, which has to observe the formal and the material norms of the Constitution, that is, it has to be a constitutional legal order. (...) the citizen may legitimately be restricted on his general freedom of action, not only by the Constitution or even only by "elementary constitutional principles" but by every formally and materially constitutional legal norm.[1115]

The BVerfG, explained that, according to the GG, this general *Gesetzesvorbehalt,* demands a range of requirements be fulfilled by the public power for the given restriction to be considered justified, referring to, *inter alia,* the value-bound order of the GG, the guarantee of human dignity, the supreme values of democracy, and the principles of the rule of law and the social state. Accordingly, only a legal norm that corresponds to these demands can be understood as part of the constitutional order. From the procedural perspective, this means:

> Everyone may file a constitutional complaint alleging that a statute restricting his freedom of action does not belong to the constitutional order because it violates (in form or content) individual constitutional provisions or general constitutional principles; therefore, that his fundamental right protected by Article 2 (1) of the Basic Law is being violated by that statute.[1116]

1115 BVerfG 6, 32, (37–38) – *Elfes* (1957). [b) Wird, wie unter 2 a) gezeigt, in Art. 2 Abs. 1 GG mit der freien Entfaltung der Persönlichkeit die allgemeine Handlungsfreiheit gewährleistet, die – soweit sie nicht Rechte anderer verletzt oder gegen das Sittengesetz verstößt – nur an die verfassungsmäßige Ordnung gebunden ist, so kann unter diesem Begriff nur die allgemeine Rechtsordnung verstanden werden, die die materiellen und formellen Normen der Verfassung zu beachten hat, also eine verfassungsmäßige Rechtsordnung sein muß (...). Der Bürger aber wird in seiner allgemeinen Handlungsfreiheit legitim eingeschränkt nicht nur durch die Verfassung oder gar nur durch "elementare Verfassungsgrundsätze," sondern durch jede formell und materiell verfassungsmäßige Rechtsnorm.]

1116 BVerfGE 6, 32 (38) – *Elfes* (1957). [Jedermann kann im Wege der Verfassungsbeschwerde geltend machen, ein seine Handlungsfreiheit beschränkendes Gesetz gehöre nicht zur verfassungsmäßigen Ordnung, weil es (formell oder inhaltlich) gegen einzelne Verfassungsbestimmungen oder allgemeine Verfassungsgrundsätze verstoße; deshalb werde sein Grundrecht aus Art. 2 Abs. 1 GG verletzt.]

3.1.2. The *Reiten im Walde* Case

Interpreting Art 2 (1) GG in the sense of its furthest-reaching extension became settled in BVerfG case law over the following years. However, some scholarship remained critical of this interpretation.[1117] The dispute came to the fore in a BVerfG judgment more than 30 years after *Elfes,* in the *Reiten im Walde* case (1989).[1118] While the majority of the First Senate deciding the case confirmed the BVerfG's case law on general freedom of action, Justice *Grimm* delivered a dissenting opinion.[1119] This reignited the old discussion on the general interpretation of Art 2 (1) GG.

The plaintiff brought a constitutional complaint before the BVerfG, stating:

> He is [was] considerably hindered by the riding regulations in (..) [respective state statutes], because he is [was] only allowed to ride on marked bridle paths and also had to obtain license plates for his horses, and pay a fee. The latter infringes the fundamental right of free development of one's personality (Article 2 (1) of the Basic Law). Citizens must be able to freely develop their interest and pleasure in riding, even in the forest. The proper and well-behaved rider does not endanger the rights of others and does not violate the constitutional order. The interests, which the challenged regulation sought to protect, could have been sufficiently safeguarded by less restrictive riding restrictions based on local conditions.[1120]

1117 BVerfGE 80, 137, (153–154) – *Reiten im Walde* (1989) describes this situation, quoting several scholars and their main reasons.

1118 BVerfGE 80, 137 – *Reiten im Walde* (1989).

1119 BVerfGE 80, 164 – *Reiten im Walde* (1989), dissenting opinion of Justice Dieter Grimm.

1120 BVerfGE 80, 137, (144) – *Reiten im Walde* (1989), description of the constitutional complaint by the BVerfG. [Er werde durch die Reitregelung in §§ 50, 51 LG 1980 erheblich behindert, weil er nur auf markierten Reitwegen reiten dürfe und außerdem Kennzeichen für seine Pferde beschaffen und eine Abgabe entrichten müsse. Dies verstoße gegen das Grundrecht der freien Entfaltung der Persönlichkeit (Art. 2 Abs. 1 GG). Der Bürger müsse sein Interesse und seine Freude am Reiten auch im Walde frei entfalten können. Der ordentliche und gesittete Reiter gefährde keine Rechte anderer und verstoße nicht gegen die verfassungsmäßige Ordnung. Den Belangen, welche die angegriffene Regelung schützen wolle, hätte durch weniger einschneidende, auf die örtlichen Gegebenheiten abstellende Reitbeschränkungen ausreichend Rechnung getragen werden können].

The BVerfG rejected the constitutional complaint but confirmed the established case law on Art 2 (1) GG, also refuting the literature that had supported the opposing view on the scope of protection of Art 2 (1) GG. Consequently, this meant that riding in the forest had to be understood as protected by the right to free development of one's personality.[1121] In its previous case law, the BVerfG had already developed the negative aspect of Art. 2 (1) GG, which in conjunction with Art. 1 (1) GG constitutes the general right of personality.[1122] However, the court explicitly affirmed that riding in the forest does not belong to the absolutely protected private area of life.[1123] Its decision entailed that the reviewed statutes that permitted restrictions on that right conformed with the "constitutional order."[1124]

The dissenting opinion, in contrast, is interesting due to its coherent and robust exposition of an alternative approach to Art. 2 (1) GG, and also because it indicates how to define the scope of protection of any basic right. Although Justice *Grimm* mostly disputed the perspective of the ruling opinion on Art. 2 (1) GG, the first paragraph of his opinion contains claims referring to all basic rights:

> Riding in the forest is not protected by basic rights. Basic rights differ from the multitude of other rights in that they protect the integrity, autonomy, and communication of the individual in their most fundamental interactions. It is precisely because of this fundamental significance of their object of protection, for an order based on human dignity, that basic rights are elevated from the plethora of rights and constitutionally endowed with enhanced guarantees vis-à-vis the public authority and,

1121 BVerfGE 80, 137, (152) – *Reiten im Walde* (1989): "According to the principles developed by the case law of the Federal Constitutional Court, Article 2.1 of the Basic Law guarantees general freedom of action in a comprehensive sense (settled case law since BVerfGE 6, 32 [36]; more recently, e.g., BVerfGE 74, 129 [151]; 75, 108 [154 f.]). Thus, not only a limited area of personal development is protected, but every form of human activity, regardless of the importance of the activity for the development of personality." [Nach den in der Rechtsprechung des Bundesverfassungsgerichts entwickelten Grundsätzen gewährleistet Art. 2 Abs. 1 GG die allgemeine Handlungsfreiheit im umfassenden Sinne (st. Rspr. seit BVerfGE 6, 32 [36]; aus neuerer Zeit etwa: BVerfGE 74, 129 [151]; 75, 108 [154 f.]). Geschützt ist damit nicht nur ein begrenzter Bereich der Persönlichkeitsentfaltung, sondern jede Form menschlichen Handelns ohne Rücksicht darauf, welches Gewicht der Betätigung für die Persönlichkeitsentfaltung zukommt.]

1122 See § 8, subsection 3.2.

1123 BVerfGE 80, 137, (155) – *Reiten im Walde* (1989).

1124 BVerfGE 80, 137, (155 ff) – *Reiten im Walde* (1989).

> in particular, with binding effect for the legislature. In this context, the understanding of what in detail deserves the intensified protection of fundamental rights may change according to historical circumstances. However, it is neither historically nor functionally the purpose of fundamental rights to place every conceivable human conduct under their special protection.[1125]

And specifically:

> Neither is such a gapless protection of fundamental rights for any human activity conveyed by Art 2 (1) GG.[1126]

Grimm justifies his position on several pages. First, Art 2 (1) GG does not, in his view, protect every human action or activity, but only those relevant to the development of personality. This may be comparable with the legal interests that special basic rights have, but concerning what they do not explicitly cover.[1127] His conclusion lies between the polar alternatives that the BVerfG considered as potential understandings of 2 (1) GG in *Elfes*: either comprehensive protection or only the core of personality.[1128] Moreover, *Grimm* argued that his third option had also been followed by the BVerfG in its case law on the GRoP, maintaining that the scope of protection of Art. 2 (1) – this time in connection with Art. 1 (1) GG – could not once and for all be defined, but must be dealt with on a case-by-case

1125 BVerfGE 80, 164, (164) – *Reiten im Walde* (1989); dissenting opinion of Justice Dieter Grimm. [Das Reiten im Walde genießt keinen Grundrechtsschutz. Die Grundrechte unterscheiden sich von der Vielzahl sonstiger Rechte dadurch, daß sie Integrität, Autonomie und Kommunikation des Einzelnen in ihren grundlegenden Bezügen schützen. Eben wegen dieser fundamentalen Bedeutung ihres Schutzobjekts für eine auf die Menschenwürde gegründete Ordnung werden sie aus der Menge der Rechte hervorgehoben und verfassungsrechtlich mit erhöhten Garantien gegenüber der öffentlichen Gewalt, insbesondere mit Bindungswirkung für den Gesetzgeber, ausgestattet. Dabei können die Auffassungen darüber, was den gesteigerten Schutz der Grundrechte im Einzelnen verdient, nach den historischen Umständen wechseln. Es ist aber weder historisch noch funktional der Sinn der Grundrechte, jedes erdenkliche menschliche Verhalten unter ihren besonderen Schutz zu stellen].

1126 BVerfGE 80, 164, (164–165) – *Reiten im Walde* Case (1989); dissenting opinion of Justice Dieter Grimm. [Ein solcher lückenloser Grundrechtsschutz für jede beliebige menschliche Tätigkeit wird auch nicht durch Art. 2 Abs. 1 GG vermittelt.]

1127 BVerfGE 80, 164, (165) – *Reiten im Walde* (1989); dissenting opinion of Justice Dieter Grimm.

1128 BVerfGE 80, 164, (165–166) – *Reiten im Walde* (1989); dissenting opinion of Justice Dieter Grimm.

basis. As a result, 2 (1) GG can be considered a catch-all right, but only for the "constitutive elements of personality," which are not protected by another individual liberty.[1129]

After referring to the procedural issues that attend the right to a general freedom of action (i.e., any infra-constitutional legal norm may be challenged by a complaint that it does not conform to the constitutional order and the banalization of basic rights that this involves),[1130] *Grimm* nonetheless recognized that his view involved the doctrinal challenge of distinguishing between freedoms important to the development of personality versus those that are not. Nevertheless, this hard determination of the scope of protection is present in most other basic rights.[1131] In the case of Art 2 (1), *Grimm* argued that the scope of protection should encompass those:

> areas of life or modes of conduct, of which the arbitrary regulation by the state may endanger the autonomy of the individual and thus foster a regime that could no longer claim to be founded on respect for human dignity. A conclusive enumeration is not possible due to changing conditions for the development of personality.[1132]

Just like other activities that the BVerfG's case law had previously regarded as protected by general freedom of action, riding in the forest does not fulfill the above-mentioned standard and therefore should not be considered protected by Art. 2 (1) GG. Therefore, the constitutional complaint, thinks *Grimm*, should have been rejected simply because 2 (1) GG does not cover riding in the forest.

But particularly crucial in *Grimm's* dissenting opinion is that the BVerfG's majority view had effects far beyond the question of the scope of

1129 BVerfGE 80, 164, (167) – *Reiten im Walde* (1989); dissenting opinion of Justice Dieter Grimm.

1130 BVerfGE 80, 164, (168–169) – *Reiten im Walde* (1989); dissenting opinion of Justice Dieter Grimm.

1131 BVerfGE 80, 164, (169) – *Reiten im Walde* (1989); dissenting opinion of Justice Dieter Grimm.

1132 ibid; dissenting opinion of Justice Dieter Grimm. [Im Kern wird es sich dabei stets um Lebensbereiche oder Verhaltensweisen handeln, deren beliebige Regulierbarkeit durch den Staat die Autonomie des Einzelnen gefährdete und damit einem System Vorschub leistete, das nicht mehr beanspruchen könnte, auf die Achtung der Menschenwürde gegründet zu sein. Eine abschließende Aufzählung scheitert am Wandel der Bedingungen für die Persönlichkeitsentfaltung.]

protection of the right to a general freedom of action.[1133] According to *Grimm*, a wide interpretation of this scope also implies a shift of power from the legislative to the constitutional jurisdiction: if Art. 2 (1) covers any human conduct not protected by a specific liberty right, a "constitutional complaint based in this fundamental right tends to extend to a general judicial review,"[1134] i.e., the BVerfG authorizes itself to potentially review any infra-constitutional norm.[1135]

3.2. The legal doctrine of guaranteed content [*Gewährleitungsgehaltslehre*]

As stated above, among the alternative approaches, *Wolfgang-Ernst Böckenförde*[1136] makes a particularly noteworthy contribution to defining the protected content of basic rights. *Böckenförde*, one of the most influential German legal scholars of the later 20th century,[1137] had criticized the doctrinal development of the understanding of basic rights in Germany for several years[1138] – not at least in his 11 *Sondervoten* (dissenting opinions) as a constitutional judge at the BVerfG.[1139] The general doctrine of basic rights had also been one of his concerns.

According to *Böckenförde*, the main issue with the traditional approach lies in how the scope of protection is conceptualized and contraposed with

1133 BVerfGE 80, 164, (168–169) – *Reiten im Walde* (1989); dissenting opinion of Justice Dieter Grimm.

1134 BVerfGE 80, 164, (168) – *Reiten im Walde* (1989); dissenting opinion of Justice Dieter Grimm. [Gewährleistet Art. 2 Abs. 1 GG die allgemeine Handlungsfreiheit im Rahmen der verfassungsmäßigen Ordnung, weitet sich die auf dieses Grundrecht gestützte Verfassungsbeschwerde tendenziell zur allgemeinen Normenkontrolle aus.]

1135 The doctrinal tension around the scope of protection of basic rights resurfaced several years later following two controversial BVerfG decisions: BVerfGE 105, 279 – *Osho* (2002); and BVerfGE 105, 252 – *Glykolwein* (2002).

1136 For another restrictive alternative, see Wolfgang Hoffmann-Riem's proposal, 'Enge oder weite Gewährleistungsgehalte der Grundrechte? [2004]' in Ino Augsberg and Sebastian Unger (eds), *Basistexte: Grundrechtstheorie* (2012).

1137 See Bernhard Schlink, 'Der Lehrer Ernst-Wolfgang Böckenförde' (2019) 58 Der Staat 441; Matthias Jestaedt, 'Glückwunsch Ernst-Wolfgang Böckenförde zum 80. Geburtstag' (2010) 65 Juristen Zeitung 890.

1138 See Böckenförde (n 420); Böckenförde, 'Grundrechte als Grundsatznormen: Zur gegenwärtigen Lage der Grundrechtsdogmatik' (n 420).

1139 Jestaedt (n 1137) 891, providing the list of the respective decisions at fn 2.

the concept of interference.[1140] This legal doctrine is especially problematic for rights that do not expressly demand a statutory basis [*Gesetzesvorbehalt*] for intrusions. In these situations, the boundaries of the scope of protection remain the unique, constitutionally acceptable tool for legislators to regulate potential conflicts between rights.

The leading scholarship and BVerfG case law deal with this problem very flexibly through the doctrine of the limits inherent in the constitution [*verfassungsimmanente Schranken*]. The treatment is so flexible, said *Böckenförde,* that almost any constitutional norm could be classified as an inherent limit.[1141] Moreover, applying these limits had generally been accepted even without a statutory basis, directly by judicial decision [*Richtervorbehalt*].[1142] Furthermore, this procedure could also be deployed for rights which, according to the constitution, may be restricted only by or pursuant to a statute [*Gesetzesvorbehalt*].[1143]

According to Böckenförde, the outcome is diametrically opposed to what supporters of the traditional approach would seek. While these scholars intended to offer the most extensive interpretation of the scope of protection, especially for rights that require no statutory basis for interferences [*vorbehaltlose Rechte*], the rights become limitable just as easily as basic rights under restriction clauses. The legislative power, which is genuinely legitimized to restrict basic rights in a democracy, thus becomes superfluous in this respect.[1144]

Against this background, *Böckenförde's* proposal has two main features that differ from the traditional approach. First, the area of life [*Sach- und Lebensbereich*] and what he calls the "guaranteed content" [*Gewährleistungsgehalt*] of the basic right should be differentiated more strictly.[1145] While the term "area of life" denotes the "thematic" ambit of the reality linked to the basic right (itself an element of the basic right's descriptive

1140 See Ernst-Wolfang Böckenförde, 'Schutzbereich, Eingriff, verfassungsimmanente Schranken. Zur Kritik gegenwärtiger Grundrechtsdogmatik' (n 1040) 166.

1141 ibid 168.

1142 ibid 169.

1143 ibid 170.

1144 ibid. For a critical-historical account of how the majority opinion came to the doctrinal solution of dealing with basic rights without legal reservation, and a description of some other proposals that were ultimately unsuccessful, see ibid 170–174.

1145 Ernst-Wolfang Böckenförde, 'Schutzbereich, Eingriff, Verfassungsimmanente Schranken. Zur Kritik gegenwärtiger Grundrechtsdogmatik' (n 1040) 174.

structure), the guaranteed content corresponds to the actual protected section of the descriptive structure of the norm. Besides, the guaranteed content may include one or more functions of basic rights (e.g., defense, protection, or participation).[1146]

Second, the guaranteed content may not be predefined in its most extensive form for all fundamental rights. Instead, each right must be interpreted independently, falling back to traditional methods of interpretation.[1147] An approach that *a priori* always aims to provide "the most extensive freedom" is inappropriate because each basic right originated from a legal reaction to concrete experiences of injustice. Thus, in this approach, the historical-genealogical canon of interpretation plays a primary role.[1148]

Böckenförde claims that this perspective is advantageous because it considerably increases legal certainty in determining the scope of protection of a right and possible constitutional justification for its restrictions.[1149] First, it reduces the need to revert to limits inherent in the constitution when dealing with those rights that do not explicitly allow for restrictions [*vorbehaltlose Rechte*], and hence contain no explicit requirement of a statutory basis for restrictions. Moreover, for rights that fall under this constitutional category, privileging the genealogical-historical canon eliminates the recourse to limits inherent in the constitution to restrict rights. Finally, defining the "guaranteed content" instead of the "scope of protection" delimits rights more precisely.

3.2.1. Critique of the doctrine of guaranteed content

Schröder lists several critiques of the doctrine of guaranteed content,[1150] centering on the excessive recourse to the historical canon of interpretation in *Böckenförde's* proposal. First, he asserts, such a vision excludes how both the risks to the individual and the views of the functions of fundamental

1146 ibid.
1147 ibid.
1148 ibid.
1149 ibid 190–192.
1150 Schröder (n 1046) 645. Also critical, Sachs (n 896) Rn. 77a, providing a list of critical literature in fn 229. Similarly, Dreier (n 888) Rn. 122, who additionally suggests that this approach misinterprets the essential meaning of basic rights as "pre-state" attributes in the sense of the primacy of individual freedom vis à vis state action.

rights have changed throughout German legal history: nowadays, an individualistic approach to basic rights is widely assumed to be closest to the spirit of the GG. Second, a broad interpretation of the scope of protection does not strip fundamental rights of their meaning, but enables a more robust control of state actions. Third, considering the manageability of basic rights, doctrinal issues over rights without restriction clauses do not need a more restrictive interpretation of the scope of protection. Moreover, balancing is a reasonable method at the stage of justification. In conclusion, though its simplicity produces some ambiguities, the traditional doctrine delivers a more straightforward method to identify the scope of protection of fundamental rights.[1151]

3.2.2. Balance

Restrictive approaches have not only received critique but also praise. *Volkmann,* for one, appraises them positively:[1152] the crisis in the doctrine of basic rights was the consequence of profound changes in the relationship between the state and the citizen; the main innovation was the development of the objective law dimension of constitutional rights.[1153] In this context, the efficacy of the canonical Three-Step Test declined. *Volkmann* argues that two phenomena in the German legal doctrine of basic rights are at fault here: the permanent and progressive expansion of what is considered the scope of protection [*Schutzbereich*]; and the extension of what is considered an interference [*Eingriff*].[1154] These factors meant that clashes between basic rights tended to be resolved increasingly at the justification level, where legal practitioners enjoy more leeway than at the level of determination of the scope of protection. The overall effect of this change has been to decrease the rationalizing utility of the traditional Three-Step Test.[1155]

1151 For an exhaustive critique, see Kahl (n 1107) 184 ff.

1152 See Volkmann (n 1035) 264–266.

1153 ibid 263.

1154 ibid 263–264. Volkmann recalls that this system enjoyed general acceptance because of its capacities in this dimension, and for that reason it imposed itself over other existing doctrinal proposals to deal with cases of basic rights.

1155 ibid 264.

Nonetheless, the traditional doctrine should, according to *Volkmann*, be retained.[1156] However, since the first step has become increasingly dysfunctional as a filter to the next, *Volkmann* proposes incorporating some substantial corrections.[1157] As suggested by *Böckenförde*, the major adjustment should be to differentiate more strictly between the normative and the descriptive content of each basic right, under particular appeal to the historical-genealogical canon, which provides a clearer outline of the scope of protection.[1158] Therefore, a presumption favoring freedom (in the sense of the most extensive interpretation of the scope of protection) should in this view apply only insofar as the given subject "remains in his legal sphere."[1159]

4. Interferences with human dignity

The challenging legal treatment of dignity is generated not only by the clause's internal doctrinal complexities, but also by external developments that could obscure its legal meaning. Correspondingly, the scholarship has emphasized the risks associated with an inflationary recourse to dignity.[1160] This phenomenon also exists outside the legal system because discourse on human dignity has become ubiquitous in the political environment.[1161] This inflationary recourse to dignity might entail a loss of its normative power in general and even its de-valorization within the legal system.[1162]

In this context, the doctrinal challenge is to identify how interferences with dignity can be tested methodically. This encompasses certain difficulties implicated in the clause's unique characteristics and the divergent approaches to its legal form. For this reason, it is beneficial to review how dignity is differently affected when considered either as a principle or a subjective right. In this latter case, though impacts on human dignity are subject to the Three-Step Test, the process has some exceptional features.

1156 ibid 265.

1157 ibid.

1158 ibid.

1159 ibid 268, in this sense, see Volkmann (n 1035). Some of the BVerfG's decisions, while not referring explicitly to these distinctions, could be perfectly reconstructed in line with them.

1160 See, e.g., Dreier (n 406) Rn. 48–49.

1161 ibid Rn. 49.

1162 ibid.

4.1. Dignity as a principle

As already examined, a minority opinion denies that human dignity has the character of a basic right.[1163] One reason for this view is that dignity cannot, in practice, be treated like other basic rights. While this seems reasonable, an alternative proposal for approaching dignity is required to legitimize the critique. In other words, since the Three-Step Test cannot be used to analyze restrictions on it, it remains unclear how an encroachment on human dignity as a norm of pure objective law content can be determined. In view of this, at least three approaches should be noted. The first of these suggests that dignity could only be infringed *together* with a particular basic right; the second, only *by* infringing a basic right; the third, depending on *how* the responsible state decision-maker acted.[1164]

Dreier's proposal can be understood in the sense that dignity as a constitutional principle could only be violated together with an individual basic right. In his approach, human dignity is "a directive principle, a maxim of interpretation, a leading principle for the understanding of basic rights (…)."[1165] As such, dignity constitutes the highest standard of state power and operates globally as a "limit to restrictions."[1166]

In a similar vein, *Isensee* suggests that constitutional dignity can be best conceptualized as an "idea" that acts within the constitution as the highest juridical norm.[1167] In *Isensee's* view (as recognized even by those who support the attribution of subjective-law content),[1168] "the objective-law form is the prime mode of the validity of Art. 1 (1) GG."[1169] In this context, human

---

1163 See § 7, subsection 3.1.

1164 The critique of the approaches of Isensee and Dreier presented in the following paragraphs draws on Manfred Baldus, 'Menschenwürdegarantie und Absolutheitsthese. Zwischenbericht zu einer zukunftsweisenden Debatte' (2011) 136 Archiv des Öffentlichen Rechts 529, 541–544.

1165 Dreier (n 406) 160.

1166 ibid Rn. 125. Similarly, Jarass, 'Art. 1' (n 406) Rn.5, who, while not denying the "basic right" character of dignity, considers its subjective law content to be of limited meaning, ibid Rn. 3. He views its protection primarily as deriving from the subsequent basic rights. Accordingly, a treatment that is not considerate of human dignity is first to be tested by the corresponding "normal" basic right. Thus, the dignity clause acts overall as a limit to restrictions: its violation represents the simultaneous violation of another basic right.

1167 Isensee, 'Würde des Menschen' (n 436) 77, Rn. 112 ff.

1168 Cf. e.g., Häberle (n 412) 327, Rn. 11.

1169 Isensee, 'Würde des Menschen' (n 436) 66. Rn. 99. [Die objektivrechtliche Form ist der primäre Geltungsmodus des Art. 1 Abs. 1 GG.]

dignity is concretized in each basic right,[1170] and as an idea, it does not allow for any relativization.[1171] However, these basic rights do not share the absoluteness of human dignity.[1172] Consequently, dignity can only be violated when, according to the conventional doctrinal methods to identify them,[1173] a fundamental right or another juridical norm in which human dignity takes form is infringed.[1174]

Finally, *Nettesheim* asserts that the relevant (state) decision-maker must always consider the interest of the affected individual and not only those of the public or third parties.[1175] In this procedural dimension, Art. 1 (1) GG guides the interpretation of constitutional and ordinary law. The exercise of state power is only legitimate when considering this procedural manifestation of the human dignity clause. While adherence to this maxim cannot be checked directly, it should be *implicitly* checked when monitoring an interference with an interest acknowledged by law, such as one protected by fundamental rights.[1176]

4.2. Dignity as a right

The prevailing opinion of dignity as a right is directly opposed to the methodological argument of the minority view described above. It is backed by BVerfG case law and supports the subjective-law character of human dignity.[1177] It claims that the only way to treat human dignity with a certain doctrinal coherence and testability is by subjecting it to the same treatment as any other defensive right.[1178] Nevertheless, in practice, the BVerfG has never tested a violation of dignity alone, but always in conjunction with another fundamental right.[1179] Since the scope of protection of dignity has previously been reviewed,[1180] the ensuing two levels of the

1170 ibid 86, Rn. 132.
1171 ibid 63–64, Rn. 95.
1172 ibid 66, Rn. 99.
1173 ibid 79–80, Rn. 118 for examples.
1174 ibid 79, Rn. 117.
1175 See Nettesheim (n 881) 98–112. This scholar also considers dignity a basic right besides its functions as a principle.
1176 ibid 102.
1177 See § 7, subsection 3.2.
1178 Hufen, 'Erosion der Menschenwürde?' (n 466).
1179 Dreier (n 406) Rn. 126.
1180 See § 7, subsection 3.2.

three-step test (interference and constitutional justification) are described next.

4.2.1. Interferences with human dignity as a right

As detailed below, the scholarship and the BVerfG case law predominantly hold that no interference with the scope of protection of the right to dignity is justifiable. However, this does not mean that interferences do not occur.[1181] The BVerfG has compatibilized these two apparently opposed ideas by insisting that nobody can take the dignity of a human being, but that the "claim of respect that arises from it [from dignity] is violable."[1182] Identifying encroachments on dignity remains an ineludible task, particularly due to the difficult of achieving a positive description of the content of the dignity clause. The most widely used method to recognize an interference with dignity is the so-called "object formula."[1183]

4.2.1.1. The object formula

4.2.1.1.1. Doctrinal antecedents and jurisprudential development

The origins of the object formula are traceable to the work of the scholar *Günther Dürig* in the mid-1950s. Following the normative consequences of Kant's[1184] conception of dignity,[1185] *Dürig* asserted that:

1181 Hufen, *Staatsrecht II. Grundrechte* (n 399) 143.

1182 BVerfGE 87, 209 (228) – *Tanz der Teufel* (1992) [Sie kann keinem Menschen genommen werden. Verletzbar ist aber der Achtungsanspruch, der sich aus ihr ergibt].

1183 Hufen, *Staatsrecht II. Grundrechte* (n 399) 143, who also warns against the apparently extended practice of confusing this formula with the scope of protection of dignity. Instead, Hufen underlines that the formula is only one way of recognizing interferences in the scope of protection.

1184 For scholarly work on this, see, e.g., Classen (n 872) 692; Hufen, 'Die Menschenwürde, Art. 1 I GG' (n 624) 6.

1185 "For all rational beings stand under the *law* so that each of them is to treat himself and all others *never merely as means,* but always *at the same time as ends in themselves,*" Kant (n 464) 41. [Denn vernünftige Wesen stehen alle unter dem *Gesetz,* daß jedes derselben sich selbst und alle andere *niemals bloß als Mittel,* sondern jederzeit *zugleich als Zweck an sich selbst* behandeln solle] (emphasis added). The BVerfG has also referred to Kant's ideas directly. In BVerfGE 45, 187

> Human dignity as such is affected when the concrete human being is degraded to an object, to a mere means, to a fungible variable. Perhaps what best shows the meaning of Art. 1 (1) is the terrible vocabulary of our time, which is based on technical ideas: Art. 1 (1) involves the degradation of the human being to a thing that can be totally "seized," "launched," "registered," "brainwashed," "replaced," "deployed," and "abandoned" (i.e., expelled)."[1186]

Dürig remarked, nonetheless, that it is unnecessary to recall obvious crimes against humanity to identify severe offences against human dignity. This is because the "perversion" of the GG's order of values begins whenever "the human being as a legal subject is disempowered."[1187] Shortly thereafter, in 1959, the BVerfG endorsed this approach for the first time.[1188] When reflecting on the right to be heard as a condition of the due process of law, it went on to say:

> [T]he dignity of the person demands that the authorities may not summarily dispose of his rights. In order to be able to influence the proceedings and their outcome, the individual shall not merely be the object of the judicial decision but shall have his say before the decision affecting his rights is made.[1189]

---

(228) – *Lebenslange Freiheitsstrafe* (1977), after repeating the *Objekt-Formel*, the court held that "the human being must always remain an end-in-himself." [Es widerspricht daher der menschlichen Würde, den Menschen zum bloßen Objekt im Staate zu machen (...). Der Satz, „der Mensch muß immer Zweck an sich selbst bleiben," gilt uneingeschränkt für alle Rechtsgebiete; denn die unverlierbare Würde des Menschen als Person besteht gerade darin, daß er als selbstverantwortliche Persönlichkeit anerkannt bleibt.].

1186 Dürig (n 471) 127. [Die Menschenwürde als solche ist getroffen, wenn der konkrete Mensch zum Objekt, zu einem bloßen Mittel, zur vertretbaren Größe herabgewürdigt wird. Am besten zeigt vielleicht der entsetzlich an technische Vorstellungen angelehnte Wortschatz unserer materialisierten Zeit, worum es in Art. 1 I geht. Es geht um die Degradierung des Menschen zum Ding, das total „erfaßt," „abgeschossen," „registriert," „im Gehirn gewaschen," „ersetzt," „eingesetzt" und „ausgesetzt" (d. h. vertrieben) werden kann.].

1187 ibid.

1188 Hufen, 'Die Menschenwürde, Art. 1 I GG' (n 624) 6, fn 56.

1189 BVerfGE 9, 89, (95) – *Gehör bei Haftbefehl* (1959). [Darüber hinaus fordert die Würde der Person, daß über ihr Recht nicht kurzerhand von Obrigkeits wegen verfügt wird; der einzelne soll nicht nur Objekt der richterlichen Entscheidung sein, sondern er soll vor einer Entscheidung, die seine Rechte betrifft, zu Wort kommen, um Einfluß auf das Verfahren und sein Ergebnis nehmen zu können.]

Some years later, in *Abhörurteil* (1970), the court substantially qualified this formula. Initially, it clarified that the general formula should not be applied uncritically to any particular case. It instead functions as a guide:[1190]

> (...) [E]verything depends on the determination of the circumstances under which human dignity can be violated. Evidently, this cannot be said in general terms, but only by observing a concrete case. General formulas such as the one that states that the "human being may not be degraded to a mere object of the state power" can only indicate the area in which cases of violation of human dignity may be found.[1191]

The court also relativized the scope to which instrumentalization was proscribed, adding that:

> Not infrequently, the human being is a mere object not only of circumstances and social development, but also of law, in the sense that he must obey it without regard to his interests. This alone does not establish a violation of human dignity. A human being must in addition be exposed to a treatment that, in principle, puts in question his quality as a subject, or, in a concrete case, the treatment must involve an arbitrary disregard of his dignity. Therefore, to be able to affect dignity, a human being's treatment by public authorities enforcing the law must be an expression of contempt for the value that belongs to the human being as such, i.e., "contemptible treatment" in this sense.[1192]

1190 According to Böckenförde, 'Die Würde des Menschen war Unantastbar' (n 420), this was indeed Dürig's intention: [Das war, ihm bewußt, nur ein Leitfaden, keine Subsumtionformel, als sie zuweilen mißverstanden und kritisiert worden ist; als Leitfaden bedurfte und bedarf sie jeweils näherer Konkretisierung. Herleitungen, die Dürig, bezogen auf Erfahrungen und Herausforderungen seiner Zeit, daraus gewann, brauchen hier nicht aufgezählt zu werden, sie sind größtenteils auch heute unbestritten.]

1191 BVerfG 30, 1, (25) – *Abhörurteil* (1970) [Was den in Art. 1 GG genannten Grundsatz der Unantastbarkeit der Menschenwürde anlangt, der nach Art. 79 Abs. 3 GG durch eine Verfassungsänderung nicht berührt werden darf, so hängt alles von der Festlegung ab, unter welchen Umständen die Menschenwürde verletzt sein kann. Offenbar läßt sich das nicht generell sagen, sondern immer nur in Ansehung des konkreten Falles. Allgemeine Formeln wie die, der Mensch dürfe nicht zum bloßen Objekt der Staatsgewalt herabgewürdigt werden, können lediglich die Richtung andeuten, in der Fälle der Verletzung der Menschenwürde gefunden werden können.]

1192 BVerfG 30, 1, (25–26) – *Abhörurteil* (1970) [Der Mensch ist nicht selten bloßes Objekt nicht nur der Verhältnisse und der gesellschaftlichen Entwicklung, sondern auch des Rechts, insofern er ohne Rücksicht auf seine Interessen sich fügen muß.

Because the court suggested that a violation of dignity requires the public power to have a particular intention ("the treatment must involve an arbitrary disregard" of dignity), the judgment has been subjected to intense criticism.[1193] Perhaps in response, this ruling was rectified in the *Großer Lauschangriff* case,[1194] where the BVerfG clarified that the threshold of a violation of dignity is satisfied by those actions of the state that, objectively considered, involve disrespect for the value of the human person.[1195] After recalling that the *Abhörurteil* ruling had acknowledged the limited capacity of the object formula, the BVerfG rephrased the wording used in that decision, stating that a violation of human dignity already occurs when public authority action "lacks respect for the value due to each human for his own sake."[1196]

More specifically, the BVerfG has applied the formula in several ways and to various cases.[1197] Thus, according to the formula, it is incompatible with dignity, *inter alia,* to "compulsorily register and catalogue the human being in his entire personality";[1198] "if cruel or inhuman processes are

---

Eine Verletzung der Menschenwürde kann darin allein nicht gefunden werden. Hinzukommen muß, daß er einer Behandlung ausgesetzt wird, die seine Subjektqualität prinzipiell in Frage stellt, oder daß in der Behandlung im konkreten Fall eine willkürliche Mißachtung der Würde des Menschen liegt. Die Behandlung des Menschen durch die öffentliche Hand, die das Gesetz vollzieht, muß also, wenn sie die Menschenwürde berühren soll, Ausdruck der Verachtung des Wertes, der dem Menschen kraft seines Personseins zukommt, also in diesem Sinne eine „verächtliche Behandlung" sein.]

1193 Classen (n 872) 192.

1194 BVerfG, 109, 279, (312–313) – *Großer Lauschangriff* (2003).

1195 Classen (n 872) 692 exposes this issue.

1196 BVerfG, 109, 279, (312–313) *Großer Lauschangriff* (2003) [Allerdings sind der Leistungskraft der Objektformel auch Grenzen gesetzt (…). Der Mensch ist nicht selten bloßes Objekt nicht nur der Verhältnisse und der gesellschaftlichen Entwicklung, sondern auch des Rechts, dem er sich zu fügen hat. Die Menschenwürde wird nicht schon dadurch verletzt, dass jemand zum Adressaten von Maßnahmen der Strafverfolgung wird, wohl aber dann, wenn durch die Art der ergriffenen Maßnahme die Subjektqualität des Betroffenen grundsätzlich in Frage gestellt wird. Das ist der Fall, wenn die Behandlung durch die öffentliche Gewalt die Achtung des Wertes vermissen lässt, der jedem Menschen um seiner selbst willen zukommt. Solche Maßnahmen dürfen auch nicht im Interesse der Effektivität der Strafrechtspflege und der Wahrheitserforschung vorgenommen werden.]

1197 Classen (n 872) 692 ff. The formula has even been applied beyond the BVerfG by some German states' constitutional courts as well as the supreme federal civil court. See overview in Häberle (n 412) 332 ff.

1198 BVerfGE 27, 1, 6 – *Mikrozensus* (1969). [Mit der Menschenwürde wäre es nicht zu vereinbaren, wenn der Staat das Recht für sich in Anspruch nehmen könnte, shown, with the intention to provide the observer a sadistic pleasure or allowing the appearance of persons or groups of persons as infra-human or unworthy";[1199] to make the criminal a "mere object of the fight against crime";[1200] or when the killing of innocents "is used as a means to rescue others."[1201] Conversely, cases such as that of a non-German whose actions lead to his or her deportation according to the law in order to "deter other foreigners from committing crimes";[1202] or of a criminal who receives a life sentence if "there remains the chance" of recovering freedom again,[1203] do not violate the proscription of instrumentalization.

4.2.1.1.2. Critique of the object-formula

Despite its generalized application, the object formula is viewed as highly deficient by some critics because its premises are untenable and it cannot provide solutions. Even in a democratic society, the individual functions as a means leading to certain ends from multiple points of view.[1204] Besides,

den Menschen zwangsweise in seiner ganzen Persönlichkeit zu registrieren und zu katalogisieren (...).]

1199 BVerfGE 87, 209, 228 – *Tanz der Teufel* (1992). [Das geschieht insbesondere dann, wenn grausame oder sonstwie unmenschliche Vorgänge gezeigt werden, um beim Betrachter ein sadistisches Vergnügen an dem Geschehen zu vermitteln oder um Personen oder Gruppen als menschenunwert erscheinen zu lassen.]

1200 BVerfGE 45, 187 (228) – *Lebenslange Freiheitsstrafe* (1977). [Der Täter darf nicht zum bloßen Objekt der Verbrechensbekämpfung unter Verletzung seines verfassungsrechtlich geschützten sozialen Wertanspruchs und Achtungsanspruchs gemacht werden.]

1201 BVerfGE 115, 118 (154) – *Luftsicherheitsgesetz* (2005). [Sie werden dadurch, dass ihre Tötung als Mittel zur Rettung anderer benutzt wird, verdinglicht und zugleich entrechtlicht; indem über ihr Leben von Staats wegen einseitig verfügt wird, wird den als Opfern selbst schutzbedürftigen Flugzeuginsassen der Wert abgesprochen, der dem Menschen um seiner selbst willen zukommt.]

1202 BVerfGE 50, 166, 176 – *Ausweisung I* (1969). [Wenn als Folge seines Tuns die im Gesetz angedrohte Ausweisung angeordnet wird, um andere Ausländer von der Begehung von Straftaten abzuhalten, so wird er damit nicht unter Verletzung seines verfassungsrechtlich geschützten Wert- und Achtungsanspruchs zum Objekt staatlichen Handelns herabgewürdigt.]

1203 BVerfGE 45, 187 (228–229) – *Lebenslange Freiheitsstrafe* (1977). [Mit einer so verstandenen Menschenwürde wäre es unvereinbar, wenn der Staat für sich in Anspruch nehmen würde, den Menschen zwangsweise seiner Freiheit zu entkleiden, ohne daß zumindest die Chance für ihn besteht, je wieder der Freiheit teilhaftig werden zu können.]

1204 Isensee, 'Würde des Menschen' (n 436) 108, Rn. 176.

the formula does not resolve the main problem of determining the dignity clause's scope of protection[1205] but merely helps identify evident violations of dignity.[1206] Finally, the formula's "normative weakness" makes it susceptible to manipulation since it can be interpreted according to personal moral, religious, or philosophical convictions wherever the constitution allows for some discretion on the part of the legislature.[1207]

4.2.1.1.3. Assessment

The legal nature of the formula is also contested. For some, it enables the scope of protection of dignity to be established by defining what it does *not* apply to. This area is to be determined on a case-by-case basis when the holder has been treated as a "mere object."[1208] Contrariwise, others remark that the formula does correspond to a standard by which to identify interferences with the scope of protection, which should therefore be explicitly determined in any case.[1209] It has also been said that the human dignity clause does not allow the scope of protection and encroachment to be strictly differentiated.[1210]

Be this as it may, scholarship and case law have developed criteria to refine the use of the formula over the years. First, not every state action that treats a human being as an object may be considered an infringement on human dignity – only those activities that deny his or her value as such.[1211] Secondly, the formula needs to be understood as delivering an overall "heuristic" function by orienting the concretization of Art. 1 (1) GG.[1212] In the same sense, it should not be applied without considering the context of a specific case.[1213]

1205 Thomas Elsner and Klara Schobert, 'Gedanken zur Abwägungsresistenz der Menschenwürde – angestoßen durch das Urteil des Bundesverfassungsgericht zur Verfassungsmäßigkeit der Sicherungsverwahrung' [2007] Das Deutsche Verwaltungsblatt 278, 281.

1206 Dreier (n 406) Rn. 55.

1207 Nettesheim (n 881) 84; similarly, Dreier (n 406) Rn. 55.

1208 Elsner and Schobert (n 1205) 280.

1209 Hufen, *Staatsrecht II. Grundrechte* (n 399) 144.

1210 Gerrit Manssen, *Staatrecht II. Grundrechte* (2021) 78.

1211 BVerfGE, 109, 279, (312–313) *Großer Lauschangriff* (2003).

1212 Kunig and Kotzur (n 1008) Rn. 34.

1213 Hufen, 'Erosion der Menschenwürde?' (n 466).

Against this backdrop, *Kingreen and Poscher* provide a balanced assessment. Though the formula leaves several questions open, it provides at least one robust orientation: not even the highest purpose can justify any measure that objectifies human beings. From this perspective, the state may not position the individual as a means to an end. From the opposite perspective, the more the human being is treated as a subject, the more respected is his or her dignity.[1214]

4.2.1.2. The negative approach

A similar approach starts from the premise that, rather than attempting to positively define the content of human dignity, one should identify actions that violate it.[1215] Lessons from concrete historical experiences, particularly those that took place during the National Socialist dictatorship, preclude the repetition of extreme forms of disrespect to the human personality. These include "defamation, discrimination, humiliation, branding, persecution, proscription, and cruel punishment."[1216]

This perspective offers security by appealing to a consensus regarding actions that have generally been acknowledged as interferences with human dignity (self-evident cases).[1217] Furthermore, while the method is based on specific infringements, each of these allows discussion of a positive definition of the protected area of dignity.[1218] In fact, the BVerfG has resorted to this method on several occasions.[1219]

Nevertheless, the benefits of the negative approach are inextricably linked to the above drawbacks. For it to function, there must be a consensus in the assessment of a concrete case.[1220] Thus, as much as this approach may avoid the repetition of past crimes, a positive description of the scope of protection of dignity is required to identify interferences as yet unen-

1214 Kingreen and Poscher (n 399) 94 Rn. 392.

1215 See § 7, subsection 1.

1216 Nettesheim (n 881) 79, quoting case law of the constitutional court of the state of Bayern (BayVerfG, BayVBL.1982, S.47 (50). [Diffamierung, Diskriminierung, Erniedrigung, Brandmarkung, Verfolgung, Ächtung und grausame Bestrafung.]

1217 Ipsen, *Staatsrecht II* (n 384) 60, 232.

1218 Elsner and Schobert (n 1205) 285.

1219 Hufen (n 133) 6, providing examples in fn 51.

1220 Dreier (n 406) Rn. 54.

countered.[1221] Based on doctrinal considerations, a positive description is required, as with any other basic right.[1222] In addition, the typical examples provided by case law and scholarship are primarily violations of some "normal" basic rights.[1223]

4.2.2. Justification of interferences

4.2.2.1. Ruling opinion: no justification possible

The BVerfG case law and most scholarship hold that no interference with the content protected by the right to human dignity may be justified.[1224] In other words, any interference means a violation of dignity.[1225] Several arguments support this rather unique conceptualization of a basic right. First, the fact that human dignity is considered the superior value within the GG's system of values favors its prevalence over any other constitutional norm, including all other fundamental rights.[1226] The main grounds for this conclusion is the word "inviolable,"[1227] contained in Article 1 (1) GG, along

1221 Nettesheim (n 881) 79.

1222 Classen (n 872) 692, fn 38.

1223 Isensee, 'Würde des Menschen' (n 436) 110.

1224 This description of the situation is supported by several scholars, *inter alia*, Kingreen and Poscher (n 399) 66; Elsner and Schobert (n 1205) 284; Nettesheim (n 881) 81; and Baldus (n 1164) 530, who provides an exhaustive list of further supporters in fn 4. For the pertinent BVerfG case law, see, e.g., BVerfGE 34, 239, (245) – *Tonband* (1973); BVerfGE 75, 369, (380) – *Strauß-Karikatur* (1987); BVerfGE 93, 266, (293) – *Soldaten sind Mörder* (1995); BVerfGE 107, 275, (284) – *Schockwerbung* (2003); BVerfGE 109, 279, (314) – *Großer Lauschangriff* (2003); BVerfGE 113, 348, (391) – *Telekommukationsüberwachung* (2005); BVerfGE 130, 1, (22) – *Wohnraumüberwachung* (2011). In most of these decisions, the inviolability of dignity is mentioned in relation to the general right of personality and its focal area of private lifestyle. See § 8, subsection 3.2 for more on this right.

1225 Dreier (n 406) Rn. 46.

1226 See, e.g, BVerfGE 50, 166 (175) – *Ausweisung I* (1979): "The dignity of the human being is the supreme value in the basic rights' system of values and belongs to the fundamental constitutional principles." [Die Würde des Menschen ist der oberste Wert im grundrechtlichen Wertsystem und gehört zu den tragenden Konstitutionsprinzipien.]

1227 Kingreen and Poscher (n 399) 63; Hufen, 'Die Menschenwürde, Art. 1 I GG' (n 624) 2; Dreier (n 406) Rn. 130. [Aus der Unantastbarkeit der Menschenwürde ergibt sich das zentrale Argument für ihre ausnahmslose Unabwägbarkeit.] For an account of the imprecision involved in the official English translation of the German word *unantastbar* as "unviolable," see Barak (n 394) 227: "untouchable" with the eternity clause prescribed by Art. 79 (3) GG.[1228] Under these conditions, dignity can only fulfill its function when its content is absolutely protected.[1229] Any other understanding might damage its unique role in the system of values established by the GG.[1230]

In any case, dignity's doctrinal treatment as an absolute right demands both restraint in applying the clause and a strict delimitation of its protected content.[1231] The appeal to dignity should be restricted to the core elements of human personality and the anthropological presuppositions of the GG.[1232]

The absoluteness of Art. 1 (1) GG has significant consequences for legal doctrine: dignity forms "measures and limits" when balancing other fundamental rights, but it cannot itself be subjected to any balancing.[1233] In the words of one critic of the foregoing: "Absolute means: not limitable, not balanceable, preferred – without exception."[1234] Thus, dignity has neither limits inherent in the constitution [*verfassungsimmanente Schranken*] nor may it be balanced against other constitutional interests.[1235]

For those who hold that the legislature must delimit the scope of protection of rights without reservation clauses, this excludes the possibility of clashes.[1236] Regarding the right to human dignity, this impossibility is strengthened by the norms in Arts. 79 (3) and 20 GG.[1237] Even for those who do not deny the plausibility of clashes, the outcome is the same: human dignity defeats any other right without legal reservation. Consequently, neither artistic nor scientific, nor religious freedom, for instance, may justify interfering with dignity. Finally, when the two sides of the right to

is a more accurate rendering. Conversely, the German equivalent to "inviolable" is the word "unverletztlich," as was correctly translated into the official English version of articles 4 (1), 10 (1), and 13 (1) GG.

1228 Kingreen and Poscher (n 399) 96.

1229 Classen (n 872) 689.

1230 Hufen, 'Die Menschenwürde, Art. 1 I GG' (n 624) 9.

1231 Classen (n 872) 689.

1232 Hufen, 'Die Menschenwürde, Art. 1 I GG' (n 624) 2. This restrictive approach demands the immediate exclusion of all the so-called "bagatelle cases." Examples of such cases are listed in Hufen, 'Die Menschenwürde, Art. 1 I GG' (n 624).

1233 Classen (n 872) 694.

1234 Baldus (n 1164) 530.

1235 Dreier (n 406) Rn.46.

1236 Kingreen and Poscher (n 399) 84.

1237 ibid.

dignity collide, a doctrinal solution can be achieved without violating the dignity of any of the affected individuals.[1238]

4.2.2.2. Minority opinion: the relativity of human dignity

A minority of scholars find the absoluteness of dignity untenable.[1239] The several who hold this view assert that the jurisprudence of the BVerfG on the matter is not entirely consistent. Several of the BVerfG's opinions have affirmed the absoluteness of dignity[1240] but have resolved the issue at hand through balancing.[1241] The hidden balancing of the BVerfG can be detected through a hermeneutic review of its statements about dignity. The recourse to some expressions typical of the proportionality test supports this claim.[1242] The inconsistency is unavoidable: a fundamental right excluded *a priori* from balancing is juridically inconceivable.[1243] Rights stand under the law of relativity.[1244] Furthermore, the BVerfG implicitly recognized the relativity of dignity when it remarked that dignity's historical meaning depends on shared understandings.[1245]

Along these lines, the BVerfG's proclamation of the absoluteness of human dignity has even been critiqued as a "distracting doctrinal maneuver" [*dogmatisches Ablenkungsmanöver*],[1246] or comprising only "rhetorical" means.[1247] Neither have scholars saved absoluteness from the inconsistencies of case law: whilst the negative approach to determining violations entails factual balancing, the aim of defining the content very restrictively

1238 For a detailed exposition of this doctrinal issue, see *infra* subsection 5.3.

1239 Baldus (n 1164) 532–536 also enumerates a list of recent scholars who have argued that the dignity clause should be considered limitable.

1240 On this, see Classen (n 872).

1241 In this vein, e.g., Robert Alexy, 'Menschenwürde und Verhältnismäßigkeit' (2015) 140 Archiv des Öffentlichen Rechts 497; Baldus (n 1164) 105 provides several examples of the BVerfG proceeding in this way. This fact has even been recognized by those who support the absoluteness of the dignity clause such as Classen (n 872) 689–692.

1242 Elsner and Schobert (n 1205) 286.

1243 Baldus (n 1164) 547.

1244 Cf. Isensee, 'Würde des Menschen' (n 436) 73, although in the context of providing an argument against considering dignity as a subjective right.

1245 Elsner and Schobert (n 1205) 286.

1246 ibid 280.

1247 Baldus (n 1164) 539.

leaves at least one scenario which can only be resolved by balancing, namely the protection versus the respect of dignity.[1248]

Besides, sticking to "inviolability" transfers the balancing process from the justification level [*Rechtfertigung*] to the determination of the scope of protection [*Schutzbereich*], producing an undesirable "mixture" of the Three-Step Test.[1249] This can be observed across several of the BVerfG's decisions,[1250] which are mostly appropriate, although their line of argument remains obscure since they aim to declare dignity inviolable.[1251]

Therefore, according to the minority, the solution is to subject dignity to the doctrine of conventional basic rights.[1252] The freedoms under Art. 1 (1) GG may be restricted according to the principle of proportionality.[1253] There is no alternative to balancing when dignity is applied under rational parameters.[1254] Consequently, human dignity does not offer the same protection to everyone and its application may vary based on the level of development of the human subjects involved.[1255]

This view holds that there also are good normative reasons, despite the concrete case law of the BVerfG, to prefer the relative conception of dignity.[1256] First of all, there are no doctrinal reasons based on the wording, legal structure, and history of the dignity clause that would necessitate an interpretation of dignity as absolute – Art. 1 (1) GG can simply be interpreted by all traditional methods of interpretation, just like any other relative basic right.[1257]

However, the minority view holds that, as a limitable right, dignity may deploy some unique functions. It can act as the final threshold, when the corresponding individual fundamental right and the subsidiary right to general freedom of action do not protect a given freedom or legal interest.[1258] Hence, human dignity represents the ultimate boundary of

1248 ibid 541, for a list of scholars who, at minimum, accept this exception to the absoluteness of dignity.
1249 Elsner and Schobert (n 1205) 281.
1250 ibid 281 ff.
1251 ibid 282.
1252 ibid 278.
1253 Nettesheim (n 881) 278.
1254 Alexy (n 1241) 512. Similarly, Baldus (n 1164) 548.
1255 Nettesheim (n 881) 105.
1256 Alexy (n 1241) 510 ff.
1257 On this, see Baldus (n 1164) 545–546.
1258 Elsner and Schobert (n 1205) 286.

protection that the basic rights system offers.[1259] As such, there are many conflicts and situations in which human dignity trumps any other clashing constitutional right or interest,[1260] even when not considered absolute.

Based on his theoretical conception of basic rights as principles of optimization,[1261] *Robert Alexy* proposes that the right to human dignity has both the structure of a principle (of optimization) and a rule.[1262] For *Alexy,* as a principle, the guarantee of human dignity may be reduced to the juridical norm that "all persons have the right to be taken seriously as persons."[1263] From another viewpoint, the dignity clause can also be interpreted as an absolute rule that can only be violated when dignity as a principle of optimization has not been correctly balanced vis à vis any clashing principle.[1264] As dignity is a semantically open concept, the constitution allows a balancing approach to be employed.[1265] The content of the rule then depends entirely on the content of the principle. Dignity's content, as a rule, is empty and it is therefore only a relative right.[1266]

5. Human dignity and restrictions on basic rights

5.1. Human dignity as an inherent limit in the constitution

According to the predominant view, the right to human dignity may not be subjected to limits inherent in the constitution. Instead, it functions itself as an inherent constitutional limit on the other basic rights. The application of human dignity in this function presupposes, first, that its scope of protection is carefully delineated and, second, that what is to be limited actually affects dignity's scope of protection.[1267] When these conditions are fulfilled, it is possible, following the general doctrine of the limits inherent

1259 Nettesheim (n 881) 88
1260 Alexy (n 1241) 510; Baldus (n 1164) 549.
1261 Alexy (n 1241) 500 ff.
1262 ibid 508–509.
1263 ibid 508. [Alle Personen haben das Recht, als Person ernst genommen zu werden.]
1264 ibid.
1265 ibid 509.
1266 ibid. Classen (n 872) 693 criticizes this "double character" approach: "dignity is always the dignity of the concrete human being. Therefore, it is not possible to conceive of an "abstract principle without a concrete human being."
1267 Hufen, *Staatsrecht II. Grundrechte* (n 399) 147, Rn. 37.

in the constitution, to restrict rights without reservation clauses by a statute or pursuant to a statute, using dignity to directly empower parliament.[1268]

Even when dignity is taken only as a principle of objective law, it may also function doubly in this category, as suggested by *Isensee*. The first function is that dignity can orient the interpretation of a concrete fundamental right that might limit another one in the event of a conflict. In this way, the possibility of appealing directly to dignity from only one side of the conflict is prevented. However, this also means that the dignity clause cannot resolve a conflict between basic rights alone.[1269] Second, the protection of dignity in its dimension as dignity of the human species can – under the preconditions of the principle of proportionality – justify the restriction of individual rights,[1270] including the general clauses of ordinary law, when they are to be interpreted according to the dignity clause.[1271]

5.2. Human dignity – unwaivable guarantee

A complex question arises when dignity conflicts with another freedom belonging to the same holder. As *Hufen* correctly phrased it, the problem is whether dignity can be justifiably restricted if the affected party consents.[1272] In this context, an appeal to the human dignity guarantee to restrict personal autonomy can be seen from two perspectives, with similar results. On one side, human dignity can serve as the constitutional basis for limiting the bearer's remaining rights. On the other side, because it is absolutely protected, not even the holder may waive his or her right to dignity: the exercise of a freedom that affects the content of one's own dignity should be considered constitutionally forbidden.[1273] In other words,

1268 ibid 147.

1269 Isensee, 'Würde des Menschen' (n 436) 88, Rn. 135, consequently clarifies that dignity alone may not be considered a limit inherent in the constitution: not even Art. 1 (1) GG can defeat the requirement of a legal basis for restrictions on basic rights.

1270 ibid 90, Rn. 138. Similarly, Häberle (n 412) 360 Rn. 85 argues that some discussions on bioethical matters are more related to dignity as dignity of the species, namely of its objective legal meaning, than to dignity as a subjective right.

1271 Isensee, 'Würde des Menschen' (n 436) 90, Rn. 139. Thus, human dignity can even serve as a basis to restrict a right without a reservation clause, but only if it fulfills the prerequisites of such clauses and the remaining steps required for justification.

1272 Hufen, 'Die Menschenwürde, Art. 1 I GG' (n 624) 10.

1273 Kingreen and Poscher (n 399) 44.

the question here is whether (and how) the holder of human dignity may also be obligated under Art. 1 (1) GG.

Although the right to dignity may plausibly be viewed as "consent-hostile" [*einwillugungsfeindlich*],[1274] the evaluation of this function is controversial. Self-determination is itself a major manifestation of human dignity[1275] and should be the first principle to be considered in this kind of situation.[1276] The "self-image" of each individual is thus co-constitutive [*mitkonstitutiv*] in defining the content of human dignity.[1277]

In this respect, an appropriate rule is that, in general, the state may neither force the individual to act "according" to human dignity nor prevent freely-decided "undignified" behaviors.[1278] Dignity may not be used against individual holders of rights for the purpose of education or improvement.[1279] Human dignity demands respect for autonomy, even when the holder uses it against him or herself,[1280] which leaves no place for a paternalistic interpretation of dignity.[1281] Even in hard cases, the principle *in dubio pro dignitate* should be applied.[1282] Acceptable exceptions, however, are those taboo behaviors restricted by the dignity clause such as the possibility of selling one's own organs or selling oneself as a slave.

However, the difference between strongly criticized "paternalistic" jurisprudence and the generally accepted taboos lies more in the intensity of shared social values and understandings of the good than in doctrinal categories.[1283] The prohibition both of selling organs and working in a "peep show"[1284] restricts contractual freedom. The challenge is to find

---

1274 Jarass, 'Vormerkungen vor Art. 1: Allgemeine Grundrechtslehren' (n 1040) Rn. 35.

1275 Hufen, *Staatsrecht II. Grundrechte* (n 399) 146–147.

1276 Isensee, 'Würde des Menschen' (n 436) 90, Rn. 138.

1277 Häberle (n 412) 357 Rn 81.

1278 Isensee, 'Würde des Menschen' (n 436) 90, Rn. 138.

1279 Ipsen, *Staatsrecht II* (n 384) 64 Rn 242.

1280 Nettesheim (n 881) 105.

1281 Hufen, 'Die Menschenwürde, Art. 1 I GG' (n 624) 4.

1282 ibid 9. Accordingly, this scholar suggests that, from the point of view of human dignity, "forcible feeding is unacceptable in the event of dignity versus life."

1283 In the same sense, Isensee, 'Würde des Menschen' (n 436) 93, Rn. 142, believes that in the case of maintaining social taboos, the recourse to dignity goes beyond the rationality of basic rights under the rule of law, as in cases of incest or consensual cannibalism. This would be the path that the BVerfG followed when it considered the penalization of incest as compatible with the GG. See BVerfGE 120, 224, (238 ff) – *Geschwisterbeischlaf* (2008).

1284 See BVerwGE 64, 274, (274) – *Peep-show* (1982): "The plaintiff applied for a permit pursuant to (…) [respective statutes] to operate a so-called "peep show." During criteria to distinguish between cases when a direct appeal to constitutional dignity to restrict a person's freedom is acceptable versus when an intended restriction must fulfill the conventional doctrinal requisites for a justified interference according to the Three-Step Test. In any case, the constitutional system of fundamental rights leaves the legislature minimal space to prevent individuals from harming themselves.[1285]

In this context, some general standards have been suggested to allow a direct application of human dignity for the restriction of autonomy: first, when the affected person renounces his or her basic rights definitively and irreversibly; second, when the interest of third parties or the public is also involved;[1286] and third, when a whole group could be jeoparadized.[1287] In any case, practices that reach the "most profound level of human humiliation" should also be forbidden based on human dignity.[1288] As a precondition of any analysis, it is essential to check whether the holder's consent was actually free.[1289]

Others suggest that what is affected in these cases is the objective-law content of Art. 1 (1) GG. In this vein, dignity acts, for example, as a criterion

this event, a woman was to show her unclothed body to the spectators, who were to be distributed in 21 individual cabins, arranged in a circle around the stage. This was to take place on a round, revolving stage with a diameter of 5 meters, and would be accompanied by music. The windows of the cabins facing the stage were each to be covered by a screen that was supposed to disappear for a certain time only after a coin was inserted and were to be covered with glass that would make the cabins invisible from the stage. The defendant [the relevant administrative office] refused to grant the requested permit." [Der Kläger beantragte, ihm eine Erlaubnis gemäß § 33 a der Gewerbeordnung – GewO – zum Betrieb einer sogenannten Peep-Show zu erteilen. Bei dieser Veranstaltung sollte auf einer runden, drehbaren Bühne mit einem Durchmesser von 5 Metern eine weibliche Person bei Musik ihren unbekleideten Körper den Zuschauern in 21 kreisförmig um die Bühne angeordneten Ein-Personen-Kabinen zeigen. Die Fenster der Kabinen zur Bühne sollten jeweils durch eine Blende abgedeckt sein, die erst nach Einwurf einer Geldmünze für eine bestimmte Zeit verschwinden sollte, und mit einem Glas versehen sein, das die Kabinen von der Bühne aus nicht einsehbar machen sollte. Der Beklagte lehnte die Erteilung der beantragten Erlaubnis ab.] The BVerwG found that not granting permission was correct because the performance would violate the woman's human dignity, and that not even her willingness to participate changed this fact. See BVerwGE 64, 274 – *Peep-show* (1982).

1285 Isensee, 'Würde des Menschen' (n 436) 134, Rn. 224.

1286 ibid 90, Rn. 138.

1287 Hufen, *Staatsrecht II. Grundrechte* (n 399) 147.

1288 Hufen, 'Die Menschenwürde, Art. 1 I GG' (n 624) 10.

1289 ibid.

for interpreting general legal clauses, such as the "public order" clause.[1290] Besides, Art. 1 (1) GG implies a moral demand on the individual to respect the dignity of the human species.[1291] Indeed, the lawmaker's margin of appreciation finds its limits in the fundamental constitutional understanding of the human being: freedoms that may endanger the normative understanding of the person as a free, autonomous, and responsible being are, therefore, constitutionally inadmissible.[1292]

5.3. Dignity versus dignity

Not only in theory but also inspired by one dramatic case,[1293] a tricky doctrinal question emerges from a suggested constellation of dignity versus dignity. In this unique case, even from the viewpoint that dignity may not be relativized, it may, at least apparently, be infringed.[1294] The problem can be summarized as whether the state may restrict the right to human dignity of one person in order to protect the right to human dignity of another. The most well-known example illustrating the complexities of this discussion is

1290 Cf., e.g., Huster (n 525) 3478; in the same sense, Isensee, 'Würde des Menschen' (n 436) 90, Rn. 138.

1291 Isensee, 'Würde des Menschen' (n 436) 134, Rn. 224, who also states, however, that these moral duties can only be imposed as legal duties under the law and in the context of regulating the scope of basic rights. Under these requisites, states Isensee, one could ensure that the principle of the dignity of the species would not be used against the freedom that the principle also concedes to the concrete individual.

1292 Nettesheim (n 881) 112, particularly concerning the possibility of manipulating human genes.

1293 In 2002, having repeatedly and unsuccessfully asked Magnus Gäfgen, the suspect, to disclose the location of a disappeared child, the deputy chief of Frankfurt's police force, Wolfgang Daschner, ordered officers to threaten him. Gäfgen had been detained as soon as he tried to collect the ransom and was threatened with torture if he continued to conceal the whereabouts of the victim. This immediately prompted him to reveal the location, but the kidnapped child was already deceased. For a detailed account in English of this tragic case and its legal aftermath, see Steven Greer, 'Should Police Threats to Torture Suspects Always be Severely Punished? Reflections on the Gäfgen Case' (2011) 11 Human Rights Law Review 67, 67–69.

1294 Dreier (n 406) Rn. 133 [Der konstruktiv einzig denkbare Ausnahmefall besteht darin, dass Würde gegen Würde steht.]

that of torture to save people's lives [*Rettungsfolter*].[1295] Here, the question is whether state officials may torture a detainee in custody to save the lives of innocent victims.

A first opinion already rejects that this constellation could factually emerge from a doctrinal point of view. By this token, *Kingreen and Poscher* remark that, although the GG establishes a duty of protection regarding dignity, it does not prescribe how this duty must be carried out in practice –[1296] as the BVerfG case law on duties of protection has clarified.[1297] Conversely, the GG already orders the state that respect for human dignity is achieved by forbidding acts that could violate it.[1298] In this sense, it is incorrect to understand the "duty of protection" (against threats emanating from third parties) under Art. 1 (1) GG as "absolute" [*nicht einschränkungsfähig*];[1299] human dignity is absolutely protected only from state actions.[1300] In addition, the end or goal of protective state measures does not justify using any means to achieve it.[1301]

However, some believe that a clash of dignity could occur,[1302] and in such eventualities, that the state must act to protect the first person, even if the

1295 A hypothetical case of a "ticking bomb" scenario is provided by Winfried Brugger, 'May Government Ever Use Torture? Two Responses from German Law' (2000) 48 The American Journal of Comparative Law 661, 662: "This hypothetical case takes place in your home city that is threatened by a terrorist armed with a bomb containing deadly chemical agents. He has hidden the bomb. After he has been tracked down and detained by the police, he states, credibly, that he has activated the timer of the bomb. The bomb will detonate in five hours and kill all of the inhabitants of your city and its suburbs. All will suffer a horrible death. Despite police pressure the terrorist refuses to disclose the bomb's location. Instead, the terrorist demands ten million dollars, the freeing of all death row inmates, and an airplane for his getaway. In addition, he wants ten hostages, so as to ensure a successful escape. The hostages must be ten prominent citizens of your home city. The police find that they are neither able to meet the terrorist's demands nor can they evacuate the city and the surrounding area in time. Only one solution seems to remain. They want to use physical force – torture – to compel the terrorist to divulge the location of the bomb. Are they allowed to use such methods?"

1296 Kingreen and Poscher (n 399) 96.

1297 See BVerfGE 46, 160, (164) – *Schleyer* (1977).

1298 Kingreen and Poscher (n 399) 96.

1299 Classen (n 872) 695 also provides more examples of the correct understanding of duties of protection for cases such as this.

1300 ibid.

1301 ibid.

1302 Dreier (n 406) Rn. 133 admits this conflict is possible, but declares there is ultimately no (doctrinal) solution to it.

other's dignity is restricted. In these cases, the dogma of the inviolability of dignity serves only as grounds for a constitutional decision on a first-come, first-served basis.[1303] Conversely, there are no constitutional grounds to prefer *a priori* the claim of respect over that of protection: both occupy the same constitutional rank.[1304] From this perspective, while the state's absolute prohibition of torture remains in place, public power must also "do everything" to prevent or stop violations of dignity by third parties.[1305] Balancing remains the unique path to resolve the dilemma: when at the stage of an "unavoidable" conflict between competing dignities, the state must favor the victim's interest(s) above the lawbreaker's.[1306]

Isensee comes to a similar conclusion in favor of the innocent, but remarks that both the right to life and the right to physical integrity are at stake here: each must be weighed against the other under the leading principle of dignity. Therefore, according to this position, *Rettungsfolter* is constitutionally justifiable from a doctrinal point of view.[1307]

6. Human dignity and limits to restrictions on fundamental rights

In this view, the dignity clause both justifies interferences with basic rights and sets limits to restrictions on them. As such, this function of dignity should be inserted in the above-mentioned list of *Schranken-Schranken*.[1308]

1303 Elsner and Schobert (n 1205) 283.

1304 Baldus (n 1164) 549. Similarly, Starck, 'Art. 1 Abs. 1' (n 406) Rn. 79.

1305 Cf. Starck, 'Art. 1 Abs. 1' (n 406) Rn. 79. [Wenn nach dieser Abwägung und weiterer Prüfung Folter als geeignet und mangels eines anderen Mittels (z.B. Hinweis auf die Höhe der zu erwartenden Strafe) als erforderlich erscheint, darf die Folter zunächst angedroht und gegebenenfalls unter Wahrung des Verhältnismäßigkeitsprinzips, das für alle polizeilichen Maßnahmen gilt, vollzogen werden.]

1306 Brugger (n 1295) 669–674, who furthermore (ibid 674 ff) argues that, in this instance, torture is not only allowed but mandatory: police have a constitutional duty to torture, given that in this case torture is the only means available to protect dignity. Similarly, Starck, 'Art. 1 Abs. 1' (n 406) Rn. 79.

1307 Isensee, 'Würde des Menschen' (n 436) 94–95, Rn. 144–145. Nonetheless, Isensee claims, the prohibition should ultimately remain in place: although the absolute prohibition of torture goes beyond the rationality of the state under the rule of law, it is also justified by the function of dignity in maintaining social-ethical taboos, which are also required by the constitutional state.

1308 See *supra* subsection 2.3.3. For a detailed description of this theory and associated case law, see the work of Mathias Hong, *Der Menschewürdegehalt der Grundrechte. Grundfragen, Entstehung und Rechtsprechung* (2019).

The main doctrinal conceptualization of this role holds that the content or substance of each fundamental right consists partly of human dignity.

6.1. The theory of the human dignity-content or human dignity-core of fundamental rights

The central statement of this theory is that the content of basic rights – at least some of them – partly comprises human dignity "substance".[1309] Occasionally, the BVerfG has referred to this content as the "human dignity core".[1310] The theory draws on the fact that human dignity is considered the foundation or root of basic rights.[1311] More specifically, the primary positive law justification of this connection is the word "therefore" [*darum*] contained in Art. 1 (2) GG.[1312]

This perspective has significant doctrinal consequences. Due to its inviolability, interfering with the human dignity content of a fundamental right may entail an unjustified restriction.[1313] Furthermore, the eternity clause of Art 79 (3) GG would state that this part of each basic right then also resists any modification by the constituent.[1314] Of course, the tricky question is how to identify the content belonging to dignity. *Stern* provides two essential distinctions.[1315] First, it is necessary to distinguish between the complete abolition versus the mere restriction of a right. For most basic rights, the first of these is inadmissible, since human dignity is so much a part of their scopes of protection that eliminating them would violate Art. 1 (1) GG.[1316] Regarding modifications, it is impossible to identify the human dignity

1309 Stern (n 401) 85. See also Herdegen, 'Art. 1. Abs. 1' (n 604) Rn. 26, who notes the particularly close connection between the dignity clause and the general right of personality and the right to life.

1310 Stern (n 401) 87.

1311 About this, see § 8, subsection 2.

1312 Hufen, *Staatsrecht II. Grundrechte* (n 399) 151 explains this point in the same way minus the same legal argument. Art. 1 (2) reads: "The German people *therefore* acknowledge inviolable and inalienable *human rights* as the basis of every community, of peace and of justice in the world" (emphasis added). [Das Deutsche Volk bekennt sich darum zu unverletzlichen und unveräußerlichen Menschenrechten als Grundlage jeder menschlichen Gemeinschaft, des Friedens und der Gerechtigkeit in der Welt.]

1313 Stern (n 401) 86.

1314 Kingreen and Poscher (n 399) 91.

1315 Stern (n 401) 86 ff.

1316 ibid 89.

content in general, but only on a case-by-case basis. Here, the interpreter must attend to the part of the fundamental right that is "indispensable" for human dignity"; namely, the part connected to the "inherent value of the human personality."[1317]

A variation of the above-mentioned approach suggests that the inviolability of the essence of any basic right prescribed by Art. 19 (2) GG is rooted in human dignity and thus enjoys the same protection. The essential and human dignity content of a right are, thus, the same.[1318] From a case-law perspective, the BVerfG's view that fundamental rights are concretizations of human dignity supports this theory.[1319] Indeed, the BVerfG has more readily referred to the human dignity content than the essential one in several decisions – yet without providing reasons for this imbalance.[1320]

6.2. Critique

Some scholars believe these approaches exhibit certain doctrinal weaknesses. For some, it is wrong to distinguish between the core and periphery of a basic right.[1321] In addition, a broadly historical interpretation should conclude that fundamental rights may not all originate in human dignity but in historical situations that preceded GG's Art. 1 (1).[1322] Furthermore, it is difficult to assert that every basic right is in part an expression of dignity - particularly with no clear criteria to define that expression.[1323]

Other critics find this disputed legal doctrine superfluous. Rather than denounce the violation of the human dignity core or content of a given right, it could simply be stated that an interference violates both the individual right and human dignity, as the BVerfG has repeatedly done.[1324] Overall, liberal democracy and basic freedoms are already secured by oth-

1317 ibid 91.

1318 This position is contested even by supporters of the theory of the human dignity content of basic rights; see, e.g., ibid 87; Herdegen, 'Art. 1. Abs. 1' (n 604) Rn. 26.

1319 Hufen, *Staatsrecht II. Grundrechte* (n 399) 151.

1320 Stern (n 401) 87, although he himself thinks they are not the same content.

1321 Dreier (n 406) 163.

1322 Hufen, *Staatsrecht II. Grundrechte* (n 399) 151.

1323 Dreier (n 406) 163.

1324 Hufen, *Staatsrecht II. Grundrechte* (n 399) 151.

er constitutional mechanisms, such as basic constitutional principles like those of the social state and the rule of law.[1325]

Isensee adds that the human dignity core theory is also problematic because it suggests that concrete basic rights possess some "branches" or "subsidiaries" [*Filiale*] of the human dignity "headquarters" located in Art. 1 (1) GG.[1326] In contrast, *Isensee* affirms, dignity does not constitute a core, but is differently realized in each basic right.[1327] In this sense, as concretizations, basic rights are separated from human dignity and remain open to modifications,[1328] which are only subject to the conventional rules of justification.[1329]

7. Conclusions and open questions

7.1. Doctrinal difficulties involved in reviewing a possible interference with the right to human dignity

7.1.1. Doctrinal perfectionism

As seen above, while the Three-Step Test is the canonical method for analyzing cases that concern fundamental rights in Germany, it is not free from critique and controversy. These difficulties only increase when it is applied to human dignity and its unique inviolability. Therefore, if the appeal to Art. 1 (1) GG is to continue aiding the resolution of juridical conflicts, a painstakingly methodical doctrinal approach is first required to review interferences with the dignity clause.

Thus, jurisdictions such as that of Chile – where there has been limited development of a general theory of basic rights[1330] – should take a restrained approach to dealing with, appealing, and applying the human dignity clause from their own domestic constitutions. Overall, considering human dignity as a basic right entails doctrinal challenges, which await satisfactory resolution even in a highly sophisticated legal environment like that of Germany. Indeed, the repeated accusation of human dignity critics

1325 Dreier (n 406) 166.
1326 Isensee, 'Würde des Menschen' (n 436) 81, Rn. 121.
1327 ibid 81, Rn. 122.
1328 ibid 97, Rn. 150.
1329 ibid 82, Rn. 123.
1330 See §§ 3, 4, 5 and 6.

in the international arena,[1331] that dignity is the door through which judges can easily introduce their own convictions, may be realized in legal environments lacking doctrinal methods to treat their dignity clauses properly.

7.1.2. "In conjunction with"

To deal with these difficulties, the BVerfG has reviewed possible interferences with dignity not in isolation but always in conjunction with [*i.V.m*] another fundamental right. Behind this strategy seems to be the court's conviction that it is difficult to decouple a violation of dignity from that of a concrete "classical" basic right.[1332]

As *Isensee* has convincingly suggested, this approach "protects the differentiation of a basic rights system from undifferentiated effects thereof,"[1333] i.e., it avoids the arbitrary recourse to human dignity to win a juridical conflict at any legal level. This approach is also necessary regarding the state's duties both to protect the individual from encroachments by private third parties through ordinary law, and to ensure the conditions of the respective reservation clauses are respected.[1334]

7.1.3. Dignity versus dignity

The complex doctrinal treatment of the human dignity clause reaches a peak when analyzing a potential conflict between the duty of protection and the obligation of respect. In general, doctrinal approaches to duties of protection [*Schutzpflichten*] regarding defensive basic rights set many challenges.[1335] The complexities increase considerably in the case of human dignity: the state must protect an absolute right. The answer to the question of how the state must comply with its obligations to respect the inviolability of dignity is, at least in theory, relatively simple: no interference with the scope of protection is justifiable. Conversely, the role of the state vis à vis

---

1331 See, e.g., Michael Rosen, 'Dignity: The Case Against' in Cristopher McCrudden (ed), *Understanding Human Dignity* (2014).

1332 Isensee, 'Würde des Menschen' (n 436) 87, Rn. 133 states that even the mention of human dignity is superfluous since the connection between each basic right and human dignity is a general fact.

1333 ibid 81, Rn. 120.

1334 ibid 131–132, Rn. 221.

1335 Hufen, *Staatsrecht II. Grundrechte* (n 399) 52–54.

third parties; namely, the protection of "inviolable" dignity, depends mostly on legislative decisions.

While it is straightforward to guarantee the duty of respecting a defensive right normatively – the GG already forbids any state action that interferes with human dignity – its protection is left to the lawmaker, whose leeway is broad. Accordingly, the most convincing approach to deal with potential clashes of dignity starts from that basis. This approach states that legislative activity may not violate an express directive of the constitution – in this case, to respect human dignity. Consequently, the protection of human dignity by a law or pursuant to a law may only be accomplished according to the rule of law [*Rechtsstaat*]. This excludes torture or any measure that violates the human dignity of a subject.

In the case of human dignity, another reason can remove all doubt from this discussion. Absoluteness can only apply to the duty of respect. The wording of the human dignity clause is generally accepted as prescriptive, so although the norm can be violated, it shall not be. However, human dignity as such, as something that precedes the state, is considered inviolable – not even the greatest self-inflicted or received humiliation can damage it.

The BVerfG has convincingly resolved the apparent contradictions implicated in all these normative statements: while human dignity is inviolable, the claim of respect that emerges from it can indeed be violated. With this clause enshrined, the state fulfills its duty to respect dignity by establishing that no action by public power that interferes with this claim may be justified. Conversely, absolute protection is impossible.

7.2. Absoluteness of human dignity from a comparative law perspective

From a comparative law perspective, several questions of doctrinal interest emerge that are useful in interpreting the Chilean Constitution. The first of these is whether human dignity should be considered inviolable in any domestic constitutional order, even though the respective constitutional clause does not say so. If yes, it is important to consider which hermeneutical methods could consistently justify this. The second is whether recognizing each human being as entitled to basic legal capacity means acknowledging the minimal content of dignity, even though the term "human dignity" is not expressly contained in a constitutional clause. The final question is to what extent the definition of the legal form or juridical nature of a dignity clause depends on the respective domestic constitutional order.

IV
Human Dignity in the Chilean Constitutional Order: A proposed understanding

§ 11 Intermediate Results

1. Introduction

The fourth and final part of this work contains three chapters. This first chapter will briefly recap the principal conclusions obtained from parts I, II, and III in order to summarize the results that inform the discussion presented in the following two chapters.

The next chapter (§ 12) proposes a set of elementary criteria for approaching a constitutional provision on human dignity in any jurisdiction. The questions of how to benefit from comparative law perspectives in general, and the German one in particular, are both discussed. Against this background, it is argued that three dimensions of the German experience of dignity are of particular importance when interpreting the human dignity clause of the Chilean Constitution: the methodological, doctrinal, and sociological.

The last chapter (§ 13) presents an original approach to understanding human dignity in the Chilean constitutional order. This proposal encompasses discussion of its legal form and content. In addition, the main functions that human dignity can play in the doctrinal categories of foundation, ownership, and the restriction of basic rights are also discussed. This original approach does not intend to be the final word on the topic but, rather, to reopen the national debate on the norm.

2. Recalling Part I: Origin of the Chilean Constitution, general theory of basic rights and system of constitutional justice

In the opening pages of this work, the reader is provided with a legal, academic, and historical context for understanding the somewhat doctrinal approach of this work in later sections. The origins of the CPR and its issue with legitimacy are also described. It is stated that the case law produced during the dictatorship, and the historical method should mostly be disregarded when interpreting the CPR.[1336]

The text then examines the limited development of the general theory of basic rights in Chile. Chilean legal practitioners lack shared methodological tools for basic rights cases, which produces considerable legal uncertainty. This problem mainly occurs due to the double character of the Chilean system of constitutional justice and the specificities of the constitutional complaints procedure prescribed in Art. 20 CPR. Although the Chilean Constitutional Tribunal has broad review competencies, constitutional complaints must be brought before the ordinary courts. Consequently, there is no unique tribunal defining the meaning of constitutional norms on basic rights. The constitutional complaints process generates great unpredictability in the relevant case law and therefore there is an obvious lack of a doctrinal corpus on fundamental rights; namely, a legal doctrine of basic rights for the Chilean Constitution. While the human dignity clause has been quoted in some rulings on constitutional complaints, they cannot give rise to general conclusions. Therefore, the analysis developed in the following chapters does not consider the content and outcome of these rulings.[1337]

3. Recalling Part II: conclusions and open questions

3.1. Content of human dignity in Chile

The treatment of human dignity in the Chilean scholarship is heterogeneous, with course books, handbooks, and general commentaries dealing with it very differently. In addition, there are relatively few individual works (journal articles or book chapters) on the topic.

1336 See § 2.
1337 See § 2.

The scholarship agrees that human dignity is a constitutional principle or value. While some scholars accord dignity the same status as other constitutional values, the ruling opinion considers dignity to be superior. The conceptualization and content of human dignity in the Chilean scholarship are redolent of traditional German doctrinal developments, but this connection is not explicitly made. Dignity is often only negatively defined with reference to specific humiliations and disempowerments or as a prohibition against treating the human being as merely a means to an end. Moreover, dignity is primarily considered a distinctive feature of human beings in the order of creation, and almost all the scholarship adheres to some version of the Theory of Dowry.

On the other hand, the CCT has repeatedly considered human dignity the supreme value or principle of the Chilean constitutional order. It also treats dignity as a quality or feature of the human being, which justifies his or her claim for respect and from which the CCT has determined the proscription of instrumentalization. Regarding basic rights, the CCT has deduced normative effects from dignity, particularly in the categories of interpretation, restriction, and the foundation of basic rights. Dignity as the foundation of basic rights has been covered most extensively in the literature.

The analysis of this section led to several critical conclusions. Among several weaknesses of the different understandings are that scholarship and jurisprudence use the term "human dignity" inconsistently; they indistinctly characterize the term as a principle, value, or even as a "precept"; they indistinctly discuss different substrates of dignity, which confuses perspectives from different disciplines. In conclusion, the major challenge remaining from this revision is to construct an operative outline of the content of human dignity with support from the positive constitutional law.[1338]

3.2. Human dignity and the foundation of basic rights in Chile

Most Chilean scholarship that addresses dignity views it as the foundation of basic rights. Some authors also consider it the grounding of the constitutional order but nearly all concur that human dignity and basic rights precede the state. Besides sharing this view, the CCT has also derived both written and implicit basic rights from dignity. It has suggested that some

1338 See § 3.

rights are closer to dignity, which it calls "strictly personal," and which warrant more robust protection by the public power. Additionally, the CCT has stated that some rights or constitutional principles are concretizations or expressions of human dignity. Finally, the CCT has also derived some implicit rights from human dignity, such as the rights to personal identity and conscientious objection.

These developments suggest that both the jurisprudence and scholarship lack a sufficiently robust justification or connection with Chilean constitutional positive law to provide human dignity with such a prominent role in this category. Hence, the task remains to convincingly construct such a connection.[1339]

3.3. Human dignity and ownership of basic rights in Chile

Chilean scholars have rarely engaged with the ownership of basic rights. Most of what has been written takes the form of reactions to specific debates on the legal status of the unborn, which have primarily focused on the concept of a "person." The point of departure has been the wording of Art. 19 (1) CPR, which guarantees the right to life to *all persons*. However, the constitution itself does not define the concept of a person. On that basis, one position claims that the interpreter must resort to the relevant civil law statutes while the other constructs a concept of a person without considering these statutes. The CCT's case law has not only supported both visions but also suggested a third perspective according to which the ownership of basic rights does not depend on any written provisions.

Both the main approaches warrant critique. They lack a disciplined and functional approach to the concept of a legal person. In addition, while they have frequently tried to identify who holds human dignity, they have rarely examined the role of Art. 1 par. 1 CPR in the ownership of fundamental rights. In conclusion, the function of human dignity in this context still requires explanation, as do its links to the concept of a legal person.

1339 See § 4.

3.4. Human dignity and restrictions on basic rights in Chile

In summary, the Chilean scholarship has ventured little further than to mention the potential relevance of human dignity in this context.[1340] Conversely, CCT case law has expressed the relevance of human dignity in defining, on the one hand, restrictions on basic rights and, on the other, limits to these restrictions. In the first instance, the CCT has said that human dignity can restrict both the right to life and the right to equality before the law. In the second, the Tribunal has affirmed that human dignity limits possible restrictions on the right to life, freedom of speech, and the privacy and confidentiality of private communications. Analogously, the Tribunal has affirmed that human dignity operates as the ultimate basis of several rules or principles that limit the state's *ius puniendi*. Overall, this chapter argues that, although the CCT may have reached some correct conclusions, it has not provided enough doctrinal arguments to justify them.

4. Recalling Part III: conclusions and open questions

4.1. Content of human dignity in Germany

The scholarship and case law on dignity in Germany are impressively well-developed. Ranging from its accepted positioning as the most important norm of the Basic Law and generally accepted inviolability, the legal doctrines surrounding the human dignity clause are highly sophisticated. The approach to Art. 1 (1) GG cannot be detached from historical facts, doctrinal practices shared by German legal practitioners, and post-war Germany's juridical innovations such as considering the GG's Bill of Rights as an objective order of values.

Compared to other constitutional provisions, the unique features of the human dignity norm hinder efforts to define its content. German scholarship has classified the multitude of grounding proposals into three main groups: the Theories of Dowry, of Recognition, and of Performance, each of which has its supporters and detractors, and is traceable in the case law of the BVerfG. No agreement has been reached regarding the legal form of

1340 See § 6, subsection 1.

human dignity, either. While some consider it only a principle or value, the ruling opinion also believes that dignity is a basic right.

The scope of protection of human dignity encompasses three main dimensions. Firstly, the respect and protection of human identity, integrity, and equality. Secondly, the guarantee of human self-determination and self-representation as well as personal honor and private intimacy. Finally, a third dimension comprises a claim of solidarity before the national community that assures the minimal means to allow the actual realization of human potentialities. Human dignity also has some strong objective law effects such as orientating the interpretation of basic rights and protecting the human species in its main features.

A first conclusion of this review is that German legal practitioners have discovered how to apply the human dignity clause in a fairly reasonable manner. Some practices support this claim: the leading role played by the BVerfG, the generalized treatment of human dignity according to the Three-Step Test, and defining the scope of protection by conjoining the main dimensions of each theory of legitimation, including the main perspectives. However, the limits of this practical compatibility become apparent when each theory provides different solutions to a particular conflict, and choosing between them is unavoidable.

The discussion on the grounding of human dignity is also linked to that on the universality or particularity of the validity of human dignity. Though it is generally held to be a universal principle, human dignity depends on concrete systems of positive law for its respect and protection. This invites the question as to whether the interpretation of human dignity in a particular legal community should be restricted to traditional sources of legitimization or whether it should also be open to other sources such as the worldviews of indigenous peoples.

Inevitably, the German debate on human dignity is shaped by the historical circumstances of widespread exclusions of human beings from legal subjectivity. In turn, the history of Chile is also marked by the fact that even today, thousands lack full entitlement to rights, notwithstanding their constitutional recognition as legal subjects. This explains why the dimension of human dignity that demands the minimal preconditions for a decent life is of particular note as it depends on economic conditions and the inclusiveness of institutions. The interaction of all these factors is to be considered when suggesting content for human dignity in the CPR.

4.2. Human dignity and the foundation of basic rights in Germany

In Germany as in Chile, there has been almost no discussion among scholars and within the jurisprudence of human dignity as the foundation of basic rights. In addition, the BVerfG, using the formula Art. 1 (1) GG *in conjunction with* another constitutional provision, has deduced two implicit rights from human dignity.

First, the BVerfG derived the GRoP from Art. 1 (1) GG in conjunction with Art. 2 (1) GG. This right emerged from successive doctrinal steps taken by the BVerfG in several rulings over several decades. It can be traced as far back as the *Elfes* case (1957), with further developments in later decisions. In the *Eppler* case (1980), the BVerfG bestowed a more precise doctrinal structure on this right, affirming that its characteristics meant its content was to be defined on a case-by-case basis. Indeed, since then, its content has continually been expanded by further concretizations.

In this context, the BVerfG case law declaring different expressions of the GRoP is significant. The scholarship has classified these expressions into related groups with different configurations. Moreover, within the scope of protection of the GRoP, the BVerfG has confirmed the existence of an absolutely protected zone as the core area of private life and has developed criteria to identify it. However, this absolutely protected area and the criteria themselves continue to be debated by scholars.

Secondly, the BVerfG recognized a constitutional right to a subsidized income in accordance with human dignity from Art. 1 (1) GG in conjunction with the social state principle. This was also the result of earlier jurisprudential developments. In the 1950s, the BVerfG had denied the possibility of deriving social claims from Art. 1 (1) GG. One big step in the opposite direction occurred several years later, when the BVerfG claimed that the state's taxation competencies had reached their limit in leaving the taxpayer a minimal income. Finally, the positive dimension of this right was added in the *Hartz IV* case (2010), where the BVerfG expressly affirmed the existence of a basic right to a minimal income in accordance with human dignity. Notwithstanding this, the BVerfG left the definition of the right's scope of protection almost entirely to the lawmaker.

Several conclusions and open questions emerge from this chapter. First, although its legal structure is sophisticated, there are good reasons to believe that the BVerfG did not affirm the right to a minimum income for doctrinal reasons alone – an important point for the Chilean case. Since the right was recognized when Germany already had a strong welfare state and the BVerfG in the *Harz IV* case restricted itself to analyzing an existing corpus of social law, one crucial question is whether this claim only appears when a given community is able to fulfill it.

Second, from a sociological perspective, while the enshrinement of a human dignity clause means that every human being is formally recognized as a holder of basic rights, the guarantee of a minimum income enables citizens to actually enjoy such rights. Conversely, societies that cannot guarantee a minimum income for all members cannot provide full integration through a human dignity clause. It is also worth mentioning the persistent doctrinal difficulties involved in defining the absolutely protected content of the GroP. Likewise, if, as is widely accepted, all basic rights are grounded in dignity, it is unclear why dignity would need to be declared as the basis of another individual right. Overall, grounding implicit rights in human dignity involves doctrinal ambiguities that are difficult to manage.

4.3. Human dignity and ownership of basic rights in Germany

Primarily due to several prominent BVerfG decisions, it is widely known that the individual receives protection via his or her basic rights – even before birth and after death. In this context, the personal scope of protection defines who the holder of a concrete basic right is. The main distinction that the GG makes is between rights applicable to any human being and those reserved for Germans. Nevertheless, before identifying who is protected by an individual basic right, one must first define who is capable of holding basic rights in the first place, i.e., who possesses basic legal capacity. While at the infra-constitutional level the determination of basic legal capacity is provided by civil law rules, the ruling opinion suggests a more extensive criterion at the constitutional level. This issue has been tackled – albeit not entirely explicitly –by the BVerfG when determining who is a holder of dignity.

Legal entities [juridical persons] are excluded from the ownership of human dignity as a matter of principle. Conversely, as a basic fact, human dignity is recognized in every human being irrespective of personal condition. Nevertheless, there are strong disagreements on the initial and final temporal thresholds of this recognition. Regarding the former, the ruling opinion attributes human dignity to the unborn, beginning at different developmental points. For the BVerfG this attribution begins at implantation, whereas several scholars argue it should apply from fertilization onwards.

In contrast, the minority opinion recognizes human dignity only in newborns, and some researchers favor intermediate time points.

Concerning the final limit, the majoritarian view holds that at least some effects of human dignity do not end with death. The contention is whether these effects originate from a subjective right to which the deceased remain entitled, or merely in duties of protection either vis à vis the deceased, their relatives, or the general interest.

The main conclusion of this chapter is that attributing human dignity entails the attribution of a basic legal capacity. Basic legal capacity, then, is the doctrinal expression of the rather theoretical conception of human dignity as "a right to have rights." Conceptualized this way, human dignity can remain an open norm able to deal with future challenges. Thus, the human dignity clause can prevent the exclusion of human beings from the community of legal persons while maintaining its core meaning.

4.4. Human dignity and restrictions on basic rights in Germany

The human dignity clause plays at least two critical roles in this doctrinal category: it may both justify restrictions on basic rights and set limits to these restrictions. The latter occurs within the context of the accepted doctrinal method to review impacts on basic rights: the Three-Step Test, which enjoys far-reaching recognition. In brief, this test consists of three successive analytical stages to identify a possible violation of a basic right. Initially, the scope of protection of the right must be identified. Next, it must be determined whether the impacts count as interference. Eventually, the existence of a constitutional justification for that interference must be checked.

The test has not escaped controversy: at the first step, debate centers on how restrictively to define the scope of protection; at the second, the discussion concerns the elements necessary for impacts on a basic right to qualify as an interference; while at the third step, the most significant contention relates to the application of the principle of proportionality in a strict sense.

Human dignity is subjected to this method when considered a basic right. Given its idiosyncrasies, which make the doctrinal treatment of dignity a challenging task, legal practitioners have developed a toolkit to identify interferences in human dignity. The most frequently applied tool is the object formula, which states that human dignity is affected when the state treats a human being as a mere means to an end, or in a way that puts a person's quality as a subject in question. The formula has been criticized for its ambiguity, but supporters suggest it at least provides a basic orientation for detecting interferences with human dignity.

There is an overwhelming consensus that no interference with human dignity may be justified. Any intrusion corresponds to a violation of the right, primarily due to the inclusion of the word "inviolable" in Art. 1 (1) GG. Human dignity is resistant to any balancing and is not subject to any limit inherent in the constitution. Yet a minority rejects this vision on the basis that absolute rights are theoretically impossible because, on principle, they are subject to the law of relativity. According to the minority, this axiom explains why the BVerfG has contradicted itself by theoretically affirming dignity's absoluteness while simultaneously subjecting it to balancing in practice.

From a doctrinal perspective, the most challenging example is the constellation "dignity v. dignity." This is repeatedly used as an example in the so-called *Rettungsfolter* constellation, which represents the confrontation of the two obligations that arise from human dignity: respect and protection. The question is whether the state may restrict the human dignity of one person (e.g., by torturing a suspect in custody) to protect the human dignity of another (e.g., a kidnapped victim). Some scholars deny the possibility of this dilemma. While the constitution already informs the state how to respect human dignity, it delegates responsibility to lawgivers on how to protect it. The measures that the lawgiver takes may not, however, contradict direct constitutional demands (respecting dignity), hence the concept of torture is automatically precluded as a possible state measure. A different view finds this constellation insoluble, with the rationality of the rule of law reaching its limits here. Finally, a minority suggests an exceptional recourse to balancing, where the victim's interest must be prioritized, thus allowing torture.

Dignity may also limit restrictions on basic rights. Since human dignity is inviolable, any intrusion that affects the human dignity core or the human dignity content of these rights would be unjustifiable. However, it is hard to define reliable criteria that would allow the interpreter to distinguish between the human dignity core of a right and its remaining content.

Finally, human dignity constitutes an inherent limit to basic rights in the constitution. As such, its application requires both careful definition of its scope of protection and identification of whether the right it restricts affects the scope of dignity in some way. A more complex question arises when considering human dignity as an unwaivable right, i.e., when human dignity is used to limit the freedom of its holder. In any case, the application of this notion should be very restrictive and confined to very few, likely extreme, cases.

The main conclusion of this chapter is that the doctrinal treatment of the right to human dignity contains many highly complex challenges. Therefore, to maintain its legitimacy in resolving juridical conflicts, the impacts on human dignity must be reviewed with the utmost care. In other words, the treatment of dignity virtually requires adjudicative perfection. In this sense, one strategy the court has resorted to is the constant analysis of a possible intrusion into human dignity in conjunction with another basic right.

5. *Summary of similarities and differences between the German and Chilean treatment of human dignity*

5.1. Antecedents

There are at least three structural reasons for the various treatments of dignity and the development of the corresponding clauses in the German and Chilean jurisdictions. First, the Chilean Constitution is faced with notorious problems of social recognition, with its legitimacy questioned by several academic, social, and political groups due to its origins in a dictatorship.[1341] One consequence of this perceived lack of legitimacy has been to question the genealogical method for interpretation.[1342] In contrast, the GG enjoys far-reaching acceptance among Germans.[1343] Recourse to the proceedings of the Parliamentary Council as an interpretive method is widely accepted,[1344] and some renowned scholars attribute particular

1341 See § 3.

1342 See § 3.

1343 A poll conducted in 2019 to mark the 70th anniversary of the GG's entry into force showed it was positively viewed by almost 90% of Germans: see <https://www.infratest-dimap.de/umfragen-analysen/bundesweit/umfragen/aktuell/70-jahre-grundgesetz/> accessed 07 July 22.

1344 See, e.g., Christian Starck, 'Maximen der Verfassungsauslegung', *Handbuch des Staatsrechts der Bundesrepublik Deutschland. Band XII* 624–628: *Normativität und Schutz der Verfassung* (2014).

importance to the proceedings for determining the scope of protection of basic rights.[1345]

Second, while the general theory of basic rights remains fairly straightforward in Chile, it has reached a highly sophisticated level of development in Germany,[1346] where each element of the general theory is addressed by abundant scholarship and case law. In particular, there is a common method of dealing with basic rights cases among legal practitioners.[1347]

Third, in Chile, both the CCT and the higher courts of the ordinary jurisdiction practice constitutional adjudication. In addition, regarding constitutional complaints (the so-called "remedy of protection"), three factors prevent the unity of jurisdiction: the procedural system, the direct effect of basic rights on third parties, and the high number of complaints that the CCT handles annually.[1348] In contrast, in Germany the BVerfG has the final word in constitutional adjudication and hears far fewer cases.

5.2. Comparison of the legal form and content of human dignity

The doctrinal treatment of dignity in Chile is relatively scarce and disparate. In the jurisprudence of the CCT, only a few cases have turned on it. In contrast, the German literature on dignity is rich, with a wealth of pertinent case law. Differences also arise regarding the legal form of human dignity. While in Chile, scholarship and case law view human dignity solely as a principle or value without exception, the ruling opinion in Germany, backed by the jurisprudence of the BVerfG, also attributes subjective law content to it. However, in both jurisdictions, the human dignity clause is considered the highest norm of the legal order.

Only a few Chilean legal scholars have suggested a different grounding for dignity than the Theory of Dowry. Traditionally, this theory has also dominated in Germany, but several scholars have used other theories as well. The protected content of human dignity is classified by the German scholarship with due consideration of relevant BVerfG case law and the theories of grounding. Some of these dimensions have also been remarked upon by Chilean scholars. However, the Chileans have not proceeded with such classifications. Lastly, German scholarship and case law have distin-

1345 See § 10.
1346 See § 10.
1347 See § 10.
1348 See § 2.

guished several normative effects of dignity, but this development has no parallel in Chile, where the literature mostly focuses on the topic of dignity as the foundation of basic rights.

5.3. Comparison of human dignity and foundation of basic rights

Further similarities can be found between the two jurisdictions in the area of dignity and the foundation of basic rights. First, in both Germany and Chile, basic rights are viewed as grounded in human dignity. Second, constitutional courts in both countries have deduced some implicit rights from dignity, with the BVerfG using the formula "in conjunction with" [*iVm*] to do so.[1349] However, there are significant differences in the depth and quantity of the doctrinal work and jurisprudence on the judicially created rights. The rights recognized by the CCT have received little attention in the scholarship or further case law; in contrast, both rights recognized by the BVerfG - especially the GRoP - have resulted from decades of jurisprudential and doctrinal development.

5.4. Comparison of human dignity and ownership of basic rights

The topic ownership of basic rights has scarcely been discussed in Chile. The scholarship has mostly discussed the issue of who can be considered a person for determining who has basic legal capacity. The CCT's case law on the topic has evolved over a number of different cases, whereas basic legal capacity has been reviewed by the BVerfG when revising cases on the ownership of dignity, showing that dignity plays an essential role in this area in Germany.

5.5. Comparison of human dignity and restrictions on basic rights

The Chilean jurisdiction follows no established methods or legal doctrine when reviewing possible restrictions on human dignity. In Germany, however, human dignity is considered a basic right, so possible impacts are treated by established doctrinal tools. Whilst the CCR has occasionally

1349 See § 4.

applied the human dignity clause to restrict rights, this has been carried out without providing doctrinal reasons. Conversely, the human dignity clause in the German jurisdiction plays at least two distinct roles in this context: justifying and setting limits to restrictions, with relevant legal doctrine developed to justify both roles.

§ 12 Elementary criteria for approaching a constitutional norm on human dignity

1. *Preliminary: the distinction between concept, content, and grounding of human dignity*

In principle, the doctrinal approach to a human dignity clause requires clearly distinguishing between three closely related but distinct issues:[1350] the first is the concept of human dignity, i.e., a definition of human dignity, such as the value of the human person. However, while a "pure" concept of human dignity alone might include the key contents to determine its normative effects, it would not say much about what these effects might be.

Accordingly, the principal normative effect of human dignity to be identified is its *protected content*. At minimum, this includes its constitutional purpose; namely, the normative reasons that caused human dignity to be incorporated into constitutional law, such as putting the human being at the center of the legal order. Both the protected content and the *legal form* of dignity help to determine its other normative effects in the legal system. These include the impacts of human dignity on the various elements of the general theory of basic rights and its role as an interpretative standard for the rest of the legal order.[1351] The third issue concerns the *grounding* of human dignity.[1352] It is necessary to identify the reasons for attributing

1350 Some content from this paragraph (§12) was previously published by Augusto Wiegand Cruz, 'El Concepto Constitucional de Dignidad Humana: Notas introductorias para una aproximación dogmática' in Gabriel Alejandro Encinas Duarte and Miguel de J. Neria Govea (eds), *Ordenamiento Jurídico: Fundamentos y Apertura* (2021).

1351 The German case represents developed doctrinal work on this topic. See §§ 7, 8, 9 and 10.

1352 Here, it is worth recalling that the questions on the foundation of human dignity vs. human dignity as the foundation of, e.g., basic or human rights must not be conflated. In addition, it is also advisable to distinguish human dignity considered as positive law from human dignity as the supra-positive foundation of those rights. On this, see Aldunate Lizana, *Derechos Fundamentales ["Fundamental Rights"]* (n 8) 96–100.

dignity to the human being: these might include because humans are made in God's image or because they possess moral autonomy.[1353]

In constitutional doctrine, these three questions are usually approached when determining the content of human dignity,[1354] indicating their relatedness: the concept of human dignity and its grounding arise together. Following this, the dimensions of the normative program of human dignity are largely defined by the chosen grounding.[1355] Despite their strong links, the theoretical distinction between the categories "concept," "content," and "grounding" of human dignity prevents them from being misapplied. The aim is to achieve the highest level of doctrinal clarity by outlining a juridical and consistent scope of the protection of human dignity, one that can be widely accepted and recognized. Although this cannot be achieved without examining its grounding and drafting a conceptualization of human dignity, these achievements are only tools to define the scope of protection.

2. First: definition of the legal form

The challenge here is to clarify whether the human dignity clause of a given constitutional order only constitutes a norm of objective law, or whether it also has the legal form of a basic right with subjective law content. In any case, given its characteristics, human dignity would probably play several essential roles thanks to its objective law effects.[1356] The interpreter must consider the likelihood that furnishing human dignity with subjective law content may increase the doctrinal challenge.[1357] For one, human dignity must fulfil the criteria of any basic right (e.g., content, ownership, addressees). In addition, a correct doctrinal review of possible restrictions on human dignity requires shared doctrinal tools with which to discipline its application by the judiciary.

1353 Thus, one may finally say that, e.g., human dignity is the value of the human being as such (concept) in virtue of his moral autonomy (grounding) that sets him or her at the center of the legal order (normative effect).

1354 See, in general, §§ 3 and 7.

1355 Well exemplified by the German experience. See § 7, subsection 2.

1356 On this point, see § 7, subsection 3.3.

1357 Greater difficulties do not necessarily mean a lower chance of achieving doctrinal correctness. For example, in Germany, several scholars hold that human dignity may only be treated with doctrinal consistency when considered as a right, see § 10, subsection 4.2.

In addition, the normative effects which human dignity as a basic right, may produce, depend on the prevailing conception of basic rights in the jurisdiction.[1358] The consequences of human dignity might differ when basic rights are considered only as defensive rights against the state versus when they are also viewed as promoting and forming an "objective order of value".[1359]

3. Second: definition of the content in accordance with its legal form

3.1. Independence

The concept of human dignity is an important topic in several disciplines.[1360] Here, the goal is to identify interpretative standards that may provide the norm with proper content specific to its constitutional context, thus achieving independence from its meaning in other fields of knowledge.

Indeed, a major challenge for constitutional doctrine is to offer a juridical treatment of notions originating from other fields of knowledge. Both sides in a legal conflict may attempt to advance their own cause by presenting themselves before the public as possessing the substantial ethical, religious, or moral value that is implied by the notion of human dignity.[1361] When legal practitioners, especially judges, are confronted with several such conceptualizations of human dignity – all of which are legitimate in a societal context – constitutional doctrine must imbue dignity with clearly defined content in order to rationalize the work of the final interpreters.[1362] The

1358 Starck, 'Maximen der Verfassungsauslegung' (n 1344) 638, recalls that one may not decide which theory to follow before the act of interpretation, as it this would mean neglecting the traditional methods of interpretation and setting basic rights outside the constitution considered in its entirety [Verfassungsganzes].

1359 See, e.g., the classification of Ernst-Wolfang Böckenförde, 'Fundamental Rights. Theory and Interpretation [1974]' in Mirjam Künkler and Tine Stein (eds), *Constitutional and Political Theory: selected writings* (2017).

1360 Hasso Hofmann, 'Methodische Probleme der juristischen Menschenwürdeinterpretation' in Ivo Appel and Georg Hermes (eds), *Mensch – Staat – Umwelt* (2008) 47.

1361 Isensee, 'Menschenwürde: Die säkulare Gesellschaft auf der Suche nach dem Absoluten' (n 437) 194, rightly remarks that "whoever determines this term dominates the legal and political terrain." [Wer diesen Begriff besetzt, beherrscht das rechtliche und politische Terrain.]

1362 On the rationalizing function of legal dogmatics, see Volkmann (n 1035) 262–264.

interpreters are then left with the hermeneutical task of avoiding the uncontrolled trespass of meaning from one discipline to another.[1363]

Modern society is composed of different functional subsystems, which operate according to their own processes and goals.[1364] Each subsystem, including that of law,[1365] "produces its own elements and through them its own structures,"[1366] and each subsystem's structures, concepts, and institutions are means to fulfil its own function.[1367] On this basis, a concept that may have operated in an undifferentiated fashion in sundry spheres of human knowledge in the past, is today treated, defined, or provided with content by each subsystem differently. Putting it another way, the concept is produced by the system itself according to its own logic and function;[1368] "the legal system must distinguish in a special way all that has to be treated as legal communications" in society.[1369]

Because human dignity is now a concept that is used simultaneously in different subsystems, any individual who intends to participate in or observe the legal system may struggle to identify which concept of human dignity belongs to the legal system.[1370] Thus a concept of human dignity that the legal system selects as relevant for its own self-constitution is

---

1363 Hofmann, 'Methodische Probleme der juristischen Menschenwürdeinterpretation' (n 1360) 47.

1364 For an overview of this approach according to systems theory, see Niklas Luhmann, 'La diferenciación de la sociedad' in Josetxo Berian and José María García Blanco (eds), *Complejidad y Modernidad* (1998) 50 ff; for a more detailed description of the social process to functional differentiation, see Niklas Luhmann, *La sociedad de la sociedad* (2006) 471–615. It is not necessary to agree with all of Luhmann's premises and conclusions to benefit from his perspective on the following ideas.

1365 According to Luhmann, *Law as a Social System*, Fatima Kastner and others eds., (2004) 148, "law deals with the function of the stabilization of normative expectations by regulating how they are generalized in relation to their temporal, factual, and social dimensions." For a strong criticism of Luhmann's social and (particularly) his legal theory, see, e.g., Mahlmann, *Rechtstheorie und Rechtsphilosophie* (n 939) 242–244.

1366 Luhmann, *Law as a Social System* (n 1365) 151.

1367 ibid 173–211.

1368 This self-production of its own concepts and distinctions is what Luhmann defines as the "operative closure" of a system (ibid 73) which leads to the autonomy of systems (ibid 95). This closure of the legal system is of a normative type. Further detail, ibid 76–142.

1369 Luhmann, *Law as a Social System* (n 1365) 74.

1370 The "dependence on legal validity is also a precondition for limiting legal argumentation exclusively to law, which has been filtered by law, and for preventing legal arguments from being derailed by moral or other prejudices" (ibid 306).

required. This should be distinguishable from other conceptions of human dignity that the legal system considers irrelevant to its own social function.

The challenge is therefore to "attribute to the human being a legal dignity that may be equivalent to his ethical dignity as a moral agent"[1371] or equivalent to any other kind of dignity as understood in a particular subsystem. Therefore, constitutional doctrine should not uncritically adopt other definitions of human dignity as a criterion for attributing meaning, and the law must develop its own concept and institution of human dignity.

3.2. Independence without isolation

In principle, a human dignity clause must be construed according to accepted methods of constitutional interpretation.[1372] Such methods are not organized in a hierarchy but are complementary.[1373] Nevertheless, given the unique characteristics of constitutional dignity, some methods may provide much more interpretive help than others.[1374] For human dignity, the proposal of considering comparative law as the "5th method of constitutional interpretation" is particularly significant.[1375] However, as shown below, the results of this process may appear insufficient to the interpreter and it may therefore be necessary to resort to other sources besides those traditionally used in legal doctrine to fully furnish the concept with content. Therefore, the interpreter will – covertly or openly – resort to a specific theory of legitimation.[1376]

1371 Kirste, 'A Legal Concept of Dignity as a Foundation of Law' (n 526) 73.

1372 On this, see, e.g., Starck, 'Maximen der Verfassungsauslegung' (n 1344) 623–637; regarding some particularities involved in the interpretation of basic rights, ibid 637–650. However, the question remains how to define, in doubtful cases, whether a norm on human dignity is or is not a basic right. The German experience shows that scholarly arguments have not only encompassed the general and the specific spheres mentioned above but also include, as *Herdegen* does, purely historical reasons for defining dignity as a basic right (see § 7, subsection 3.2).

1373 Starck, 'Maximen der Verfassungsauslegung' (n 1344) 627.

1374 Hofmann, 'Methodische Probleme der juristischen Menschenwürdeinterpretation' (n 1360) 47–49, apropos of the German case, describes how little one might obtain from only the wording of Art. 1 (1) GG.

1375 See Peter Häberle, 'Grundrechtsgeltung und Grundrechtsinterpretation im Verfassungsstaat – Zugleich zur Rechtsvergleichung als "fünfter Auslegungsmethode"' (1989) 44 Juristenzeitung 913, 916–918.

1376 See, e.g., the discussion on the grounding of dignity in the German context in § 7, subsection 2.

As can be seen, the interpreter must balance the autonomy of legal doctrine and its necessary embeddedness in its social environment: "Constitutional openness implies a cognitive openness of the legal system towards the reality that is the object of its formation."[1377] In other words, the legal system is normatively (operationally) closed, but cognitively open.[1378] Human dignity is one of those cases where the protected content of the norm is hard to grasp simply by referring to the constitutional text.[1379] Against this backdrop, some preliminary steps for attributing meaning to a human dignity clause will be proposed. First, it will be suggested that, among the conventional means of constitutional interpretation, the historical-genealogical method, when understood in a broad sense, is particularly constructive because:

> (…) individual fundamental rights arose from concrete rejection of injustice or the struggle for certain rights. In a historical-genetic perspective, they gained their purpose and developed their substantive profile from this source.[1380]

Here, the subjective ideas on human dignity that the authors of a given norm held (i.e., which grounding they give it) are considered less decisive than the legal aim that its juridification should serve. More specifically, the crux is to identify the protective purpose for which human dignity

1377 Francisco J. Bastida Freijedo and others, *Teoría General de los Derechos Fundamentales en la Constitución Española de 1978* (2004) 57.

1378 See Luhmann, *Law as a Social System* (n 1365) 106 ff. Regarding the legal system itself, ibid 22.

1379 Starck, 'Maximen der Verfassungsauslegung' (n 1344) 628, frames this problem differently, asserting that "the fact that the constitutional text is supposed to function as an outer limit of interpretation is not a sufficient safeguard of the normativity of the constitution, because in many cases the normative content (only this content can be binding) of the text is in need of interpretation." [Dass der Verfassungstext als äußere Grenze der Interpretation fungieren soll, ist keine hinreichende Sicherung der Normativität der Verfassung, weil in vielen Fällen der normative Gehalt (nur dieser kann binden) des Textes interpretationsbedürftig ist.]

1380 Ernst-Wolfang Böckenförde, 'Schutzbereich, Eingriff, verfassungsimmanente Schranken. Zur Kritik gegenwärtiger Grundrechtsdogmatik' (n 1040) 174. [Denn die einzelnen Grundrechte sind entstanden aus konkreter Unrechtsabwehr oder der Erkämpfung bestimmter Rechte, haben historisch-genetisch von daher ihre Zielrichtung erhalten und ihr sachliches Profil ausgebildet]. For this approach, see ibid 174 ff.

was introduced into the law.[1381] The goal is to find a primary reference around which further doctrinal work can be built.[1382] The next step involves sketching an overview of possible theoretical sources to complement the minimal content already identified by the first step. Each source's main advantages and drawbacks in grounding human dignity should also be noted. Finally, some criteria should be used to foster a disciplined approach to the abundant sources on human dignity in comparative case law and scholarship (see below).

3.2.1. The minimal protective purpose of the constitutional concept of human dignity[1383]

Lawrence Rosen has pointed out the link between legal concepts and culture: law is "an excellent storehouse of stories."[1384] The meaning of frequently used concepts in the legal sphere develops from the experience of legal practitioners, from legal logic itself, and from broader agreements within a given culture of which law forms a part.[1385]

The Canadian philosopher Charles Taylor has explored the origins of modern Western identity in detail.[1386] For Taylor, the content of individual subjectivity in modernity is determined by the characteristics of "inward-

1381 From a different perspective, but in a very similar sense, Hofmann, 'Methodische Probleme der juristischen Menschenwürdeinterpretation' (n 1360) 66 suggests a hermeneutic "(...) in the sense of an extended objective-teleological interpretative intention, to ask about the purpose that had, according to the state of things in 1949, to place the guarantee of human dignity at the top of the constitutional work; that is where, at the time of Weimar, the revolutionary overthrow of the monarchy had been sealed with the definition of the republican form of state." [(...) im Sinne einer erweiterten objektiv-teleologischen Interpretationsabsicht nach dem Zweck fragen, den es nach Lage der Dinge im Jahre 1949 hatte, die Menschenwürdegarantie an der Spitze des Verfassungswerks zu platzieren, also dort, wo man seinerzeit in Weimar mit der Festlegung der republikanischen Staatsform den revolutionären Sturz der Monarchie besiegelt hatte].

1382 ibid.

1383 Some ideas already presented in Júlio Carvalho and Augusto Wiegand Cruz, 'The Augustan Novel and the Cultural Foundations of Human Dignity' (2022) 108 Archiv für Rechts- und Sozialphilosophie 108, 118–121 are further developed in this subsection.

1384 Lawrence Rosen, *Law as Culture* (2006) xii.

1385 ibid 6–7.

1386 See Charles Taylor, *The Sources of the Self* (1989).

ness, freedom, individuality, and being embedded in nature."[1387] Taylor stresses that although the sources of these attributes are controversial, there is a profound agreement about the moral standards that emerged as a consequence of this subjective structuring of the modern self.[1388] One such standard is a universal demand for respect by human beings.[1389] While Taylor believes this demand is not exclusive to the modern West, its concretization through the language of rights is unique to Western modernity.[1390]

This concretization was rooted in the work of thinkers in the natural law tradition who began to use the language of rights to express universal moral norms at the dawn of modernity.[1391] When the first philosophers of the modern era conceived the concept of subjective fundamental rights as defensive rights of the individual against the state, they combined the ancient idea that human life must be respected with the modern focus on individual autonomy.[1392] Taylor underlines that "the moral world of moderns is significantly different from that of previous civilizations."[1393]

Taylor argues that the merging of these two moral discourses resulted in a novel legal conception: henceforth, respect for the human meant recognizing the status of everyone as a subject of law – not simply as a passive object of legal rules ("no one may kill another") but also as an active participant.[1394] In this sense, Taylor emphasizes, while the condemnation of murder was assuredly not born with modernity, the latter's innovation was to express that ancient standard through the concept of the "right to life."[1395]

1387 ibid xi.

1388 ibid 11 ff. This is reminiscent of the discussions on the grounding of legal human dignity. Despite differences in justification, their normative results are, broadly speaking, highly similar.

1389 ibid 6: "We are all universalists *now* about respect for life and integrity, but this means not just that we happen to have such reactions or that we have decided in the light of the present predicament of the human race that it is useful to have such reactions (...). It means rather that *we believe it would be utterly wrong and unfounded to draw boundaries any narrower than around the whole human race*" (emphasis added).

1390 ibid 11. According to Taylor, this preferred formulation of the principle of respect in terms of rights "has become central to our legal system – and in this form has spread around the world."

1391 ibid.

1392 ibid 12.

1393 ibid 11.

1394 Cf. ibid 11–12.

1395 Cf. ibid.

The inner logic of this development triggered a long-lasting and potentially permanent process. On the one hand, the "natural" rights proclaimed by those thinkers became enshrined in legal documents, thus inaugurating the history of human rights in positive law.[1396] On the other, increasing numbers of rights and the bearers of these rights were recognized over time, not least thanks to the countless struggles waged by excluded social groups demanding their recognition as equals before the established power.[1397] These struggles played out alongside their theoretical foundations in politics or law and were modulated in distinctly religious, philosophical, or moral languages.[1398]

However, the process was far from smooth, with innumerable groups excluded: in general, women were denied the same rights as men until very recently.[1399] Even among men, important rights were reserved only for those that owned property.[1400] Privileges for the aristocracy were still

---

1396 On this, see, e.g., Stephan Kirste, 'Transpositive Foundations of Positive Human Rights' in João Maurício Adeonato (ed), *Human Rights and the Problem of Legal Injustice. Annals of the Preparatory Meeting for the XXVI World Congress of the International Association of Philosophy of Law and Social Philosophy* (2013); Frotscher and Pieroth (n 384) 9–46. Against this background, Starck, 'Maximen der Verfassungsauslegung' (n 1344) 638, remarks on the importance of the "history of the development of basic rights since the first proclamations of basic rights" for their interpretation. [Geschichte der Entwicklung der Grundrechte seit den ersten Grundrechtsproklamationen, inbesondere die deutsche Grundrechtesgeschichte, ist für deren Auslegung heranzuziehen (...)]

1397 For an overview of the development of basic rights in Germany, see Hufen, *Staatsrecht II. Grundrechte* (n 399) 19–30.

1398 For an overview of different groundings of human rights, see Mahlmann, *Rechtstheorie und Rechtsphilosophie* (n 939) 354-363. From a sociological perspective, this process coincides with the transition from stratified to modern, functionally differentiated societies. At least from the 18th century onwards, stratification can no longer justify inequalities and is repeatedly confronted with the demands of equality qua the equal value of each and every human being. On this, see Luhmann, *la Sociedad de La Sociedad* (n 1364) 612ff. Luhmann, 'la Diferenciación de la Sociedad' (n 1364) 59, further remarks that a crucial characteristic of societies that have left behind the primacy of stratifications as the main model of differentiation, i.e., modern society, emerges "when any person (...) has the same legal status."

1399 The fact that equality before the law has been achieved, at least formally, does not mean an end to deep-rooted and substantial obstacles for the full inclusion of women: this has been a historical feature of even the most inclusive societies – not to mention in the rest of the world. About this, see Mahlmann, *Rechtstheorie und Rechtsphilosophie* (n 939) 249–250.

1400 E.g., regarding the right to vote in Chile, while census suffrage was abolished in 1874, a minimum level of literacy was required until 1970. See Samuel Valenzuecommon in Europe until recently.[1401] Even in the United States until the middle of the 19th century, slavery was not only legal, but widespread in several states.[1402] However, the main setback for the moral standard described so far occurred during World War Two and through the heinous crimes that characterized it. Thus, the concept of human dignity in law seems to have developed as a reaction to dark periods of human history.[1403] Although some legal texts had previously incorporated the concept of human dignity,[1404] one can safely argue that the point of departure in modern constitutionalism was dignity's incorporation at the very start of the UN's Universal Declaration of Human Rights (1948) and in the GG (1949).[1405]

After World War Two, it became imperative to legally guarantee a minimum content of equal and unconditional recognition and protection for all human beings, despite differences about the theoretical grounding for that recognition. The proceedings of the UN's Universal Declaration of Human

---

la, 'La Ley Electoral de 1890 y la Democratización del Régimen Político Chileno' (1998) 71 Estudios Públicos 265; about the German *Zensuswahlrecht* in its several configurations, see Anna-Lena Strelitz-Risse, *Das Zensuswahlrecht. Erscheinungsformen, Begründung und Überwindung am Beispiel Frankreichs und Deutschlands* (2018) 156–396.

1401 The upper chamber of the British Parliament, the House of Lords, currently includes a small proportion of hereditary peers among its members. Further information is available on the webpage of the Parliament of the United Kingdom, see <https://members.parliament.uk/parties/lords/by-peera> accessed 07 July, 2022.

1402 At federal constitutional level, slavery was abolished in the US in 1865, with the 13th Amendment. In this regard, Luhmann, *Law as a Social System* (n 1365) 150, emphasizes the crucial importance of the positivization of moral standards; with the example of post-independence America in mind, he states: "whether or not norms can be maintained when they are pitted against a reality that differs from their expectations on a massive scale is a question that only the theory of operatively closed systems can address meaningfully. The history of human rights, which was launched in a society engaged in the slave trade with its considerable suppression of political opposition and drastic restrictions on the freedom of religion, in short, in the American society of 1776, is proof that norms can still prevail."

1403 Barak (n 394) 34. Also taking into account the experience of its extended incorporation into the new democratic constitutions of East European countries after the collapse of the Soviet Union, Christoph Möllers, 'Democracy and Human Dignity: Limits of Moralized Conception of Rights in German Constitutional Law' (2009) 42 Israel Law Review 416, 421, suggests that human dignity "seems to be a problem-solving mechanism for politically traumatized, new democratic orders, which were forced to turn to law when politics had previously failed (...)."

1404 See, e.g., Art. 6 of the Constitution of Finland (1919); preamble of the Constitution of Ireland (1937). A detailed overview is given in Barak (n 394) 49–50.

1405 Möllers (n 1403) 421–422.

Rights show that this idea was a milestone in its first Article.[1406] In turn, the Parliamentary Council redacted the norm on human dignity under the influence of the corresponding UDHR experience,[1407] while accounting for the extreme crimes of the Nazi dictatorship.[1408] Similarly, the importance of enshrining basic rights as justiciable subjective rights was first manifested at this time, not only in the proceedings of the Parliamentary Council but also in several norms of the GG itself.[1409]

Against this background, the establishment of human dignity in Art. 1 (1) GG was:

> (...) a sign of turning away from a criminal regime and its totalitarian disregard for the individual, a sign of the return to the individualistic culture of freedom in the West, and at the same time, in this sense, it was the guiding manifesto of a German statehood that, literally, had to be renewed from the ground up. Article 1 (1) of the Basic Law is, as Konrad Hesse has formulated it, the "normative foundation of this historical-concrete polity."[1410]

1406 Tore Lindholm, 'Article 1' in Gudmundur Alfredsson and Eide Asbjørn (eds), *The Universal Declaration of Human Rights. A Common Standard of Achievement* (1999).

1407 Hofmann, 'Methodische Probleme der juristischen Menschenwürdeinterpretation' (n 1360) 48.

1408 Mahlmann, 'The Basic Law at 60 – Human Dignity and the Culture of Republicanism' (n 395) 10, advances the position that "[N]azism still legitimizes the guarantee of human dignity today by the abominable, vivid barbarism of its negation." The constitutions of some *Länder* even make this connection expressly. So, e.g., the preamble of the Constitution of the Free State of Bavaria; or even more explicit, the preamble of the Constitution of the Free Hanseatic City of Bremen.

1409 Starck, 'Maximen der Verfassungsauslegung' (n 1344) 644.

1410 Hofmann, 'Methodische Probleme der juristischen Menschenwürdeinterpretation' (n 1360) 67. [Es war ein Zeichen der Abkehr von einem verbrecherischen Regime und seiner totalitären Missachtung des Individuums, ein Zeichen der Rückkehr zur individualistischen Freiheitskultur des Westens und zugleich das in diesem Sinn richtungweisende Manifest der buchstäblich von Grund auf zu erneuernden deutschen Staatlichkeit. Art. 1 Abs. 1 GG ist so, wie Konrad Hesse formuliert hat, die „normative Grundlegung dieses geschichtlich-konkreten Gemeinwesens"]. Hofmann also recounts the importance of distinguishing the universal idea of dignity from its concrete meaning for an actual state (ibid, fn 61). [Damit ist auch die Differenz zwischen der abstrakten und universalen Menschenwürdeidee und der konkreten und begrenzten Bedeutung der Menschenwürdegarantie eines bestimmten Staates bezeichnet. Manche haben offenbar Schwierigkeiten, diesen Unterschied zu begreifen.] This idea is further considered below.

From these two foundational documents for legal human dignity, the concept was recognized in a succession of international documents and domestic constitutions during the second half of the 20th century.[1411] Indeed, this process is not yet complete, as recent constitutions continue to add a human dignity clause into their texts.[1412]

The legal genealogy of the concept descends from the universal attribution of legal personality wherein every human being, without exception, must be recognized as a holder of fundamental rights.[1413] In this sense, the legal meaning of dignity as recognizing any human being as a legal person corresponds to the juridification of an ethical standard characteristic of Western modernity: the universal recognition of the value of every human being. This time, however, what is recognized is the value of the human being in the legal system: his or her legal personhood. In other words, it corresponds to the desire to stabilize an ethical norm – a kind of normative expectation without legal quality – by its juridification, transforming it into a norm resistant to deceptions.[1414]

Recognizing human dignity in law provides a "greater prospect of success and stability"[1415] to the modern moral standard of respect. When recog-

1411 A detailed exposition of this impressive development can be found in Barak (n 394) 34–65.

1412 ibid 58–59.

1413 Similarly, among the Chilean scholarship, Aldunate Lizana, *Derechos Fundamentales* (n 8) 99.

1414 See Luhmann, *Law as a Social System* (n 1365) 151 ff. One should recall here that, according to Luhmann (ibid 142), "law deals with expectations that are directed at society and not at individuals (...). 'Expectation', then, does not refer to an actual state of consciousness of a given individual human being, but to the temporal aspect of the meaning of communications." Law, adds Luhmann (ibid 148), "deals with the function of the stabilization of normative expectations by regulating how they are generalized in relation to their temporal, factual, and social dimensions."

1415 This is the effect that Luhmann, in *Law as a Social System* (n 1365) 152, attributes to the positivization of normative expectations. The practical meaning of the latter in the case of a conflict is significant: "there may be an argumentative advantage in certain situations, when problems of interpretation occur and one can refer to allegedly uncontested moral values, and morality always has significant rhetorical benefits. One cannot, however, refer to it if one wants to equip normative expectations with greater prospects of success and stability. In this case, the norm, which is to be brought into this safety zone, has to be juridified. And if this is not done in spite of an opportunity to do so, then one should anticipate the question: why not?" In the case of human dignity, after World War Two, the opportunity was taken. Describing Luhmann's theory, Johann Braun, *Einführung in die Rechtsphilosophie* (2011) 349, comments that although the positivization of nized in the legal system, human dignity can stabilize normative expectations regarding the recognition of every human being as a legal person; each human being possesses basic legal capacity and holds (fundamental) rights and duties.[1416] Hence, in any jurisdiction, this can be considered the minimum content to be covered by a norm that refers to human dignity.[1417]

The ongoing inquiry into the motivation behind the institutionalization of the concept of human dignity protects the normativity of the clause.[1418] It reduces the possibility that the relevant theory of constitutional interpretation becomes a completely closed instrument and, therefore, ideological. Moreover, it prevents the uncritical adaptation of its meaning to "time trends" [*Zeitströmungen*], which might not represent the majority opinion, but those of minorities that can influence the corresponding "Zeitgeist."[1419] Thus, keeping in mind the genealogy of human dignity as a constitutional concept allows us to maintain its elementary connection with social reality without forgetting its primary purpose.

---

law allowed expectations to be stabilized at a previously unimaginable level of precision, the possibility of reform or change remains. In this respect, one may say that the eternity clause contained in Art. 79 (3) GG that protects Art. 1 (1) from any reform constitutes a reinforced stabilization of expectations regarding human dignity.

1416 In this sense, Luhmann, *Law as a Social System* (n 1365) 269 ff, remarks that the concept of subjective rights substantially contributed to the legal system's adaptation to its environment – the recognition of legal capacity, with the independence of any individual conditions, was achieved thanks to this conception, which is thus the most "important achievement of law in modern times."

1417 Beyond this minimal protective meaning, the content of human dignity may vary depending on the respective jurisdiction, thus achieving more or less coverage: see Matthias Mahlmann, 'The Good Sense of Dignity. Six Antidotes to Dignity Fatigue in Ethics and Law' in Christopher McCrudden (ed), *Understanding Human Dignity* (2013) 598. This is proven by German legal doctrine, wherein the preferred grounding of human dignity determines whether more or fewer dimensions of the core of human personality are protected (§7, subsection 3.2).

1418 In this sense, Mahlmann, 'The Basic Law at 60 – Human Dignity and the Culture of Republicanism' (n 395) 10, states that "for many, human dignity epitomizes the core of the normative project of human rights and civilized constitutionalism that was the imperative of the new beginning after 1945."

1419 In this sense, see Starck, 'Maximen der Verfassungsauslegung' (n 1344) 630, who criticizes the negative effects on legal doctrine that Haberle's thesis of the "open society of constitutional interpreters" may produce. [Offene Gesellschaft der Verfassungsinterpreten].

3.2.2. Theoretical sources for completing human dignity's content: the legitimation of human dignity

The previous sections provide an indicative basis for fully determining the content of a given norm on human dignity. The next step must overcome the fact that the constitutional concept of human dignity is repeatedly accused of not functioning in a way that avoids its partisan manipulation;[1420] in *Taylor's* terms, of being endowed with content by recourse only to one of the fragmented moral bases of modern identity, about which views are deeply divergent. This explains why one of the most frequent discussions on human dignity concerns how to ensure its neutrality[1421] without jeopardizing its strength.[1422] The two main epistemological roots of the legal concept of human dignity[1423] view it either as a human property (or quality) or a human construct. The ramifications of these two main starting points differ significantly.[1424]

First, viewed as a human quality, dignity can be justified transcendently using theological models as an act of divine bestowal.[1425] It may also have an immanentist justification, based on man's innate qualities and their accompanying normative principles.[1426] Within the latter group, one can

1420 See powerful critiques in, e.g., Mirko Bagaric and James Allan, 'The vacuous concept of Dignity' (2006) 5 Journal of Human Rights 257; Ruth Macklin, 'Dignity is a Useless Concept' (2003) 327 British Medical Journal 1419; Rosen (n 1331); Steven Pinker, 'The Stupidity of Dignity' *The New Republic* (2008).

1421 A classic example is the concise view of Theodor Heuss, see Pikard and Werner (n 407) 72, that dignity is a "non-interpreted thesis."

1422 In this regard, Christoph Enders, 'Right to Have Rights – The German Constitutional Concept of Human Dignity' (2010) 253 NUJS Law Review 253, 12, asks whether the current devotion to dignity will remain valid in a globalized world.

1423 Oliver W. Lembcke, 'Human Dignity – a Constituent and Constitutional Principle. Some Perspectives of a German Discourse' in Stephan Kirste and Winfried Brugger (eds), *Human Dignity as a Foundation of Law: Proceedings of the Special Workshop held at the 24th World Congress of the International Association for Philosophy of Law and Social Philosophy in Beijing, 2009* (2013) 209.

1424 There are several classifications of the main grounding theories of human dignity. As shown above, German constitutional scholarship tends to present this classification in three (not two) main groups: see § 7. Mahlmann, 'The Good Sense of Dignity. Six Antidotes to Dignity Fatigue in Ethics and Law' (n 1417) 64–65, also classifies them in three groups, but with partially different content; Lembcke (n 1423) 209–210, as quoted above, suggests two main groups, each one containing three subgroups. The following paragraphs rest mainly on these classifications.

1425 See Barak (n 394) 114–116 for a short description of these models.

1426 See § 7, subsection 2.1.1., for a description of the Theory of Dowry.

distinguish between theories that require the actual presence or development of such qualities in order to attribute dignity,[1427] and those for whom potentiality, i.e., humanity alone, is sufficient.[1428] Second, some theories view human dignity only as a product of human social interaction,[1429] i.e., as the contingent result of discursive creations,[1430] either as "the result of achievements of presentation"[1431] or constituted as social recognition through the positive valuation of reciprocal demands of respect.[1432] Because such different understandings of human dignity exist, it is critical to determine whether there are "reasons normatively to prefer one concretization over another."[1433] This is of utmost importance because determining the doctrinal elements of the constitutional concept of human dignity, such as its ownership and inviolability, will depend on the chosen model.[1434] While constructivist theories of human dignity dispel any suspicion of a metaphysical or religious foundation, their contingent characterization of human dignity may devalue the unconditional protective content that led to its entry into law. On the other side of the spectrum, theological models of interpretation - despite their important role in the unfolding of the moral notion of radical equality among all members of the human family and their granting of normative certainties to the members of their communities - are unacceptable in a secular state.[1435] Therefore, those theories that recognize the unconditional dignity of every human being[1436]

1427 See, e.g., the proposal by Julian Nida-Rümelin, 'Why Human Dignity Rests upon Freedom' in Stephan Kirste and Winfried Brugger (eds), *Human Dignity as a Foundation of Law: Proceedings of the Special Workshop held at the 24th World Congress of the International Association for Philosophy of Law and Social Philosophy in Beijing, 2009* (2013).

1428 So, e.g., Dürig (n 471).

1429 According to Lembcke's classification (n 1423) 209.

1430 See Mahlmann's classification in 'The Good Sense of Dignity. Six Antidotes to Dignity Fatigue in Ethics and Law' (n 1417) 606.

1431 See Niklas Luhmann, *Los Derechos Fundamentales como Institución* (Oak Editorial 2010) 157 ff. See also § 7, subsection 2.1.2.

1432 As in Hofmann, 'Die versprochene Menschenwürde' (n 405) 364. See also § 7, subsection 2.1.3.

1433 Mahlmann, 'The Good Sense of Dignity. Six Antidotes to Dignity Fatigue in Ethics and Law' (n 1417) 602.

1434 Lembcke (n 1423) 210.

1435 Ernst-Wolfgang Böckenförde, 'El Poder Constituyente del Pueblo. Un Concepto Límite del Derecho Constitucional', *Estudios sobre el Estado de Derecho y la Democracia* (2000) 180.

1436 Cf., also Mahlmann, 'The Good Sense of Dignity. Six Antidotes to Dignity Fatigue in Ethics and Law' (n 1417) 607–609.

without recourse to sacred texts or ontological essentialisms may be those best equipped to determine and shape a given norm of human dignity in light of its core protective purpose.

In conclusion, it is worth reiterating the risk of unnecessary polemic arising when excessive prominence is assigned to grounding theories. Therefore, it is necessary to delimit the territory of constitutional law, and what properly belongs to legal theory or the philosophy of law. Just as the legal system must differentiate itself from its environment, so legal doctrine must distinguish itself from other specialized legal fields or self-descriptions within the legal system.[1437]

3.2.3. Approach to scholarship and jurisprudence from a comparative law perspective – legal transfer, comparison, and interpretation

Since its enshrinement in post-war international human rights documents and the German Basic Law, the concept of human dignity has begun and continues to be incorporated in many constitutional orders. This process has occurred primarily through the expanding international influence of German doctrine and jurisprudence on the concept[1438] and has been described as a remarkable process of legal transfer.[1439]

Constitutional jurisdictions that have recently begun doctrinal work around a dignity clause will, of course, seek guidance from those engaged in this process for longer.[1440] This interest goes far beyond simply knowing the

1437 On the existing fields and self-description of the legal system, see Luhmann, *Law as a Social System* (n 1365) 211–229; 305–356;423–463.

1438 On this, see Christopher McCrudden, 'Human Dignity and Judicial Jnterpretation of Human Rights' (2008) 19 European Journal of International Law 655; Botha (n 395); Barak (n 394) 94.

1439 Cf. Art. 1 (1) GG with, e.g., Constitution of Lithuania. "Article 21. The human person shall be inviolable. Human dignity shall be protected by law (...)"; the Fundamental Law of Hungary. "Article II (Freedom and Responsibility) Human dignity shall be inviolable. Every human being shall have the right to life and human dignity (...)"; Art. 1 (1) of the Charter of Fundamental Rights of the European Union "Human dignity shall be inviolable. It must be respected and protected." However, the concept of legal transfer is not free of ambiguities: see Alexander Graser, 'Rechtstransfer: Begriffe, Kontexte und Deutungen' in Alpay Hekimler (ed), *Festschrift für Otto Kaufman* (2021) 4–5.

1440 Hofmann, 'Methodische Probleme der Juristischen Menschenwürdeinterpretation' (n 1360) 48, recalls that such guidance was unavailable to German jurists in 1949: at that moment there was very little comparative legal scholarship on human "origin" of the norm: it includes investigating its legal treatment in its country of origin and comparing, as this may illuminate its content and purpose in one's own jurisdiction.[1441] Human dignity is consequently a privileged case for utilizing comparative law as the "5th method of interpretation:"[1442] legal transfer and comparative law are closely connected.[1443]

At the same time, the centrality of the specific positive constitutional text must be emphasized; this is particularly valid when both norms have similar wordings.[1444] A legal transfer can only be comprehended when observed as a complex process.[1445] Accordingly, the legal doctrine developed around a specific positivization of a norm on human dignity cannot be brought into one's own legal order without any mediation.[1446]

Now, the challenge is to define the content of human dignity and attribute to it a certain form or legal nature. The corresponding normative and doctrinal consequences are then drawn, supported by the unique characteristics of the concrete positive norm on dignity, taken within its frame of reference, i.e., the constitution to which it belongs.

dignity that could be utilized to interpret the human dignity clause of the GG, except mostly Art. 1 UDHR of the UN, which in fact, as previously mentioned, the Parliamentary Council had considered.

1441 Graser (n 1439) 1 correctly recalls that, in the context of continuous change in legal orders, legal transfers are of considerable importance, but this is not always noted since it commonly appears more urgent to "discuss the content and practicality of a norm, not its origin" [über Inhalt und Zweckmäßigkeit einer Norm zu diskutieren, nicht über deren Herkunft].

1442 See Häberle (n 1375) 916–918.

1443 Cf. Alexander Graser, 'Zombie mit Potential' [2018] Rechtswissenschft 136, 150, who adds that "in practice, such a reception will often actually be preceded by a process of comparative reflection, even if the conditions of simultaneous reception can vary greatly." [In der Praxis dürfte einer solcher Rezeption oft auch tatsächlich ein vergleichender Reflexionsprozess vorangegangen sein, auch wenn die Bedingungen zeitgleicher Rezeption stark variieren können].

1444 Häberle (n 1375) 917–918.

1445 Graser (n 1439) 10.

1446 Häberle (n 1375) 918.

3.2.3.1. Three lessons from Germany for the doctrinal treatment of the Chilean provision on dignity

The interpretation of the German human dignity clause cannot be used uncritically to interpret that of the Chilean Constitution.[1447] The potential scientific utility of comparing both experiences depends not least on one's perspective.[1448] As a starting point, *Graser's* "basal" understanding of comparative law will be followed here – comparative law emerges "when a person with knowledge of one legal system engages with a further one."[1449] This is likely to trigger a "reflective process," understood in a broad sense.[1450] In the present context, this perspective encourages the analyst to seek inspiration from the German experience, but do so in a selective and cautious fashion.

Accordingly, rather than simply allotting partially or in full the same content to the Chilean human dignity clause as that of its German counterpart, as well as the same normative effects it was granted in the reviewed elements of the general theory of basic rights, it is more promising to consider how to approach a constitutional norm on dignity based on the German experience. In this regard, three dimensions are proposed for consideration: the methodological, the grounding, and the sociological. Indeed, the German understanding of human dignity is embedded in a concrete methodological, philosophical-historical, and sociological context.[1451] Therefore, when using the German work on human dignity to interpret the Chilean norm, one should consider at least these three dimensions.

1447 This is an important risk, given the considerable heterogeneity of the doctrinal work on the provision on dignity in Germany.

1448 Graser (n 1443) 143.

1449 ibid 139. [Rechtsvergleichung ist, wenn ein Mensch mit Kenntnissen in einer Rechtsordnung sich mit einer weiteren befasst.]

1450 ibid. [Denn dann – so vermute ich – stellt sich fast zwangsläufig ein Reflexionsprozess ein. Es fallen Gemeinsamkeiten und Unterschiede auf, die regelmäßig bereits die kognitive Einordnung des neu erlernten Rechts beeinflussen werden, daneben wahrscheinlich neue Gedanken über das bekannte Recht und womöglich auch darüber hinaus des Betrachtenden Blick auf diese beiden Ordnungen prägen.]

1451 Of course, the human dignity clause of the GG has been involved in other dimensions or contexts, which may also warrant attention. The selection presented here is what appears to be most relevant to the Chilean context based on the author's research to date.

3.2.3.1.1. Grounding dimension

In 1949, the very inclusion of the guarantee of human dignity in the GG conveyed a definitive message of great moral significance for the new German state. However, the legal challenge of interpreting the human dignity clause using doctrinal methods had just begun. Although the legal concept of human dignity was a recent innovation, behind it were two thousand years of theological and philosophical reflection. Scholars rapidly agreed that human dignity was the central norm of the GG. The language they used to describe this conception was impressive and original;[1452] the BVerfG, for its part, followed a similar path.[1453]

Nonetheless, the complicated task of determining the content of human dignity remained. Over the years, as the legal literature on the subject expanded and became more refined, the particular nature of human dignity came into focus since it was apparent it could not be interpreted using traditional legal methods alone. The interpreters had to refer to some philosophical, ideological, or theological corpora. These attempts represented the different worldviews of their holders, which could, nevertheless, be reduced to a few groupings until, after a number of years, a particular classification gained widespread acceptance. This classification distinguishes between the Dowry, Achievement, and Recognition theories. While these theories postulate different dimensions of dignity, the literature found them consistent enough to forge a doctrinal interpretation of constitutional dignity to solve legal disputes. The content of dignity results from the sum of the dimensions that each theory includes.

Consequently, the German experience provides a valuable lesson for any jurisdiction regarding the content of a given human dignity clause. First, the traditional means of interpretation are insufficient and the recourse to the history of ideas is thus unavoidable. Second, the different theories for grounding human dignity can be approached productively. Despite some potential incompatibilities, polemical clashes of the different positions can typically be avoided. Each theory provides valuable dimensions that deserve consideration since each recognizes the plurality of visions of the good that may coexist within a given society. The interpretation of human

1452 See § 7, subsection 3.
1453 See § 7, subsection 3.

dignity thereby remains open to new dimensions; it is able to develop just as society and its ideas do.[1454]

3.2.3.1.2. Sociological dimension

Luhmann claims that fundamental rights play a functional role by avoiding the de-differentiation of social subsystems – more specifically, by avoiding the politicization of the whole society.[1455] If, for example, the right to freedom of religion or conscience is guaranteed, the political subsystem cannot dominate the religious one,[1456] enabling these subsystems to remain autonomous and differentiated from each other. From the individual's viewpoint, this means the state cannot tell anyone what he or she should believe. However, because basic legal capacity is a prerequisite for participating in these autonomous subsystems, whoever lacks such capacity cannot participate freely in society. In other words, social inclusion only exists for those entitled to basic rights.[1457]

1454 As stated above, this openness to plurality has, however, an insuperable limit: regardless of the plurality of sources that advocate a particular and perfectly valid interpretation of human dignity, the basic fact that any human being is entitled to basic rights must remain unalterable.

1455 See Luhmann, *Los Derechos Fundamentales como Institución* (n 1431) 99, 161, 297, 308, 312.

1456 Cf. ibid 325.

1457 Luhmann 'Inclusión y Exclusión' in Josetxo Berian and José García Blanco (eds), *Complejidad y Modernidad* (1998) 126 claims that modern society does not uniformly regulate inclusion – each subsystem regulates the conditions for communicating within its own boundaries. Modern society, says Luhmann, describes this predisposition to inclusion with the "semantics" of civil and human rights. However, exclusion from one system "almost automatically" involves exclusion from the others (ibid 134); consequently, the codes of each subsystem are both valid and invalid for the same society (ibid 155), leaving the distinction between inclusion/exclusion as a "meta-code." Against this background, the idea presented here is that the normative content of human dignity, as a right to have rights or as the attribution of basic legal capacity, can be understood as the intention to provide the conditions for inclusion to each human being. However, Luhmann himself did not consider human dignity in this sense. For the role that he attributes to human dignity in the German doctrine of basic rights, i.e., under the GG, see Luhmann, *Los Derechos Fundamentales como Institución* (n 1431) 139–177; for the role of human dignity in the international law of human rights – in the context of which global legal normativity may be found in global society, see Luhmann, *Law as a Social System* (n 1365).
486 ff.

This viewpoint clarifies that human dignity, as a right to have rights, formally enables everyone to freely participate in the different subsystems by enabling every individual to invoke the respective fundamental right whenever the state (or the political system) attempts to interfere with their freedom. The formal inclusion of all people in society is a decisive legal step and reflects the continued development of law in the West.[1458]

Nevertheless, simply possessing a right to have (basic) rights (i.e., a basic legal capacity) has limited meaning for the individual. Scientific or professional freedom is minimally useful if one cannot even attend elementary school; the basic right to own property is necessary, but means almost nothing to one who does not have enough to eat. The fact that the police are not allowed to enter one's home without court authorization represents progress, but the ability to enjoy the inviolability of one's home presupposes that one has a home in the first place.[1459] Thanks to human dignity, each human may potentially participate in any subsystem (such as those of the economy, religion, or science); but actually doing so requires meeting additional criteria. To interpret human dignity only as formal inclusion is insufficient to guarantee the factual participation of the individual in society.[1460]

1458 See *supra* subsection 3.2.1.

1459 Luhmann, *Law as a Social System* (n 1365) 487 ff, explains that the difference between inclusion/exclusion (i.e., the possibility that human beings can even participate in society at all) works as a distinction that operates before the distinction ("code") with which each subsystem selects which communications belong to it (in the case of the legal system, this refers to which communications the code legal/illegal can be applied). Thus, while the existence of a global society is a fact, the differences in development between different states (territorially defined) may be attributed to the different level of participation of their populations in society according to "inclusion/exclusion" meta-code. Where a population is largely excluded, the distinction between inclusion/exclusion becomes dominant. So, exclusion "from one functional area prevents inclusion in others" (ibid 489) and this happens even when somebody is not *formally* excluded: "Illiterate persons," claims Luhmann, "whether formally excluded or not, are prevented from participation in politics." For further detail on the meaning of the "inclusion/exclusion" distinction in societies where many are excluded, see Luhmann, *La Sociedad de La Sociedad* (n 1364) 488 ff.

1460 Although the Basic Law prescribes the principle of the social state, which commands the legislator to achieve social justice and security, the principle itself lacks subjective content. If, despite all welfare state [Sozialsstaat] measures, the individual still lacks the minimum resources needed to participate in the subsystems, he may not directly invoke the social state principle to obtain such resources from the state. For futher detail on the social state principle, see § 8 subsection, 3.1.1.

When the Federal Republic came into being, some German scholars stated that the protective promise of human dignity also guaranteed everyone a decent existence.[1461] Nevertheless, as early as 1951, the BVerfG rejected the idea that the GG included an fundamental individual right "to a legal regulation of entitlements to an adequate social care through the state."[1462] While qualifying this ruling over time, it decisively changed its view only sixty years later. In *Hartz IV*,[1463] the court stated that Art. 1 (1) GG, in conjunction with the social state principle, guarantees "to any individual in need the material preconditions which are imperative for his physical existence as well as a minimum level of participation in social, political, and cultural life."[1464]

Art. 1 (1) GG included the individual in society, both formally and materially. However, while Art. 1 (1) alone attributes basic legal capacity and, therefore, the potential to freely participate in social subsystems, it requires the social state principle to provide the minimal resources to actually be able to do so. However, the BVerfG did not create this right from nothing. The legislature had developed minimal provisions for a decent existence over the course of decades. When the court reviewed an existing social law corpus in the *Hartz IV* case, the protective force of that corpus was questioned due to the liberalizing measures the German state had taken in 2005 (the so-called "Agenda 2010").[1465] Hence, it can be said that one dimension of the dignity clause is an order to the public power to create decent conditions for everyone. These conditions, however, were not created from the constitution alone, but also from the German state's continued political efforts to build and maintain a welfare state.

In the light of these developments, the following conclusions arise from a comparative perspective. Human dignity's normative program aims to include all human beings fully in society. This means not only formal inclusion *qua* recognition of every human being as a legal person but also the guarantee of a minimum income, which is a prerequisite for exercising freedoms; namely, being included materially in society.[1466] Human dignity

1461 See § 8, subsection 3.1.

1462 BVerfG 1, 97 (97) – *Hinterbliebenenrente I* (1951), 4th headnote.

1463 BVerfG 125, 175 – *Hartz IV* (2010).

1464 One may note that the formulation of the BVerfG indicates an understanding based on the perception of different subsystems.

1465 See § 8, subsection 3.1.2.1.

1466 In this sense, Luhmann, 'Inclusión y Exclusión' (n 1457) 123, recalls that inclusion refers to the idea of human beings treated as "persons."

demands the state prioritize creating the conditions that allow the institutionalized provision of a minimum income for all. However, the existence of a guaranteed minimum income is the result of complex institutional structures and not an *a priori* doctrinal construction of the BVerfG.

3.2.3.1.3. Doctrinal dimension

A third outcome of the German experience relates to its illuminating doctrinal treatment of human dignity. The main doctrinal fact is that human dignity is considered an absolute right by the ruling opinion and the BVerfG. Although the latter's view is far from uncontested, German legal practitioners apply it using widespread doctrinal tools that enable human dignity to be precisely and predictably processed as a right. Therefore, most of the criticism leveled at legal dignity that has appeared in the international arena or other jurisdictions is of limited relevance to the German case.

Initially, the German courts rejected most of those dignity-based claims that the international debates found unjustified. Several scholarly articles are critical of human dignity as a legal concept, recalling its use as a basis for several ridiculous complaints in the German courts. However, their authors sometimes neglect to mention that these claims were eventually unsuccessful. Likewise, the BVerfG's jurisprudence on human dignity tends to be restrained, as evidenced by the fact it has deduced only one social right from dignity.[1467] Moreover, the wording of the norm strongly supports interpreting the human dignity clause as a subjective right.[1468] Other jurisdictions that do not fulfill these characteristics should exercise great caution if considering whether to attribute subjective law content to the dignity clause.

1467 See § 8, subsection 3.1.
1468 See § 7, subsection 3.2.

§ 13 Bases for the understanding of human dignity in the Chilean constitutional order

1. Reconstruction of the concept of human dignity based on Art. 1 in conjunction with Art. 5, par. 2. CPR

1.1. Juridical norm

1.1.1. The dignity clause as a preamble

The Chilean dignity clause is worded in a way that resembles a preamble.[1469] Its structure is akin to a moral proclamation: it intends to mobilize.[1470] Indeed, it is remarkably similar to the first sentence of Art. 1 UDHR,[1471] a similarity that increases the rhetorical force of the clause. In the light of the human rights tradition, the provision suggests that the validity of those rights–along with human dignity, freedom, and equality –does not depend on their positivization.[1472] Nonetheless, this does not prevent human rights from assuming the form of positive subjective rights within the CPR.[1473]

1469 Art. 1, par. 1, CPR: "Persons are born equal in dignity and rights."

1470 On the characteristics of preambles, see Javier Tajadura Tejada, 'La Función Política de los Preámbulos Constitucionales' (2001) 5 Cuestiones Constitucionales 235; for preambles in Latin American texts, see Orlando Pardo Martínez, 'Metarrelatos Políticos: los Preámbulos Constitucionales Latinoamericanos (2018) 20 Reflexión Política.

1471 However, this similarity arose almost by chance. Regarding the genealogy of Art. 1, par. 1 CPR and its reforms, see § 2, subsection 4.2.

1472 On the supra-positive validity and form of human rights, see Stephan Kirste, '§ 204 Die naturrechtliche Idee überstaatlicher Menschenrechte' in Josef Isensee and Paul Kirchhof (eds), *Handbuch des Staatsrechts der Bundesrepublik Deutschland. Band X.* (2012) 5 ff.

1473 ibid.

1.1.2. The openness of the constitutional text

As described above, Art. 1, par. 1 CPR establishes the opening of the constitutional text onto reality, preventing a completely self-referential legitimation of its norms; the CPR recognizes that human value does not ultimately depend on any positive-law provision, not even those of the greatest significance. However, this does not mean the CPR had decided upon the definitive grounding of human dignity.[1474] Apart from aligning itself with the human rights tradition of modern constitutionalism, the CPR leaves the question of grounding open to interpretation.[1475]

1.1.3. Legal character

However, none of the above-mentioned characteristics should be understood as a rejection of the juridical power of Art. 1 par. 1 CPR. The indicative grammatical structure within the CPR is also the strongest form of the imperative.[1476] Art. 1, par. 1 belongs to the first chapter of the CPR. This establishes the CPR's main normative principles, which are then concretized by further constitutional dispositions. There are no reasons to exclude Art. 1, par. 1 CPR from this normativity.[1477]

Some concrete effects of the clause are soon declared. In Art. 1 par. 4 CPR, the first sentence prescribes that "the State is at the service of the human person." This phrase could even be seen as redundant, since simply incorporating dignity in the CPR has that effect on the state.[1478]

1474 See § 4.

1475 Böckenförde, 'El Poder Constituyente del Pueblo. Un Concepto Límite del Derecho Constitucional' (n 1435) 180. While most of the Chilean constitutional drafters (see § 2) took a similar approach to the grounding of basic rights, this issue remains open. As Mahlmann, 'The Good Sense of Dignity. Six Antidotes to Dignity Fatigue in Ethics and Law' (n 1417) 600, recalls, "a plurality of background ideas" were present when "norms constitutive of modern dignity law were drafted" – see, e.g., Lindholm (n 1406).

1476 For further detail on the meaning of this Isensee statement, see § 7.

1477 This vision is also supported by the ruling opinion. See § 3, subsections 1 and 2.

1478 Similarly, Hofmann, 'Methodische Probleme der Juristischen Menschenwürdeinterpretation' (n 1360) 67, suggests this is also the main implicit meaning of Art. 1 (1) GG. Here, the wording of Art. 1 of the "Chiemseer Entwurf" should be recalled [Artikel 1. (1) Der Staat ist um des Menschen willen da, nicht der Mensch um des Staates willen. (2) Die Würde der menschlichen Persönlichkeit ist unantastbar.

In addition, the remaining paragraphs of Art. 1 CPR concretize several implications of placing the individual at the center of the legal order. First, the family is declared the core of society (Art. 1, par. 2 CPR). As such, it enjoys the state's protection, which seeks to strengthen it (Art. 1, par. 5 CPR). Second, other human associations enjoy recognition, protection, and autonomy (Art. 1, par. 3 CPR). Third, the state must promote the material and spiritual flourishing of the individual (Art. 1, par. 4 CPR), which includes creating equal opportunities for all (Art. 1, par. 5 CPR).

1.1.4. Juridical interpretation

The recognition of human dignity *qua* its institutionalization[1479] necessitates its interpretation through constitutional doctrine. In other words, while incorporating human dignity into the CPR may be understood as recognizing a supra-positive reality, Art. 1, par. 1 CPR must be interpreted as a positive-law clause when already in the CPR. Art. 1, par. 1 CPR does not make a biological, ontological, or metaphysical declaration,[1480] but is a normative attribution:[1481] at least for the constitutional order, human beings enjoy these characteristics. The consequences thereof are juridically developed in the rest of the constitutional text.

1.2. Rank

1.2.1. Supreme constitutional norm

Human dignity is the supreme norm of the Chilean constitutional order. Although the CPR may appear to have awarded freedom, equality, and dignity the same rank, the superiority of human dignity must be affirmed for reasons set out below.[1482]

Die öffentliche Gewalt ist in allen ihren Erscheinungsformen verpflichtet, die Menschenwürde zu achten und zu schützen.]

1479 See Lembcke (n 1423) on the consequences of the institutionalization of dignity.

1480 See the ruling opinion in § 3, subsection 1.5. for a different view on this

1481 See Mahlmann, 'The Good Sense of Dignity. Six Antidotes to Dignity Fatigue in Ethics and Law' (n 1417) 604.

1482 While the Chilean ruling opinion concurs, it mostly does so without doctrinal arguments to support this idea on the positive text: see § 3, subsection 1.3.

From a constitutional point of view, human freedom and equality are not biological realities but normative assumptions. The CPR only recognizes that human value precedes the state. Consequently, human beings must be granted the highest possible status within the constitutional order: that of legal persons, i.e., subjects capable of holding rights, beginning with fundamental rights. Because the state exists for the sake of human beings, all human beings are legal persons within the legal system.[1483] If each human being is equal in holding the basic legal capacity to use constitutional freedoms, then individuals are "free and equal in rights." The CPR organizes this freedom in its Bill of Rights, which identifies several basic rights.[1484] The more complex a society is, the more freedom must be differentiated into diverse basic rights. Differentiation also acknowledges the fact that some thematic areas of freedom require stronger protection and any restriction on the associated rights must therefore be more strongly justified.[1485] Recognizing human dignity makes all human beings legal persons, equal before the law, and, as holders of basic rights, (legally) free.

1.2.2. Human nature and human dignity

Art. 5 par. 2 CPR supports the above view. The provision stipulates that the exercise of state power reaches its limit in the "essential rights that emanate from human nature."[1486] However, the language used could have used the more precise concept that the state is bound to basic rights,[1487] because the

1483 This is the minimal content of every norm on dignity, as has already been described. See § 12, subsection 3.2.1.

1484 See Art. 19 CPR.

1485 Thus, rights linked to religion, artistic expression, assembly, or scientific discovery could be part of a general right of freedom. The differentiation depends on historical and doctrinal reasons. For an overview of the history of basic rights in Chile, see Fernando Muñoz León, 'Historia de los Derechos Fundamentales in Pablo Contreras Vásquez and Constanza Salgado Muñoz (eds), *Manual sobre Derechos Fundamentales* (2017). However, the main doctrinal difference among them corresponds to spheres of freedom that deserve stronger protection qua stricter justification of restrictions. An overview of the legal doctrine for restrictions on fundamental rights in Chile is given in Aldunate Lizana, *Derechos Fundamentales* (n 8) 234–239.

1486 See § 2, subsection 5.2 for a summary of the main discussions in Chilean legal doctrine and case law on this clause (Art. 5 par. 2 CPR).

1487 On the genealogy of this provision, see an overview in Aldunate Lizana, *Derechos Fundamentales* (n 8) 316–319; 422–423.

meaning of both, "essential" and "human nature" are highly debatable and open to undisciplined interpretations.

These difficulties are not, however, excuses for doctrinal inaction, since law must not remain indeterminate. Although unable to define "human nature" from a biological or philosophical point of view, the law must assign it a juridical meaning. In this sense, within the constitution, the "nature" of the human being must be understood as an attribute that the law recognizes as prior to the state, i.e., dignity. In other words, the *nature* of the human being as a legal person is his or her ownership of basic rights.[1488] This confirms the above claim that if (essential) rights emanate from human dignity, human dignity is more prominent in the constitutional order than other constitutional rights or principles such as freedom and equality.

1.3. Legal form

1.3.1. Constitutional principle

The dignity clause of the CPR is a constitutional principle[1489] that occupies a different doctrinal category to the basic rights prescribed by the CPR.[1490] The arguments supporting this position are listed below.

1.3.1.1. Grammar

Art. 1, par. 1 CPR does not have the structure of a basic right; its wording does not suggest the existence of subjective-law content. Moreover, its form resembles that of a preamble. However, given that it has normative force, it must be understood as a constitutional principle.

1488 Equally, Kirste, 'A Legal Concept of Dignity as a Foundation of Law' (n 526) 77, believes that these "persons are not created out of bones and flesh; their body consists of rights and duties."

1489 This is in line with practically all Chilean scholarship and case law, although most use the term "value." See § 3, subsection 1.3.

1490 On the Bill of Rights of the CPR and its location, see § 2.

1.3.1.2. Location

Art. 1, par. 1 opens the CPR's chapter "Institutional Foundation," which establishes several constitutional principles and no fundamental rights.[1491] Systematically analyzed, the human dignity clause shares this legal form when no strong reasons suggest the opposite.

1.3.1.3. Genealogy

The full record of constitutional proceedings suggest that all the drafters involved in the discussion considered the dignity clause only as a principle or a value.[1492]

1.3.1.4. Remedy of protection

Neither the norm's wording nor its location, nor its genealogy definitively excludes human dignity from the Bill of Rights of the CPR. All these obstacles could be overcome if Art. 20 CPR had considered the human dignity clause within the catalog of norms in which protection is guaranteed by the remedy of protection – the CPR's constitutional complaint mechanism.

The remedy of protection may be brought before the courts only for those rights expressly listed in the CPR as protected from interference by that remedy. However, the omission of human dignity from that list of rights, in conjunction with the reasons stated above, support the conclusion that human dignity does not have the character of a basic right. This interpretation is confirmed by scholarship and case law.[1493]

1491 On this section of the CPR, see more details in § 2, subsection 4.1.
1492 For the genealogy of the norm, see § 2, subsection 4.2.
1493 See § 3, subsections 1.3. and 2.1.

1.4. Content of human dignity

1.4.1. Minimal content: Basic legal capacity

The previous chapter (§12) suggests that, at minimum, a constitutional norm on human dignity means recognizing every human being as a legal person.[1494] This is valid for any jurisdiction, including the Chilean one.[1495] Conversely, any limitation of this guarantee would entail the exclusion of a group of individuals from legal subjectivity and must be understood as directly contradicting the aforementioned juridical minimal content. Its absoluteness can be enforced by considering human dignity as a principle of objective law.[1496]

1.4.2. Elementary minimal constitutive factors for the enjoyment of basic legal capacity

In addition, as part of the content protected by human dignity, it is also essential to consider the constitutive elements of personality that allow the exercise of the freedoms guaranteed by basic rights. Without the protection of these constitutive elements of personality, the formal inclusion of the human being in the legal system as a legal person has no practical meaning.

1.4.2.1. The traditional theories of legitimation

The constitutive elements of human personality are not accessible by interpreting Art. 1, para. 1 CPR by canonic means alone. In this sense, the theories of the grounding of human dignity used in Germany can inform the interpretation of Art. 1, par. 1 CPR.[1497] On the one hand, these theories

1494 Aldunate Lizana, *Derechos Fundamentales* (n 8) 99, interprets it this way, both in general and for the Chilean case.

1495 For an interesting reflection on questions associated with the universal validity of dignity (in the strict sense), and good reasons for maintaining it, see Mahlmann, 'The Good Sense of Dignity. Six Antidotes to Dignity Fatigue in Ethics and Law' (n 1417) 615.

1496 Regarding the objective law effects of the human dignity clause in the German context, see § 7, subsection 3.3.

1497 See § 12, subsection 3.2.3.1. For the current grounding of dignity in Chilean legal doctrine, see § 3, subsection 1.4.

are congruent in many areas regarding the content protected by human dignity, making them essentially compatible.[1498] On the other, they highlight various aspects of human personality, which may hold implications for the protected content. A pragmatic understanding of human dignity should not strictly prefer one theory over another as a matter of principle,[1499] thereby allowing the application of any theory to cases when it may provide clearer answers.[1500] However, when the theories provide different solutions to a particular case, the interpreter will have to prioritize among them.[1501]

According to the perspective being defended here, the various dimensions of the protected content of human dignity provided by the distinct theories of grounding must be understood as the constitutive elements of personality that imbue basic legal capacity with practical meaning. They can also be understood as the minimal negative freedoms that are preconditions for legal subjectivity before the state. Usually, these freedoms are recognized separately in other constitutional provisions and are occasionally expressed as norms that admit no restriction, i.e., the absolute prohibition of torture[1502] or slavery.[1503] Frequently, they also receive support from international human rights law; in the CPR this occurs explicitly thanks to its Art. 5, par. 2.[1504]

1.4.2.1.1. Defensive sphere

The defensive dimension of these constitutive elements of personality may coincide with the scope of protection of some concrete individual basic rights. However, the protection of the former does not depend on the explicit establishment of these latter rights in the CPR. Basic legal capacity may not be understood as a completely empty box. When considering dignity's juridical goals, it would not be sufficiently protective to provide a legal person with basic legal capacity in the abstract but no rights in

1498 See § 12, subsection 3.2.3.1.1.
1499 See § 12, subsection 3.2.3.1.1.
1500 See § 12, subsection 3.2.1
1501 Criteria for facilitating this process are described in §12.
1502 Art. 19 no. 1, par. 4 CPR.
1503 Art. 19 no. 2, par. 1 CPR.
1504 See § 2, subsection 5.2.

practice.[1505] Therefore, basic legal capacity presupposes some minimum of guaranteed freedoms.[1506] In cases where the CPR does not prescribe concrete positive norms to protect these dimensions, the corresponding freedom must be deduced from Art. 1, par. 1 in conjunction with Art. 5, par. 2 CPR.[1507]

1.4.2.1.2. Protective sphere

Although there is no written duty of protection, the CPR demands the state protect human dignity against third parties. It is possible to reconstruct this duty from Art. 1, par. 1 CPR, in conjunction with the first sentence of Art. 1 par. 4 CPR, which prescribes that the "State is at the service of the human being." Accordingly, the state must protect the legal subject from attacks by third parties that could jeopardize those constitutive elements of personality that stand as preconditions for the factual enjoyment of basic legal capacity. In protecting these dimensions, the state has less margin of appreciation than in protecting other individual basic rights. The former must be protected more strongly by ordinary law – human dignity is the superior norm of the CPR.

1.4.2.1.3. Benefit sphere

Art. 1, par. 4 CPR reads:

> [T]he State is at the service of the human being and its end is to promote the common good, for which it must help create the social conditions which may allow each and every one of the members of the national community his greatest possible spiritual and material realization, with

---

1505 For a different perspective on this point, see Kirste, 'A Legal Concept of Dignity as a Foundation of Law' (n 526) 80, where he states that "human dignity is a right to be respected as having potential to have further rights and does not mean to actually have them."

1506 This also corresponds to the dimensions of the content of human dignity in Germany, on most accounts. See § 7, subsection 3.2.

1507 More detail *infra* in subsection 2.1.2. The CCT has indeed proceeded in this manner when deducing some implicit fundamental rights from dignity. See § 4, subsection 2.2.2.

total respect for the rights and guarantees that this Constitution establishes.[1508]

It might initially be concluded that this provision is already comparable with the GG's principle of the social state. However, on closer examination, Art 1. par. 4 alone does not constitute a similar obligation on the Chilean state. The paragraph does not differentiate between those who already enjoy the social conditions necessary for minimal spiritual and material development and those who do not. Accordingly, the state would have to act equally to allow all citizens their *greatest possible* realization.

Only when interpreted in conjunction with the human dignity clause does the lawmaker's primary task appear. If the normative program of human dignity is to fully include all individuals in society, it can be deduced that the primary aim of the norm of human dignity is to include those that *remain* excluded. Faced with two possibilities – namely, to pursue either those conditions that allow everyone to realize their *maximal* potential, or to create conditions that enable everyone's *minimal* spiritual and material realization – human dignity requires the legislator to choose the second option. This means the claim to advance the material and spiritual development of those who already enjoy minimal conditions is not equal before the state to the claim of those who do not yet enjoy these conditions.

Therefore, from Art. 1, par. 1 in conjunction with Art. 1, par. 4 CPR, a norm relating to the social state for the CPR can be formulated, explicitly based on human dignity. To develop its own understanding, the Chilean jurisdiction may use German doctrine and case law on the social state principle as a helpful starting point.[1509] Essentially, the German legal doctrine on this principle demands that the state achieve a balance between freedom and equality, thereby creating the preconditions that allow the factual exercise of freedom for all.[1510]

From its positive dimension, this doctrinal construction must be understood as a norm of objective law, which assigns the Chilean lawgiver its most urgent mandatory task: achieving not only formal, but also substan-

1508 [El Estado está al servicio de la persona humana y su finalidad es promover el bien común, para lo cual debe contribuir a crear las condiciones sociales que permitan a todos y a cada uno de los integrantes de la comunidad nacional su mayor realización espiritual y material posible, con pleno respeto a los derechos y garantías que esta Constitución establece.]

1509 See § 8, subsection 3.1.1.

1510 See § 8, subsection 3.1.1.

tive or material inclusion of all individuals in society.[1511] For everyone to participate in society, merely recognizing certain freedoms in the CPR is not enough. Instead, complex institutional mechanisms must be developed to create the social conditions that allow everyone the minimal resources needed to exercise their freedom.[1512]

The institutional pursuit and achievement of this aim becomes a major task of Chile's political system, thanks to Art. 1 par. 1 in conjunction with Art. 1 par. 4 CPR. The CPR delegates responsibility for complying with the command to the democratic political process. While the CPR does not decide how lawmakers execute the task, it demands that the institutionalization of social inclusion is a primary outcome.[1513]

However, the CPR itself obstructs the completion of this task. While it requires the democratic lawmaker to achieve the aforementioned conditions, it neglects to supply the political tools for the job. For example, until very recently the CPR contained a set of rules that complicated the majoritarian democratic lawmaker's pursuit of a social agenda, as the minority could block such proposals easily. Although recent reforms have alleviated this problem, it has not been completely resolved.[1514] This is one of the CPR's more significant democratic deficits, which, furthermore, cannot and must not be overcome by constitutional interpretation alone as that would mean fighting for democracy with means that contradict the democratic constitutional principle.[1515]

1511 See § 12, subsection 3.2.3.1.2 for more on dignity and full inclusion in society.

1512 A similar recognition of this dimension of dignity is to be found in Nogueira Alcalá, *Dogmática Constitucional* (n 43) 108.

1513 See also § 8, subsection 3.1.

1514 See § 2, subsection 1. In addition to the issues described in the aforementioned subsection, the current Chilean political system is characterised by highly fragmented and weakened political parties. This hinders the formation of consistent majorities and collaboration between the opposition and the government. However, this topic goes far beyond the scope of the present work. For more information, see Luis Eugenio García-Huidobro and Lucas Sierra (eds.), *Diez Miradas sobre el Sistema de Gobierno: Diagnósticos y Propuestas para la Nueva Constitución* (2022).

1515 Starck, 'Maximen der Verfassungsauslegung' (n 1344) 617, correctly summarizes this tension: "In a democratic state, the political process requires that the substantive questions are subjected to the decision of the majority and that not all are predecided by the constitution (...). [Der politische Prozeß in einem demokratischen Staat verlangt, daß substantielle Fragen der Mehrheitsentscheidung unterworfen sind und daß nicht alle durch die Verfassung in der Gestalt, die sie durch die Interpretation des Verfassungsgerichts gefunden hat, vorentschieden sind.]

Hence, at least when considered cumulatively, such counter-majoritarian rules contradict the order deduced from Art. 1, par. 1 in conjunction with Art. 1, par. 4 CPR – and, indirectly, the human dignity clause as well. Since human dignity is the CPR's supreme norm, there is an urgent need to reform this counter-majoritarian set of rules to overcome this internal contradiction of the CPR.

1.4.2.2. Universality of human dignity and the particularity of the Chilean community that guarantees it

First of all, human dignity must be understood as a universally valid criterion for attributing basic legal capacity. In addition, it is feasible to utilize traditional theories on the grounding of human dignity to define more fully what is protected by the CPR's human dignity clause. In doing so, the same content should not be attached to each norm on human dignity in every jurisdiction. Instead, it should be recognized that these sources of interpretation are, in essence, inseparably attached to legal dignity and without them, it would be impossible to complement the latter's minimal content.

However, each norm on human dignity must be enforced by a concrete jurisdiction.[1516] Thus, a relative conceptualization of dignity may be required alongside the universal. This universal meaning of human dignity is not displaced by the relative understanding but instead complements it in each community, which supplies a specific meaning that may have no significance for any other setting.

In the Chilean case, the meanings that native peoples ascribe to "human dignity" or functionally similar terms must be considered.[1517] These mean-

1516 See Hofmann, 'Die versprochene Menschenwürde' (n 405) on the difference between the universality of human dignity and its concreteness regarding the state responsible for guaranteeing it, in reference to the German case.

1517 See Mahlmann, 'The Good Sense of Dignity. Six Antidotes to Dignity Fatigue in Ethics and Law' (n 1417) 596–597. This may hold, for example, for the concept of *buen vivir* [good living], practiced by several indigenous peoples in Latin America, including Chile, e.g., *suma qamaña* [Aymara People] or *Küme mogen* [Mapuche People]. For a detailed explanation of this connection, see Viviana Bohórquez Monsalve and Javier Aguirre Román, 'Las Tensiones de la Dignidad Humana: Conceptualización y Aplicación en el Derecho Internacional de los Derechos Humanos' (2009) 6 Sur. Revista Internacional de Derechos Humanos 41, 46.

ings should also be considered when furnishing Art. 1, par. 1 CPR with content, at three different levels.

First, this worldview should complement the interpretation of Art. 1 par. 1 CPR that results from the traditional theories of grounding. Second, the dimensions of human dignity contributed by this worldview must also be valid when interpreting ordinary law, especially the so-called general clauses.[1518] Third, these indigenous concepts – which are functionally similar to human dignity – frequently emphasize both the special relationship between these peoples and nature and the need for autonomy from traditional state authorities to develop that relationship properly.[1519] This tripartite approach can also guide the transference of some competencies from the central state to self-government by the native communities, including the possibility of applying their own normative systems among them in certain areas.[1520]

1518 These two levels can be classified as access to justice in conditions of "interculturality," which is one of the main demands of indigenous peoples in this area; see Marie-Christine Fuchs and Hartmut Rank (eds), 'Elementos Formales. Fundamentos de la Jurisdicción Indigena', *Manual de Pluralismo Jurídico para la Práctica de la Justicia Intercultural* (2022) 80. The other corresponds to what is presented in this paragraph of the present text as the third level; namely, the recognition of spaces for indigenous jurisdiction.

1519 Fuchs and Rank (n 1518) 106 argue that "it is important that the indigenous culture, with its principles, spirituality, and relationship with nature, also has a space for the interpretation of fundamental rights. (...)."

1520 A grounding for legal pluralism in the Latin American context, from several perspectives, can be found in Fuchs and Rank (n 1518). Their proposal, however, does not always maintain enough critical distance from its subject. See e.g., ibid 80, where the authors somewhat relativize the seriousness of corporal punishment within some indigenous traditions, by affirming that it is also "true that in many cases corporal punishment is still used, such as, inter alia, forced community work, the use of sticks, whipping, nettles, and cold water baths. These produce situations that must first be understood in order to know which legal values are protected by these institutions, and then assessed from an intercultural human rights perspective (...)." [También es cierto que en muchos casos se siguen usando penas corporales, como trabajo comunitario, uso de cepos, azotes, ortiga, baños de agua fría, entre otros, que generan situaciones que deben ser primero comprendidas para saber cuál o cuáles son los valores jurídicos protegidos por esas instituciones y, después, valoradas desde una perspectiva intercultural de los derechos humanos (...)].

2. *Human dignity in the general theory of basic rights*

The preceding pages have already described the desirable role of human dignity regarding various elements of the legal doctrine of basic rights in the Chilean constitutional order, which are the topic of this work. A summary of these results is provided below.

2.1. Foundation of basic rights

2.1.1. Grounding of basic rights in a general sense

Chilean scholarship and case law unanimously believe that human dignity is the foundation of basic rights.[1521] This conclusion is correct. However, such a strong statement must be justified from a doctrinal perspective. To reiterate: the CCT has held that human dignity makes a person worthy of respect inasmuch as it is the source of the rights he or she enjoys.[1522] However, a different formulation would be more appropriate; namely, the main way that the CPR respects those who are bestowed with human dignity is by recognizing their rights.

From Art. 1 par. 1 CPR alone, robust positive-law support for considering human dignity as the foundation of basic rights is undetectable. But when the dignity clause of the CPR is considered in conjunction with Art. 5, par. 2 CPR, and the concept of "human nature" contained therein is mapped to that of human dignity, this grounding can be doctrinally sustained in a consistent fashion.[1523]

2.1.2. Grounding of implicit rights

Both the CCT and most scholars have argued that, consistent with Art. 5, par. 2 CPR, the constitutional catalog of rights must not be considered exhaustive.[1524] According to the approach defended in the current work,

1521 See § 4, subsections 1 and 2.1.

1522 CCT Rol 389–2003, par. 17. More details in § 3, subsection 2.2.

1523 See *supra* subsection 1.2.2. A similar doctrinal proposal is formulated by Aldunate Lizana, *Derechos Fundamentales* (n 8) 349.

1524 See § 4, subsections 1 and 2.2.2.

a direct deduction of subjective rights from human dignity is not only possible, but indeed mandatory in some cases. Nonetheless, this deduction must be restricted to protecting those constitutive elements of personality without which basic legal capacity would become an empty attribute. If such negative freedoms are not expressly considered by the Bill of Rights of the CPR, they must be deduced from Art. 1, par. 1 in conjunction with Art. 5, par. 2.[1525]

This process of deduction can be outlined as follows: firstly, Art. 5, par. 2 CPR leaves the catalog of rights open to those that emanate from "human nature." Secondly, human nature refers, as previously explained, to the concept of human dignity prescribed in Art. 1, par. 1 CPR. Thirdly, to the extent that the constitutive elements of personality are not expressly stated by the constitution, they can be deduced from the human dignity clause. Finally, the different theories of grounding provide a means to determine these elements. In most relevant aspects, these theories lead to the same results, but if an incompatibility is discovered, it is necessary to prioritize using the criteria described in §12. In practice, the main responsibility for concretizing these dimensions lies with the CCT.

2.2. Ownership of basic rights

The primary function of human dignity is to attribute basic legal capacity or legal personhood to any human being,[1526] and the Chilean case is no exception.[1527] This affirmation does not immediately resolve some of the most controversial legal conflicts of our times,[1528] but transfers their doctrinal treatment to the level of the concrete individual rights in question.

Accordingly, Art. 1 par. 1 CPR in conjunction with Art. 5 par. 2 CPR represents the point where the constitutional system opens onto cognitive reality. The conjunction of these two articles places the individual in the center of the legal order by declaring him or her a legal person. One could phrase this constitutional recognition in the language of rights, i.e., as a

1525 See *supra* subsection 1.2.2. The CCT reached comparable conclusions when it deduced some implicit rights, albeit without providing the aforementioned doctrinal justification. See § 4, subsection 2.2.3.

1526 See § 12, subsection 3.1.

1527 See *supra* 1.1.2.2.1.

1528 See § 5 and § 9.

right to be recognized as a legal person or as a *right to have rights*.[1529] This claim is the only constitutional right of the human being as such; all other rights follow from the status as a legal person.[1530] In the case of the CPR, this status is provided by a norm of objective law. Should this basic legal capacity be questioned in a concrete case, the individual as a legal person may claim its validity through the guarantee of concrete constitutional rights contained in the CPR's Bill of Rights or through one of the implicit rights that can be deduced from the dignity clause.

2.3. Restrictions on basic rights

2.3.1. Restrictions on human dignity

Understanding human dignity as the attribution of basic legal capacity has absolute validity.[1531] Any limitation on this normative effect of human dignity would effectively exclude a particular group of human beings from the ownership of basic rights.[1532] The constitutive elements of personality, which in law usually take the form of defensive freedoms, are also, in principle, not limitable. Occasionally, they are recognized as absolute prohibitions, such as a minimum of physical integrity (prohibition of torture) or of freedom (prohibition of slavery).

1529 On these conceptions of *Kirste* and *Enders*, see § 7, subsection 3.1.

1530 Stephan Kirste, 'Die Hermeneutik der Personifikation im Recht' (2015) 101 Archiv für Rechts- und Sozialphilosophie 473, 482 ff.

1531 The present work does not aim to propose a doctrinal treatment of restrictions on basic rights of the CPR, i.e., an equivalent of the German *Drei-Stufen-Prüfung*, but it must be remembered that such a doctrine – shared, simple, and accepted by legal practitioners – is a prerequisite for correctly applying human dignity in this context. See § 12, subsection 3.2.3.1.3. The development of this dimension remains precarious in Chile; see § 2, subsection 2.

1532 See Mahlmann, 'The Good Sense of Dignity. Six Antidotes to Dignity Fatigue in Ethics and Law' (n 1417) 611, for a similar grounding for the absoluteness of human dignity in any jurisdiction.

2.3.2. Human dignity as an inherent limit in the constitution

While the literature has only mentioned that human dignity plays a role as an inherent limit in the constitution in the Chilean context,[1533] the CCT has used human dignity as a basis both for restricting fundamental rights and for limiting those restrictions, in several cases.[1534] Although the results of this case law may sometimes be accurate, the CCT is yet to build a doctrinal argument that would make them predictable.[1535]

Following the categories developed in Germany, appealing to human dignity to directly justify a restriction on fundamental rights equates to viewing human dignity as an inherent limit in the Constitution.[1536] Human dignity can also play this role in the Constitution of Chile – the human dignity clause of Art. 1, par. 1 is the supreme principle of the CPR.[1537] It therefore prevails over other constitutional provisions, including those with subjective-law content as basic rights.

Nevertheless, correctly applying human dignity in this role requires careful determination of its content as a main prerequisite, as outlined above.[1538] In addition, a watertight process rests on established legal doctrine regarding the limits inherent in the constitution. Developing or proposing such doctrine for the Chilean constitution exceeds the scope of this work. Nonetheless, the German experience in this matter is one possible point of departure. Accordingly, the reflections presented in the relevant chapter of this work[1539] can be considered in the Chilean discussion.[1540]

2.3.3. Human dignity as a limit to restrictions on basic rights

Art. 1 par. 1 CPR may also justify limits to restrictions on basic rights. However, this does not necessarily rely on a theory of the human dignity content

1533 See § 6, subsection 1.
1534 See § 6, subsection 2.
1535 See this critique in more detail in § 6, subsection 3.
1536 See § 10, subsection 5.1.
1537 See *supra* subsection 1.4.
1538 See *supra* section 1.
1539 See § 10, subsection 5, e.g., dignity as an inherent limit in the constitution; dignity versus dignity; dignity as an unwaivable guarantee.
1540 For example, one of the main doctrinal questions here is whether the limits inherent in the constitution may be directly applied by the courts. See § 10, subsection 2.3.2 and 5.1.

of fundamental rights. Art. 19, no. 26 CPR already proclaims a guarantee of inviolability of the essence of basic rights – equivalent to the guarantee of 19 (2) GG.[1541] The interpretation of this clause may be ambiguous,[1542] but it already provides enough protection against grotesque transgressions of basic rights, in any case.

In this light, there is no reason to assume that the basic rights of the CPR contain a core of human dignity. The criticism that this theory has received in Germany applies to the Chilean case, as well:[1543] support for it is doctrinally inconvenient and even unnecessary. Human dignity is concretized differently in every right of the CPR,[1544] so it is preferable to locate the possible human dignity content of each basic right directly in Art. 1, par. 1 CPR. Impacts on the content of human dignity would violate both dignity itself and the right in question. In such cases, human dignity acts as a limit on restrictions; for instance, should the prohibition of torture not be included directly in the Bill of Rights, it must be considered forbidden by Art. 1, par. 1 CPR.

When considering human dignity as a limit on the restrictions of basic rights, its limiting effect on legal pluralism is of particular interest to the Chilean jurisdiction.[1545] While the content of dignity may guide the transfer of self-government competencies, including the possibility of applying traditional systems of normativity within any given indigenous community, it also sets boundaries on this process. The supremacy of the human dignity clause places it above any other set of rules, whether they stem from the state or indigenous norms. The supremacy of human dignity, in this case, also represents the supremacy of the entire CPR in relation to other normative orders.

1541 Art. 19 (2) GG: "In no case may the essence of a basic right be affected." [In keinem Falle darf ein Grundrecht in seinem Wesensgehalt angetastet werden.]

1542 See an overview in Aldunate Lizana, *Derechos Fundamentales* (n 8) 264.

1543 See § 10, subsection 6.1.

1544 Isensee, 'Würde des Menschen' (n 436) 81, Rn. 122.

1545 Act N°19.253 of 1993, which "establishes norms for the protection, promotion, and development of the Indigenous and creates the National Agency for Indigenous Development" recognizes, in a limited fashion, the validity of legal pluralism. E.g., Art. 54 states that customary law is valid in trial when its parties belong to the same indigenous people, and such law is not contrary to the CPR. The CPR itself recognizes neither indigenous peoples nor legal pluralism. For an overview of the constitution and legal regulation of legal pluralism in several other Latin American countries, see Fuchs and Rank (n 1518) 116–169.

Maintaining the predominance of human dignity, however, demands the fulfillment of several standards. The first of these is that traditional or customary rules applying only to relevant indigenous peoples must conform to the constitutional counterparts. Because the lack of written rules might generate severe conflicts, codification should be promoted.

Second, members of indigenous communities affected by legal pluralism must not be dispossessed of their constitutional rights.[1546] This criterion will have the effect of retaining indigenous persons under the corpus of ordinary law that protects basic rights against attacks from third parties. Furthermore, if the state concedes jurisdictional competencies to indigenous authorities,[1547] the latter may not unconstitutionally restrict the scope of protection of basic rights.[1548] Moreover, it should be discussed whether these authorities also become addressees of fundamental rights and are directly bound to them. Each member of an indigenous community must be entitled to decide which corpus of law (statal or indigenous) should apply to his or her case.[1549] Finally, to maintain the supreme character of Art. 1, par. 1 CPR, there must be remedies available in the ordinary courts for the decisions of indigenous tribunals or similar organs that administer justice.

1546 See some possible examples of conflicts in hypothetical cases based on real facts in Marie-Christine Fuchs and Hartmut Rank (eds), *Manual de Pluralismo Jurídico para la Práctica de la Justicia Intercultural* (2022) 42–48.

1547 However, according to Fuchs and Rank (n 1518) 100, a clear distribution of competencies is rare in the Latin American experience. States have frequently gone no further than the constitutional recognition of legal pluralism or the signing of the International Labor Organization's Indigenous and Tribal Peoples Convention (n°169 of 1989).

1548 ibid 102 correctly describes this tension.

1549 ibid 102 shows that this option is not, however, free of complexities.

Deutschsprachige Zusammenfassung

Die vorliegende Arbeit befasst sich mit der Rechtsdogmatik zur Menschenwürde. Sie soll einen Beitrag zur Grundrechtstheorie liefern – sowohl zur allgemeinen als auch speziell zu jener in der chilenischen Rechtswissenschaft. Zu diesem Zweck untersucht sie, wie das verfassungsrechtliche Konzept der Menschenwürde in Deutschland behandelt wird, wo die Rechtslehre zur Menschenwürde eine beispiellose Entwicklung genommen hat.

Das Buch gliedert sich in vier Teile. Neben der Einleitung (§ 1) wird im ersten Teil ein Überblick über den rechtlichen, wissenschaftlichen und historischen Kontext gegeben, in dem das Konzept der Menschenwürde in Chile steht (§ 2).

Im zweiten Teil (§§ 3, 4, 5, 6) werden die Ergebnisse einer umfassenden Untersuchung darüber vorgestellt, wie die chilenische Verfassungslehre und Rechtsprechung den Begriff der Menschenwürde behandelt haben. Hinsichtlich dessen Rolle in der Grundrechtslehre fokussiert die Untersuchung dabei auf drei Dimensionen: das Fundament der Grundrechte, die Grundrechtsberechtigung und Grundrechtseinschränkungen. Jeder Abschnitt endet mit einer Kritik an der jeweiligen Entwicklung und identifiziert die entscheidenden Punkte, die später im vierten Teil des Buches behandelt werden.

Der dritte Teil (§§ 7, 8, 9, 10) unternimmt dasselbe für die deutsche Rechtsordnung. Er beschränkt sich dabei auf eine Darstellung der zentralen Diskussionsstränge, da im Rahmen einer Dissertation die deutsche Literatur und Rechtsprechung zur Menschenwürde nicht umfassend behandelt werden könnten und dies angesichts der Ziele der vorliegenden Arbeit auch nicht notwendig ist. Die Untersuchung folgt insofern keiner symmetrischen vergleichenden Methodik. Der deutsche Kontext wird herangezogen, um die Untersuchung der chilenischen Lage zu beleuchten.

Der vierte und letzte Teil besteht aus drei Kapiteln, in deren erstem (§ 11) kurz die wichtigsten Schlussfolgerungen aus den vorangegangenen Teilen in Erinnerung gerufen werden. Ziel ist es, jene Ergebnisse zusammenzufassen, die die Arbeit in den folgenden Kapiteln bestimmen.

Im anschließenden Kapitel (§ 12) werden einige elementare Kriterien vorgeschlagen, mithilfe derer die Analyse von Verfassungsnormen zur Menschenwürde in einem beliebigen Rechtssystem erfolgen kann. Es wird erörtert, wie man von rechtsvergleichenden Perspektiven im Allgemeinen und der deutschen im Besonderen profitieren kann. Vor diesem Hintergrund sind drei Dimensionen der deutschen Erfahrung für die Auslegung der Menschenwürdeklausel der chilenischen Verfassung von besonderer Bedeutung, die sich aus drei unterschiedlichen Perspektiven ergibt: der methodischen, der dogmatischen und der soziologischen.

Im letzten Kapitel (§ 13) wird ein neuer Ansatz zum Verständnis der Menschenwürde in der chilenischen Verfassungsordnung vorgestellt. Dieser Vorschlag umfasst insbesondere die Erörterung ihrer rechtlichen Form und ihres Inhalts. Darüber hinaus werden die wichtigsten Funktionen erörtert, welche die Menschenwürde in den dogmatischen Dimensionen des Fundaments, der Berechtigung und der Einschränkung von Grundrechten spielen kann. Dieser neue Ansatz will nicht das letzte Wort zu diesem Thema sein, sondern vielmehr die chilenische Debatte über die Norm neu eröffne

Bibliography

1. Scholarship and Proceedings

Accatino Scagliotti, Daniela: "La Interpretación de los Derechos Fundamentales y la Seguridad Jurídica. Una Mirada a la Practica Constitucional Chilena ["Interpretation of Fundamental Rights and Legal Certainty. A view on the Chilean Constitutional Practice"]" in Andrés Bordalí Salamanca (ed), *Justicia Constitucional y Derechos Fundamentales ["Constitucional Justice and Fundamental Rights"]* (1st ed., Lexis Nexis 2006)

Aillapán Quinteros, Juan Eduardo: "El Derecho a la Propia Imagen: ¿Derecho Personalísimo?, ¿Derecho Fundamental? Precisiones Terminológicas para el Ordenamiento Jurídico Chileno ["The Right to One's Own Image: Strictly Personal Right? Basic Right? Terminological Precisions for the Chilean Juridical Order"" (2016) 43 Revista Chilena de Derecho 433

Aldunate Lizana, Eduardo: "La Titularidad de los Derechos Fundamentales ["Ownership of Fundamental Rights"]" (2003) 1 Estudios Constitucionales 187

——, "Tutela Jurisdiccional y Configuración Constitucional del Derecho de Propiedad ["Jurisdictional Protection and Constitutional Configuration of the Right to Property"]" in Andrés Bordalí Salamanca (ed), *Justicia Constitucional y Derechos Fundamentales ["Constitucional Justice and Fundamental Rights"]* (1st ed., Lexis Nexis 2006)

——, *Derechos Fundamentales ["Fundamental Rights"]* (1st ed., Thomson Reuters 2008)

Alexy, Robert: "Menschenwürde und Verhältnismäßigkeit" (2015) 140 Archiv des Öffentlichen Rechts 497

Alvear Téllez, Julio: "La Persona en la Constitución de 1980: Fundamento de los Derechos y Garantías Constitucionales ["The Person in the Constitution of 1980: Foundation of the Constitutional Rights and Guarantees"]" in Enrique Navarro Beltran (ed), *20 Años de la Constitución Chilena: 1981–2001 ["20 years of the Chilean Constitution:1981–2001"]* (1st ed., Editorial Jurídica Conosur 2001)

Álvez Marín, Amaya: "Norma y Tipicidad Iusfundamental ["Norm and Legal Description in Fundamental Rights"]" in Pablo Contreras Vásquez and Constanza Salgado Muñoz (eds), *Manual sobre Derechos Fundamentales ["Handbook of Fundamental Rights"]* (1st ed., LOM 2017)

Araya, Rodrigo (ed): *Doscientas mil voces: Ecos y Aprendizajes del proceso constituyente de Michelle Bachelet ["Two Hundred Thousand Voices: Echoes and Learnings from Michelle Bachelet's Constituent Process"]* (1st ed., Ediciones Abierta 2020)

Atria Lemaitre, Fernando: *Los Peligros de la Constitución ["The Dangers of the Constitución"]* (1st ed., Universidad Diego Portales 1997)

Badura, Peter, "Generalprävention und Würde des Menschen" (1964) 19 Juristenzeitung 337

Bagaric, Mirko and Allan, James: "The Vacuous Concept of Dignity" (2006) 5 Journal of Human Rights 257

Baldus, Manfred: "Menschenwürdegarantie und Absolutheitsthese. Zwischenbericht zu einer zukunftsweisenden Debatte" (2011) 136 Archiv des Öffentlichen Rechts 529

——, *Kämpfe um die Menschenwürde. Die Debatten seit 1949* (1st edn, Suhrkamp 2016)

Barak, Aharon: *Human Dignity. The Constitutional Value and the Constitutional Right* (1st ed., Cambridge University Press 2015)

Bascuñan Rodríguez, Antonio: "Después de la Píldora ["After the Pill"]" [2006] Anuario de Derechos Humanos 2006 ["Yearbook on Human Rights (2006)"] 235

——, "Simposio Aborto y Derechos Humanos ["Abortion and Human Rights Symposium"]" (2015) 11 Anuario de Derechos Humanos 58

Bassa Mercado, Jaime: *El Estado Constitucional de Derecho: Efectos sobre la Constitución Vigente y Derechos Sociales ["The Constitutional Rule of Law: Effects over the Constitution and Social (Welfare) Rights"]* (1st ed., Lexis Nexis 2008)

——, "La Pretension de Objetividad en la Interpretación Constitucional ["The Pretension of Objetivity in Constitutional Interpretation"]" in Jaime Bassa Mercado, Juan Carlos Ferrada Bórquez and Christian Viera Álvarez (eds), *La Constitución Chilena ["The Chilean Constitution"]* (1st ed., LOM 2015)

Bassa Mercado, Jaime; Ferrada Borquéz, Juan Carlos; and Viera Álvarez, Christian (eds): *La Constitución Chilena ["The Chilean Constitution"]* (1st ed., LOM 2015)

Bastida Freijedo, Francisco José and others: *Teoría General de los Derechos Fundamentales en la Constitución Española de 1978 ["A General Theory of Fundamental Rights in the Spanish Constitution of 1978"]* (1st edn, Tecnos 2004)

Benda, Ernst: "Verständigungsversuche über die Würde des Meschen" (2001) 54 Neue Juristische Wochenschrift 2147

Böckenförde, Ernst-Wolfgang: "Grundrechte als Grundsatznormen: Zur gegenwärtigen Lage der Grundrechtsdogmatik" (1990) 29 Der Staat 1

——, "Kritik der Wertbegründung des Rechts [1976]," *Recht, Staat, Freiheit: Studien zur Rechtsphilosophie, Staatstheorie und Verfassungsgeschichte* (Suhrkamp 1991)

——, "El Poder Constituyente del Pueblo. Un Concepto Límite del Derecho Constitucional," *Estudios sobre el Estado de Derecho y la Democracia* (1st ed., Trotta 2000)

——, "Menschenwürde als normatives Prinzip. Die Grundrechte in der bioethischen Debatte" (2003) 58 Juristenzeitung 809

——, "Schutzbereich, Eingriff, verfassungsimmanente Schranken. Zur Kritik gegenwärtiger Grundrechtsdogmatik" (2003) 42 Der Staat 165

——, "Die Würde des Menschen war unantastbar" *Frankfurter Allgemeine Zeitung* (Frankfurt am Main, September 3, 2003) 33

——, "Einspruch im Namen der Menschenwürde" *Frankfurter Allgemeine Zeitung* (2011)

——, “Fundamental Rights. Theory and Interpretation [1974]” in Mirjam Künkler and Tine Stein (eds), *Constitutional and Political Theory: Selected writings. Volume I* (1st ed., Oxford University Press 2017)

Bogdandy, Armin: “German Legal Hegemony?” (2020) 2020–43 Mpil Research Paper Series 2

Bohórquez Monsalve, Viviana and Aguirre Román, Javier: “Las Tensiones de la Dignidad Humana: Conceptualización y Aplicación en el Derecho Internacional de los Derechos Humanos [“The Tensions of Human Dignity: Conceptualization and Adjudication in International Human Rights Law”]” (2009) 6 Sur. Revista Internacional de Derechos Humanos 41

Bordalí Salamanca, Andrés: “La Tutela de los Derechos Fundamentales Bajo un Sistema Dual de Justicia Constitucional [“The Protection of Fundamental Righs under a Dual System of Constitutional Justice”]” in Andrés Bordalí Salamanca (ed), *Justicia Constitucional y Derechos Fundamentales [“Constitucional Justice and Fundamental Rights”]* (1st ed., Lexis Nexis 2006)

Botha, Henk: “Human Dignity in Comparative Perspective” (2009) 20 Stellenbosch Law Review 171

Braun, Johann: *Einführung in die Rechtsphilosophie* (2nd ed., Mohr Siebeck 2011)

Brugger, Winfried: “May Government Ever Use Torture – Two Responses from German Law” (2000) 48 The American Journal of Comparative Law 661

Bulnes Aldunate, Luz: “Principios y Valores Constitucionales. La Dignidad de la Persona frente a la Jurisprudencia [“Principles and Values. The Dignity of a Person vis à vis Case Law”]” (2004) 10 Actualidad Jurídica. La Revista de Derecho de la Universidad del Desarrollo

Bundesministerium für Arbeit und Sozialordnung, “Zweistufenplan der Bundesregierung für kunden- und wettbewerbsorientierte Dienstleistungen am Arbeitsmarkt” [2002] Pressemitteilung, 22. Februar 2002

Candia Falcón, Gonzalo: “Analizando la Tesis de los Derechos Implícitos: Comentario a la Sentencia del Tribunal Constitucional Recaída sobre el Requerimimiento de Inaplicabilidad Rol N°2408–2013 [“Analizing Implicit Right’s Thesis”]” (2014) 21 Revista de Derecho (Universidad Católica del Norte) 497

Carvalho, Julio and Wiegand Cruz, Augusto: “The Augustan Novel and the Cultural Foundations of Human Dignity” (2022) 108 Archiv für Rechts- und Sozialphilosophie 108

Cea Egaña, José Luis: “Dignidad, Derechos y Garantías en el Régimen Constitucional Chileno [“Dignity, Right and Duties in the Chilean Constitutional Order”],” *Práctica Constitucional y Derechos Fundamentales [“Constitutional Practice and Fundamental Rights”]* (1st ed., Corporación Nacional de Reparación y Reconciliación 1996)

——, “Un caso real de Violación de la Dignidad Humana [“Human Dignity: A Real Case of Incroachment”],” *XXV Jornadas de Derecho Público. Tomo II.* (1st ed., Edeval 1995)

——, *El Sistema Constitucional Chileno: Síntesis Crítica [“The Constitutional Chilean System”]* (1st ed., Facultad de Ciencias Jurídicas y Sociales de la Universidad Austral de Chile 1999)

——, "Dignidad de la Persona y Discrecionalidad Estatal ["Dignity of the Person and State Discretion"]" (2001) 4 Ius Publicum 201

——, *Derecho Constitucional Chileno. Tomo I. ["Chilean Constitutional Law. Vol. I."]* (3rd ed., Ediciones Universidad Católica de Chile 2017)

——, *Derecho Constitucional Chileno. Tomo II. Derechos, deberes y garantías ["Chilean Constitutional Law. Vol. II. Rights, Duties and Guarantees]* (3rd ed., Ediciones Universidad Católica de Chile 2019)

Classen, Claus Dieter: "Die Menschenwürde ist - und bleibt - unantastbar" (2009) 2009 Die Öffentliche Verwaltung 689

Collier, Simon and Sater, William F.: *A History of Chile, 1808–2002* (2nd ed., Cambridge University Press 2004)

Comisión de Estudios de la Nueva Constitución ["Commission of Studies of the New Constitution"]: *Actas Oficiales de Comisión Constituyente ["Proceedings of the Constituent Commision"] Tomo VIII*

——, *Actas Oficiales de la Comisión Constituyente ["Proceedings of Constituent Commision"] Tomo I*

——, *Actas Oficiales de la Comisión Constituyente ["Proceedings of Constituent Commision"] Tomo III*

——, *Actas Oficiales de la Comisión Constituyente ["Proceedings of Constituent Commision"] Tomo IX*

——, *Actas Oficiales de la Comisión Constituyente ["Proceedings of the Constituent Comission"] Tomo V*

——, *Actas Oficiales de la Comisión Constituyente ["Proceedings of the Constituent Commision"] Tomo XI*

Consejo de Estado [State Council]: "Actas del Consejo de Estado [Proceedings of the State Council], 111th session, 22 July 1980"

——, "Actas del Consejo de Estado [Proceedings of the State Council], 54th session, 14 November 1978"

——, "Actas del Consejo de Estado [Proceedings of the State Council], 56th session, 28 November 1978"

Contreras Vásquez, Pablo: "Titularidad de Derechos Fundamentales ["Ownership of Fundamental Rights"]" in Pablo Contreras Vásquez and Constanza Salgado (eds), *Manual sobre Derechos Fundamentales ["Handbook of Fundamental Rights"]* (1st ed., LOM 2017)

——, "¿Derechos Implícitos? Notas Sobre la Identificación de Normas de Derecho Fundamental ["Implicit Righs? Notes on the Identification of Norms Concerning Fundamental Rights"]" in José Ignacio Núñez Leiva (ed), *Nuevas perspectivas en derecho público ["New Perspectives on Public Law"]* (1st ed., Librotecnia 2011)

——, "Titularidad de los Derechos Fundamentales ["Ownership of Fundamental Rights"]" in Pablo Contreras Vásquez and Constanza Salgado (eds), *Manual sobre Derechos Fundamentales ["Handbook of Fundamental Rights"]* (1st ed., LOM 2017)

Contreras Vásquez, Pablo and Salgado Muñoz, Constanza: "Introducción ["Introduction"]" in Pablo Contreras Vásquez and Constanza Salgado Muñoz (eds), *Manual sobre Derechos Fundamentales ["Handbook of Fundamental Rights"]* (1st ed., LOM 2017)

Corral Talciani, Hernán: "El Respeto y Protección de la Vida Privada en la Constitución de 1980 [The Respect and Protection of Private Life in the Constitution of 1980]" in Enrique Navarro Beltrán (ed), *20 Años de la Constitución Chilena: 1981–2001 ["20 years of the Chilean Constitution:1981–2001"]* (1st ed., Editorial Jurídica Conosur 2001)

——, "El Concepto Jurídico de Persona y su Relevancia para la Protección del Derecho a la Vida ["The Juridical Concept of a Person and its Relevance to the Protection of the Right to Life"]" (2005) 11 Ius et Praxis 37

Covarrubias Cuevas, Ignacio: "¿Puede la Dignidad Humana Ser un Principio Comúnmente Compartido en Materia de Adjudicación Constitucional? ["Capability of Human Dignity as a shared Constitutional Principle in Constitutional Adjudication"]" (2014) 29 Actualidad Jurídica 147

Dederer, Hans-Georg: "Menschenwürde des Embryo in vitro?" (2002) 127 Archiv des Öffentlichen Rechts 2

——, "Die Garantie der Menschenwürde (Art. 1 Abs. 1 GG) Dogmatische Grundfragen auf dem Stand der Wissenschaft" (2009) 57 Jahrbuch des öffentlichen Rechts der Gegenwart. Neue Folge (JöR) 89

Di Fabio, Udo: "Art. 2 Abs. 1" in Theodor Maunz and Günter Dürig (eds), *Kommentar zum Grundgesetz* (Stand 92, Beck-online 2020)

Díaz de Valdés Juliá, José Manuel: "Bases de la Institucionalidad: una Revisión Propositiva ["Institutional Foundation: a Purposive Review"]" in José Francisco García García (ed), *Nueva Constitución o Reforma ["New Constitution or Reform"]* (1st ed., Thomson Reuters 2014)

Diez Urzúa, Sergio: *Personas y Valores. Su Protección Constitucional ["The Constitutional Protection of Persons and Values"]* (1st ed., Editorial Jurídica de Chile 1999)

Dorn Garrido, Carlos: "La Dignidad de la Persona: Límite a la Autonomía Individual ["Dignity of the Person: a Limit to Individual Autonomy"]" (2011) 26 Revista de Derecho 71

Dreier, Horst: "Art. 1 Abs. 1" in Horst Dreier (ed), *Grundgesetz, Band I (Art. 1 – 19)* (3rd edn, Mohr Siebeck (Beck-online) 2013)

——, "Vorbemerkungen vor Art. 1 GG" in Horst Dreier (ed), *Grundgesetz, Band I (Art.1 – 19)* (3rd edn, CH Beck (Beck-online) 2013)

Dürig, Günter: "Der Grundrechtssatz von der Menschenwürde. Entwurf eines praktikablen Wertsystems der Grundrechte aus Art. 1 Abs. 1 in Verbindung mit Art. 19 Abs. II des Grundgesetz" (1956) 81 Archiv des Öffentlichen Rechts 117

Eifert, Martin: "Das Allgemeine Persönlichkeitsrecht des Art. 2 Abs. 1 GG" (2015) 11 Juristische Ausbildung 1181

Elsner, Thomas and Schobert, Klara: "Gedanken zur Abwägungsresistenz der Menschenwürde – angestoßen durch das Urteil des Bundesverfassungsgericht zur Verfassungsmäßigkeit der Sicherungsverwahrung" [2007] Das Deutsche Verwaltungsblatt 278

Enders, Christoph: *Die Menschenwürde in der Verfassungsordnung: Zur Dogmatik des Art. 1 GG* (1st ed., Mohr Siebeck 1997)

——, "Right to Have Rights – The German Constitutional Concept of Human Dignity" (2010) 253 NUJS Law Review 253

Epping, Völker: *Grundrechte* (8th ed., Springer 2019)

Evans de la Cuadra, Ernesto: *Los Derechos Constitucionales. Tomo I. ["The Constitutional Rights. Vol. I"]* (2nd ed., Editorial Jurídica de Chile 1999)

Fernández González, Miguel Ángel: "La Dignidad Humana ante la Jurisprudencia de la Corte Suprema ["Human Dignity vis à vis the Case Law of the Supreme Court"]" in Arturo Fernandois Vöhringer (ed), *Principios, Valores e Instituciones ["Principles, Values, Institutions"].* (1st ed., Ediciones Universidad Católica de Chile 2016)

Figueroa García Huidobro, Rodolfo: "Concepto de Persona, Titularidad del Derecho a la Vida y Aborto ["A Concept of a Person, Entitlement to the Right to Life and Abortion"]" (2007) 20 Revista de derecho (Valdivia) 95

Frotscher, Werner and Pieroth, Bodo: *Verfassungsgeschichte* (18th ed., CHBeck 2019)

Fuchs, Maria-Christine (ed.): "Elementos Formales. Fundamentos de la Jurisdicción Indigena," *Manual de Pluralismo Jurídico para la Práctica de la Justicia Intercultural* (2nd ed., Konrad Adenauer Stiftung 2020)

—— (eds), *Manual de Pluralismo Jurídico para la Práctica de la Justicia Intercultural* (2nd ed., Konrad Adenauer Stiftung 2020)

García-Huidobro, Luis Eugenio and Sierra, Lucas (eds.), *Diez Miradas sobre el Sistema de Gobierno: Diagnósticos y Propuestas para la Nueva Constitución* (1st ed., Hueders 2022)

Geis, Max-Emanuel: "Der Kernbereich des Persönlichkeitsrechts" 46 Juristenzeitung 112

Gómez Bernales, Gastón: *Derechos Fundamentales y Recurso de Protección ["Fundamental Rights and the Remedy of Protection"]* (1st ed., Ediciones Universidad Diego Portales 2005)

——, *Las Sentencias del Tribunal Constitucional y sus Efectos sobre la Jurisdicción Común [The Decisions of the Constitutional Court and its Effects on the Ordinary Courts"]* (1st ed., Ediciones Universidad Diego Portales 2013)

Graser, Alexander: "Zombie mit Potential" [2018] Rechtswissenschaft 136

——, "Rechtstransfer: Begriffe, Kontexte und Deutungen" in Alpay Hekimler (ed), *Festschrift für Otto Kaufman* (2021)

Greer, Steven: "Should Police Threats to Torture Suspects Always be Severely Punished? Reflections on the Gäfgen Case" (2011) 11 Human Rights Law Review 67

Häberle, Peter: "Grundrechtsgeltung und Grundrechtsinterpretation im Verfassungsstaat – Zugleich zur Rechtsvergleichung als 'fünfter Auslegungsmethode'" (1989) 44 Juristenzeitung 913

——, “Die Menschenwürde als Grundlage der staatlichen Gemeinschaft” in Josef Isensee and Paul Kirchhof (eds), *Handbuch des Staatsrechts der Bundesrepublik Deutschland. Band II: Verfassungsstaat* (3rd ed., CF Müller 2004)

Habermas, Jürgen: *Die Zukunft der menschlichen Natur. Auf dem Weg zu einer liberalen Eugenik?* (4th ed., Suhrkamp 2002)

Hartz, Peter and others: “Moderne Dienstleistungen am Arbeitsmarkt” [2002] Bericht der Kommission zum Abbau der Arbeitslosigkeit und zur Umstrukturierung der Bundesanstalt für Arbeit, 16. August 2002 343

Hauer, Katharina M.: *Die Fürsorgeentscheidung des Bundesverwaltungsgerichts (BVerwGE 1, 159) aus rechtshistorischer Sicht* (1st ed. Nomos Verlag 2020)

Henríquez Viñas, Miriam: “Jerarquía de los Tratados de Derechos Humanos: Análisis Jurisprudencial desde el Método de Casos. [Hierarchy of Human Rights' Treaties: Jurisprudential Analisys from a Method of Cases]” (2008) 6 Estudios Constitucionales 73

Herdegen, Matthias: “Die Menschenwürde im Fluß des bioetischen Diskurses” (2001) 56 Juristen Zeitung 773

——, “Art. 1. Abs. 1” in Theodor Maunz and Günther Dürig (eds), *Kommentar zum Grundgesetz* (CH Beck 2020)

——, “Art. 1. Abs. 3” in Theodor Maunz and Günter Dürig (eds), *Kommentar zum Grundgesetz* (CH Beck (Beck-online) 2020)

Heun, Werner: “Embryonenforschung und Verfassung – Lebensrecht und Menschenwürde des Embryos” (2002) 57 Juristen Zeitung 517

Hoerster, Norbert: “Kompromisslösungen zum Menschenrecht des Embryos auf Leben” [2003] Juristische Schulung 529

Hoffmann-Riem, Wolfgang: “Enge oder weite Gewährleistungsgehalte der Grundrechte? [2004]” in Ino Augsberg and Sebastian Unger (eds), *Basistexte:Grundrechtstheorie* (1st ed., Nomos 2012)

Höfling, Wolfram: “Menschenwürde und gute Sitten” (1983) 36 Neue Juristische Wocheschrift 1582

——, “Art. 1” in Michael Sachs (ed), *Grundgesetz Kommentar* (9th edn, Beck-online 2021)

Hofmann, Hasso: “Die Grundrechte 1789 – 1949 – 1989” [1989] Neue Juristische Wocheschrift 3177

——, “Die versprochene Menschenwürde” (1993) 118 Archiv des Öffentlichen Rechts 253

——, “Methodische Probleme der juristischen Menschenwürdeinterpretation” in Ivo Appel and Georg Hermes (eds), *Mensch – Staat – Umwelt* (1st edn, Duncker & Humblot 2008)

Hong, Mathias: *Der Menschenwürdegehalt der Grundrechte. Grundfragen, Entstehung und Rechtsprechung* (1st ed. Mohr Siebeck 2019)

Hörle, Tatjana: “Menschenwürde und Lebenschutz” (2003) 89 Archiv für Rechts- und Sozialphilosophie 318

Huber, Peter M.: "Die Informationstätigkeit der öffentlichen Hand — ein grundrechtliches Sonderregime aus Karlsruhe?" (2003) 58 Juristen Zeitung 290

Hufen, Friedhelm: "Erosion der Menschenwürde?" (2004) 59 Juristen Zeitung 313

——, "Die Menschenwürde, Art. 1 I GG" [2020] Juristische Schulung 1

——, *Staatsrecht II. Grundrechte* (8th ed., CHBeck 2020)

Huster, Stefan: "Individuelle Menschenwürde oder öffentliche Ordnung? Ein Diskussionsbeitrag anlässlich 'Big Brother'" [2000] Neue Juristische Wocheschrift 3477

Ibaceta Medina, David: "Protección de la Dignidad de las Personas Privadas de Libertad en el Bloque de Constitucionalidad ["Protection of Inmates' Dignity according to the Contitutional Block"]" (2008) 70 Revista de Derecho Público 149

Ipsen, Jörn: "Der 'verfassungsrechtliche Status' des Embryos in vitro" (2001) 56 Juristen Zeitung 989

——, "Grundzüge einer Grundrechtsdogmatik" (2013) 52 Der Staat 266

——, *Staatsrecht I. Staatsorganisationsrecht* (27th ed., Vahlen 2015)

——, *Staatsrecht II* (22nd ed., Vahlen 2019)

Isensee, Josef: "Menschenwürde: die säkulare Gesellschaft auf der Suche nach dem Absoluten" (2006) 131 Archiv des Öffentlichen Rechts 173

——, "Der grundrechtliche Konnex von Menschenleben und Menschenwürde" (2009) 18 Zeitschrift für Lebensrecht 114

——, "Würde des Menschen" in Detlef Merten and Hans-Jürgen Papier (eds), *Handbuch der Grundrechte in Deutschland und Europa Band IV Grundrechte in Deutschland: Einzelgrundrechte* (1st ed., CF Müller 2011)

Jakab, András: "The Fading International Influence of German Constitutional Thinking" (2020) 2020–43 Mpil Research Paper Series 27

Jana Linetzki, Andrés: "La Eficacia Horizontal de los Derechos Fundamentales ["The Effects on Third Parties of Fundamental Righs"]" in Departamento de Derecho Privado de la Facultad de Derecho de la Universidad de Chile [Private Law Department Law Faculty of the University of Chile] (ed), *Derecho Civil y Constitución [Civil Law and Constitution]* (1st ed., Tirant Lo Blanch 2021)

Jarass, Hans: "Art. 1" in Hans Jarass and Bodo Pieroth (eds), *Grundgesetz für die Bundesrepublik Deutschland* (16th ed., CH Beck (Beck-online) 2020)

——, "Art. 19" in Hans Jarass and Bodo Pieroth (eds), *Grundgesetz für die Bundesrepublik Deutschland* (16th ed., CH Beck (Beck-online) 2020)

——, "Art. 20" in Hans Jarass and Bodo Pieroth (eds), *Grundgesetz für die Bundesrepublik Deutschland* (16th ed., CH Beck (Beck-online) 2020)

——, "Vormerkungen vor Art. 1: Allgemeine Grundrechtslehren" in Hans Jarass and Bodo Pieroth (eds), *Grundgesetz für die Bundesrepublik Deutschland* (16th ed., CH Beck (Beck-online) 2020)

Jarass, Hans: "Das Allgemeine Persönlichkeitsrecht im Grundgesetz" [1989] Neue Juristische Wocheschrift 857

Jestaedt, Matthias: "Glückwunsch Ernst-Wolfgang Böckenförde zum 80. Geburtstag" (2010) 65 Juristen Zeitung 890

Kahl, Wolfgang: "Vom weiten Schutzbereich zum engen Gewährleistungsgehalt: Kritik einer neuen Richtung der deutschen Grundrechtsdogmatik" (2004) 43 Der Staat 167

Kaltenborn, Bruno; Knerr, Petra; and Kurth-Laatsch, Sylvia: "Hartz-Evaluierung: Ausgangslage" [2004] Erster Zwischenbericht im Auftrag des Bundesministeriums für Wirtschaft und Arbeit (BMWA), Dezember 2004 80

Kant, Immanuel: *Groundwork of the Metaphysics of Morals* (Mary Gregor ed, 1st ed., Cambridge University Press 1997)

Kielmansegg, Sebastian Graf von: "Die Grundrechtsprüfung" [2008] Juristische Schulung 23

Kingreen, Thorsten and Poscher, Ralf: *Grundrechte Staatsrecht II* (32nd ed., CF Müller 2016)

Kirchhof, Ferdinand: "Die Entwicklung des Sozialverfassungsrechts" [2015] Neue Zeitschrift für Sozialrecht 1

Kirste, Stephan: "Die naturrechtliche Idee überstaatlicher Menschenrechte" in Josef Isensee and Paul Kirchhof (eds), *Handbuch des Staatsrechts der Bundesrepublik Deutschland. Band X.* (3rd ed., CF Müller 2012)

——, "A Legal Concept of Dignity as a Foundation of Law" in Winfried Brugger and Stephan Kirste Brugger (ed), *Human Dignity as a Foundation of Law: Proceedings of the Special Workshop held at the 24th World Congress of the International Association for Philosophy of Law and Social Philosophy in Beijing, 2009* (1st ed., Steiner 2013)

——, "Transpositive Foundations of Positive Human Rights" in João Maurício Adeonato (ed), *Human Rights and the Problem of Legal Injustice. Annals of the Preparatory Meeting for the XXVI World Congress of the International Association of Philosophy of Law and Social Philosophy* (1st ed., Noeses 2013)

——, "Die Hermeneutik der Personifikation im Recht" (2015) 101 Archiv für Rechts- und Sozialphilosophie 473

Kloepfer, Michael: "Humangentechnik als Verfassungsfrage" (2002) 57 Juristen Zeitung 417

Knoepffler, Nicolaus: *Würde und Freiheit. Vier Konzeptionen im Vergleich* (1st ed., Verlag Karl Alber 2018)

Kommers, Donald P. and Miller, Russell A.: *The Constitutional Jurisprudence of the Federal Republic of Germany* (3rd ed., Duke University Press 2012)

Kunig, Philip and Kotzur, Markus: "GG Art. 1" in Ingo von Münch and Philip Kunig (eds), *Grundgesetz-Kommentar* (7th ed., CH Beck (Beck-online) 2021)

Leisner, Walter: "Darf der Staat gütig sein? – Förderung und Hilfe zwischen Sozialstaat und Rechtstaat" [2001] Neue Juristische Wocheschrift 1329

Lembcke, Oliver W.: "Human Dignity – a Constituent and Constitutional Principle. Some Perspectives of a German Discourse" in Stephan Kirste and Winfried Brugger (eds), *Human Dignity as a Foundation of Law: Proceedings of the Special Workshop held at the 24th World Congress of the International Association for Philosophy of Law and Social Philosophy in Beijing, 2009* (1st ed., Steiner 2013)

Lenz, Stefan: "Das Elfes-Urteil des Bundesverfassungsgericht von 1957" (2016) 2 Rechtswissenschft 149

Lindholm, Tore: "Article 1" in Gudmundur Alfredsson and Eide Asbjørn (eds), *The Universal Declaration of Human Rights. A Common Standard of Achievement* (1st ed., Kluwer Law International 1999)

Luhmann, Niklas: *Grundrechte als Institution* (2nd ed., Duncker & Humblot 1974)

——, "Inclusión y Exclusión" in Josetxo Berian and José María García Blanco (eds), *Complejidad y Modernidad* (1st ed., Herder 1998)

——, "La Diferenciación de la Sociedad" in Josetxo Berian and José María García Blanco (eds), *Complejidad y Modernidad* (1st ed., Herder 1998)

——, *Law as a Social System* (Fatima Kastner and others eds, 1st ed., Oxford University Press 2004)

——, *La Sociedad de la Sociedad* (1st ed. in Spanish, Herder 2006)

——, *Los Derechos Fundamentales como Institución* (Oak Editorial 2010)

Macklin, Ruth: "Dignity is a Useless Concept" (2003) 327 British Medical Journal 1419

Mahlmann, Matthias: *Elemente einer ethischen Grundrechtstheorie* (1st ed., Nomos 2008)

——, "The Basic Law at 60 – Human Dignity and the Culture of Republicanism" (2010) 11 German Law Journal 9

——, "The Good Sense of Dignity. Six Antidotes to Dignity Fatigue in Ethics and Law" in Christopher McCrudden (ed), *Understanding Human Dignity* (1st ed., Oxford University Press 2013)

——, *Rechtstheorie und Rechtsphilosophie* (6th ed., Nomos 2021)

Manssen, Gerrit: *Staatrecht II. Grundrechte* (18th ed., CH Beck 2021)

Martínez Estay, José Ignacio: "Valor de la Incorporación de Conceptos Meta-jurídicos al Lenguaje del Derecho Constitucional. El Caso de la Dignidad Humana ["The Worth of the Incorporation of Meta-juridical Concepts to the Language of Constitutional Law. The Case of Human Dignity"]" (2001) XXII Revista de Derecho de la Universidad Católica de Valparaíso 115

McCrudden, Christopher: "Human Dignity and Judicial Interpretation of Human Rights" (2008) 19 European Journal of International Law 655

Meinke, Monika M.: *In Verbindug mit* (1st ed., Duncker & Humblot 2006)

Hailbronner, Michaela: "Rethinking the Rise of the German Constitutional Court: From Anti-Nazism to Value Formalism" (2012) 12 Internationational Journal of Contitutional Law 626

Molina Guaita, Hernán: "La Dignidad del Hombre es Sagrada ["Human Dignity is Sacred"]" (1994) LXII Revista de Derecho (Universidad de Concepción) 93

——, *Derecho Constitucional [Constitutional Law]* (7th ed., Lexis Nexis 2006)

Möllers, Christoph: "Democracy and Human Dignity: Limits of a Moralized Conception of Rights in German Constitutional Law" (2009) 42 Israel Law Review 416

Müller-Franken, Sebastian: "Vormerkung vor Art. 1 Allgemeine Grundrechtslehren," *Kommentar zum Grundgesetz* (14th ed., Carl Heymanns Verlag 2017)

Muñoz León, Fernando: "Historia de los Derechos Fundamentales ["A History of Fundamental Rights in Chile"]" in Pablo Contreras Vásquez and Constanza Salgado Muñoz (eds), *Manual sobre Derechos Fundamentales ["Handbook of Fundamental Rights"]* (1st ed., LOM 2017)

Navarro Beltrán, Enrique: "El Divorcio y la Dignidad de la Persona a la Luz de la Constitución de 1980 ["Divorce and Dignity of the Person in the Chilean Constitution"]," *XXV Jornadas de Derecho Público. Tomo II.* (Valparíso 1995)

Nettesheim, Martin: "Die Garantie der Menschenwürde: zwischen metaphysischer Überhöhung und bloßem Abwägungstopos" (2005) 130 Archiv des Öffentlichen Rechts 71

——, "Leben in Würde" (2019) 74 Juristenzeitung 1

Neumann, Ulfrid: "Die Tyrannei der Würde: Argumentationstheoretische Erwägungen zum Menschenwürdeprinzip" (1998) 84 Archiv für Rechts- und Sozialphilosophie 153

Nida-Rümelin, Julian: "Why Human Dignity Rests upon Freedom" in Stephan Kirste and Winfried Brugger (eds), *Human Dignity as a Foundation of Law: Proceedings of the Special Workshop held at the 24th World Congress of the International Association for Philosophy of Law and Social Philosophy in Beijing, 2009* (1st ed., Franz Steiner Verlag 2013)

Nogueira Alcalá, Humberto: *Dogmática Constitucional ["Constitutional Doctrine"]* (1st ed., Editorial Universidad de Talca 1997)

——, "El Derecho a la Vida en el Ordenamiento Jurídico Chileno ["The Right to Life in the Chilean Juridical Order"]" [1997] Gaceta Jurídica

——, "Dignidad de la Persona y Bloque Constitucional de Derechos ["Dignity of the Person and Constitutional Block of Rights"]" (2006) 13 Revista de Derecho (Universidad Católica del Norte) 67

——, *Lineamientos de Interpretación Constitucional y del Bloque Constitucional de Derechos ["Guidelines of Constitutional Interpretation and of the Constitutional Block of Rights"]* (1st ed., Librotecnia 2006)

——, "Dignidad de la Persona, Derechos Fundamentales y Bloque Constitucional de Derechos: una Aproximación desde Chile y América Latina. ["Dignity of the Person, Fundamental Rights and Constitutional Block of Rights. An Approach from Chile and Latinamerica"]" (2010) 5 Revista de Derecho (Universidad Católica de Uruguay) 79

——, *Derechos Fundamentales y Garantías Constitucionales. Tomo I ["Fundamental Rights and Constitutional Guarantees. Vol I."]* (5th ed., Librotecnia 2018)

——, *Derechos Fundamentales y Garantías Constitucionales. Tomo III ["Fundamental Rights and Constitutional Guarantees. Vol. III"]* (3rd ed., Librotecnia 2019)

Núñez Poblete, Manuel A.: "Titularidad y Sujetos Pasivos de los Derechos Fundamentales ["Ownership and Adressees of Fundamental Rights"]" (2001) 63 Revista de Derecho Público 200

Orrego Sanchéz, Cristobal: "Vigencia de los Derechos Esenciales que Emanan de la Naturaleza Humana y su Reconocimiento en el Ordenamiento Jurídico Chileno ["Natural Human Rights Validity and its Recognition in the Chilean Juridical Order"]" 20 Revista Chilena de Derecho 59

Pabst, Heinz-Joaquim: "Der postmortale Persönlichkeitsschutz in der neueren Rechtsprechung des BVerfG" [2002] Neue Juristische Wocheschrift 999

Pardo Martínez, Orlando: "Metarrelatos Políticos: los Preámbulos Constitucionales Latinoamericanos. [Political Metanarratives: The Latin American Constitutional Preambles]" (2018) 20 Reflexión Política

Paredes Paredes, Felipe: *La Garantía Jurisdiccional de los Derechos Fundamentales ["The Jurisdictional Guarantee of Fundamental Rights"]* (1st ed., Thomson Reuters 2014)

Peña Torres, Marisol: "La Jurisprudencia de Valores del Tribunal Constitucional ["Constitutional Tribunal's Jurisprudence of Values"]" in Arturo Fernandois Vöhringer (ed), *Principios, Valores e Instituciones. [Principles, Values, Institutions"]* (1st ed., Ediciones Universidad Católica de Chile 2016)

Pfeffer Urquiaga, Ernesto: "Algunos Criterios que Permiten Solucionar el Conflicto Derivado de la Colisión de Derechos ["Some Criteria to Solve a Clash of Rights"]" (1998) Número Esp. Revista de Derecho 225

——, "El Recurso de Protección y su Eficacia en la Tutela de los Derechos Constitucionales en Chile ["The Remedy of Protection and its Effectiveness in the Protection of Constitutional Rights in Chile"]" (2006) 4 Estudios Constitucionales 87

——, "Breves Reflexiones y Algunas Propuestas en Torno a los Derechos, Garantías y Deberes Constitucionales ["Reflections and Some Proposals on Constitutional Rights, Guarantees and Duties"]" in José Francisco García García (ed), *Nueva Constitución o Reforma ["New Constitution or Reform"]* (1st ed., Thomson Reuters 2014)

Pfeffer Urquiaga, Enrique; Bulnes Aldunate, Luz; and Verdugo Marinkovic, Mario: *Manual de Derecho Constitucional. Tomo I. [Handbook of Constitutional Law: Volume I.]* (1st ed., Editorial Jurídica de Chile 1985)

Pikard, Eberhard and Werner, Wolfram: "Nr. 5 Vierte Sitzung des Ausschusses für Grundsatzfragen 23. September 1948" in Eberhard Pikard and Wolfram Werner (eds), *Der Parlamentarische Rat 1948 – 1949. Akten und Protokolle. Band 5. Ausschuß für Grundsatzfragen* (1st ed., De Gruyter 1993)

Pinker, Steven: "The Stupidity of Dignity" *The New Republic* (2008)

Ponce de León Solís, Viviana: "El Nudge, su Aplicación en el Derecho Chileno y sus Potenciales Problemas de Constitucionalidad [Nudge, its Application in Chilean Law and its Potential Constitutional Issues"]" (2019) 46 Revista Chilena de Derecho 345

Poscher, Ralf: "Die Würde des Menschen ist unantastbar" (2004) 59 Juristenzeitung 756

——, "Meschenwürde und Kernbereichsschutz" (2009) 64 Juristenzeitung 269

——, "Menschenwürde" in Matthias Herdegen and others (eds), *Handbuch des Verfassungsrechts* (1st ed., CH Beck (Beck-online) 2021)

Quinzio Figuereido, Jorge Mario: *Tratado de Derecho Constitucional ["A Contitutional Law Treaty"]* (2nd ed., Lexis Nexis 2006)

Rennert, Dominik: "Die verdrängte Werttheorie und ihre Historisierung" (2014) 53 Der Staat 31

Rodríguez Collao, Luis: "Honor y Dignidad de la Persona ["Honor and Dignity of the Person"]" (1999) 20 Revista de Derecho de la Pontificia Universidad Católica de Valparaíso 9

Rosales Rigol, Cecilia: "Algunas Reflexiones en Torno a la Dignidad y a la Vida Humana a Propósito de una Posible Reforma Constitucional ["Some Reflections on Human Life and Dignity Considering a Prospect of Constitutional Reform"]" (2007) 69 Revista de Derecho Público 118

Rosen, Lawrence: *Law as Culture* (1st ed., Princeton University Press 2006)

Rosen, Michael: "Dignity: The Case Against" in Christopher McCrudden (ed), *Understanding Human Dignity* (1st edn, Oxford University Press 2014)

Ruiz-Tagle Vial, Pablo: "Una Visión Democrática y Liberal de los Derechos Fundamentales para la Constitución Chilena del Bicentenario ["A Democratic and Liberal Vision of Fundamental Rights for the Bicentenary Chilean Constitution"]" in Andrés Bordalí Salamanca (ed), *Justicia Constitucional y Derechos Fundamentales ["Constitucional Justice and Fundamental Rights"]* (1st ed., Lexis Nexis 2006)

Sachs, Michael: "Vorbemerkungen zu Abschnitt I" in Michael Sachs (ed), *Grundgesetz Kommentar* (8th ed., Beck-online 2018)

Schapp, Jan: "Grundrechte als Wertordnung" (1998) 53 Juristenzeitung 913

Schlink, Bernhard: "German Constitutional Culture in Transition" (1992) 14 Cardozo Law Review 711

——, "Proportionality in Constitutional Law: Why Everywhere But Here?" (2012) 22 Duke Journal of Comparative and International Law 291

——, "Der Lehrer Ernst-Wolfgang Böckenförde" (2019) 58 Der Staat 441

Schmidt am Busch, Birgit: "Postmortaler Würdeschutz und gesetzgeberische Gestaltungsfreiheit" (2010) 49 Der Staat 211

Schmidt, Rolf: *Grundrechte* (24th ed., Dr Rolf Schmidt 2019)

Schröder, Gerhard: "Mut zum Frieden und zur Veränderung" [2003] Regierungserklärung des Bundeskanzlers - 14.03.2003

Schröder, Ulrich Jan: "Der Schutzbereich der Grundrechte" [2016] Juristische Ausbildung 641

Schroth, Ulrich: "Forschung mit embryonalen Stammzellen und Preimplantationsdiagnostik im Lichte des Rechts" (2002) 57 Juristen Zeitung 170

Seiler, Christian: "Das Grundrecht auf ein menschenwürdiges Existenzminimum" (2010) 10 Juristenzeitung 500

Silva Bascuñan, Alejandro: *Tratado de Derecho Constitucional. Tomo IV. ["A Constitutional Law Treaty: Volume IV"]* (2a ed., Editorial Jurídica de Chile 1997)

Smend, Rudolf: *Verfassung und Verfassungsrecht* (1st ed., Duncker & Humblot 1928)

Soto Kloss, Eduardo: "La Dignidad de la Persona. Fundamento de los Derechos Humanos. Antecedentes Veterotestamentarios. ["The Dignity of the Person. The Foundation of Human Rights. Old Testament Antecedents"]" [1987] Revista de Derecho Público 49

——, "La Noción de Persona en la Constitución ["The Constitutional Notion of a Person"]" (1991) 50 Revista de Derecho Público

Spellbrinck, Wolfgang: "Zur Bedeutung der Menschenwürde für das Recht der Sozialleistungen" (2011) 126 Deutsches Verwaltungsblatt 661

Spilker, Bettina: "Postmortaler Schutz durch das Grundgesetz" [2014] Die Öffentliche Verwaltung 637

Starck, Christian: "Menschenwürde als Verfassungsgarantie im modernen Staat" (1981) 36 Juristenzeitung 457

——, "Verfassungsrechtliche Grenzen der Biowissenschaft und Fortpflanzungsmedizin" (2002) 57 Juristen Zeitung 1065

——, "Maximen der Verfassungsauslegung" in Josef Isensee and Paul Kirchhof (eds), *Handbuch des Staatsrechts der Bundesrepublik Deutschland. Band XII: Normativität und Schutz der Verfassung* (3rd ed., CF Müller 2014)

——, "Art. 1. Abs. 2" in Hermann von Mangoldt, Friedrich Klein and Christian Starck (eds), *Kommentar zum Grundgesetz* (7th ed., Beck-online 2018)

——, "Art. 1 Abs. 1" in Hermann von Mangoldt, Friedrich Klein and Christian Starck (eds), *Kommentar zum Grundgesetz* (7th ed., Beck-online 2018)

——, "Art. 1 Abs. 3" in Hermann von Mangoldt, Friedrich Klein and Christian Starck (eds), *Kommentar zum Grundgesetz* (7th ed., Beck-online 2018)

Stern, Klaus: *Das Staatsrecht der Bundesrepublik Deutschland, Band IV/1* (1st ed., CH Beck (Beck-online) 2006)

——, "Einleitung. Die Hauptprinzipien des Grundrechtssystems des Grundgesetzes" in Klaus Stern and Florian Becker (eds), *Grundrechte Kommentar* (3rd edn, 2019)

Stöcker, Hans A.: "Menschliche Würde und kritische Jurisprudenz" (1988) 23 Juristenzeitung 685

Stone Sweet, Alex and Mathews, Jud: "Proportionality Balancing and Global Constitutionalism" (2008) 47 Columbia Journal of Trasnational Law 68

Störring, Lars Peter: *Das Untermaßverbot in der Diskussion. Untersuchung einer umstrittenen Rechtsfigur* (1st ed., Duncker & Humblot 2009)

Strelitz-Risse, Anna-Lenn: *Das Zensuswahlrecht. Erscheinungsformen, Begründung und Überwindung am Beispiel Frankreichs und Deutschlands* (1st ed., Duncker & Humblot 2018)

Suhr, Dieter: "Gleiche Freiheit. Allgemeine Grundlage und Reziprozitätsdefizite in der Geldwirtschaft" [2001] Fragen der Freiheit 5

Susnjar, Davor and Greiser, Johannes: "Zur dogmatischen Einordnung des Grundrechts auf ein menschenwürdiges Existenzminimum" (2018) 20 Das Deutsche Verwaltungsblatt 1329

Tajadura Tejada, Javier: "La Función Política de los Preámbulos Constitucionales ["The Political Function of the Constitutional Preambles"]" (2001) 5 Cuestiones Constitucionales 235

Tapia Rodríguez, Mauricio: "Dignidad Humana en el Derecho Civil ["Human Dignity and Civil Law"]" in Departamento de Derecho Privado Facultad de Derecho Universidad de Chile (ed), *Derecho Civil y Constitución [Civil Law and Constitution]* (1st ed., Tirant Lo Blanch 2021)

Taylor, Charles: *The Sources of the Self* (1st ed., Harvard University Press 1989)

Undurraga, Verónica: "Derecho a la Autonomía Personal y Libre Desarrollo de la Personalidad" in Pablo Contreras and Constanza Salgado Muñoz (eds), *Curso de Derechos Fundamentales* (1st ed., Tirant Lo Blanch 2021)

Valenzuela, Samuel: "La Ley Electoral de 1890 y la Democratización del Régimen Político Chileno" (1998) 71 Estudios Públicos 265

Verdugo Marinkovic, Mario; Pfeffer Urquiaga, Enrique; and Nogueira Alcalá, Hector: *Derecho Constitucional. Volume I* (2nd Ed., Editorial Jurídica de Chile 2002)

Viale Costa, Gino: "Derecho Penal del Enemigo y Dignidad Humana ¿Es Posible Conciliar Ambos Institutos? ["Criminal Law for the Enemy and Human Dignity. Are these two Institutions Compatible?"]" (2012) 25 Revista de Derecho (Universidad Católica de la Santísima Concepción) 71

Vivanco Martínez, Angela: "El Derecho a la Vida y a la Integridad Física y Psíquica en la Carta Fundamental de 1980 ["The Right to Life and to Physical and Psychic Integrity in the Constitution of 1980"]" in Enrique Navarro Beltrán (ed), *20 Años de la Constitución Chilena: 1981–2001 ["20 years of the Chilean Constitution: 1981–2001"]* (1st ed., Editorial Jurídica Conosur 2001)

——, *Curso de Derecho Constitucional. Vol. II. ["A Constitutional Law Course. Vol. II."]* (1st edn, Ediciones Universidad Católica de Chile 2006)

——, "La Pildora del Día Después ['Morning-After Pill']" (2008) 35 Revista Chilena de Derecho 543

——, *Disposición sobre la Vida Humana y Principios Constitucionales ["Dealing with Human Life and Constitutional Principles"]* (1st edn, Ediciones Universidad Santo Tomás 2014)

——, "La Importancia del Concepto Constitucional de Persona y la Protección de la Vida en la Carta Fundamental de 1980 ["The Importance of the Constitutional Concept of a Person and the Protection of Life in the Constitution of 1980"]" in José Francisco García García (ed), *Nueva Constitución o Reforma ["New Constitution or Reform"]* (1st ed., Thomson Reuters 2014)

Volkmann, Uwe: "Veränderung des Grundrechtsdogmatik" (2005) 60 Juristen Zeitung 261

——, "Allgemeine Grundrechtslehre" in Matthias Herdegen and others (eds), *Handbuch des Verfassungsrechts* (1st ed., CH Beck (Beck-online) 2021)

Voßkuhle, Andreas and Kaiser, Anna-Bettina: "Grundwissen – Öffentliches Recht: Der Grundrechtseingriff" [2009] Juristische Schulung 313

Voßkuhle, Andreas and Wischmeyer, Thomas: "Grundwissen – Öffentliches Recht: Das Sozialstaatsprinzip" [2015] Juristische Schulung 693

Wiegand Cruz, Augusto, "Die aktuelle Prozess des Verfassungswandels in Chile" (*JuWissBlog*, 2020) 3

——, "El Concepto Constitucional de Dignidad Humana: Notas Introductorias para una Aproximación Dogmática ["The Constitutional Concept of Human Dignity"]" in Gabriel Alejandro Encinas Duarte and Miguel de J. Neria Govea (eds), *Ordenamiento Jurídico: Fundamentos y Apertura* (1st ed., Derecho Global 2021)

Williams Benavente, Jaime: "La Dignidad de la Persona Humana en la Constitución de 1980 ["The Dignity of the Human Person in the Chilean Constitution"]" (2001) 2 Actualidad Jurídica. La Revista de Derecho de la Universidad del Desarrollo 31

Wölfl, Bernd: "Sphärentheorie und Vorbehalt des Gesetzes" [2002] NVwZ 49

Zacharias, Diana: "Zur Abgrenzung von Menschenwürde und allgemeinem Persönlichkeitsrecht" [2001] Neue Juristische Wochenschrift 2950

Zapata Larraín, Patricio: "Persona y Embrión Humano. Nuevos Problemas Legales y su Solución en el Derecho Chileno ["Person and Human Embryo"]" (1998) 15 Revista Chilena de Derecho

2. Case Law

2.1. Chilean Constitutional Tribunal [Tribunal Constitucional - CCT]

CCT Rol 19–1983, decision of 29.10.1983.

CCT Rol 46–1987, decision of 21.12.1987.

CCT Rol 53–1988, decision of 05.04.1988.

CCT Rol 226–1995, decision of 30.10.1995.

CCT Rol 245–1996, decision of 02.12.1996.

CCT Rol 389–2003, decision of 28.10.2003.

CCT Rol 433–2005, decision of 25.01.2005.

CCT Rol 521–2006, decision of 01.08.2006.

CCT Rol 591–2006, decision of 11.01.2007.

CCT Rol 740–2007, decision of 18.04.2008.

CCT Rol 834–2007, decision of 13.05.2008.

CCT Rol 943–2007, decision of 10.06.2008.

CCT Rol 976–2007, decision of 26.06.2008.

CCT Rol 1185–2008, decision of 16.04.2009.

CCT Rol 1287–2008, decision of 08.09.2009.

CCT Rol 1340–2009, decision of 29.09.2009.

CCT Rol 1348–2009, decision of 27.04.2010.

CCT Rol 1683–2010, decision of 04.01.2011.

CCT Rol 2273–2012, decision of 04.07.2013.

CCT Rol 2410–2013, decision of 29.08.2013.

CCT Rol 3062–2016, decision of 27.03.2017.

CCT Rol 3329–2017, decision of 23.08.2018.

CCT Rol 3364–2017, decision of 14.09.2017.
CCT Rol 3372–2017, decision of 15.05.2018.
CCT Rol 3421–2017, decision of 18.12.2018.
CCT Rol 3422–2017, decision of 18.12.2018
CCT Rol 3542–2017, decision of 15.05.2018.
CCT Rol 3581–2017, decision of 05.10.2017.
CCT Rol 3729–2017, decision of 28.08.2017.
CCT Rol 4384–2018, decision of 29.05.2018.
CCT Rol 4572–2018, decision of 13.06.2019.
CCT Rol 5278–2018, decision of 06.06.2019
CCT Rol 5572–2018, decision of 18.01.2019.
CCT Rol 5677–2018, decision of 02.01.2019.
CCT Rol 6294–2019, decision of 13.06.2019.
CCT Rol 6462–2019, decision of 24.09.2019.
CCT Rol 7620–2020, decision of 04.06.2020.
CCT Rol 8452–2020, decision of 09.06.2020.
CCT Rol 8892–2020, decision of 10.12.2020.
CCT Rol 11428–2021, decision of 19.10.2021.

2.2. German Federal Constitutional Court [Bundesverfassungsgericht – BVerfG]

BVerfGE 1, 14 – *Neugliederung* (1951)
BVerfGE 1, 97 – *Hinterbliebenenrente* I (1951)
BVerfGE 1, 322 – *Erzwungene Staatsangehörigkeit* (1952)
BVerfGE 2, 1 – *SRP-Verbot* (1952)
BVerfGE 3, 225 – *Gleichberechtigung* (1953)
BVerfGE 5, 85 – *KPD-Verbot* (1956)
BVerfGE 6, 32 – *Elfes* (1957)
BVerfGE 7, 198 – *Lüth* (1958)
BVerfGE 9, 89 – *Gehör bei Haftbefehl* (1959)
BVerfGE 21, 362 – *Sozialversicherungsträger* (1967)
BVerfGE 22, 180 – *Jugendhilfe* (1967)
BVerfGE 28, 386 – *Kurzzeitige Freiheitstrafe* (1970)
BVerfGE 27, 1 – *Mikrozensus* (1969)
BVerfGE 27, 344 – *Ehescheidungakten* (1970)
BVerfGE 30, 1 – *Abhörurteil* (1970)
BVerfGE 30, 173 – *Mephisto* (1971)

BVerfGE 32, 98 – *Gesundbeter* (1971)
BVerfGE 32, 373 – *Ärztliche Schweigepflicht* (1980)
BVerfGE 34, 228 – *Tonbandaufnahme* (1973)
BVerfGE 39, 1 – *Schwangerschaftsabbruch* I (1972)
BVerfGE 34, 269 – *Soraya* (1973)
BVerfGE 44, 353 – *Durchsuchung Drogenberatungsstelle* (1977)
BVerfGE 45, 187 – *Lebenslange Freiheitstrafe* (1977)
BVerfGE 46, 160 – *Schleyer* (1977)
BVerfGE 47, 46 – *Sexualkundeunterricht* (1977)
BVerfGE 48, 127 – *Wehrpflichtnovelle* (1977)
BVerfGE 49, 286 – *Transsexuelle I* (1978)
BVerfGE 50, 166 – *Ausweisung I* (1979)
BVerfGE 54, 148 – *Eppler* (1980).
BVerfGE 54, 208 – *Böll* (1980)
BVerfGE 54, 341 – *Wirtschatsasyl* (1980).
BVerfGE 2 BvR 166/81 – *Lügendetektor* (1981) [Decision of the *Vorprüfungsausschuss*]
BVerfGE 59, 231 – *Freie Mitarbeiter* (1982)
BVerfGE 64, 261 – *Hafturlaub* (1983)
BVerfGE 65, 1 – *Volkszählung* (1983)
BVerfGE 75, 369 – *Strauß-Karikatur* (1987)
BVerfGE 79, 256 – *Kenntnis der eigenen Abstammung* (1989)
BVerfGE 80, 137 – *Reiten im Walde* (1989)
BVerfGE 80, 164 – *Reiten im Walde* (1989), dissenting opinion of justice Dieter Grimm.
BVerfGE 80, 367 – *Tagebuch* (1989)
BVerfGE 82, 60 – *Steuerfreie Existenzminimum* (1983)
BVerfGE 86, 288 – *Strafaussetzung bei lebenslanger Freiheitsstrafe* (1992)
BVerfGE 87, 207 – *Tanz der Teufel* (1992)
BVerfGE 88, 203 – *Schwangerschaftsabbruch II* (1993)
BVerfGE 93, 266 – *Soldaten-sind-Mörder* (1995)
BVerfGE 96, 375 – *Kind als Schaden* (1997)
BVerfGE 99, 216 – *Familienlastenausgleich II* (1998)
BVerfGE 101, 361 – *Caroline von Monaco II* (2000)
BVerfG, Judgment of the First Chamber of the First Senate of 25 August 2000 – 1 BvL 2707/95
BVerfG, Judgment of the First Chamber of the First Senate of 5 April 2001 – 1 BvL 932/94
BVerfGE 105, 279 – *Osho* (2002)
BVerfGE 107, 275 – *Schockwerbung* II (2003)
BVerfGE 109, 279 – *Großer Lauschangriff* (2003)

BVerfGE 113, 348 – *Vorbeugende Telekommunikationsüberwachung* (2005)

BVerfGE 115, 118 – *Luftsicherheitsgesetz* (2005)

BVerfG, Judgment of the First Chamber of the First Senate of 22 August 2006 – 1 BvL 1168/04

BVerfGE 119, 1 – *Roman Esra* (2007)

BVerfGE 120, 224 – *Geschwisterbeischlaf* (2008)

BVerfGE 120, 274 – *Online-Durchsuchungen* (2008)

BVerfGE 121, 175 – *Transsexuelle* II (2008)

BVerfGE 124, 43 – *Beschlagnahme von E-Mails* (2009)

BVerfG, Judgment of the First Chamber of the First Senate of 4 February 2010 – 1 BvR 369/04

BVerfGE 125, 175 (222) – *Hartz IV* (2010).

BVerfGE 130, 1 – *Wohnraumüberwachung* (2011)

BVerfGE 132, 134 – *Asylbewerberleistungsgesetz* (2012)

BVerfGE 137, 34 – *Existenzsichernder Regelbedarf* (2014)

BVerfG, Judgment of the Third Chamber of the First Senate of 14 July 2015 – 1 BvR 1127/14

BVerfGE 140, 317 – *Identitätskontrolle* (2015)

BVerfGE 141, 220 – *Bundeskriminalamtsgesetz* (2016)

BVerfG, Judgement of the Second Chamber of the Second Senate of 06 September 2016 – 2 BvR 890/16

BVerfGE 144, 20 – *NPD-Verbotsverfahren* (2017)

BVerfG, Judgment of the First Senate of 5 November 2019 – 1 BvL 7/16

BVerfGE 153, 182 – *Suizidbeihilfe* (2020)

2.3. Supreme Court of Justice [Bundesgerichthof - BGH]

BGHZ 13, 334 – *Veröffentlichung von Briefen* (1954)

2.4. Federal Administrative Court [Bundesverwaltungsgericht – BVerwG]

BVerwGE 1, 159 – *Fürsorgeentscheidung* (1954)

BVerwGE 64, 274 – *Peep-show* (1982)

BVerwGE 87, 37 – *Diethylenglykol* (1990)

BVerwGE 90, 112 – *Osho II* (1992)